FOREWORD TO THE FIFTY-SECOND EDITION

In what has been a long career in farming and farming politics I have lived and worked through periods of major change. Perhaps the greatest of those changes occurred as we joined the European Common Market in 1973. The mirror image of that change is of course in play now as we chart a course for UK agriculture as past members of what has become the European Union. With devolution, the four countries of the United Kingdom are moving ahead at different speeds. England is most advanced with its agricultural transition plan aiming to have removed the Basic Payment Scheme by 2028. Recent announcements point to a patchwork of new funding streams from Government focused predominantly on public payments for public goods.

The current period of significant change, like others before, will provide an impetus for many farm operators to consider whether it is time for them to cease farming. Proposals, again at least in England, for a lump sum exit scheme for farmers will undoubtedly provide an incentive to retire. At the same time, there will be many new entrants and progressive farmers who will see this period of change as an opportunity either to get a foot on the farming ladder or to seek the development of their businesses. Either way, those decisions need to be informed by sound farm business analysis backed up with good data, the like of which can be found in the pages of this Pocketbook. It was a desire to ensure that quality, accessible farm business data was available as a planning tool to farm operators that drove John Nix to develop his idea for a Pocketbook. John has left a powerful legacy in the Pocketbook of which I would encourage all considering their future in farming to make regular and detailed use.

Henry Plumb.

The Lord Plumb of Coleshill D.L.

July 2021

iii

FOREWORD TO THE FIRST EDITION

This booklet is intended for farmers, advisers, students and everyone else who, frequently or infrequently, find themselves hunting for data relating to farm management - whether it is for blunt pencil calculations on the back of an envelope or for feeding into a computer. The material contained is based upon the sort of information which the author finds himself frequently having to look up in his twin roles as adviser and teacher in farm management. There are several excellent handbooks already in existence, but this pocketbook endeavours to cover a wider field and thus to be substantially more comprehensive. It is intended that most of the data herein contained will have a national application, although there is inevitably some bias towards conditions in the south-eastern half of the country.

The development of farm planning techniques in recent years has outstripped the quality and quantity of data available. It is hoped that this booklet will go a little further in supplying the type of information required. It cannot, however, claim to be the ultimate in this respect. For example, there are many variations in labour requirements according to farm conditions and sizes and types of machine used and there are many more variations in sheep and beef systems than are dealt with here. More detailed data on these lines are gradually becoming available from various sources. It is hoped further to refine the material in this booklet and to keep it up to date in subsequent editions, as the information becomes available. As a help towards this end, any comments or criticisms will be gratefully received.

The author wishes to thank his many friends and colleagues who have given him so much time and help in compiling this information.

John Nix
October 1966

First published October 1966
Fifty second Edition September 2021

£31·00

630·
68
RED

This b[...]
last [...]

John Nix
Pocketbook

FOR FARM MANAGEMENT

For 2022
Fifty-Second Edition

Graham Redman

Published September 2021

Copies of this book may be obtained from:
The Pocketbook, 2 Nottingham Street
Melton Mowbray, Leicestershire LE13 1NW
Tel: 01664 564 508
Available at   www.thepocketbook.co.uk/
        and   theandersonscentre.co.uk/shop/

Price £31.00 + **£3.00 p&p**
5 to 19 copies: £30.00
Over 20 copies: *call us*
Postage & Packaging free for 5 or more copies in single deliveries

ISBN 978-1-9196-545-0-8

Acknowledgement:

The author is exceedingly grateful to all the people who have given, generously of their time and expertise to compile this book. It takes contributions from many people to put this book together. In particular, thanks goes to Richard King, Caroline Ingamells and Joe Scarratt, without who, it would not have been possible to complete this book to the standard and deadlines required.

Suggested Citation:

Redman, G., 2021. *The John Nix Pocketbook for Farm Management 2022*. 52nd Edition. *Published:* Melton Mowbray: Agro Business Consultants

CONTENTS

I. GENERAL

1. DATES AND FIGURES IN THE BOOK

Figures in this book are projected for 2022 unless otherwise stated. Thus, the crops data relate to the 2022 harvest. The livestock data relate mostly to the 2022/23 year (e.g. for winter-finished beef or the milk year). The yields and prices assume a 'normal' or average season, based on trends. Looking 6-18 months ahead to 2022/23, no one can know what the actual average yield and price for that particular year will be for any commodity. For this reason, we cannot refer to the figures in this book as forecasts, rather sensible forward prices for budgeting and planning purposes. It is not the intention of The Pocketbook to include 'historical data', except for some of the material in the Agricultural Statistics section and where highlighted.

When using the figures, they can be adjusted as appropriate according to circumstances (personal historic performance, soil fertility, livestock genetics for examples), and price and cost differences. For most of the figures quoted, single figures are used to represent what is in fact a large range of possibilities. This variation can be because of many factors including farmer's ability, environmental conditions (e.g., weather), (local) market prices, enterprise size and level of mechanisation and many others. This means that the figures should be adapted for personal situations to accommodate local conditions.

SOURCES OF DATA

The sources of data used in this book are wide and multiple, totalling over 50 separate contributors. Data sourced and used in this book are interpreted ahead of publication: it is not simply a matter of reciting data sourced from elsewhere. The interpretation might be to consider it for the forthcoming year rather than historic years, cross examine it against other data sources, test it against economic principles or historic performances, particularly when from sources potentially with a bias or commercial interest. It might also be to test it against the practicalities of farming. The contributions are considered according to their reliability, validity, relevance, and suppliers' commercial interests. The following list categorises into groups, the information sources used in this book. They are not in order of relevance; all are very important, and the author is very grateful for the support of each source, without which, this book would not be possible.

- Published and peer reviewed academic material such as Farm Business Survey, Pesticide Usage Survey
- Defra statistical publications such as June Survey of UK Farming, British Survey of Fertiliser Practice and RB209
- Published price data from impartial sources, including AHDB
- Commercial quotes for some goods such as fertiliser and spray prices
- Expertise from consultants and other specialists focussed on their own fields for example seed specialists, dairy consultants, niche enterprise farmers and suppliers.
- Historic data, with analysis to identify forward trends
- Industry surveys, such as NAAC contractors' rates

2. THE USE OF GROSS MARGINS

DEFINITION

The data on the crop and livestock enterprises in the Pocketbook are based on gross margins. The gross margin of an enterprise is its output less its variable costs. Enterprise output includes the market value of production retained on the farm. The variable costs must (a) be specific to the enterprise and (b) vary in proportion to the size of the enterprise, i.e. number of hectares or head of stock. The main items of variable costs are: Crops: fertiliser, seed, sprays, casual labour and contract work specific to the crop. Non-Grazing Livestock: concentrate feed, vet. and med., marketing expenses. Grazing Livestock is as for non-grazing livestock, plus forage crop variable costs.

POINTS TO NOTE

1. The gross margin is not a profit figure. The 'fixed costs' (rent, labour, machinery, general overheads) have to be covered by the total farm gross margin before arriving at a profit. For whole farm costings and net margins, refer to chapter IX.

2. The gross margin of an enterprise will differ from season to season, because of yield and price differences affecting output and also because variable costs will vary, e.g., the number and type of sprays required. Different soils and other natural factors, as well as level of management, will also cause differences between farms.

3. Variable costs vary from farm to farm, e.g., some farmers have greater weed control costs than others; some farmers employ a contractor to combine their cereals (a variable cost), others use their own equipment (a fixed cost); some employ a contractor to deliver their sugar beet to the factory (a variable cost), others have their own lorry (a fixed cost). These differences must be borne in mind in making inter-farm comparisons.

4. Provided points 2 and 3 are borne in mind, comparison of gross margins (particularly averages over several seasons) with standards are a useful check on technical performance.

5. The other main use of gross margins is in farm planning. This is not simply a matter of substituting high gross margin enterprises in place of low ones. The gross margin is only one feature of an enterprise. It says nothing about the call the enterprise makes on the farm resources - labour at different times of the year, machinery, buildings, working capital, etc. All these factors and more have to be considered in the planning process.

6. Complete allocation of many farm expenses is generally only possible arbitrarily since they are shared by multiple farm enterprises. Allocation can hence be misleading. The same can be true when regular labour and machinery are employed on specific enterprises. This is because when enterprises are substituted, expanded, contracted or deleted, the variable costs for each enterprise will vary in proportion to the size of that enterprise, but other costs will not, except possibly fuel and some repair costs. 'Fixed' costs may change at a different rate to the enterprise size - and often not smoothly in small amounts at a time. Either the same regular labour force will cope with a new enterprise size or revised number of workers will be needed. The same is true of tractors, other machines and buildings. The only point of making such calculations is for efficiency comparisons, e.g., labour cost per cow.

7. Allocating fixed costs at a flat rate (e.g., per hectare) between enterprises is misleading. It ignores the whole problem of enterprise inter-relationships, differences between enterprises in total and seasonal requirements for labour, machinery and capital, and other factors such as different quality land on the same farm.

8. Changes in the scale of an enterprise will affect its gross margin per unit, e.g., increasing the area of winter wheat from 30% to 55% on a farm will mean more second and third crop wheats being grown, and a smaller proportion of the crop being drilled in the best conditions; hence yields may fall. Even if yields remain the same, variable costs (e.g., fertiliser) may be higher.

9. Gross margins used for planning future changes should also take account of possible changes in price, and the effect of changes in production techniques.

LOW, AVERAGE AND HIGH LEVELS

The levels of production given for many crop and livestock enterprises indicate differences in natural factors, soil productivity etc., and particularly managerial skill. They refer to an average for each level. Higher variable costs do not necessarily mean greater output but depend on other factors too such as timing of applications.

Some variable costs in the schedules are calculated according to output (P and K fertiliser is based on the average yield taken off the land and haulage and packaging are linked to output). But for the most part, variable costs demonstrate minimal change between high yielding and low yielding fields or farms. Hence the majority of costs do not vary according to yield, which is true in many sectors of farming.

The book is written with the progressive and business-orientated farm manager in mind, those wanting to improve their businesses both technically and commercially. It therefore has high performance figures for most gross margins. We do not simply take Defra's published average yields but seek more evidence where possible or necessary. These figures are achievable in most farm businesses.

COMPLETE ENTERPRISE COSTINGS

Gross margins are extremely useful for simple benchmarking and comparative tests. However, more than half of the variation in performance between farms (of all sectors) is in their overheads so will not show up on gross margin schedules. This means examining farm structure and overhead costs is crucial and understanding full costs of production is useful for business planning.

Almost everybody calculates the cost of production per litre or tonne differently thereby giving different answers to the same question. Much arbitrary allocation of 'joint costs' is required to attempt fully costed net margins, and the results are often of limited use in making farm decisions. Another problem in 'complete enterprise costing' is where to stop. For example, should interest on capital be included, whether borrowed or not? If so, further problems of asset valuation and allocation are involved. Variations between farms in their financial situations are considerable as, ranging from the farmer who owns all his land without any mortgage and has no other borrowings to the one with both a rent to pay for all his land and heavy borrowings in addition.

It is natural to want to know 'unit costs' to compare, for example, with prices received. Sometimes these calculations clarify particular costs and therefore efficiency gains that could be made. For these reasons costs per litre of milk are included, although the calculation of some of the 'fixed cost' items is difficult. If a farm has only one enterprise such calculations on that farm are obviously straightforward. But these farms are rare; even dedicated dairy farms usually have youngstock and home-grown forage, which are separate enterprises to milk production.

If required, a cost per tonne of combinable crops can be calculated by adding the fixed costs per hectare of mainly cereals farms (according to size range, given on page 211) to the variable costs per hectare given in the enterprise gross margin data and dividing by the selected yield. Such calculations need to be interpreted with caution because the allocation of fixed costs per hectare is inevitably crude. At The Andersons Centre (the Pocketbook's owner), allocation of labour and machinery is made according to fuel use per hectare. This makes the resulting margins more comparable; for example, grass seed with potatoes. This is not a perfect science but attributes the various costs more accurately than per hectare or per unit of yield.

The allocation of specific labour (e.g. a full-time cowman), machinery (e.g. a potato harvester) and buildings (e.g. a grain store) is relatively simple to allocate and can provide useful information both for efficiency comparisons and partial budgeting. For some enterprises on many mixed farms, there are few such specific items and the question of the other so-called fixed cost items remains if a full costing is attempted.

GROSS MARGIN MAIN ASSUMPTIONS

Budgeting future prices, by necessity requires making assumptions about how they are likely to move in the future from current levels (July 2021). This Edition of the Pocketbook uses the following key assumptions for 2022:

- *Sterling:* The pound: euro exchange rate throughout the book is £1 = €1.18, equivalent to €1 = 85p.

- *Wheat Price:* Feed wheat price (from which many other commodity prices are benchmarked), is £160/tonne. This is an ex-farm price for grain harvested in 2022, and delivery averaged throughout the year and typical marketing dates.

- *Fertiliser prices:* Prices for nitrogen (N), phosphate (P) and potash (K) are the same throughout and are detailed in a full schedule of fertiliser valuations on page 274. To calculate the gross margins, the following are used:

  o   N: 79.7 p/kg   (£275/t 34.5% N)   (UK Ammonium Nitrate)

  o $P_2 O_5$:   87.0 p/kg   (£400/t 46% P_2O_5)   (Triple Super Phosphate)

  o K_2O: 41.7 p/kg   (£250/t 60% K_2O)   (Muriate of Potash)

  Standard fertiliser recommendations from RB209 have been used, assuming an average soil type with mineral and nitrogen indexes of 2. Each gross margin accounts for the replacement of the minerals taken off the field by the harvested crop (excluding straw which is costed as incorporated).

- *Seed:* In the gross margin data, HSS refers to Home Saved Seed, C2 refers to certified (Merchant bought) seed. Hy refers to Hybrid seed. Seed rates vary according to soil, season, variety, drilling date etc. HSS cost includes grain value, cleaning, dressing, testing and BSPB (British Society of Plant Protection) levy (refer to p 285).

- *Sprays:* Refer to Agrochemical Rates on page 283. PGR refers to Plant Growth Regulators

- *Tractor Diesel:* Farm machinery fuel price (red diesel) is taken to be 55ppl.Note the contractor's prices include it at 50ppl (page 182).

II. ENTERPRISE DATA

1. CROPS

WHEAT

Feed Winter Wheat

Production level	Low	Average	High	
Yield: t/ha (t/ac)	7.25 (2.9)	8.60 (3.5)	9.75 (3.9)	
	£	£	£	£/t
Output at £160/t	1,160 (470)	1,376 (557)	1,560 (632)	160
Variable Costs £/ha *(£/ac)* :				
Seed......................		68 (28)		8
Fertiliser..................		220 (89)		26
Sprays.....................		255 (103)		30
Total Variable Costs		543 (220)		63
Gross Margin £/ha (ac)	**617** (250)	**833** (337)	**1,017** (412)	97

Fertiliser Basis 8.6t/ha					Seed:		Sprays £/ha:	
Nutrient	Kg/t	Kg/Ha	£/Ha	£/t C2	£430	Herbicides	£103
N	22	190	£151	Kg/Ha	175	Fungicides	£121
P	6.5	56	£49	% HSS	30%	Insecticides	£8
K	5.5	47	£20	£/t HSS	£301	PGRs	£18
						Other	£6

1. *Yields.* The average yield is for all winter feed wheat, i.e. all varieties and 1ˢᵗ and subsequent wheats. See over for more on First and Second Wheats. The overall yield used for feed and milling wheats including spring varieties calculates as 8.4t/ha, the national average all-wheat yield (ex-2020).

2. *Straw* is costed as incorporated. Average yield and price are approximately 4.2 tonnes per hectare at £55/tonne (£5 more in small bales); variable costs (string) approx. £3.70 per tonne. Unbaled straw (sold for baling): anything from £50/ha (£20/acre) to £100/ha (£40/acre), national average around £85/ha (£34/acre). Account for minerals and organic matter taken from soil if removing straw.

3. *Seed* is costed with a single purpose dressing. Up to a third of growers require additional seed treatments, specifically to supress BYDV. This can add £140 per tonne of seed (£24.80/ha). This has not been added in the gross margins so should be considered.

4. This schedule does not account for severe *grass weed infestations* such as Black Grass or Sterile Brome. Costs associated with managing such problems can amount to up to £160/hectare additional agrochemical costs. Yield losses increase as infestation rises:

Yield losses from Black Grass Infestations

Grass plants/m²	Yield loss t/Ha	% yield loss	References:
8-12	0.2-0.4	2-5%	Roebuck, J.F. (1987).
12-25	0.4-0.8	5-15%	B.C.P.C. and
100	1-2	15-25%	Blair A, Cussans J,
>300	+3	37%	Lutman P (1999).

Milling Winter Wheat

Production level	Low	Average	High	
Yield: t/ha (t/ac)	6.75 (2.7)	7.90 (3.2)	9.00 (3.6)	
	£	**£**	**£**	**£/t**
Output at £171/t	1,154 (467)	1,351 (547)	1,539 (623)	*171*
Variable Costs £/ha *(£/ac)* :				
Seed......................		73 (30)		*9*
Fertiliser...................		262 (106)		*33*
Sprays.....................		264 (107)		*33*
Total Variable Costs		599 (243)		*76*
Gross Margin £/ha (ac)	**555** (225)	**752** (304)	**940** (381)	*95*

Fertiliser Basis 7.9t/ha				Seed:		Sprays £/ha:	
Nutrient	Kg/t	Kg/Ha	£/Ha	£/t C2	£450	Herbicides	£103
N	*32*	250	£199	Kg/Ha	175	Fungicides	£127
P	6.5	51	£44	% HSS	25%	Insecticides	£8
K	5.5	43	£18	£/t HSS	313	PGRs	£18
						Other	£9

5. The average *milling price* is based on a 'full specification' (Group 1) premium of £17.00 over feed wheat, a 'biscuit' grade (Group 2) milling specification of £5 and a 20% failure rate of achieving the specification. The average milling wheat rose in 2020. Full specification is defined as Group 1 wheat with a minimum Hagberg of 250, 13% protein and a bushel weight of at least 76kg/hl.

6. *Milling v. Feed.* The yield of bread and biscuit wheat (generically known as milling) was historically about 8% below feed wheat but is now less than 3% (*AHDB*). The price premium varies according to quality and scarcity. Not all deliveries achieve full specification. Group 2 yields are slightly higher than Group 1. Wheat group 1 varieties accounted for about 24% of 2020 wheat area.

Comparison between First and Second Feed Wheat Crops

Production level	Average		High	
Year (after break)	First	Second	First	Second
Yield: t/ha (t/ac)	8.71 (3.5)	7.90 (3.2)	10.24 (4.1)	9.28 (3.8)
	£	**£**	**£**	**£**
Output	1,394 (565)	1,263 (512)	1,638 (664)	1,485 (601)
Variable Costs £/ha *(£/ac)* :				
Seed...........................	67 (27)	114 (46)	67 (27)	114 (46)
Fertiliser......................	226 (92)	205 (83)	266 (108)	240 (97)
Sprays.........................	252 (102)	272 (110)	252 (102)	272 (110)
Variable Costs	545 (221)	591 (239)	584 (237)	626 (254)
Gross Margin £/ha (ac)	**849** (344)	**673** (272)	**1054** (427)	**858** (348)

7. First v. Second (Feed) Wheat. Different types and lengths of rotational breaks affect subsequent wheat yields as well as weather, soils and varieties etc. The table above assumes a yield reduction of 7% for second wheats compared with first. Third wheats could yield 10% below second wheats; variable costs are likely to be similar. Heavy, well-structured, well-drained clay soils are best suited to second wheats.

Spring Wheat

Production level	Low	Average	High	
Yield: t/ha (t/ac)	5.25 (2.1)	6.20 (2.5)	7.00 (2.8)	
	£	£	£	£/t
Output at £171/t	898 (364)	1,060 (429)	1,197 (485)	*171*
Variable Costs £/ha *(£/ac)* :				
Seed........................		84 (34)		*14*
Fertiliser..................		196 (79)		*32*
Sprays.....................		151 (61)		*24*
Total Variable Costs		431 (175)		*70*
Gross Margin £/ha (ac)	**467** (189)	**629** (255)	**766** (310)	*101*

Fertiliser Basis 6.2t/ha					Seed:		Sprays £/ha:	
Nutrient	Kg/t	Kg/Ha	£/Ha	£/t C2	£450	Herbicides	£65
N	24	150	£120	Kg/Ha	200	Fungicides	£55
P	8.5	53	£46	% HSS	20%	Insecticides	£8
K	12	74	£31	£/t HSS	312	PGRs	£18
						Other	£6

1. *Price:* In general, see Winter Wheat (previous pages). A higher proportion of spring wheat is sold for milling compared with winter wheat (95% here). Here we assume 20% failure rate to feed price for 2022 harvest.

2. *Yield.* Here, spring wheat yield is 80% of winter second milling wheat.

3. *Straw:* See Winter Wheat but yields are lower (3t/ha).

4. *Area.* It is thought usually 5% of UK wheat area is a spring sown although it was as much as 13% in 2020 (measured by drilling date). It is popular after root crops or after a wet autumn. The area has risen in recent years to manage grass weeds and some new spring varieties have long planting windows. New varieties that can be grown as winter or spring wheats are blurring the distinction between the crops, and perhaps will become one crop in the near future.

Red Wheat is a very hard spring wheat crop which was grown in the UK under contract until 2015 harvest. At its peak it covered several thousand hectares but is not grown in the UK any longer in any substantial way.

BARLEY

Winter Feed Barley

Production level	Low	Average	High	
Yield: t/ha (t/ac)	6.25 (2.5)	7.30 (3.0)	8.25 (3.3)	
	£	£	£	£/t
Output at £142/t	888 (360)	1,037 (420)	1,172 (475)	142
Variable Costs £/ha *(£/ac)* :				
Seed......................		78 (31)		11
Fertiliser..................		198 (80)		27
Sprays....................		195 (79)		27
Total Variable Costs		471 (191)		65
Gross Margin £/ha (ac)	**417** (169)	**566** (229)	**701** (284)	78

Fertiliser Basis 7.3t/ha				Seed:		Sprays:	
Nutrient	Kg/t	Kg/Ha	£/Ha	£/t C	410	Herbicides	£81
N	19	140	£112	£/t HSS	283	Fungicides	£83
P	8.5	62	£54	Kg/Ha	175	Insecticides	£8
K	10.5	77	£32	£/Ha Hy	110	PGRs	£18
				C:Hy:HSS	45:30:25	Other	£6

1. *Prices*. Feed barley has a lower nutritional value to wheat so is normally discounted to feed wheat, by about 8% as used here (the average over 5 and 20 years is 7.5%).

2. *Hybrid Varieties*. Increasing amounts of winter feed barley is hybrid seed. For this, we could expect seed costs of about £100 per hectare and yields of about 10% higher than the conventional varieties. Fertiliser is adjusted accordingly.

Winter Malting Barley

Production level	Low	Average	High	
Yield: t/ha (t/ac)	5.75 (2.3)	6.70 (2.7)	7.75 (3.1)	
	£	£	£	£/t
Output at £156/t	897 (363)	1,045 (423)	1,209 (490)	156
Variable Costs £/ha *(£/ac)* :				
Seed......................		69 (28)		10
Fertiliser..................		158 (64)		24
Sprays....................		195 (79)		29
Total Variable Costs		422 (171)		63
Gross Margin £/ha (ac)	**475** (192)	**623** (252)	**787** (319)	93

Fertiliser Basis 6.7t/ha				Seed:		Sprays £/Ha:	
Nutrient	Kg/t	Kg/Ha	£/Ha	£/t C2	£430	Herbicides	£81
N	15	100	£80	Kg/Ha	175	Fungicides	£83
P	8.5	57	£50	% HSS	25%	Insecticides	£8
K	10.5	70	£29	£/t HSS	296	PGRs	£18
						Other	£6

3. *Straw* is costed as incorporated. Average yield is approx. 3.6 tonnes per hectare, value £60 per tonne baled ex-field, higher in the West, (£10/t more in small bales); variable cost (string) approximately £3.70 per tonne. Prices rise in years of forage shortage.

4. *Prices.* Winter Malting Barley generally has a lower malting specification to spring barley. Here, winter malting barley has a £15.00 per tonne premium over feed barley. The gross margin accounts for some that do not meet malting standards. For the best malting barleys, the premium in the past has been £25 or more in some years.

Spring Malting Barley

Production level	Low	Average	High	
Yield: t/ha (t/ac)	5.00 (2.0)	5.70 (2.3)	6.50 (2.6)	
	£	£	£	£/t
Output at £157/t	785 (318)	895 (362)	1,021 (413)	157
Variable Costs £/ha *(£/ac)* :				
Seed......................		69 (28)		12
Fertiliser...................		134 (54)		24
Sprays....................		151 (61)		27
Total Variable Costs		354 (144)		62
Gross Margin £/ha (ac)	**431** (175)	**540** (219)	**666** (270)	**95**

Fertiliser Basis 5.7t/ha				Seed:		Sprays:	
Nutrient	Kg/t	Kg/Ha	£/Ha	£/t C2	£440	Herbicides	£65
N	14	80	£64	Kg/Ha	175	Fungicides	£55
P	8.5	48	£42	% HSS	35%	Insecticides	£8
K	12	68	£28	£/t HSS	301	PGRs	£18
						Other	£6

1. *Prices.* Most spring barley grown is malting varieties, grown for a premium. Spring malting premiums usually exceed those for winter varieties. Here the premium over feed barley is £23.00 per tonne. This also allows for 20% failed samples making feed price at £157 per tonne.

2. Straw: as per Winter Barley, but with lower yield, costed as incorporated. Account for minerals and organic matter if removed.

Naked Barley.

Naked barley, suitable for roasting, flaking or milling as pearl barley, is now rarely heard of. It is grown like normal barley, but yields are about 15% lower. It could be either autumn or spring sown

OATS

Winter Oats

Production level	Low	Average	High	
Yield: t/ha (t/ac)	5.25 (2.1)	6.10 (2.5)	7.00 (2.8)	
	£	£	£	£/t
Output at £142/t (feed)	746 (302)	866 (351)	994 (403)	142
Variable Costs £/ha (£/ac) :				
Seed......................		70 (28)		11
Fertiliser..................		160 (65)		26
Sprays....................		131 (53)		22
Total Variable Costs		361 (146)		59
Gross Margin £/ha (ac)	**385** (156)	**505** (204)	**633** (256)	83

Fertiliser Basis 6.1t/ha				Seed:		Sprays:	
Nutrient	Kg/t	Kg/Ha	£/Ha	£/t C2	£450	Herbicides	£57
N	21	130	£104	Kg/Ha	175	Fungicides	£44
P	8	49	£43	% HSS	30%	Insecticides	£8
K	5.5	34	£14	£/t HSS	279	PGRs	£17
						Other	£6

1. *Price:* Feed price quoted. Milling specification requires a minimum bushel weight of 50kg/Hl. Conservation grade milling oats may obtain a premium of £10-20/tonne.

2. *Straw* is costed as incorporated here. Average yield is 3.4 tonnes per hectare; value £60 per tonne according to region and season; variable costs (string) £3.70 per tonne.

Spring Oats

Production level	Low	Average	High	
Yield: t/ha (t/ac)	4.75 (1.9)	5.60 (2.3)	6.50 (2.6)	
	£	£	£	£/t
Output at £142/t (feed)	675 (273)	795 (322)	923 (374)	142
Variable Costs £/ha (£/ac) :				
Seed......................		74 (30)		13
Fertiliser..................		108 (44)		19
Sprays....................		93 (38)		17
Total Variable Costs		275 (111)		49
Gross Margin £/ha (ac)	**400** (162)	**521** (211)	**648** (263)	93

Fertiliser Basis 5.6t/ha				Seed:		Sprays:	
Nutrient	Kg/t	Kg/Ha	£/Ha	£/t C2	£450	Herbicides	£37
N	13	70	£56	Kg/Ha	185	Fungicides	£34
P	8	45	£39	% HSS	30%	Insecticides	£7
K	5.5	31	£13	£/t HSS	279	PGRs	£9
						Other	£6

3. *Winter or Spring?* 50% oats are winter crops (*PUS report 284 2019*). The proportion of spring oats has been rising in recent years; spring oats dominate further north with an estimated 70% winter oats in England/Wales but 20% in Scotland.

Naked Oats

Production level	Low	Average	High	
Yield: t/ha (t/ac)	4.5 (1.8)	5.10 (2.1)	6.50 (2.6)	
	£	£	£	£/t
Output at £200/t	900 (365)	1,020 (413)	1,300 (527)	200
Variable Costs £/ha *(£/ac)* :				
Seed......................		63 (26)		12
Fertiliser...................		144 (58)		28
Sprays....................		140 (57)		27
Total Variable Costs		347 (141)		68
Gross Margin £/ha (ac)	**553** (224)	**673** (273)	**953** (386)	*132*

Fertiliser Basis 5.1t/ha				Seed:	
Nutrient	Kg/t	Kg/Ha	£/Ha	£/t C2	640
N	20	100	£80	Kg/Ha	100
P	9	50	£43	% HSS	5%
K	16.5	50	£21	£/t HSS	358

1. *Price:* based on contracts offering premiums 30% above the average feed wheat price. The premium can be reduced according to husk content. Contracts require a maximum moisture content of 14%, which is also recommended for long-term storage. A 15% failure rate to feed wheat has been included.

2. *Inputs* are lower than for wheat or barley. The agronomy is similar to that of husked oat varieties. Oats provide a break in the take-all cycle.

3. Naked oats have a higher protein, energy and oil content than husked oats, but the fibre content is lower – as the husk is removed during harvesting.

4. The area grown is increasing steadily. Naked oats account for about 10% of the traded tonnage of UK oats (i.e. excluding those grown for on-farm use). The traditional markets such as racehorse feed, dog food, and bird feed markets are all increasing. Over recent years the human consumption market has developed so that at least half the crop is now sold for health foods, artisan breads and breakfast cereals.

5. Around a third of plantings are spring and this proportion rises after a wet autumn. The margin above is winter cropping. NIAB data suggest spring yields average 20%-25% less than conventional oats. The actual difference will depend on the particular season but are likely now to be in the range 15%-20%.

6. Harvest is just after winter barley. Care needs to be taken with both the timing of harvest, and the set-up of the combine, to ensure a clean, saleable sample.

OILSEED RAPE

Winter Oilseed Rape

Production level	Low	Average	High	
Yield: t/ha (t/ac)	3.00 (1.2)	3.50 (1.4)	4.00 (1.6)	
	£	£	£	£/t
Output at £380/t	1140 (462)	1,330 (539)	1,520 (616)	380
Variable Costs £/ha (£/ac) :				
Seed......................		64 (26)		18
Fertiliser..................		210 (85)		60
Sprays.....................		234 (95)		67
Total Variable Costs		508 (206)		145
Gross Margin £/ha (ac)	**632** (256)	**822** (333)	**1,012** (410)	235

Fertiliser Basis 3.5t/ha				Seed:		Sprays:	
Nutrient	Kg/t	Kg/Ha	£/Ha	£/Ha C	60	Herbicides	£113
N	54	190	£151	£/Ha Hy	80	Fungicides	£80
P	14	49	£43	£/Ha HSS	20	Insecticides	£8
K	11	39	£16	C:Hy:HSS	25:25:50	PGRs	£18
	Seed write-off		7%	Kg/Ha	5.5	Other	£15

1. *Prices.* The price used for the 2022 crop is £385/tonne plus oil bonuses at 44% oil content. The bonus is paid on the percentage of oil over 40 percent, at 1.5 times the sale value of the crop and an equal but opposite penalty below 40%. For example, in this case, the bonus is on 4% oil x £385 x 1.5 = £23. (Figures are rounded to the nearest £5.00 in the margin)

Spring Oilseed Rape

Production level	Low	Average	High	
Yield: t/ha (t/ac)	2.00 (0.8)	2.28 (0.9)	2.50 (1.0)	
	£	£	£	£/t
Output at £380/t	760 (308)	865 (350)	950 (385)	380
Variable Costs £/ha (£/ac) :				
Seed......................		68 (28)		30
Fertiliser..................		102 (41)		45
Sprays.....................		152 (61)		67
Total Variable Costs		322 (130)		141
Gross Margin £/ha (ac)	**438** (177)	**543** (220)	**628** (254)	239

2. *Inputs: Seed* as per WOSR, but 45% conventional, 5% HSS, 50% hybrid. *Fertiliser:* N/P/K at 80/32/25 kg/ha. *Sprays,* Herbicides. £54, Fungicides, £57, Insecticides £8, PGRs £18 and Others £15/ha

3. *Winter Versus Spring*: As little as 8,000 hectares of spring OSR are grown in the UK which is 2.5% of the entire crop. As can be seen, the financial reward is slim compared with other combinable crops.

LINSEED

Spring Linseed

Production level	Low	Average	High	
Yield: t/ha (t/ac)	1.50 (0.6)	1.75 (0.7)	2.00 (0.8)	
	£	£	£	£/t
Output at £430/t	645 (261)	753 (305)	860 (348)	430
Variable Costs £/ha (£/ac) :				
Seed......................		90 (36)		51
Fertiliser..................		73 (30)		42
Sprays....................		66 (27)		38
Total Variable Costs		229 (93)		131
Gross Margin £/ha (ac)	**416** (168)	**524** (212)	**631** (256)	**299**

Fertiliser Basis 1.75t/ha				Seed:		Sprays:
Nutrient	Kg/t	Kg/Ha	£/Ha	£/t C2	2000	
N	29	50	£40	Kg/Ha	45	
P	14	30	£26	% HSS	0%	
K	11	10	£4	£/t HSS		
S			£3			

1. The *price* is OSR price plus 13%. Contract prices are normally tied to a standard 38% oil and 9% moisture. Some specialist contracts for specific varieties such as Yellow Linseed can be worth more.

2. Most *linseed is spring-sown* (about 24,000 hectares but varies considerably), drilling mid-March to mid-April, no more than 1 year in 5. Too much nitrogen (over 130 kg/ha) can cause lodging, delayed maturity and excessive weed growth causing difficult harvesting, poor quality and lower yields. Harvesting: spring normally end Aug-early Sept. Harvest moisture content 12-16%: Dry to 9% for storage.

Winter Linseed

Production level	Low	Average	High	
Yield: t/ha (t/ac)	1.75 (0.7)	2.00 (0.8)	2.25 (0.9)	
	£	£	£	£/t
Output at £430/t	753 (305)	860 (348)	968 (392)	430
Variable Costs £/ha (£/ac) :				
Seed......................		95 (38)		48
Fertiliser..................		105 (43)		53
Sprays....................		80 (32)		40
Total Variable Costs		280 (113)		140
Gross Margin £/ha (ac)	**473** (192)	**580** (235)	**688** (278)	**290**

3. *Winter Linseed Output:* Price as per Spring. *Inputs:* Seed rate fractionally higher, fertiliser N/P/K 90/28/22 kg/ha.

4. *Winter Linseed* area is currently about 4,000 hectares grown in the UK. Yield can be higher than springs but is affected by frost heave, disease and thrips (thunder-bugs), most varieties susceptible to lodging; pigeons can be troublesome. Early sowing (early to mid-Sept) is best.

FIELD PEAS

Blue Peas

Production level	**Low**	**Average**	**High**	
Yield: t/ha (t/ac)	3.50 (1.4)	4.00 (1.6)	4.50 (1.8)	
	£	**£**	**£**	*£/t*
Output at £230/t	805 (326)	920 (373)	1,035 (419)	*230*
Variable Costs £/ha *(£/ac)* :				
Seed........................		91 (37)		*23*
Fertiliser...................		48 (19)		*12*
Sprays......................		157 (64)		*39*
Total Variable Costs		296 (120)		*74*
Gross Margin £/ha (ac)	**509** (206)	**624** (253)	**739** (299)	*156*

Fertiliser Basis 4t/ha				**Seed:**		**Sprays:**	
Nutrient	Kg/t	Kg/Ha	£/Ha	£/t C2	525	Herbicides	£81
N	*0*	0	£0	Kg/Ha	200	Fungicides	£55
P	9.0	36	£31	% HSS	30%	Insecticides	£11
K	10	40	£17	£/t HSS	298	PGRs	£0
						Other	£10

1. *Price.* All peas are grown for a premium market (not stock-feed) with only a small proportion of low-grade samples (30%) compounded for feed. Feed value is therefore not relevant as a base price.

   The overall price for *Blue Peas* of £230/tonne, takes account of human consumption values (£250/tonne) and a 70% pass rate with feed price of £185. Most peas (70%) are Blues, used for micronizing (largely for pet food) and exports.

Marrowfats

Production level	Low	Average	High	
Yield: t/ha (t/ac)	3.00 (1.2)	3.60 (1.5)	4.25 (1.7)	
	£	**£**	**£**	**£/t**
Output at £325/t	975 (395)	1,170 (474)	1,381 (559)	*325*
Variable Costs £/ha *(£/ac)* :				
Seed......................		164 (66)		*46*
Fertiliser..................		43 (17)		*12*
Sprays....................		195 (79)		*54*
Total Variable Costs		402 (163)		*112*
Gross Margin £/ha (ac)	**573** (232)	**768** (311)	**979** (397)	*213*

Fertiliser Basis 3.6t/ha					Seed:		Sprays:	
Nutrient	Kg/t	Kg/Ha	£/Ha	£/t C2	575	Herbicides	£70
N	*0*	0	£0	Kg/Ha	300	Fungicides	£97
P	9.0	32	£28	% HSS	20%	Insecticides	£11
K	10.0	36	£15	£/t HSS	435	PGRs	£0
						Other	£17

2. *Price:* Marrowfats can achieve higher prices than Blues and in recent years have achieved considerable premiums over other combinable crops. However, they are subject to a small illiquid market. They are not priced with a premium over wheat, as the markets bear no relationship. However, for the grower, this relationship is important as all crops will, in effect, be competing for space in the arable rotation.

3. Marrowfat Peas are used for canning, packets and export trade. They are almost entirely grown on a contract thus production is restricted by demand although this is growing. They yield about 10% less than Blue Peas. The average price in this gross margin is £325/tonne being £360/tonne for 80%, £185 for the 20% that fails quality specification.

FIELD BEANS

Winter Beans

Production level	Low	Average	High	
Yield: t/ha (t/ac)	3.75 (1.5)	4.30 (1.7)	5.00 (2.0)	
	£	**£**	**£**	**£/t**
Output at £195/t	731.3 (296)	839 (340)	975 (395)	*195*
Variable Costs £/ha *(£/ac)* :				
Seed......................		98 (40)		*23*
Fertiliser..................		63 (26)		*15*
Sprays....................		132 (54)		*31*
Total Variable Costs		293 (119)		*68*
Gross Margin £/ha (ac)	**438** (177)	**545** (221)	**682** (276)	*127*

Fertiliser Basis 4.3t/ha				Seed:		Sprays:	
Nutrient	Kg/t	Kg/Ha	£/Ha	£/t C2	500	Herbicides	£65
N	0	0	£0	Kg/Ha	250	Fungicides	£50
P	11	47	£41	% HSS	50%	Insecticides	£8
K	12	52	£22	£/t HSS	283	PGRs	£0
						Other	£10

1. *Price.* This is based on a human consumption price of £205/tonne achieved by 60% and feed specification for the rest at £185/tonne. *All beans* are grown with a potential for sale into a human consumption market. However, insect damage, dis-colouring or other damage means some is sold for feed.

Spring Beans

Production level	Low	Average	High	
Yield: t/ha (t/ac)	3.25 (1.3)	3.90 (1.6)	4.50 (1.8)	
	£	**£**	**£**	**£/t**
Output at £205/t	666 (270)	800 (324)	923 (374)	*205*
Variable Costs £/ha *(£/ac)* :				
Seed......................		103 (42)		*26*
Fertiliser..................		57 (23)		*15*
Sprays....................		130 (53)		*33*
Total Variable Costs		290 (117)		*74*
Gross Margin £/ha (ac)	**376** (152)	**509** (206)	**632** (256)	*131*

Fertiliser Basis 3.9t/ha				Seed:		Sprays:	
Nutrient	Kg/t	Kg/Ha	£/Ha	£/t C2	510	Herbicides	£65
N	0	0	£0	Kg/Ha	250	Fungicides	£44
P	11	43	£37	% HSS	45%	Insecticides	£11
K	12	47	£20	£/t HSS	293	PGRs	£0
						Other	£10

2. *Price.* Spring beans are all grown for the human consumption market. It is only the poor-quality beans (predominantly Bruchid beetle damaged) that are rejected and redirected to feed compounders. Damaged samples can be cleaned if the premium justifies it. A large proportion of the crop is exported (to North Africa). Average spring bean price is budgeted here at £205/tonne comprising 60% at £215/tonne and the rest at £185/tonne (for feed).

Winter versus Spring Beans.

The key determinant between which to crop is soil type. Winter beans are more suited to heavy soils and springs on lighter land. As the schedules illustrate, there is little real difference between the gross margins. Spring crops are retained in many rotations to help manage grass weed problems. The Arable Pesticide Usage Survey 2019 (284) suggests that in 2018, 53% of beans planted were spring beans.

Peas or Beans?

Combinable pea area is about 40,000 hectares in the UK, comparable with vining peas. Combinable pea area fell from a high in 2001 of 100,000 hectares. The field bean area varies considerably from year to year, between 100,000 to 200,000 hectares. High quality and good yields can return high gross margins and offer wider benefits to the farming system through added soil nitrogen and organic matter, although they can be difficult to grow, and the unpredictability of pulses has put several growers off in previous years.

Beyond the Gross Margin

Page 2 explains that the gross margin is only a partial measure of crop contribution and cost to the farm business. Amongst the combinable crops this is particularly true for the legumes such as peas and beans. They fix nitrogen into soil which is then available for uptake by subsequent crops either saving input costs into the following crop or raising its yield. The amount fixed is very difficult to predict but varies from almost nothing to over 200kg/ha in the extreme cases based on soil type, crop health, growing conditions and other factors too. A useful average figure used by the PGRO for additional nitrogen available for the following crop after a pulse crop is 50kg/ha (worth £40/ha in 2022 at budgeted fertiliser prices). The associated input savings from the following crop, or the additional yield it achieves should therefore, for management purposes be attributed to the leguminous crop.

Other Pulses?

Lentils, Chickpeas and *peanuts* are all pulses, grown in warmer climates than the UK offers. There are not viable varieties for the UK to cultivate commercially at present and the UK market is currently relatively small. However, these might become more important foods for the future, being high in vegetable protein and versatile ingredients in home cooking and future processing techniques.

VINING PEAS

Vining Peas

Production level	**Low**		**Average**		**High**		
Yield: t/ha (t/ac)	4.00 (1.6)		4.80 (1.9)		5.50 (2.2)		
	£		**£**		**£**		**£/t**
Output at £270/t	1080 (437)		1,296 (525)		1,485 (601)		*270*
Variable Costs £/ha *(£/ac)* :							
Seed......................			250 (101)				*52*
Fertiliser..................			12 (5)				*3*
Sprays.....................			157 (64)				*33*
Contract Vining...........			143 (58)				*30*
Total Variable Costs			562 (228)				*117*
Gross Margin £/ha (ac)	**518** (210)		**734** (297)		**923** (374)		*153*

Fertiliser Basis 4.8t/ha				Seed:		Sprays:	
Nutrient	Kg/t	Kg/Ha	£/Ha			Herbs	£81
N	*0*	0	£0			Fungs	£55
P	1.5	7	£6			Insect	£11
K	3	14	£6			PGRs	£0
						Other	£10

The table relates to vining peas grown on contract for 2022

1. The *price* ranges from £210 to £380/tonne ex farm depending primarily on quality. Here we use an average of £270/tonne. The average yield is taken as 4.80 tonnes per hectare; the national average (fresh weight) for the last five years has ranged between 3.6 and 5.1 although growers are paid on frozen weight. Top quality ('150 minute') peas have to be grown within 40 miles of the factory. More distant 'long haul' peas will be in the lower price range.

   The average yield of petit pois is lower but the price averages 12 to 15% more.

2. *Fertiliser*. Many growers use no fertiliser; but RB209 suggests P&K as per the gross margin.

3. *Sprays*. Both herbicide and aphicide are commonly used with fungicides being used dependant on seasonal requirements.

4. *Harvest*: A pea viner costs in the region of £460,000, and on average covers about 600 hectares per year over a 40 to 60-day harvest period. Contracting costs are estimated as typical actual costs based on this information. Different cooperative and producer organisations cost their machinery in different ways.

5. Total UK area drilled in 2019 was 39,684 hectares with 36,162 vined with a view to vining a 140,000-tonne crop for frozen and canned use. A small surplus might be grown that exceeds contracted requirements

   Acknowledgement: Thanks to British Growers Association

LUPINS

Production level	Low	Average	High	
Yield: t/ha (t/ac)	2.25 (0.9)	3.00 (1.2)	3.75 (1.5)	
	£	£	£	£/t
Output at £275/t	619 (251)	825 (334)	1,031 (418)	275
Variable Costs £/ha:				
Seed...................		152 (62)		51
Fertiliser..............		78 (32)		26
Sprays.................		80 (32)		27
Total Variable Costs		310 (126)		103
Gross Margin £/ha (ac)	309 (125)	515 (209)	721 (292)	172

Fertiliser Basis 3t/ha				Seed:	
Nutrient	Kg/t	Kg/Ha	£/Ha	£/t C2	£800
N	8	25	£20	Kg/Ha	190
P	15	45	£39	% HSS	0%
K	15	45	£19	£/t HSS	-

1. *Price* used here is £300 per tonne (White lupins). Few lupins are traded on the open market, but the value tends to be higher than feed beans due to higher protein content (34% to 38% for white lupins) which means the price is closer to soya values.

2. A leguminous spring crop grown on light land. They are a good substitute for non-GM soya bean meal in livestock feed. Around three-quarters of UK lupins are whole-cropped for silage, but they can also be crimped or milled and fed directly to stock or the grain traded as a cash crop. Growing costs will be similar for all end uses.

3. Around 2,000 hectares (5,000 acres) are grown in the UK, about 60-70% are white (mostly in South and East), 15-20% blue and the remainder yellow (North and Scotland due to their shorter growing season).

4. Lupins need a good cereal seedbed and pre-emergence weed control. Anthracnose is a potentially serious threat, but plant health measures have so far kept it under control.

5. Appropriate variety choice is important depending on area of the country, soil pH, intended end use and growth habit required. There are three distinct species of spring lupins; white, blue and yellow. White lupins have higher protein and potentially greater yield than blues but require a longer growing season. Yellow lupins fall between blue and white on both counts.

Lupin characteristics

	White *Lupinus Albus*	Yellow *Lupinus Luteus*	Blue *Lupinus Angustifolius*
Flower Colour	white or blue	yellow	white or blue
Growth habit	semi-determinate	semi-determinate	fully or semi-determinate
pH tolerance	5 to 7.6	4.6 to 6.8	5 to 6.8
Protein	34-38%	36-40%	30-34%
Oil content	10%	5%	6%
Yield	3.0-3.5 t/ha	2.5-3.0 t/ha	3.0-3.5 t/ha

Acknowledgement: Thanks to - Soya UK.

HERBAGE SEEDS

	Intermediate Perennial Ryegrass		Late Perennial Ryegrass	
	Average	High	Average	High
	£	£	£	£
Yield (tonnes per ha)	1.3	1.7	1.1	1.5
Price per 50 kg (£)	57		60	
Output	1,482	1,938	1,320	1,800
Variable Costs:				
Seed	60		60	
Fertiliser	211		211	
Sprays	175		175	
Cleaning / Certification...........	182	230	158	206
Total Variable Costs	628	676	604	652
Gross Margin per ha	**854**	**1,262**	**716**	**1,148**
Gross Margin per acre	346	511	290	465

1. *Prices* are for certified seed for 2022 harvest. They show an average for diploid/tetraploid varieties (diploid command slightly higher prices). High sugar varieties have a premium of £5-£10 over the values quoted. Amenity grasses also command a premium (around £5-£15 per 50 kg above the agricultural price).

2. No allowance has been made above for *by-products*. Some crops produce 4 to 5 tonnes of threshed hay, which is of low feeding value, potentially worth £300 per hectare. Some grasses, especially spring-sown ryegrass, also provide good autumn and winter grazing.

3. *Yields* are for cleaned certified seed. The crop is risky, i.e. yields are highly variable, depending especially on the weather at, and precise timeliness of, harvesting. The margin assumes the use of growth regulators and stripper headers which reduces the risk. Most grasses give their highest yield in their first harvest year, assuming good establishment. Crops are usually replaced after two harvests.

4. *Inputs: Seed* margin assumes 10kg per hectare (for tetraploid types) at £12 per kg with cost split over two harvest years. Spring planted seed rates are lower. If the seed crop is undersown, the seed rate for the cover crop is reduced and nitrogen applications restricted.

5. *Chemical* costs. The margins assume an autumn-sown crop; spring costs are lower.

6. The following were the number of hectares grown for certified seed production for the main grasses and clovers in the UK for the 2020 harvest;

Italian / Westerwold Ryegrass ..	377	Cocksfoot	Nil
Early Perennial Ryegrass	57	Red Fescue	540
Inter. Perennial Ryegrass	2,528	White Clover	Nil
Late Perennial Ryegrass	2,747	Red Clover..............................	96
Amenity Perennial Ryegrass.....	758	Common Vetch.......................	95
Hybrid Ryegrass	863	Timothy..................................	57

The ryegrasses total 7,330 ha (*18,112 acres*).
All herbage seeds total 8,118 ha (*20,060 acres*).

7. *Labour*: see page 161.

Acknowledgement: Thanks to - Herbage Seed Services; NIAB.

RYE

Production level	Low	Average	High	
Yield: t/ha (t/ac)	4.0 (1.6)	5.50 (2.2)	7.00 (2.8)	
	£	£	£	£/t
Output at £170/t	680 (275)	935 (379)	1,190 (482)	170
Variable Costs £/ha:				
Seed......................		91 (37)		17
Fertiliser................		190 (77)		35
Sprays...................		137 (55)		25
Total Variable Costs		418 (169)		76
Gross Margin £/ha (ac)	262 (106)	517 (209)	772 (313)	94

Fertiliser Basis 5.5t/ha				Seed:	
Nutrient	Kg/t	Kg/Ha	£/Ha	£/t C2	650
N	25	140	£112	Kg/Ha	140
P	7.8	50	£43	% HSS	0%
K	5.6	85	£35	£/t HSS	250

1. The *price* of £170 per tonne for 2022 harvest is based on a £10 per tonne premium over feed wheat price at the point of sale. It assumes the milling specification is achieved. Feed grade price achieves between feed wheat and feed barley. Only a very small percentage of the crop is grown for the free market.

2. Rye is autumn-sown, drought tolerant and very hardy. It can withstand low temperatures and starts growing early in the spring. It has all-round resistance to wheat and barley diseases, e.g. eyespot, and suffers less from take-all than wheat – hence it is a possible replacement for third or fourth wheat. Its vigour keeps weeds down. Its herbicide, fungicide and fertiliser requirements are lower than for other cereals, except for growth regulators. Rye is harvested earlier than winter wheat (useful for following with oilseed rape).

3. Largely grown on light, low fertility, sandy or stony soils, not suited to other cereals. The average yield in the UK has historically been around 6 tonnes per hectare but can be quite variable.

4. The area grown in the UK ranged between 6,000 and 7,000 ha for many years but has recently risen to nearer 30,000 hectares. The additional area is mainly whole-cropped for use in anaerobic digestion plants. For rye grain, crispbread is the major outlet. It is also milled into flour, used in mixed-grain bread and muesli. About two-thirds of the UK grain requirements are imported, mainly from Canada (which produces the highest quality), Denmark, Germany and Spain.

5. *Drawbacks*: it sprouts in a wet harvest: must therefore harvest early, at relatively high moisture. It grows very tall and lodges easily: hence high levels of nitrogen are not possible; but growth regulators help. Its heavy straw crop means slow combining (twice as long as wheat and barley), and difficult straw incorporation. Hybrid varieties, with shorter, stiffer straw resolve many of these problems.

6. Drilling: 2nd and 3rd weeks September. Harvesting: by mid-August at relatively high moisture content, then dry to 14-15% (no drying costs included in margin). Whole-crop rye is cut at 30-35% dry matter around the end of June or start of July.

TRITICALE

Production level	Low	Average	High	
Yield: t/ha (t/ac)	3.00 (1.2)	4.50 (1.8)	6.50 (2.6)	
	£	£	£	£/t
Output at £155/t	465 (188)	698 (283)	1,008 (408)	155
Variable Costs £/ha:				
Seed.....................		61 (25)		14
Fertiliser...............		165 (67)		37
Sprays...................		85 (34)		19
Total Variable Costs		311 (126)		69
Gross Margin £/ha (ac)	**154** (62)	**387** (157)	**697** (282)	**86**

Fertiliser Basis 4.5t/ha				Seed:	
Nutrient	Kg/t	Kg/Ha	£/Ha	£/t C2	425
N	28	125	£100	Kg/Ha	160
P	7.8	50	£43	% HSS	40%
K	5.6	50	£22	£/t HSS	310

1. The *price* of £155 per tonne for 2022 harvest is based on a £4-£6 per tonne discount on the feed wheat price.

2. A 'man-made' cross between rye and hard wheat. It combines the hardiness of rye and the marketability of feed wheat. It is used in livestock feed, particularly pig and poultry rations, having high levels of lysine (an amino acid). After a rise to nearly 15,000 ha, the cropped UK area has settled at around 10,000 ha in recent years.

3. The average yield in the UK has historically been just over 4 tonnes per hectare; the low yield resulting from being grown on light land. In these circumstances, it frequently out-yields wheat or barley, and with lower input requirements. It is less prone to damage than other cereals where rabbit grazing is a problem.

4. Less fungicide is needed because of its good disease resistance, except for ergot, but including take-all (making it a good replacement for a third or fourth wheat). It is a tall crop, which helps to suppress weeds, but it is susceptible to lodging; growth regulators are beneficial.

5. The crop is best drilled early (September) on light, drought-prone soils; otherwise, October is satisfactory. Harvesting is at the same time as wheat. There is more straw, which slows combining, and incorporation is difficult; this is less of a problem on poor soils as there is less straw.

Spring Triticale

Varieties with no vernalisation requirement can be sown through into the spring (mid-April). Spring sown triticale is mostly seen in livestock areas – the north and west of England, as well as western Scotland, Wales and N. Ireland. Being a spring crop means winter water logging is not an issue and can be grown on a wider range of soils. In total up to 5,000 hectares of spring triticale is grown in the UK: either on its own or as part of a mixture. The crop has lower yields than winter triticale (80-90%). However, most is whole cropped to produce an 'arable forage'. Often it is grown in a mixture with a protein crop. Inputs for spring triticale are lower than those for winter varieties.

BORAGE

Production level	Low	Average	High	
Yield: t/ha (t/ac)	0.1 (0.0)	0.4 (0.2)	0.7 (0.3)	
	£	£	£	£/t
Output at £2900/t	290 (117)	1,160 (470)	2,030 (822)	2,900
Variable Costs £/ha:				
Seed....................		170 (69)		425
Fertiliser...............		109 (44)		273
Sprays..................		55 (22)		138
Total Variable Costs		334 (135)		835
Gross Margin £/ha (ac)	-44 -18	826 (335)	1,696 (687)	2065

Fertiliser Basis 0.4t/ha				Seed:	
Nutrient	Kg/t	Kg/Ha	£/Ha	£/Kg C2	£10.00
N	200	80	£64	Kg/Ha	17
P	87.5	35	£30	% HSS	0%
K	87.5	35	£15	£/t HSS	-

1. Borage is indigenous to Britain (or at least here since Roman times); it has both grown in the wild and been cultivated for centuries. It is produced principally for use as a dietary supplement, but it may also be used in cosmetics and pharmaceuticals. The oil has a high gamma linolenic acid (GLA) content.

2. It was first grown as a field crop in the UK in the early 1980's. The area grown in the UK was traditionally around 5,000 hectares. However, due to a world-wide surplus of GLA, few, if any, contracts were offered in the years 2009 to 2011. The area has recovered since, but not to previous levels. Contracts are available for harvest 2022.

3. The harvest crop price assumed is £2,900 per tonne for the 2022 crop. Values have been up to £3,000 per tonne but have settled slightly lower in the last couple of seasons. The market tends to be volatile; it is essential for a grower to have a buy-back contract with a reputable company. The crop should not be grown speculatively.

4. The crop is spring sown (April-May) into a good seedbed. Its aggressive growth gives good weed control with a high plant density. There are no significant pests and diseases, except for powdery mildew. Low rainfall areas are preferred owing to harvesting difficulties in wet conditions. It is combined in late July/early August, after swathing and drying, which takes a minimum of two weeks. The costs of swathing are not included in the margin above. Harvesting can be difficult and seed shedding at maturity is a problem. Seed should be promptly dried to 10% for safe storage. Cleaning may be necessary.

5. Borage should only be considered by those prepared to invest sufficient time in the crop's husbandry, harvest and storage. Borage is a low yield / high risk crop – yields are from virtually nothing to 0.75 tonnes per ha (6cwt per acre); average 0.4 (3.2).

Acknowledgement: Thanks to – Frontier; Fairking; Premium Crops.

MINORITY CROPS

Camelina Sativa

Camelina, Gold of Pleasure, or False Flax is a fast-growing spring (or occasionally winter) sown crop. It is easily grown and harvested and is drought tolerant. The oil contains a range of essential fatty acids. It can be used as a food supplement or in industry as a drying oil. There is limited commercial scale production in the UK and the crop should only be grown with a contract in place. Current domestic usage requirements could support around 1,000 ha of the crop in the UK. Yields are in the 1.0-2.5 tonne per ha range with a contract price for harvest 2022 likely to be around £650 per tonne. Growing costs are in the region of £300 per hectare.

Crambe - Abyssinian Mustard

Crambe is an industrial oilseed that contains high levels of erucic acid. Converted into erucamide it is used as a slip agent in plastics and is a constituent of heat sensitive dyes. The area of crambe in the UK had grown to around 5,000 ha in the early 2000's. However, the major promoter/buyer of the crop went into receivership and little or none is being currently grown commercially.

Crambe is a cruciferous spring crop managed in a similar way to spring oilseed rape. It has a short growing season, requiring only 100-120 days to reach maturity after emergence. As with oilseed rape, timely harvesting is important. Crambe can be combined direct, desiccated and combined or swathed. The crop should be stored and marketed at a moisture content of 9% or less. Yields are in the 2.5 tonne per ha range. Contract prices offered in the past were £180 per tonne. Growing costs are likely to be around £300-£350 per hectare.

Durum Wheat

As well as pasta, durum is used to produce semolina, couscous, biscuits, and is widely used in North African and Middle Eastern cooking. Domestic demand is met almost completely by imports as UK-grown crops struggle to compete on cost and there is currently no premium for domestic production.

The crop was first grown in England in the late 1970s and reached a high point of 11,000 ha (27,000 acres) in 1984. Since then, the area has declined to virtually nothing as no contracts are being offered to produce durum in the UK. There may be scope for individual growers to develop their own niche markets.

The crop is likely to be grown only in the driest parts of the east/south east, where it can best compete with second and third wheats. It may be either autumn or spring sown; with around two-thirds autumn sown historically. On average a winter crop should yield 75%-80% of conventional feed wheat in the same situation. The crop is very sensitive to stress and frost-kill in severe winters; the spring-sown crop is more reliable, and cheaper to grow, but the yield is usually 15-20% lower. Spring crops also allow more opportunities for black grass control. The crop has a higher disease resistance than other wheats, except for eyespot and ergot.

Harvesting is a critical operation; it needs to be done as soon as the crop reaches 20% moisture content, or at most 18%: it is very prone to sprouting and the quality for semolina is reduced if harvest is delayed. Durum must be dried (slowly) to 15%. It is easier and quicker to dry than normal wheat. The straw is of poorer quality and lesser quantity than conventional wheat straw and is therefore rarely baled. In the past, an ex-farm premium for 'Grade A' durum of £50 per tonne over feed wheat was offered. Growing costs are likely to be around £400-£500 per hectare.

Echium

Echium is a member of the Boraginacea family like Borage. Similar that crop, it has high concentrations of gamma linolenic acid (GLA) but is also rich in stearidonic acid, which is used in cosmetic creams to reduce skin wrinkling and the effects of sunburn.

In the past, there has been around 1,000 ha or so grown in the UK. A global glut of the active ingredient led to no contracts being offered in the years 2009 to 2019. It is believed that a small area of contracts will be offered for harvest 2022. Current demand for Echium oil is low as it is uncompetitive against marine oil alternatives. It is essential for a grower to have a buy-back contract with a reputable company, and the crop should not be grown speculatively. In the past prices have collapsed to almost nothing due to over-supply in the market.

The crop can be grown as far north as Yorkshire. It has a husbandry programme similar to that of borage but does not shed its seed as readily as borage. The seed is relatively small in size. Echium is suitable for light to medium land whereas borage performs better on a wider range of soil types.

The crop is sown in April and should come to harvest in July/August. There appear to be no significant pests of the crop. Harvesting is carried out with the use of a swather. Yields are approximately 250kg per ha (100kg per acre). Contract prices have been around £3,800 per tonne of clean seed. Growing costs are likely to be around £300-£350 per hectare.

Evening Primrose

This crop is an important source of gamma linolenic acid (GLA), but it is no longer grown in the UK and very little is cultivated elsewhere in Western Europe – it has been largely superseded by borage, which is easier to grow. The crop is still widely grown in China where the climate is more suitable, and labour costs are lower. Previous editions have given details of the crop and possible gross margin data.

Flax (cut flax for industrial fibre)

Flax was re-introduced into the UK during the 1990s, not as the traditional, pulled, long fibre variety used for linen textiles but as a cut, combinable crop producing shorter fibres for industrial uses – 'short-fibre flax'. As a natural, biodegradable fibre and a renewable resource it was promoted as a 'green' alternative to synthetic fibres and plastics. New markets were developed, and several processing plants set up – the area of flax expanded to 20,200 ha in 1996. Following low prices and reform of the subsidy regime, the area fell to less than 2,000 ha by 2003, and the one remaining processing facility in Wales was closed. Little, if any, is currently grown.

The agronomy of flax is similar to that of linseed, but it is harvested earlier. It is spring sown, suitable for most soil types although lighter soil is preferred. It is a low input crop but weed control is essential. It grows best in areas of high rainfall such as Wales and the South-west. There are several harvesting options (described in earlier editions). The preferred option is desiccation followed by combining. The straw is left to rett in the field and then baled. Retting takes 10-21 days, depending on weather conditions. The price paid for straw will reflect quality. The fibre content of a reasonable crop is 20-30%.

Hemp

The traditional use for hemp was in canvas and rope manufacture. New uses have developed over recent years in building materials (insulation) and producing internal car panels for the automotive industry. The core or pith of the plant is used for horse or poultry bedding. If the plants are left to mature, then the seed heads can be harvested. The seeds can be used in cooking, bird food and fishing bait. If pressed, the resulting 'hemp oil' has markets as a high value cooking oil, and in nutritional supplements and cosmetics. Finally, the flowers, stems and leaves of the plant can be chemically processed to produce 'CBD' oil which has 'nutraceutical' properties.

The area planted had been stable at around 1,000 ha. However, the UK's sole commercial processor of the crop went into administration in autumn 2013 and no contracts were available for some years. A small number of farmers have continued to grow the crop and market the output themselves. The crop has good 'green' credentials and would be useful agronomically as a break crop. Efforts are being made to re-establish commercial processing in the UK, but these are still at an early stage. There may be limited contracts available for the 2022 harvest. However, the crop is bulky, and it is likely that it will only be viable to grow the crop close to a processing site.

Hemp is drilled in late April/May and the fibre crop grows 3 to 3.5m (10-12 feet) tall. A minimum area of 10 ha is suggested to prevent predator (pigeon) damage to seedlings. A well-grown crop should have no weed or pest problems. Being a fast-growing, high volume crop, it requires adequate fertiliser applications to reach its potential. As a non-food crop though, sewerage sludge, digestate etc. are often used. The crop is cut in mid to late August; either mowed or with a modified forage harvester. The crop is then left to dry, bleach, and partially rett for 3-4 weeks, after which it is baled. Average yields should be around 7.5 tonne per ha (*3.0t per acre*), with target yields at 9.5 tonnes per ha (*3.8t per acre*). The crop must be stored under cover.

In the past, a delivered price of £160 per tonne was offered. Growing costs are likely to be around £400-£450 per hectare.

Dual Hemp

Hemp may also be grown as a dual-purpose crop. In the past, up to 10-15% of the national hemp crop was of this type. The crop is left to mature longer, and then the top can be combined for the seed before the straw is mown and retted. A yield of 1.0-1.2 tonne per ha (*0.4-0.5t per ac*) of seed is possible. The seed was worth around £500 per tonne. However, the yield of straw is lower at 5-6 tonnes per ha (*2.0-2.4t per ac*), with the price being same as 'conventional' hemp (see above). Agronomy and costs are likely to be similar to a fibre crop. Because of the time needed to let the seed heads mature, an earlier-maturing variety is used. The later harvest also means that this crop is more suitable for early land in the East and South.

Grain Maize

Maize is one of the major global grains – with world output being higher than that for wheat. However, the climate of the UK has made it difficult to ripen the crop and most maize is grown for forage rather than grain. A combination of earlier varieties, the development of machinery that copes better with wet conditions, and even possibly the effects of warmer summers has improved the prospects of this crop.

There is market potential, as well over a million tonnes of grain maize are imported annually. It is used in animal rations, human foods, and in industrial processes. Marketing the UK crop is a problem at present as consignments are generally not big enough to interest the major buyers. The animal feed market is the likeliest outlet for domestic production - a specialised or local market can be developed, for example feed for pigeons or corn-fed chickens. The basis of pricing in the margin is a £10-£20 per tonne premium over feed wheat. This assumes sale into a 'niche' premium market – as a 'commodity' maize is generally worth less than wheat.

There is no fundamental difference between forage and grain maize – the same varieties are simply left in the field for 3-6 weeks longer to let the cobs mature. A Defra survey in 2019 suggested less than 5% of the total maize area was for grain.

The crop can be grown south of a line from Bristol to East Anglia, excluding the far south-west. Fields should be below 500ft in elevation and south facing. To maximise heat units, the crop should be drilled as soon as soil temperatures are above 8°c − usually late April/May. Harvest by conventional combine with an adapted header in October/ November. In UK conditions grain maize seldom drops below 30% moisture. The crop needs to be dried to 15% for storage which can be expensive and time-consuming. On good land the crop can yield 8-10 tonnes per hectare, but the average is not likely to be so high.

Grain Maize Gross Margin Schedule

	£/ha	(£/ac)
Yield 7.5t/ha (3.0t/acre), Price £175/t ex-farm		
Output	1,313	(532)
Variable Costs:		
Seed	190	(77)
Fertiliser	117	(47)
Sprays	54	(22)
Total Variable Costs	360	(146)
Gross Margin per ha (acre)..	**952**	(386)
But note high drying costs:		
£15-25/t on-farm; £20-30/t off-farm	113-225	(46-91)

The majority of grain maize is currently stored as a crimped product. The crop is cut at 30-35% moisture from mid-October to early November with the 'wet' grain being processed, and an additive added (usually an organic acid). The overall cost of crimping and preservative is around £12-£15 per tonne. The grain is clamped or put into large bales or bags. It provides a very digestible dairy feed of high nutrition content. Yields can be 11-13 tonnes per hectare, and it sells for £160-£220 per tonne ex-farm.

Acknowledgement: Thanks to - Maize Growers Association.

Millet

Millet describes a range of small-seeded grain plants covering a number of different species. The most commonly grown type in the UK is proso (also called white or common) millet. Millet has been cultivated since prehistoric times. It is a major food source in arid and semi-arid parts of the world; predominantly India, China, and parts of Africa. The crop has been grown in the UK for game cover for many years, but it has recently been commercialised to supply grain to the bird seed market.

Millet Gross Margin Schedule

	£/ha	(£/ac)
Yield 3.0t/ha (1.2t/acre), Price £250/t ex-farm		
Output	750	(304)
Variable Costs:		
Seed	100	(41)
Fertiliser	121	(49)
Sprays	65	(26)
Total Variable Costs	286	(116)
Gross Margin per ha (acre)..	**464**	(188)

The UK currently imports approximately 15,000 tonnes of millet for bird and pet feed each year. Domestic plantings over the last five years have ranged from below 500 to 1,000 hectares. With the current market size, there is the potential to grow the area to around 2,000 hectares. Full import substitution is likely to be difficult as UK crop cannot compete with the very white colour of the best French white millets.

The crop can be grown on a range of soil types, but as it is drought tolerant, it is often planted on lighter land. It does not grow well in heavy or very chalky soils. The crop requires warm temperatures to ripen and is therefore best suited to the southern half of England. The crop is late drilled, usually in May once the soil has warmed up sufficiently. It can be planted as late as June. It requires a fine seedbed. The crop grows to about a metre high and is ready to harvest after 4½ months in mid to late September. The crop is usually desiccated before harvesting with a conventional combine harvester.

Yields are in the range 2.5-4.0 tonnes per ha. The contract price for 2022 is not known at the time of writing. However, contract values have recently been around £80-£100 per tonne above the feed wheat price and a price of £250 per tonne is assumed.

Acknowledgement: Thanks to - Premium Crops and Soya UK.

Navy Beans

Navy beans are the basis for the familiar canned 'baked beans'. Over 100,000t of these are consumed annually in the UK – with the vast majority of these being imported from North America. A few years ago, there was some interest in the crop, as varieties adapted to the soil types and climate of the UK were introduced. However, disappointing prices, variable yields, and the lack of area aid discouraged growers. It seems unlikely that the economics will encourage a resurgence of production in the foreseeable future.

The crop requires good fertile land and some care in growing. Sowing is in mid-May when there is no further frost risk. Harvesting is late August/early September. The target yield is 3.0 tonnes per hectare, but the average is likely to be substantially less. When budgeting, an average of around 2.0 tonnes per ha (*0.8t per acre*) could be assumed. There is very little market information available on price, but it is likely to be in the region of £250-£300 per tonne. Variable costs are likely to be in the range £300-£350 per ha.

Poppies

Commercial growing of poppies in the UK began in the early 2000's with poppy heads being processed to produce morphine for pharmaceutical purposes and the seeds being sold into the culinary market. Around 2,000 ha of the crop were grown in 2016 – all on contract to the sole UK processor. However, UK production ceased in 2017. There may be future opportunity to grow poppy seeds for the culinary market in the future, but current seed prices mean this is unlikely to be financially viable at the present time.

The crop needs free-draining alkaline soils; it is planted in the second half of March and is harvested in early to mid-August. Under the previous contracts, the processor undertook the harvesting operation with a specialised machine. Seed was included as part of the contract, as was agronomy advice (the processor specified the pesticides to be used). The grower needed to be able to offer on-floor drying facilities. Average yields are between 1.5 and 2.5 tonnes per ha. In 2016 a basic fee of £100 per ha was paid by the processor, which was then topped-up by a bonus based on the yield of the alkaloid from the crop. This figure was not publicly stated but was likely to equate to around £1,200 per ha for an average crop. Growing costs are around £350-£400 per hectare excluding the costs of seed which was provided by the processor.

Soya Beans

Soya is a sub-tropical crop in origin, grown mainly in North and South America, but also to a smaller extent in southern and eastern Europe. The UK imports three quarters of a million tonnes each year as beans and almost a further 2 million tonnes as meal, all for animal feed, so there would appear to be a ready market for the home-grown product.

Various attempts have been made to commercialise the crop in the UK. In the late 1990's new varieties were introduced and by the early 2000's the area expanded to 1,700 ha, but after several difficult years the planted area declined with less than 100 ha per year. The plant breeding process has continued and further varietal improvements in yield and earliness have been made. Problems with flea beetle in oilseed rape and soya's ability to deal with blackgrass has seen its popularity as a break crop rise again. High soya prices have made the economics more attractive at the same time. An expansion in area has been seen in the last couple of years, with the 2020 area thought to be over 3,000 ha.

Soya Bean Gross Margin Schedule

	£/ha	(£/ac)
Yield 2.2t/ha (0.9t/acre), Price £400/t ex-farm		
Output	880	(356)
Variable Costs:		
Seed	140	(57)
Fertiliser	69	(28)
Sprays	95	(38)
Total Variable Costs	304	(123)
Gross Margin per ha (acre)...	**576**	(233)

The crop is sown in late April or early May, depending on soil temperature, into a fine moist seedbed. The crop has a requirement for high temperatures and cumulative day-degrees of heat (similar to maize). This effectively restricts the crop to the southern half of England. The crop is combine harvested in September, usually after desiccation. The crop should be cleaned and dried to 14% moisture and 2% admixture.

As a legume, soya is a good alternative break crop, largely fixing its own nitrogen. Maintenance P and K is required plus 10-20kg of N to get the crop started. Spray costs also tend to be low.

Target yield is 3.0 tonnes per hectare, but the average is likely to be less; an average of 2.2 tonnes per ha (*0.9t per acre*) is assumed. The price is largely determined by the price of imported crop. The UK crop is GM free, for which a premium is paid. A further premium may be paid for Identity Preserved UK crop which goes into human consumption or for organically grown soya. For 2022 harvest the price is estimated to be £400 per tonne.

Sunflower

Over the past decade the UK has imported between 30-80,000 tonnes of sunflower seed annually, plus over half-a-million tonnes of sunflower oil and meal. No seed is commercially crushed in the UK. There has been continued interest in sunflower, but late harvests and low yields have restricted the development of the crop. It is unclear how much of the crop is currently commercially grown in the UK, but it is likely to be less than 500 ha. This would produce some 1,000 tonnes of seed. Almost all UK production goes into bird seed. Some attempts have been made to cold-press sunflowers to produce a UK-sunflower oil, but this market is still restricted to local and small-scale production. Producers should satisfy themselves of the end-market before planting the crop.

Extra-early maturing semi-dwarf hybrid varieties are the most suitable to conditions in the UK. The crop needs a relatively mild climate and is best grown south-east of a line from the Wash to east Dorset. Sowing is from April to early May when the soil temperature is 7-8°C. Although sunflower will grow on a broad range of soil types, its capacity to do well in dry and sandy soils and areas of low rainfall is a recommendation. Pre-emergence weed control may be necessary; at the right plant density weeds should not subsequently be a problem. As it is a broad row crop, chemical or mechanical weed control is possible.

Sclerotina and botrytis, in a wet season, may affect the crop. On areas of less than 6 ha bird damage can be serious. Sunflower has a low nitrogen requirement.

Harvesting is from mid-September to early-October by combine harvester. Yields of up to 2.5 tonnes per ha with oil content of 44% are possible. The crop is dried to 8-9% for safe storage, which can be expensive. There is little or no trade in UK-produced sunflower seed and growers are likely to have to develop their own markets. On European markets, sunflower seed is priced close to the value of rapeseed (often a small premium). Growing costs will be in the region of £350-£400 per hectare.

Others

Other crops that have been in the news in recent years as possible new crops for the future (or present crops capable of substantial development) include the following: chickpeas and lentils, ahiflower, lunaria, fenugreek, meadowfoam, cuphea, peppermint, quinoa, buckwheat, honesty and herbs for their essential oils. At present there are no reliable data for these crops on average yield expectations and little on prices or variable costs, when grown on a commercial scale in this country. A number of them are either for the health food market or are sources of oil for industry as replacements for marine oils and light mineral oils. Research continues on many of them. More details may be available from the NNFCC.

POTATOES

Maincrop Potatoes

Production level	Low	Average	High	
Yield: t/ha (t/ac)	43.0 (17.4)	50.4 (20.4)	58.0 (23.5)	
	£	£	£	£/t
Output at £165/t	7,095 (2,873)	8,314 (3367)	9,570 (3876)	165
Variable Costs £/ha *(£/ac)* :				
Seed..........................		980 (397)		19
Fertiliser.....................		379 (153)		8
Sprays.......................		582 (236)		12
Sundries		103 (42)		2
Contracting...................		1625 (658)		32
Total Variable Costs	3,669 (1,486)	3,669 (1,486)	3,669 (1,486)	
Gross Margin £/ha (ac)	**3426** (1,388)	**4646** (1,882)	**5901** (2,390)	**92**

Fertiliser Basis 50.390243902439t/ha				Seed:		Sprays:	
Nutrient	Kg/t	Kg/Ha	£/Ha	£/t C2	370	Herbicides	£32
N	3.6	179	£143	Kg/Ha	3,000	Fungicides	£200
P	1.0	50	£43	% HSS	40%	Insecticides	£50
K	5.8	292	£122	£/t HSS	280	PGRs	£0
MgO		40	£71	Kg/Ha	2,800	Other	£300

1. *Prices*. The price used above is £165 per tonne for ware and £35 for stock feed (assumed 5%), which gives £160 per tonne for the whole crop. The average price for wares between 2010 and 2020 was £165/tonne. Variations according to quality and market are considerable.

2. *Sprays*: herbicide, Blight control, and haulm destruction. Includes Nematode (PCN) spray, which accounts for about 60% of potato land.

3. *Casual Labour*. Casual labour has been removed from the gross margin. This cost varies considerably on end-use and therefore processing and storage requirements. It could vary from nothing to £23/tonne.

4. *Contracting*: Includes destoning, ridging, planting and harvest and carting. For other contract work see page 182.

5. *Sundries:* Assume £50/ha agronomy, £42.62 AHDB Levy and miscellaneous costs.

6. *Potato Land Rentals* range depending on the year, location, soil and water availability, ranging from over £650/ha (£260/acre) to as much as £1,200/ha (£500/acre), depending on terms as well as soil type such as irrigation maintenance. The late harvested potatoes depress following crop yields. As a result, some have tried to increase potato rents on back of increased cereal prices.

7. *Specialised Equipment Prices*: see page 176 and *Potato Store Costs*: see page 219.

8. *Labour*: see p. 161.

Early Potatoes

Production level		Low		Average	High	
Yield: t/ha (t/ac)		22.0	(8.9)	26.0 (10.5)	30.0 (12.2)	
		£		**£**	**£**	**£/t**
Output at £240/t		5,280 (2,138)		6,240 (2527)	7,200 (2916)	*240*
Variable Costs £/ha *(£/ac)* :						
Seed...........................				895 (362)		*34*
Fertiliser......................				200 (81)		*8*
Sprays........................				406 (164)		*16*
Sundries ....….............				103 (42)		*4*
Contracting ....….............				1,625 (658)		*63*
Total Variable Costs		3,229 (1,308)		3,229 (1,308)	3,229 (1,308)	*124*
Gross Margin £/ha (ac)		**2051** (831)		**3011** (1,220)	**3971** (1,608)	*116*

Fertiliser Basis 26t/ha				Seed:		Sprays:	
Nutrient	Kg/t	Kg/Ha	£/Ha	£/t C2	270	Herbicides	£17
N	*4.4*	113	£90	Kg/Ha	3,400	Fungicides	£103
P		31	£27	% HSS	10%	Insecticides	£26
K	5.8	151	£63	£/t HSS	245	PGRs	£0
MgO			£20	Kg/Ha	2,800	Other	£260

1. *Prices* and *Yields*. The price assumed above is an average of £250 per tonne for a 24 tonne/ha yield. Yields increase, and prices fall as the season progresses. Thus, both depend on the date of lifting, e.g., late May 7t/ha, June, 15t/ha; July 20 to 30 t/ha. Prices in late May to mid-June can be up to three times those in July; the earliest crops (early May) can exceed £1,000 per tonne, but the price could be down to £500 by mid-May and to £250 by early June. So, an average output of £6,000 given above could be obtained from 10 tonnes at £600 per tonne, 15t at £400, 20t at £300 or 30t at £200.

2. *Sprays*: herbicide, blight control, and haulm destruction. Includes Nematode (PCN) spray, which accounts for about 60% of potato land.

3. *Contracting*: Includes destoning, ridging, planting and harvest and carting. For other contract work see page 182.

4. *Sundries*: as above

5. *Labour*: see p. 161.

Early and Maincrop Potatoes

About 80% of potatoes in the UK are maincrop (harvest in August or later), with 12% seed and the rest as earlies (defined as harvested before 1 August).

SUGAR BEET

Production level	Low		Average	High	
Yield: t/ha (t/ac)	65.5	(26.5)	77.0 (31.2)	88.5 (35.8)	
	£		£	£	£/t
Output at £25.55/t	1,674 (678)		1,967 (797)	2,261 (916)	26
Variable Costs £/ha *(£/ac)* :					
Seed..........................			207 (84)		2.7
Fertiliser.....................			238 (96)		3.1
Sprays........................			244 (99)		3.2
Sundries......................			44 (18)		0.6
Contract Harvest.............			215 (87)		2.8
Total Variable Costs			948 (384)		12
Gross Margin £/ha (ac)	**726** (294)		**1,019** (413)	**1,313** (532)	13

Fertiliser Basis 77t/ha				Seed:		Sprays:	
Nutrient	Kg/t	Kg/Ha	£/Ha	£/unit	180	Herbicides	£160
N		100	£80	Unit/Ha	1.15	Fungicides	£38
P	0.8	62	£54	% HSS	0%	Insecticides	£39
K	1.7	131	£55	£/t HSS		PGRs	£0
MgO			£50	Transport £/t	£5.60	Other	£7

Yield = 'Adjusted tonnes' at standard 16% sugar content

1. These figures are for the crop drilled in 2022, harvested and delivered in 2022/23. New whole crop weights are now included in yields.

2. *Prices*. The 'all-in' price is not yet known. £25.40 per adjusted tonne has been used plus Late delivery allowances less levies. This is based on 100% sold 'in contract'. Sugar bonus may be payable (see below).

3. Late delivery allowances of 40p/tonne. Late delivery bonus: 26 December - 7 January: 0.8% of price; thereafter, the rate rises by 0.3% per day and at 0.4% per day from 1 March. Transport bonus is excluded as equivalent costs are not in this gross margin.

4. A bonus has been available (not included in the gross margin) for growers when the average EU sugar price exceeds a trigger €375/t. This margin is converted into beet (16% sugar), sterling at the exchange rate set, and growers committing to 3-year contracts earn 25% of uplift, 1-year commitments earn 15%. For example:

   - EU sugar price of €500/t. €450-€375 = €75/t.
   - Conversion to beet (6.4t per tonne of sugar) = €11.72/t
   - Convert to sterling (at say 85p/€) = £9.96/t
   - 1-year contract earns 15%, so £1.49/t, 3- year earns 25% so £2.49/t

5. *Seed*; includes a standard seed dressing.

6. *Contract*. Excludes carting, British Sugar provides harvesting at this rate. For other contract work see page 182.

7. *Transport*. Contract haulage charges vary according to distance to factory, typically about £5.60 per (unadjusted) tonne of unwashed beet including loading and cleaning (dirt and top tare assumed at 14% in total).

TOP FRUIT

The figures indicate a range within which the performance of most (established) orchards falls. The gross margins are calculated as lower yields less lower costs and higher yields less higher costs. This direct link is not always the case, although several post-harvest costs are relative to the amount of fruit marketed. Production costs are not the main cost in top fruit production, the grading, packing and storage are far more significant.

	Dessert Apples		*Culinary Apples*		*Pears*	
Production level	Low	High	Low	High	Low	High
Yield: tonnes per ha	30	50	30	55	20	45
Price £/tonne	580	1,000	390	715	610	1,000
	£	£	£	£	£	£
Output	17,400	50,000	11,700	39,325	12,200	45,000
Variable Costs:						
Orchard Depreciation	1,100	2,310	880	1,850	705	1,295
Pruning & Husbandry	1,350	1,550	1,080	1,240	820	1,845
Fertiliser/spray	1,038	2,076	983	2,185	759	1,857
Crop Sundries	477	796	477	849	371	849
Harvesting	2,250	3,750	1,860	3,410	1,500	3,375
Contract Packing	4,800	8,000	4,800	8,800	3,200	7,200
Packaging	2,460	6,150	960	4,510	1,440	5,085
Transport	1,980	4,290	1,190	3,630	1,190	3,265
Commission/Levies	1,565	4,500	1,055	3,540	1,100	4,050
Total Variable Costs	17,020	33,421	13,286	30,014	11,086	28,821
Gross Margin per ha	**380**	**16,579**	**-1,586**	**9,311**	**1,114**	**16,179**

1. *Price*: Average of all grades. Price is influenced by grade-out, variety, customer and pack format (which in turn may affect packing and packaging costs).

2. *Orchard Depreciation*: Establishment costs vary, depending on the type of top fruit and method of production. Costs include land preparation, fencing, trees, posts, stakes and guards, planting labour and irrigation installation.

3. *Orchard Longevity*: Varies on factors including tree performance, new varieties, outcompeting older ones and consumer preference. As a guide, dessert; 12 to 20 years, culinary; 15 to 30, cider; 15 to 45 and pears; 15 to 40. More recently planted denser apple and pear systems likely to be shorter-lived, with full cropping reached in years 3-5 (6-9 for traditional systems). Figures above include an allowance for 5% immature trees.

4. *Pruning & Husbandry*: This is a labour cost. The differentiation between winter pruning and summer thinning is less clear than historically, and highly dependent on variety.

5. *Crop Sundries*: Include bin depreciation, tree replacement (dependant on canker susceptibility of variety), associated tree ties, rabbit guards, stake replacement, bee hire, picking hods and other harvest aids.

6. *Harvesting*: Based on £75/t average (including supervision, Employer's NI & holiday allowance) for dessert apples and pears and £62/t for culinary. Varies significantly with variety, yield, fruit size and quality, etc.

7. *Grading and Packing*: Most packing is undertaken off-farm with contract packing. Costs average about £155 per tonne plus transport for dessert apples.

8. *Packaging*: £82/t and £123/t used here for desserts, £33-£82 for culinary and £72-£113 for pears, although may be higher with specialist formats. Considerable variations arise from both crop quality (i.e. grade-out), customer and pack format.

9. *Transport*: allowance for farm to final customer, haulage to and from store and packer could double these figures.

10. *Commission/levies*: Including both marketer's and retailer's commission, as well as levies (e.g. English Apples and Pears, AHDB), 9% has been used here. Charges vary between 2 and 25% dependant on system and organisation. Varietal royalties and Producer Organisation levies are excluded.

SOFT FRUIT

The figures, for both soil-grown and a table-top substrate crop, indicate a range in which the performance of most, but not all crops falls. The gross margins are lower yields less lower costs and higher yields less higher costs. In practice, costs are not all linked to yields although most of the costs are incurred at or after harvest and are therefore affected by volume.

	Strawberries Raised Bed		Tabletop Ever-bearers		Raspberries	
Production level	Low	High	Low	High	Low	High
Yield: tonnes per ha	18	23	28	44	8	15
Price £/tonne	2,750	3,680	2,750	3,680	5,750	7,760
	£	£	£	£	£	£
Output	49,500	84,640	77,000	161,920	46,000	116,400
Variable Costs:						
Plants, Planting	5,478	5,478	10,720	10,720	1,008	1,008
Structures	5,953	5,953	9,533	9,533	5,953	5,953
Fertiliser/Predators...	1,500	2,500	3,000	5,500	1,750	3,500
Fieldwork	2,179	4,825	3,612	9,650	1,575	6,195
Harvesting	15,390	19,665	16,464	25,872	18,960	35,550
Grading/Packing	5,580	7,130	8,680	13,640	4,360	8,175
Packaging	7,525	9,615	11,705	18,390	4,160	7,800
Transport	3,780	4,830	5,880	9,240	2,080	3,900
Commission	4,455	7,620	6,930	14,575	4,140	10,475
Total Variable Costs	51,839	67,615	76,524	117,120	43,986	82,556
Gross Margin per ha	**-2,339**	**17,025**	**476**	**44,801**	**2,014**	**33,844**

Strawberry Raised Bed Notes

1. *Plants & Planting:* including plants and substrate. *Plants;* 35,000 per hectare with 60-day cropping in year 1 followed by 2 further years in main season production. Plants/planting/sterilisation written off over crop life of 3 years. Bed making not included as a variable cost.

2. *Structures:* average cost per year. Annual cost of poly-tunnels including land preparation, irrigation installation, metalwork (all w/o over 10 years) and plastic (w/o 5 years). Costs included for erection, dismantling and venting. Currently high increase in steel price is adding to new structures beyond figures quoted here.

3. *Fertiliser, Sprays, Predators:* Recent increases due to greater predator usage

4. *Fieldwork:* weeding, runner removal, leaf thinning etc.

5. *Harvesting*- including supervision, Employer' s NI & holiday allowance. Ranges from £650 to £1,300/tonne, £855 used here.

6. *Grading/Packing £310/t. Packaging at £418/t, Transport at £210/t.*

7. *Commission/levies:* Including both marketeer's and retailer's commission, as well as levies (e.g. AHDB). A total of 9% has been used, although charges vary considerably. N.B. This does not include levy payments under the Producer Organisation regime.

Strawberries - Table-top Ever Bearer Notes:

1. *This system* holds plants off the ground for ease of management and harvest, in substrates, rather than soil. About 80% of strawberries are now grown in this format on substrate and the percentage is rising annually. Between 45 and 60% of turnover of June- bearing raised bed strawberries is spent on labour, whereas it falls to 30 to 40% for ever-bearers.

2. *Plants*: assumes 40,000 per hectare. Plants/planting written off over crop life of one year. Cost of substrate bags w/o 2 years; sometimes replaced annually.

3. *Structures:* poly-tunnel cost as for June-bearers, together with annual cost of table- top system (estimated as £32,000 plus installation w/o 10 years, table-top system costs vary considerably). Currently high increase in steel price is adding to new structures beyond figures quoted here.

4. Fieldwork- weeding, runner removal, leaf thinning and tucking, truss support etc.

5. *Harvesting*: including supervision, Employer's NI & holiday allowance. Ranges from £450 to £750/tonne, £588 used here.

6. *Grading, Packing, Packaging, Transport & Commission* - as for June bearers.

Raspberries Notes:

1. *Raspberries* UK crop area 1,500 hectares but are worth more than Blackcurrants (2,500 Ha)

2. *Plants* - 8000/ha at 48p per plant. Planting at 15p per plant. Land preparation and irrigation, £655 to £1,090/ha

3. *Structures*- as for strawberries, including irrigation.

4. *Wirework*- to include material and labour.

5. *Plants/planting/wirework* written off over crop life of, say 5 years. Crop life typically 4 to 7 years although some systems are annual replacement.

6. *Harvesting* (including supervision, employer's NI & holiday allowance) - Ranges from £1,650 to £2,700/tonne, £2,370 used here (£2.25/kg). Includes supervision & transport to packhouse.

7. *Grading/Packing*: £545 per tonne (54.5p/kg).

8. *Packaging:* £520 per tonne (52 p/kg).

9. *Transport:* £260 per tonne (26 p/kg).

10. *Commission/levies:* Including both marketeer's and retailer's commission, as well as levies (e.g. AHDB), 9% has been used, charges can vary considerably. This does not include levy payments under the Producer Organisation regime.

FRUIT FOR PROCESSING

This section puts cider apples and blackcurrants together as their production systems are closer to each other than to their biologically closer crops. Harvest represents the end of the process with these crops, so packing, grading and storage costs are minimal. Yield is the key consideration for these crops.

	Cider Apples		*Blackcurrants*	
Production level	Low	High	Low	High
Yield: tonnes per ha	15	55	5.5	7.5
	£	£	£	£
Price £/tonne	125	125	660	765
Output	1,875	6,875	3,630	5,738
Variable Costs:				
Depreciation	448	673	854	1,196
Fertiliser/spray/Sundry	382	964	460	460
Husbandry Labour	161	161	161	161
Contract Harvesting	630	2,310	230	315
Transport	160	580	60	85
Commission/Levies	55	205	110	170
Total Variable Costs	1,836	4,892	1,875	2,386
Gross Margin per ha	**39**	**1,983**	**1,755**	**3,351**

Cider Apples

Although a top fruit, this crop is grown for processing so has fundamentally different customer requirements and therefore costs to other top fruit. This is currently the largest top fruit sector by area but not value. Some orchards are appearing specifically for juicing (Jonagold particularly). Establishment costs approximately £9,350 plant and planting costs, with another £4,100 land preparation, and irrigation set up costs. Orchards can last over 40 years, but this example depreciated over 30. Machine harvested and collected (tree shaker, sweep and collector) at £40/tonne. Fruit transport £10.50/ tonne.

Blackcurrants

Although a soft fruit, this crop is much more of a field crop grown on arable farms with machine harvesting. All UK blackcurrant crop is processed into cordial drink. Establishment costs approximately £8,000/ha for bushes with full production in year 2 followed by up to 10 years cropping. Contracts with processors are required. Blackcurrants are grown on about 2,500 hectares in the UK, by 45 growers. Establishment costs are an illustration of a 10-year system but can be far shorter. Contract harvesting £42/tonne. Transport is £11.00/tonne and levies are 3% output.

VINEYARDS

The planted area under vines in England and Wales in 2021 is estimated to be 3,750 hectares, five times greater than it was in 2004 when the figure was 761 hectares. The area had fallen from a previous high of 1,065 hectares in 1993 when the Britain grew mainly Germanic grape varieties which then fell out of fashion. Wine Standards (WS), a branch of the Food Standards Agency, keeps the Vineyard Register (VR) and in June 2020 it estimated that there were over 750 'commercial' vineyards (vineyards of 0.10 ha or more), plus several smaller ones run as hobbies and not selling wine. The average size of vineyards in Britain is now around 5.0 ha, although there several producers with over 100 ha of vineyards and the 25 largest account for 50% of production; more if you only consider sparkling wine. In the last decade, the vineyard area has been expanding by between 7.5% and 10% per year. At present, around 30% of the vineyard area is not fully cropping as the vines are too young. There is no restriction on planting vines in Britain and almost any variety may be legally planted.

The 2020 vintage produced 8.81 million 75cl bottles of wine, both still and sparkling and in the last three years (2018-2020) a total of 32.4 million bottles has been produced. Whilst average annual yields have risen in the last three years to 3,534 litres per ha, the ten-year average yield is 2,524 l/ha. This is a low figure compared to world yield levels, reflecting the many young vineyards in the UK, plus some under-performing and poorly sited and managed vineyards (Bordeaux averages around 7,000 l/ha.) However, yields in well-run, well located vineyards are two to three times these average GB levels. Crop yields depend on conditions around flowering (mid-June to mid-July) and these can be extremely variable in our maritime climate. Because of the large plantings in recent years which are now coming into production, the number of bottles produced each year is rising and stocks of wine, both still and sparkling, are now at an all-time high. However, in a rapidly expanding vineyard region the amount of the amount of sparkling wine available for sale in any one year is smaller than the amount produced, as bottle-fermented sparkling wines take 2 to 5 years to mature after bottling and many new vineyards are still building up stocks or only just releasing their first vintages. Still wines come to the market faster and can be on sale within 3 years of planting vines, whereas sparkling wine producers typically have several years' worth of stock to store (and finance) before they start selling wines. A stock equal to at least 5 times the annual sales would be usual for a sparkling wine producer in Britain (average stock levels in Champagne stand at 4 years and 2 months' worth of sales), with those selling long-aged and prestige cuvées carrying significantly higher stock levels of those wines. Sparkling wines from 2010 and 2011 vintages are still available from some British producers.

Most of the wines produced in Britain used to be white, but the proportion of red (and mainly) rosé wines, both still and sparkling, has risen to around 15% of the total. It is estimated that around two-thirds of the harvest is made into sparkling wine, a figure that will increase as many of the new, sparkling-only vineyards start cropping. Since the very warm year of 2003, plantings of Champagne-style varieties (Chardonnay, Pinot Noir and Meunier) have increased significantly. Chardonnay and Pinot Noir are now the most widely planted varieties (around 1,150 ha each) and these, together with Meunier (375 ha), account for around 70% of the total vine area. Bacchus, with 400 ha, is the most widely planted still-wine variety, and is becoming recognised as one from which excellent top-quality still wines can be made. The variety is expanding and accounts for around 8.5% of the UK vineyard area. The other most widely planted varieties are Seyval Blanc, Reichensteiner, Blauer Frühburgunder, Solaris, Rondo, and Ortega. Together these ten varieties account for around 85% of all vineyards.

Many producers find that, at least initially, before they have built up a reputation for the quality of their wines, selling from the 'farm-gate' is their best route to market and helps introduce their wines to the public. However, over the last twenty years, the reputation of English and Welsh sparkling wines has improved considerably and with the rising availability of these wines, more outlets, both on-trade and off-trade, now stock them. All wines sold in Britain bear the same VAT and duty irrespective of their origin and value, and the duty on sparkling wines is higher than for still-wines. British-grown wines only account for around 0.3% of the domestic wine market.

The market in Britain for all sparkling wines is around 215 million bottles a year and growing. Around two-thirds of this is Prosecco (now much bigger by volume and value than Champagne), Cava, Asti Spumante and other less expensive wines. Champagne (for which Britain is the biggest export market) accounts for just under 27 million bottles a year (having fallen from 36 million bottles in 2008) and it is into this sector of the sparkling wine market that British producers need to sell their wines if their enterprises are to be profitable. Current sales of English and Welsh wines are around 5 to 6 million bottles, with exports accounting for around 5% of that total. Despite the disruption to the hospitality industry since March 2020, most vineyards report good direct-to-consumer sales for 2021.

Although the amount of English and Welsh sparkling wine available for sale today is still quite small, given the amount of land already planted with Champagne varieties, this will rise from today's estimated 3-4 million bottles available for sale to around 6-8 million by 2025 as the recent larger vintages mature. It is estimated that around half of the sparkling wine vineyards currently planted do not yet have wine on the market as they are too young to crop, or the wine they have produced is still ageing. What impact this increase in supply will have upon prices of English and Welsh sparkling wines, currently matching those of Champagne and other top-quality sparkling wines, is unknown. The amount currently exported is estimated to around 10% of all sales by volume and this might well increase as available volumes increase. One sector which is increasing is the production of sparkling wines from non-traditional methods such as the Charmat (or tank method) used for Prosecco and other cheaper sparkling wines and of wines that have been carbonated. From small beginnings, producers of these wines, which are appearing in both bottles and cans, are expanding and with their lower production costs, and much shorter time-to-market, are being more widely seen. What pressure these less-expensive wines will have on other wines has yet to be seen.

A Quality Wine Scheme for England and Wales was introduced in 1991 and a Regional Wine Scheme in 1997, but in 2010 these were replaced with a new system of wine classification based upon the terms Protected Designation of Origin (PDO) and Protected Geographical Indication (PGI). PDO wines are broadly the same as Quality Wines and PGI wines the same as Regional wines. All PDO and PGI wines have to go through a testing and tasting procedure before they can use the relevant names. There are also 'Varietal Wines' which have to be 'certified' and can then be labelled with the name of the grape variety and vintage, but not vineyard name. Wines outside of these three categories are known as 'UK Wines' and may not bear vintage or variety names, although they can state their origin. There is also a PDO for sparkling wines made from certain vine varieties which allows the term 'English Quality Sparkling Wine' to be used. Wines of Great Britain (WineGB – formerly the UK Vineyards Association) promotes all English and Welsh wines and organise tastings and events such as the annual trade and press tasting held in September, English Wine Week at the end of May, the annual English and Welsh Wine of the Year Competition in July, plus other services to members. WineGB does not directly market wines.

The quality of any wine depends on the site and, in a cool maritime climate like Britain's, the best sites are on south-facing, well-drained land, sheltered from prevailing south-westerly winds and usually less than 100 metres above sea level. Coastal sites are often too windy. The best sites are in the southern half of England or Wales with the counties of Essex, Kent, East and West Sussex, Hampshire and Surrey; the traditional fruit and hop growing counties. Success should be defined not only by wine quality, but also by yield. Low to very low yields in many vineyards, whilst they might contribute to wine quality, do not usually help business viability. Most of the longest-established and most successful UK vineyards sell some of their wine direct to the consumer and often have tea-rooms, restaurants and even hotels as part of their enterprise. They also offer guided tours, weddings, parties and corporate entertaining. Sites for vineyards should be selected with these activities in mind.

High quality vineyard management and marketing ability are both essential for a successful vineyard enterprise. There is no minimum area for profitable production and a small vineyard selling wine at the farm gate and locally may be just as profitable per pound or hour invested as a larger one selling wine (at a much lower return) through wholesalers and retailers. Some vineyards grow grapes under contract for other wineries, and there is also a 'spot' market for grapes and prices fluctuate according to vintage. 2021 saw the creation of two grape and wine trading platforms which in itself is an indication of an increase in availability of grapes and wine. The very poor harvest in 2012 caused grape prices to rise between 2013-17, but the high yielding 2018 and 2019 harvests have brought grape prices down. Given the very large number of vineyards planted in recent years, many of which are now starting to crop, many producers believe that grape prices (as well as wine prices) will fall in coming years.

Most vineyards in Britain are planted with a row width of 1.75 to 2.25 metres, an intervine distance of between 1.0 m and 1.4 m and use the Guyot cane-pruned system, either two-cane Double Guyot or single-cane Single Guyot. A vine density of 4,000 to 5,000 vines per hectare gives the best quality grapes and economic yield in our weather conditions. Cane-pruned vines, with good establishment, should be partially cropping in their third summer and fully yielding by their fourth, although much will depend on how they establish. Growers on fertile soils often get a small crop in year two.

Suitable land for vineyards is often hard to find and is becoming increasingly expensive, especially if you are looking for larger areas of south-facing land deemed 'perfect for vines'. In recent years some buyers have been prepared to pay a considerable premium for good sites for vines, and whereas once £30,000 per ha would have been quoted, some producers have paid over £60,000 per ha. Capital for vineyard establishment (including planting materials and labour) of £25,000 to £30,000 per ha is typical, although fencing and drainage increases this figure. These prices are affected by the £-€ rate as all vines, and some trellising materials and vineyard equipment are imported from the Euro-zone. A suitable tractor, mower, sprayer etc. are also required to manage the vines and together these cost at least £75,000 and often considerably more.

There were 190 wineries registered in Britain for processing home-grown grapes for the 2020 harvest. Whilst many are small and in modest buildings, the best are as modern and well-equipped as any in the world, costing several millions to build. Many smaller vineyards take their grapes to be made into wine under contract to one of the established wineries or to one of the contract-only wineries of which several have been set up in recent years. Either way, using an established winery gives small growers access to state-of-the-art equipment and experienced winemakers. Temperature controlled storage space for wines to mature, especially sparkling wines, is also required, whether or not you have your own winery.

Depending on the quality of the site, the vine varieties grown, and the style of wine produced, a well-sited, well-managed vineyard should yield on average at least 7.5 tonnes per ha (*3 tonnes per acre*) of grapes, with higher yields possible. For still wine production, around 950 x 75cl bottles will be produced from 1 tonne of grapes. For sparkling wine, production will be between 675 and 800 bottles per tonne, depending on quality, with some additional juice/wine available which will not be suitable for sparkling wine, but might be blended into still wine, depending on the vintage.

There is also a market for selling grapes to wineries. Grape prices vary according to the variety and the vintage and whether growers are under contract or not. Prices range from £1,500 to £2,500 per tonne delivered to a winery, with still varieties being less valuable and good Pinot Noir or Chardonnay for sparkling wine at the higher end.

The costs below refer to a commercial enterprise on a suitable site producing sparkling wine sold via retailers from a broad variety range. Any direct sales to the public will have higher profit margins. The cost structure for small-scale still wine producers is different. A retail price for still wine of at least £12 per bottle is required to cover outgoings, capital and profit, assuming a grower uses a contract winery and sells wine at full price to the consumer with no sales costs..

Sparkling Wine - White (Double Guyot)

Production level	Low	Average	High
Yield: Tonnes per ha (acre)	4.00 (1.6)	7.50 (3.0)	11.00 (4.5)
Bottles per ha (acre)	3,000 (1,215)	5,625 (2,278)	8,250 (3,341)
	£	£	£
Output at £11.14 per bottle	33,420 (13,535)	62,663 (25,378)	91,905 (37,222)
Variable Costs:			
Establishment (over 25 years).........		1,320 (535)	
Annual Material Costs		1,500 (608)	
Labour (Growing)		6,500 (2,633)	
Labour (Harvesting) at £250/t...	1,000 (405)	1,875 (759)	2,750 (1,114)
Winery Costs at £7.5/bottle........	22,500 (9,113)	42,188 (17,086)	22,500 (9,113)
General Overheads		2,500 (1,013)	
Total Costs	35,320 (14,305)	55,883 (22,632)	37,070 (15,013)
Returns per ha (acre)	**-1,900** -770	**6,780** (2,746)	**54,835** (22,208)

Sales		Establishment	/ha	/acre
Bottles per tonne of grapes	750	Crop longevity (years)		25
Retail price of bottle	25.00	Plants/Ha(Ac)	3000 to	1215 to
Less: Retail margin at 30%	17.50		5000	2025
Less: VAT at 20% and Duty		Materials	18,000	7,290
at £2.86 per bottle	*11.14*	Labour	15,000	6,075
		Total Establish.	*33,000*	*13,365*

1. If wines are sold via a wholesaler and/or retailer, gross profit margin of at least 10% (wholesaler) and 30% (retailer) on duty-paid prices must be allowed for.

2. Sparkling wine of 8.5% and up to 15% or more has a duty rate of £2.86 per 75cl bottle; still wines of the same alcoholic strength, £2.23 per 75cl bottle (2021 rates).

3. Establishment costs would be more if the site has to be drained and provided with windbreaks and rabbit and deer fencing. Annual growing costs can also be significantly greater, depending on planting density, variety, yield, labour costs and management.

4. Harvesting costs are yield dependent

5. Assumes wine is made at contract-winery. This includes materials, labour, storage an transport. Having still wine made under contract costs at least £5.00 a bottle.

Acknowledgements: Stephen Skelton MW, Viticultural Consultant www.englishwine.com and the UK Vineyards Association, Mrs Jo Cowderoy: jo@ukva.org.uk

2. FORAGE PRODUCTION

FORAGE VARIABLE COSTS

Grassland	1-2 year Ley		Intensive 3-5 year Ley		Long Term Ley		Improved Permanent Pasture		Low Input Pasture	
Yield t/ha *(ac)*	50	*(20)*	47	*(19)*	42	*(17)*	35	*(14)*	27	*(11)*
Years Ley	2		4		7		-		-	
Kg/ha *(units/acre)*										
N	250	*(199)*	200	*(159)*	150	*(120)*	100	*(80)*	50	*(40)*
P	35	*(28)*	33	*(26)*	29	*(23)*	25	*(20)*	19	*(15)*
K	120	*(96)*	113	*(90)*	101	*(80)*	84	*(67)*	65	*(52)*
Costs £/ha *(£/ac)*										
Seed *per year*	54	(22)	36	(15)	24	(10)	7	(3)	3	(1)
Fertiliser	280	(113)	235	(95)	187	(76)	136	(55)	83	(34)
Sprays	15	(6)	10	(4)	5	(2)	2	(1)	0	(0)
Total *£/ha/Yr*	348	(141)	281	(114)	216	(87)	145	(59)	87	(35)
cost £/t fresh weight	6.96		5.98		5.14		4.14		3.21	

Other Forages	Unimproved Pasture		Maize		Clover Ley		Kale		Swedes	
Yield t/ha (t/acre)	18	*(7)*	40	*(16)*	40 (16)		45 (18)		70 (28)	
Costs £/ha *(£/ac)*										
Seed			190	(77)	34	(14)	49	(20)	160	(65)
Fertiliser			117	(47)	39	(16)	142	(58)	104	(42)
Sprays			54	(22)	10	(4)	11	(4)	11	(4)
Total £/ha (£/ac)	0	(0)	360	(146)	82	(33)	202	(82)	275	(111)
Cost £/t fresh weight	0.00		9.01		2.06		4.48		3.93	

	Fodder Beet		Forage Rape	Maincrop Turnips	Stubble Turnips
Yield t/ha (t/acre)	70	*(28)*	35 (14)	65 (26)	35 (14)
Costs £/ha *(£/ac)*					
Seed	210	(85)	37 (15)	57 (23)	20 (8)
Fertiliser	201	(81)	110 (45)	143 (58)	120 (49)
Sprays	107	(43)	20 (8)	11 (4)	11 (4)
Total £/ha (£/ac)	518 (210)		167 (68)	211 (85)	151 (61)
Cost £/t fresh weight	7.40		4.78	3.25	4.32

Forage Notes

1. *Seed costs:* vary according to the proportion of permanent pasture and length of leys.

2. *Fertiliser* is assumed to come partially from manure as well as bagged fertiliser. It is often less on permanent pasture, depending on management style which also affects stocking rates and productive levels per animal.

3. *Contract work* on maize, silage and cultivations: Refer to Page 182.

4. *Labour:* forage and conservation labour, pages 161

5. *Conservation machinery:* page 176.

6. *Standing maize* crops are typically sold for £750 to £1,000/ha (£300-400/acre), depending on the potential yield of the crop and local supply and demand which has become volatile with local demand from anaerobic digestion plants.

7. An appropriate combination of these forage gross margins is used to calculate the forage costs of all the grazing livestock margins throughout the book. For simplicity, only the grass (appropriate combination of all 5 types), maize and stubble turnips are used. Each livestock gross margin explains which forage crops are used.

8. *Plastic wrap* for baled silage = £1.90/ round bale (120cm), £5.20 to £6.50 for contract wrapping (4-6 layers).

9. *Net wrap* for bales = £0.70/round bale.

8. *Whole Crop (feed wheat).* Variable costs are as for combined crop (page 5) plus contract harvesting and clamping at £165 per ha (£65/ac.) see contractors charges page 182. Fresh yield averages 27.5 tonnes per ha (11 t/ac.) harvested in late June at 35% dry matter. Urea treatment (for higher dry matter) for whole crop alkalage: £8.30/treated tonne. For urea treated grain, add £16.70 per tonne. Standing wheat auctions for about £1,100 per hectare (£445/acre). This is based on 8.5t/ha at £150 which is the opportunity cost of harvesting as grain less harvesting (£90/ha), carting (est. £20/ha) and storage costs (£5-8/tonne).

TOTAL COSTS OF FORAGE

Linked to previous schedule, grass silage using 'Intensive 3-5 year' and assumes 2-cuts and a 4-year ley with 47 fresh tonnes per hectare from 2 cuts.

Cost of Preserved Forage **2 cuts**	Clamped Grass Silage *	Wrapped Grass Silage *	Hay *	Clamped Maize	*Grazed Grass*
Variable Costs £/ha	281	281	281	360	*281*
Operational Costs					
Mowing		60	60		
Turning		35	70		
Raking		37	37		
Harvest, Clamp/Gather	374	242	198	174	
Drilling	9	9	9	51	9
Land Preparation	93	93	93	371	93
Fertilising & Spraying	53	53	53	26	53
Land based Costs £/ha	809	809	800	982	*435*
Total Costs £/fresh t	19.26	19.26	19.05	23.39	*10.36*
Fresh DM	18%	18%	18%	28%	*18%*
Preserved DM %	25%	30%	85%	30%	*18%*
Preserved weight t	36	28	9	33	27
Sub-total £/t Preserved	27	32	90	25	*10*
Baling/wrapping £/bale		£10	5		
Wrap £/bale		1.90			
sheet £/t	1.65			1.65	
Bale Weight		600	400		
Total Costs £/t Preserved	**28**	**52**	**103**	**27**	*10.36*
Total Costs £/t dry weight	**114**	**174**	**121**	**89**	*58*
MJ per kg DM	*10.9*	*10.9*	*8.8*	*11.0*	*11.5*
£/MJ kg DM	**1.04**	**1.59**	**1.37**	**0.81**	*0.50*

Total Forage Cost Notes:

1. *Variable Costs*: Linked to previous schedule, with 47 tonnes per hectare from the 'Intensive 3-5 year' margin, assuming 2-cuts and a 4-year ley.

2. *Operational Costs:* Taken from contractor's charges, page 182, land preparation and drilling divided by length of rotation.

3. *All costs* are charged to the forage, despite possible late season grazing.

4. *Conserved Grass* (*) figures are based on 2 cuts.

5. Neither *land rent or the Basic Payment Scheme* costs and incomes are included in this schedule. Depending on its use, will depend on whether you should include them in your costings. But if one is in, the other should be in most cases.

Sale Value of hay and (far less common because of its bulk) silage vary widely according to the region and season (supply/demand situation), quality and time of year:

a. *Hay* (pick-up baled) has an average ex-farm sale value of £60 to £140 per tonne, average £75. Seed hay £100 to £120 per tonne and £70-£90 per tonne for meadow hay; prices are higher in the west than the east and more after a dry summer. Prices tend to be higher for horses as quality is higher. Big bale hay is £20 to £30/tonne cheaper.

b.   *Grass silage* is typically about £34.5 per tonne delivered (higher when forage is very short in an area and *vice versa*), maize silage approx. £33.00 per tonne.

Relative Costs of Grazing, Conserved Grass, etc.

	£/t Fresh Weight	Yield DM tonnes/ha (acre)	Cost per tonne DM (£)	MJ per kg DM	Pence per MJ of ME in DM
Grazed Grass	9.12	7.6 (3.1)	£51	12.8	0.40
Grass Silage	25.24	7.6 (3.1)	£101	10.9	0.93
Big Bale Silage	37.03	7.6 (3.1)	£123	10.8	1.14
Hay	70.11	7.6 (3.1)	£82	8.8	0.94
Kale (direct drilled)	17.62	6.8 (2.7)	£117	11	1.07
Forage Turnips (d.d.)	12.39	6.8 (2.8)	£118	10.2	1.16
Brewer's Grains	42.00	-	£175	11.7	1.50
Concentrates	275.00	-	£320	12.8	2.50

1.   In interpreting the above figures for use in planning feed use on farm, own land, labour and capital for equipment are included here for home-produced fodder but not for purchased feed, and much more storage is required.

2.   The consumption of fodder is limited by its bulk and its quality/digestibility.

3.   The cost of forage will vary enormously depending on growing conditions, soil fertility and type, intensity of farming practice and management ability.

GRAZING LIVESTOCK UNITS (GLU)

Large, high-yield dairy cow....	1.60			
Small, low yield dairy cow	1.00	Lowland ewes	0.11	
Beef cows (excl. calf)	0.75	Upland ewes............................	0.08	
Heifers in calf (rearing)	0.80	Hill / LFA ewes......................	0.06	
Bulls	0.65	Breeding ewe hoggets:		
		½ to 1 year	0.06	
Other cattle (excl. intensive beef):		Other sheep, over 1 year..........	0.08	
0-1 year old.............................	0.34	Store lambs, under 1 year........	0.04	
1-2 years old	0.65	Rams......................................	0.08	
2 years old and over................	0.80			
Breeding sows	0.44	Broilers	0.0017	
Gilts in pig..............................	0.20	Other table chicken	0.004	
Maiden gilts............................	0.18	Turkeys	0.005	
Boars	0.35	Ducks, geese, other poultry .	0.003	
Other pigs...............................	0.17	Horses	0.80	
Cocks, hens, pullets in lay	0.017	Breeding nanny goats..........	0.16	
Pullets, 1 week to point of lay.	0.003	Other goats...........................	0.11	

Source: as advised by DEFRA for the Farm Business Survey.

1.   *Total livestock units on a farm* should be calculated by multiplying the above ratios by the monthly livestock numbers averaged over the whole year.

2.   *The ratios are based on feed requirements.* Strictly speaking, when calculating stocking density, allowances should also be made for differences in output (e.g., milk yield per cow or liveweight gain per head), breed (e.g., Friesians v. Jerseys) and quantities of non-forage feed consumed.

3. GRAZING LIVESTOCK

DAIRY COWS

General Notes:

The notes below detail the general points that are pertinent to completing costings for all dairy enterprises. A number of gross margins are then presented with specific detail relating to each production system.

1. *Yield per cow:* Increases in this are usually (though not necessarily) associated with more 'intensive' farming operations. 'Intensification' generally focuses on higher gross margins per hectare, although more intensive systems will incur higher variable and overhead costs (specifically machinery and labour requirements). Higher milk yields require different cow genetics (usually Friesian / Holstein's) and higher concentrate feeding (kg/litre), as well as other inputs. Higher yielding cows often have fewer lactations, see page 51.

2. *Yield:* The yield is annual herd production divided by the average number of cows and calved heifers in the herd. The average yield given for each type of production system is an estimated national figure for sizeable herds.

3. *Milk Price:* the average milk price for the 2022/23 milk year (April to March) is budgeted at 29p for a standard litre. The prices used for each gross margin are averages for the year, after deducting transport & levy costs. It incorporates adjustments for milk composition and seasonality assuming a 1 million litre per year herd (the volume standard litres are calculated despite the average herd producing 1.4 million litres).

Milk price variations between contracts are about 2.5 pence per litre (ppl). Milk supply contracts and the pricing of the milk is notoriously complicated with many variables, of varying importance depending on end-use of the milk.

Delivery Volume; Smaller herds receive smaller volume bonuses and pay higher transport charges. The average price received by individual producers also depends on seasonality of production and compositional quality.

Seasonality Price Adjustments: These vary between milk buyers. Some have payment formulae that encourage a level monthly production, with deductions and bonuses related to the individual producer's spring and autumn deliveries. Others have simple monthly adjustments per litre or on a percentage basis. The average adjustments below are for a selection of companies operating conventional adjustments are as follows in 2022/23 in pence per litre:

April	May	June	July	Aug	Sept	Oct	Nov	Dec	Jan– Mar
–4.6	–5.0	–4.5	0.8	+2.1	+3.6	+3.3	+0.7	+1.0	0.3

Some buyers also offer a premium for a level delivery option if supplies in a calendar month are within 10% of an agreed daily volume.

Some milk buyers have an 'A' and 'B' production payment system, where deliveries greater than an agreed volume (perhaps based on the previous year's deliveries) are paid the open market price for milk rather than the contracted price.

Paying for Milk Solids: Milk price calculations depend on the buyer and its end market. For example, cheesemakers mostly pay for butterfat and protein whereas a liquid processor pays largely base price per litre with small adjustments for butterfat. As a result, constituent values vary widely between buyers. More buyers are moving to this payment system.

A *standard litre* is typically 4·10% butterfat and 3·30% protein. A typical cheesemaker might calculate milk price summarised as follows:

	% Content	Pence per 1%	Price paid
Butterfat	4.10	3.6	14.8
Protein	3.30	4.0	13.2
Total ppl			28*

* *Other adjustments are made to this price such as delivery volumes, collection rates, haulage hygiene and cleanliness and seasonality.*

Within Breed Quality Variation: For Holstein Friesians, without going to extremes, the range can easily be: 3.5% to 4.1% butterfat and 3.1% to 3.4% protein. The difference in value between these levels combined can be up to 3.5p per 1 percent of milk solids depending on milk contract. This is being achieved by both breeding and feeding for milk quality to meet varying contractual requirements.

Proportional Split of Dairy Breeds and milk Compositions:

	Cows %	Butterfat %	Protein %
Holstein / Friesian	82	3.95	3·3
Cross Breeds	10	4.6	3.6
Jersey	3.9	5·4	3·9
Guernsey	0.5	4·7	3·6
Ayrshire	2·4	4·1	3·3
Others	1.2	3·9	3·3
All Breeds		4.0	3·3

Data from Dairy Co. & CDI

Hygiene Price Adjustments: These have been becoming more demanding in recent years and vary widely between the different milk buyers. A typical current example is as follows:

A. *Bactoscan (bacteria measure)*

Bactoscan reading	Price Adjustment (ppl)
0- 30,000	0.0
30,001-50,000	-0.25
50,001-75,000	-1.25
75,001-100,000	-4.00
100,001-250,001	-8.00
> 250,000	-15p

B. *Somatic Cell Count (Mastitis)*

Count	Price Adjustment (ppl)
0-225,000	0.0
225,001 – 250,000	-0.25
250,001-300,000	-1.75
300,001 - 400,000	-6.0
Over 400,000	-15.0

Top hygiene banded milk used to attract bonuses; now top-quality milk is expected as the norm in order to receive the standard litre price.

C. *Antibiotics.* Milk in a consignment that fails an antibiotics test is commonly charged 125 to 200 percent the value of the milk plus costs in excess of £300.

4. *Concentrate Price:* An average of £255/t has been used for dairy concentrate. This includes blends and straights which are typically lower cost than compounds by £10 to

£15 per tonne. Spring calving herds have lower protein concentrate as grazed grass has more protein than conserved feeds; conversely, autumn calvers receive higher protein concentrate. An average of £240/t has been used for spring calving herds.

All-Year-Round Calving Friesian/Holsteins (per cow per year)

	Average		High	
Yield Per Cow (litres)	8,000		9,500	
	£/Cow	ppl	£/Cow	ppl
Milk Output @ 29 ppl	2,320	29.0	2,755	29.0
Calf Value	139	1.7	139	1.5
Cull Value	168	2.1	189	2.0
Less, Replacement Cost @ 25% & 28% per year	-414	-5.2	-477	-5.0
Total Output	**2,213**	**27.7**	**2,606**	**27.4**
Variable Costs:				
Concentrate Costs £255/t @ 2.6t & 3.5t/cow	663	8.3	893	9.4
Purchased Bulk Feed	23	0.3	23	0.2
Vet & Med	85	1.1	88	0.9
Bedding	76	1.0	76	0.8
AI	60	0.8	62	0.7
Recording, Parlour Consumables, Sundries	82	1.0	82	0.9
Total Variable Costs	989	12.4	1,224	12.9
Gross Margin per cow Before Forage Costs	**1,224**	**15.3**	**1,382**	**14.5**
Forage Costs @ 2.1 Cows Per Forage Hectare	142	1.8	142	1.5
Gross Margin per Cow After Forage Costs	**1,082**	**13.5**	**1,240**	**13.1**
Gross Margin Per Forage Hectare	2,273		2,604	
Margin of Milk Over Concentrates	1,657	20.7	1,863	19.6
Sensitivity Analysis per cow				
Concentrate Price +/- £10/tonne	+- 26.0		+- 35.0	
Milk Price +/- 0.50 ppl	+- 40.0		+- 47.5	

All-year-round calving herds have higher costs of production than seasonal producers and so aim to sell their milk on a liquid premium based (supermarket supply) contract. Both vet and med and A.I. costs tend to increase with higher milk yield due to greater pressure on the cow and poorer fertility. As a result, herd replacement rates are also considerably higher. About 85% of the UK dairy herd calves all year round.

See notes on page 50.

Autumn Calving Friesian/Holsteins (per cow per year)

Yield Per Cow (litres)	Average 6,000		High 7,000	
	£/Cow	ppl	£/Cow	ppl
Milk Output @ 29 ppl	1,740	29.0	2,030	29.0
Calf Value	128	2.1	128	1.8
Cull Value	120	2.0	120	1.7
Less, Replacement Cost @ 23% per year	-324	-5.4	-324	-4.6
Total Output	**1,664**	**27.7**	**1,954**	**27.9**
Variable Costs:				
Concentrate Costs £255/t @ 1.5t and 1.8t/cow	383	6.4	459	6.6
Purchased Bulk Feed	21	0.4	21	0.3
Vet & Med	54	0.9	59	0.8
Bedding	62	1.0	62	0.9
AI	49	0.8	51	0.7
Recording, Parlour Consumables, Sundries	55	0.9	55	0.8
Total Variable Costs	624	10.4	707	10.1
Gross Margin per cow Before Forage Costs	**1,041**	**17.3**	**1,247**	**17.8**
Forage Costs @ 2.2 Cows Per Forage Hectare	132	2.2	132	1.9
Gross Margin per Cow After Forage Costs	**909**	**15.2**	**1,116**	**15.9**
Gross Margin Per Forage Hectare	2,000		2,454	
Margin of Milk Over Concentrates	1,358	22.6	1,571	22.4

Sensitivity Analysis per cow

Concentrate Price +/- £10/tonne	+- 15.0	+- 18.0
Milk Price +/- 0.50 ppl	+- 30.0	+- 35.0

Autumn calving herds (80% or more calvings between August and November within a 12-week period) tend to have higher overheads than spring calving herds, mainly associated with winter housing and feeding – buildings, greater silage requirements, slurry and muck handling, plus labour. The decision between being a spring or autumn calving producer depends largely on specific circumstances, such as building facilities available, the ability of the farm to grow forage (wet or dry land) and the nearby milk buyers' requirements.

See notes on page 50.

Spring Calving Friesians (per cow per year)

	Average		High	
Yield Per Cow (litres)	*5,250*		*6,000*	
	£/Cow	*ppl*	*£/Cow*	*ppl*
Milk Output @ 28.5 ppl	1,496	28.5	1,710	28.5
Calf Value	123	2.3	123	2.0
Cull Value	94	1.8	94	1.6
Less, Replacement Cost @ 20% per year	-267	-5.1	-267	-4.4
Total Output	**1,447**	**27.6**	**1,660**	**27.7**
Variable Costs:				
Concentrate Costs £240/t @ 0.8t and 1.2t/cow	192	3.7	288	4.8
Purchased Bulk Feed	0	0.0	0	0.0
Vet & Med	50	1.0	55	0.9
Bedding	46	0.9	47	0.8
AI	49	0.9	53	0.9
Recording, Parlour Consumables, Sundries	55	1.0	60	1.0
Total Variable Costs	392	7.5	503	8.4
Gross Margin per cow Before Forage Costs	**1,055**	**20.1**	**1,157**	**19.3**
Forage Costs @ 2.3 Cows Per Forage Hectare	122	2.3	122	2.0
Gross Margin per Cow After Forage Costs	**932**	**17.8**	**1,035**	**17.3**
Gross Margin Per Forage Hectare	2,238		2,485	
Margin of Milk Over Concentrates	1,304	24.8	1,422	23.7
Sensitivity Analysis per cow				
Concentrate Price +/- £10/tonne	+- 8.0		+- 12.0	
Milk Price +/- 0.50 ppl	+- 26.3		+- 30.0	

Spring calving herds (80% or more calvings between February and May within a 12-week calving period) typically have a lower annual average yield than other systems due to a smaller, hardier cow type but higher milk solids, typically by 10 percent ideal for a cheese/ manufacturing contract. As a result, replacement rates are lower than other systems despite the reductions from seasonality. These systems have lower overhead costs (labour, buildings and machinery) and focus on milk from grazed grass. Lower costs reflect the lower milk price received.

Block-calved, especially spring calved cows tend to be smaller than all-year-round calvers, requiring far less maintenance feed, and can therefore also be stocked at considerably higher stocking rates. They also have lower milk yield though.

See notes below.

Dairy Gross Margins Notes:

1. *Value of Calves:* Average annual value per calf at 10-20 days old, allowing for 7% mortality and an average calving index of 400 days for all year-round calving (AYR) and 385 days for seasonal calving herds. The average value assumed for spring and autumn calving (Seasonal) herds is comprised equally:

Calf Value (net):

	AYR	Seasonal (A/S)	Channel Islands
Dairy bull calf (dairy x dairy)	£50	*£40*	*£30*
Dairy heifer calf (dairy x dairy)	£200	£200	£200
Cross bred bull (beef x dairy)	£230	*£180/170*	*£90*
Cross bred heifer (beef x dairy)	£140	*£130/120*	*£80*
Calving Interval (days)	*400*	*385*	*385*
Calf Mortality	*7%*	*7%*	*7%*
Average*	***£139***	***£128/123***	***£91***

* The advent of sexed semen on a third of herds means they are not having many dairy bull calves. For that third of herds, a quarter of calves represent the heifer replacement, and the others are beef calves or a small number (5%) of dairy bull calves.

Calves for all-year-round calving herds with higher milk yields sometimes have less beef genetics meaning dairy bull calves and beef cross animals are less valuable but higher value dairy calves.

2. *Replacement Costs:* The table below demonstrates herd replacement costs.

	AYR		Autumn	Spring	Bull
Yield per cow	*8,000*	*9,500*	*6,000*	*5,250*	
Value of new heifers (bull) (a)	1,630	1,680	1,380	1,300	2,000
Replacement Rate (b)	25%	28%	23%	20%	25%
Bull Depreciation per cow (c.)	6.84	6.84	6.84	6.84	
Herd Depreciation (a x b +c = d)	**414**	**477**	**324**	**267**	**500**
Cull Cow Value (net) (e)	702	702	540	486	800
Casualty Rate (f)	4%	4%	3%	3%	4%
Cows per Bull (g)					45
Annual Cull Value (b x e x (1-f) = h)	**168**	**189**	**120**	**94**	**192**
Calf Value/cow/yr (see above) (i)	139	139	128	123	
Net Replacement Cost (d-h-i)	107	149	76	50	
Cost of Bull Per cow ((a-e) x b x (1-f) / g)					6.84

Herd depreciation is the annual cost of replacing the herd i.e. the cost of a down-calving heifer divided by its life expectancy in years (or multiplied by the annual replacement rate). When the value of cull cows and calves are added (both adjusted for casualty and mortality allowance), the net replacement cost can be calculated.

3. *Concentrate Costs:*

	AYR		Autumn		Spring	
Yield per cow	*8,000*	*9,500*	*6,000*	*7,000*	*5,250*	*6,000*
Tonnes / Cow	2.60	3.50	1.50	1.80	0.80	1.20
Kg feed / Litre	0.325	0.368	0.250	0.257	0.152	0.200
Milk From Forage	2,722	2,395	2,955	3,346	3,626	3,564
Concentrate Cost (ppl)	8.29	9.39	6.38	6.56	3.66	4.80
Conc. cost p/marginal L		15.30		7.65		12.80

Costs of concentrate per marginal (additional) litre. The cost of the extra feed required to move from the first yield to the second yield in each category. The yield difference in the spring and autumn groups is small, but the yield rise for AYR herds is considerable, the cost of the last litre (e.g., to 9,500 l) is always dearest and will be more than the figure shown.

Yield from forage per cow. Calculated using takeaway basis 1kg feed = 2.03 l milk so take yield and deduct milk from concreate giving yield from forage. E.g., Spring 5,250 l with 800kg gives 1624 l milk so 3626 litres from forage.

4. *Concentrate Feeding:* The table below is an example of annual concentrate use for an all-year-round calving herd.

Typical Monthly Variation in Concentrate Feeding (kg per litre, 8,000 litre herd)

Winter		Summer	
October	0.36	April	0.29
November	0.38	May	0.20
December	0.39	June	0.20
January	0.39	July	0.26
February	0.38	August	0.30
March	0.34	September	0.33
Average winter: 0.37		Average summer: 0.26	
Weighted average whole year: 0.325kg/l			

The distribution on farm varies according to factors such as seasonality of calving, milk yield, summer grazing productivity, the quality of grass, winter forages, bulk feeds, as well as turnout and housing dates. The March figure in particular will be affected by type of soil and seasonal rainfall.

Yield without concentrate and good silage can be 4,000 litres for spring calvers.

5. *Margin over Concentrates (MOC) and Concentrates per litre:* It is important to highlight in the above gross margins the differences between the margin (of milk value) over concentrates per cow; the same large variation can occur with widely differing combinations of milk yield and quantity of concentrates fed.

In the following table, for each production system, figures are given for *(a)* margin of milk value over concentrates per cow (£) and *(b)* concentrates per litre (kg).

Margin Over Concentrates (MOC) and Concentrates per Litre (C/L)

Milking System	All-Year-Round Calving				Autumn Calving		Spring Calving	
Milk Yield (litres)	8,000		9,500		6,000		5,250	
	MOC	C/L	MOC	C/L	MOC	C/L	MOC	C/L
Concentrates per cow	£	kg	£	kg	£	kg	£	kg
0.65 tonne (£156)	-	-	-	-	-	-	1340	0.12
0.75 tonne (£180)	-	-	-	-	-	-	1316	0.14
0.90 tonne (£216)	-	-	-	-	-	-	1280	0.17
1.05 tonne (£252)	-	-	-	-	1,488	0.18	1244	0.20
1.60 tonne (£408)	-	-	-	-	1,332	0.27	-	-
1.80 tonne (£459)	-	-	-	-	1,281	0.30	-	-
2.00 tonne (£510)	1,810	0.25	-	-	1,230	0.33	-	-
2.20 tonne (£561)	1,759	0.28	-	-	-	-	-	-
2.45 tonne (£625)	1,695	0.31			-	-	-	-
2.70 tonne (£689)	1,631	0.34	2066	0.28	-	-	-	-
3.00 tonne (£765)	-	-	1990	0.32	-	-	-	-
3.35 tonne (£854)	-	-	1901	0.35	-	-	-	-
3.75 tonne (£956)	-	-	1799	0.39	-	-	-	-

6. *Stocking Rate and Forage Costs:* The stocking rates used assume nearly all forage/bulk foods are obtained from the forage area, i.e. little is bought in. The stocking rates of 2.1, 2.2 and 2.3 cows per forage hectare (AYR, autumn calving and spring calving respectively) assume good grassland management. Higher stocking rates are achievable, particularly in the West where natural conditions favour forage production. Typically, this would be where forage dry matter of 13 tonnes per hectare can be produced. About 55 per cent of forage area is grazed and 45 per cent conserved for an AYR calving herd.

Spring calving herds rely much less on conserved forage. Some high yielding herds are housed all-year and fed 100 percent conserved feed.

Forage costs are taken from the *Forage Variable Costs* on page 42 as follows:

	Grass	Maize	Grass	Maize	Grass	Maize
£ Cost /Ha	281	360	£/Ha		£/cow	
Spring calving	100%	0%	281	0	122	0
Autumn calving	89%	11%	250	40	114	18
All year round calving	78%	22%	219	79	104	38

An increase in stocking density can be obtained not only by intensifying grassland production, but also by buying in bulk fodder (assuming the same level of concentrate feeding). A zero-grazed farm buying in forage needs no land. In this situation, the gross margin per hectare would be extreme (and meaningless), although the cost of hauling in forage would be high.

Overheads such as labour and building depreciation are likely to increase per hectare as stocking density rises. Management challenges occur with higher stocking rates such as poaching which can be alleviated with good cow tracks. Cross Compliance and Nitrate Vulnerable Zone regulations must still be adhered to.

7. *Labour*: see page 172.

8. *Building Costs*: see page 219.

Costs of Milk Production Summary (Pence per Litre)

Production Type	AYR Calving	Autumn Calving	Spring Calving
Litres per cow	*8,000*	*6,000*	*5,250*
	Pence Per Litre		
Concentrates	9.39	6.56	4.80
Forage and Bought Bulk Feed	1.74	2.18	2.04
Other Variable Costs	3.48	3.54	3.58
Total Variable Costs	**14.62**	**12.28**	**10.42**
All Labour (inc. unpaid)	4.95	5.81	5.55
Power and Machinery*	6.55	7.15	5.87
General Overheads	1.26	1.40	1.39
Total Overhead Costs	**12.76**	**14.36**	**12.81**
Less, Net Replacement Cost	1.33	1.26	0.94
Total Costs of Production	**28.71**	**27.90**	**24.17**

* *inc electricity & parlour repairs*

1. This schedule only compiles the costs of milk production. Adding milk price to it does not constitute a profit or loss as other components of the farm should be included such as BPS, youngstock enterprises, rent and finance.

2. The *Variable Costs* per litre are derived from the data (and therefore the assumptions made) under high performance in the dairy gross margin tables for each system.

3. The *Overhead Costs* assume above average financial performance. They are adapted from the medium-sized 'mainly dairying' farm data in the Overhead Costs Section on page 209. Within each system, there is a marked difference between the costs achieved by the top 10% and the bottom 10% of producers (over 10ppl). The difference is mainly due to management ability. *Labour* includes the farmer and unpaid family labour but

there is no management charge included. *Power and machinery* covers all machinery and equipment costs, including the use of farm vehicles, depreciation, etc. *General overheads* similarly relate to the whole farm, including electricity and property repairs. *Rent/Rental Equivalent and Finance* assumes a modest rental charge on all land plus interest charges on a modest amount of working capital. No long-term debt is included.

4. All-year-round calving herds will have the highest overheads in absolute terms. However, well-managed high yielding herds can compete with block calving systems due to higher output. Spring calving herds may have the lowest total overheads due to a shorter housing period, less demand for winter forage and lower muck handling costs. Costs per litre might be higher though as yields are lower. Rental costs, in pence per litre terms, will be higher though due to the fixed land charge and lower output (litres) per unit area of land unless stocking rates are raised.

Channel Island Breeds (per cow per year)

Production Type	AYR Average	AYR High	A. Calving	S. Calving
Milk Yield per Cow (litres)	*5,450*	*6,250*	*5,000*	*4,150*
	£	£	£	£
Milk Value per Cow at 37 ppl	2,017	2,313	1,850	1,536
Calf Value	91	91	91	91
Cull Value	98	110	90	79
Less, Replacement Cost	-325	-364	-299	-260
Total Output	**1,881**	**2,150**	**1,733**	**1,445**
Variable Costs:				
Concentrate Costs	455	624	364	239
Purchased Bulk Feed	27	27	27	27
Vet & Med	53	57	49	45
Bedding	45	45	45	40
AI	34	36	34	32
Parlour Consumables, Sundries etc.	59	59	59	59
Total Variable Costs	**673**	**848**	**578**	**442**
Gross Margin Before Forage Costs	**1,208**	**1,302**	**1,155**	**1,004**
Forage Costs @ 2.5 Cows Per Forage Ha	147	147	112	112
Gross Margin After Forage Costs	**1,061**	**1,154**	**1,042**	**892**
Gross Margin Per Forage Hectare	2,652	2,886	2,606	2,229
Margin of Milk Over Concentrates	**1,562**	**1,689**	**1,486**	**1,297**

1. *Yield.* Average of Jerseys and Guernseys. See Note 1 and 2 for Holstein Friesians (page 46). Guernsey yield averages slightly higher than Jerseys and Jerseys achieve a higher butterfat and protein (see page 47).

2. *Milk Price.* This is 36p per litre (average of Jerseys and Guernseys for a level profile). This is based upon a milk solid content. Milk buyers are increasingly paying for solids, rather than a separate Channel Island contract.

3. *Concentrate Costs.* The average price taken (for 2022) is £260 per tonne (for all-year-round calving herds), £255 per tonne average for spring calving herds and £265 per tonne for autumn calving herds.

Amounts	*Milk Group*	*AYR ave.*	*AYR High*	*Autumn*	*Spring*
	kg/litre	0.321	0.384	0.280	0.217
	tonnes/cow	1.75	2.40	1.40	0.90
	pence / litre (ppl)	8.35	9.98	7.28	5.75
	pence/ marginal litre*		21.13		

* *This is the additional cost of feed between yield groups, and the cost of the additional feed divided by the additional litres of production.*

4. *Net Annual Replacement Cost*: Calculated as follows:

	AYR Average	AYR High	A. Calving	S. Calving
Yield per cow	*5,450*	*6,250*	*5,000*	*4,150*
Value of new heifers (a)	1,300	1,300	1,300	1,300
Replacement Rate (b)	25%	28%	23%	20%
Bull Depreciation per cow (c.)	6.8	6.8	6.8	6.8
Herd Depreciation (a x b +c = d)	**332**	**371**	**306**	**267**
Cull Cow Value *(e)	405	405	405	405
Casualty Rate (f)	3%	3%	3%	3%
Annual Cull Value (b x e x (1-f) = g)	**98**	**110**	**90**	**79**
Calf Values (h)	**91**	**91**	**91**	**91**
Net Replacement Cost (d-g-h)	**142**	**169**	**124**	**97**

*Cull cow prices for Guernseys are about £40 higher than for Jerseys.

** Allowing for calving index of 400 days and calf mortality; mixture of pure-bred calves and beef crosses. Guernsey calves, especially crosses, are worth more than Jersey calves, averaging perhaps £10 more per head and substantially more for some Guernsey beef crosses.

5. *Forage Costs and Stocking Rate.* See, in general, Note 6 for Holstein Friesians (page 52). See forage section for details of improved temporary grass used here. At the average stocking rate given above for combined Channel Island breeds (2.5 cows per forage hectare) the average figure for Jerseys would be approximately 2.60 and that for Guernseys 2.40 cows per forage hectare.

Once a Day and Three Times a Day Milking.

All other schedules assume twice a day milking. A growing number of farms are now milking either once a day (*OAD*) or three times a day (*TTAD*).

	OAD		TTAD	
Yield Per Cow (litres)	*3,500*		*10,000*	
	£/Cow	*ppl*	*£/Cow*	*ppl*
Milk Output @ 32.6 and 29ppl respectively	1,141	32.6	2,900	29.0
Calf Value	123	3.5	139	1.4
Cull Value	102	2.9	231	2.3
Less, Replacement Cost @ 15% & 35% per year	-251	-7.2	-595	-5.9
Total Output	**1,115**	**31.9**	**2,675**	**26.8**
Variable Costs:				
Concentrates £240/t @ 0.2t and £280 @ 4t/cow	48	1.4	960	9.6
Purchased Bulk Feed	0	0.0	45	0.5
Vet & Med	33	0.9	96	1.0
Bedding	45	1.3	50	0.5
AI	38	1.1	76	0.8
Recording, Parlour Consumables, Sundries	28	0.8	107	1.1
Total Variable Costs	192	5.5	1,334	13.3
Gross Margin per cow Before Forage Costs	**923**	**26.4**	**1,341**	**13.4**
Forage Costs @ 2.4 & 2.0 Cows / Forage Ha	120	3.4	152	1.5
Gross Margin per Cow After Forage Costs	**802**	**22.9**	**1,189**	**11.9**
Gross Margin Per Forage Hectare	1,926		2,378	
Margin of Milk Over Concentrates	1,093	31.2	1,940	19.4
Sensitivity Analysis per cow				
Concentrate Price +/- £10/tonne	+- 2.0		+- 40.0	
Milk Price +/- 0.50 ppl	+- 143.5		+- 50.0	

Notes on Once a Day (OAD) and Three times a day (TTAD) Milking

1. OAD milking is centred on cost stripping, as well as a lifestyle choice for the farmer. It means block calving, low yields and minimal concentrate feeding. Cows are small with low maintenance costs and almost always associated with spring calving herds. The transition to OAD can take 3 seasons as cows adjust.

2. Milk solids increase considerably in OAD, meaning milk price should be much higher (hence the higher milk price) depending on milk contract. OAD milking often has a higher stocking rate to account for the reduction in milk per cow.

3. TTAD cows are larger and produce very high yields but with very high marginal costs of production. It is often associated with robotic milking. Observation and cow management is still required so costs per cow often rise but can fall per litre. Vet and replacement costs rise considerably as well as concentrate feed. Cows are often fully housed.

4. OAD milking systems can work on farms where fields are distant from the parlour or difficult terrain such as hills. Equally, TTAD milking systems must keep the cows close to the parlour at all times.

Acknowledgement ~ thanks to National Once a Day Farms via Pasture to Profit.

DAIRY FOLLOWERS

(per Heifer reared)

Production Type	AYR		Autumn		Spring	
	£		£		£	
Value of heifer (allowing for culls)	1543		1339		1261	
Less Value of calf	210		210		210	
Output £/head	1333		1129		1051	
Variable Costs:						
Concentrate Costs	324		133		91	
Bedding	90		76		62	
Vet & Med	28		26		24	
Other Costs	18		17		16	
Total Variable Costs £/head exc. forage	460		252		193	
Gross Margin £/Heifer, before forage	873		877		858	
Forage Variable Costs £/Head	126		126		126	
Gross Margin £/Heifer	746		751		732	
Stocking Rate: Heifers reared/Ha (acre)	1.4	(3.5)	1.4	(3.5)	1.4	(3.5)
Gross Margin £/Forage Hectare (acre)	1066	(431)	1072	(434)	1045	(423)

B. Channel Island Breeds

Production Type	AYR		Autumn		Spring	
	£		£		£	
Value of heifer (allowing for culls)	1170		1170		1170	
Less Value of calf	96		96		96	
Output £/head	1074		1074		1074	
Variable Costs:						
Concentrate Costs	241		116		80	
Miscellaneous inc. Bedding, Vet Med.	116		101		87	
Total Variable Costs £/head exc. forage	357		217		166	
Gross Margin £/Heifer, before forage	717		857		908	
Forage Variable Costs £/Head	114		114		114	
Gross Margin £/Heifer	604		743		794	
Stocking Rate: Heifers reared/Ha (acre)	1.5	(3.8)	1.5	(3.8)	1.5	(3.8)
Gross Margin £/Forage Hectare (acre)	929	(376)	1143	(463)	1222	(494)

N.B. on average Channel Island heifers calve about three months younger than Holstein

1.   *Heifer values* are based on the purchase price of calving heifers into the dairy herd less 3% mortality with a 3 percent allowance for culls and barren animals sold at £300. Most heifers are home reared. If heifers are reared for sale, the price of whole batches is likely to be lower than the values given in the tables, by 10 or 15 percent. On the other hand, the purchaser will often take the batch a few months before the average expected calving date, thus reducing the costs incurred by the rearer.

2.   *Calf Value*: is based on the cost of a heifer dairy calf, increased to account for mortality of 5 percent.

3. *Concentrate cost* Other things being equal, a lower calving age requires higher levels of feeding. Feeding schedule laid out below:

		AYR	Autumn	Spring
Milk Substitute				
£1780/T	g/day	750	600	500
	days fed	63	63	63
	£/calf	£84	£67	£56
Weaning Nuts (18%)				
£295/T	kg/day	1.5	1.0	1.0
	days fed	84	42	35
	£/calf	£37	£12	£10
Grower Nuts (16%)				
£245/T	kg/day	2.2	2.0	2.0
	days fed	365	98	42
	£/calf	£197	£48	£21
Total Conc (£/calf)		**£318**	**£128**	**£87**
Bedding				
	t/heifer	1.3	1.1	0.9
	£/t	69	69	69

4. *Forage variable costs.* Grass for both grazing and conservation, at £216/ha, assuming all home produced. This is the variable costs for long term leys and improved permanent pasture (combined in equal parts) in the forage section on page 42, thus assuming less productive grassland is used to rear dairy heifers with the best pasture being retained for the dairy cows.

5. *A "replacement unit"* (i.e. calf + yearling + heifer) equals about 1·25 livestock units with an average calving age of 2 years 4 months. The three stocking rates used above are equivalent to approximately 0.75, 0·6 and 0·5 forage hectares (1.85, 1.48, 1.24 acres) respectively per Holstein Friesian cow (Livestock Unit). Note, this is a 2-year gross margin. It can be treated as a gross margin over a longer period of time or a margin per replacement unit, not per animal on the farm per year.

6. *Higher gross margin per hectare* figures can be achieved by intensive grazing methods, particularly if combined with alternative winter feeding systems, such as out-wintering on forage crops such as Fodder Beet or Kale.

7. *Contract Rearing*: see page 76.

8. *Labour*: see page 172.

SELF-CONTAINED DAIRY HERD: COWS AND FOLLOWERS

At average annual replacement rates (25 per cent of the milking herd), nearly one-third of a replacement unit is required for each cow in the herd, i.e. roughly one calf, yearling and heifer for every three cows (including calved heifers), allowing for mortality and culling. At average stocking rates for both, this means more than 1 hectare devoted to followers for every 3 hectares for cows. Surplus youngstock are often reared and frequently the stocking rate is less intensive, the ratio often exceeds this in practice. 1:3 is about the minimum where all replacement heifers are reared, unless their winter feeding is based largely on straw and purchased supplements, or unless there is a combination of long average herd life and early calving, i.e. all at 2 years old.

The table below shows the combined gross margin per forage hectare (acre) for the whole herd (i.e., Cows and Followers combined) for four different dairy systems assuming the same stocking rate for the dairy cows and three levels of performance, including different stocking rates, for the followers. This assumes a 3:1 land use ratio (dairy cows' area: followers' area) and relates to the dairying systems (gross margins) shown earlier in this section. It is important to note, however, that these are only a guide as the figures (ratio of land areas assumed) do not take account of the different herd replacement rates for each dairying system. In practise, it is likely that the amount of land required for the followers for a block spring calving herd would be less than that for a high yielding all-year-round calving herd; this is due to the fact that typically a high yielding herd would have a higher herd replacement rate and as such require more heifers and therefore land on which to rear them.

Gross Margin per Forage Hectare for Cows and Followers Combined

			G.M per Forage Hectare (acre) Dairy Cows			
		System Litres	AYR Ave. 8,000	AYR High 9,500	Autumn 6,000	Spring 5,250
			£	£	£	£
G.M. per Forage Hectare (acre) Followers			2273 (920)	2604 (1055)	2000 (810)	2238 (906)
	AYR	1075 (435)	1973 (799)	2222 (900)		
	Aut.	1079 (437)			1770 (717)	
	Spr.	1051 (426)				1941 (786)

As an example, the above table indicates that for an all-year-round 8,000 litre dairy herd (AYR Average) and AYR followers, the whole farm-system gross margin per hectare (acre) figure is £1,973 (799) compared with £2,273 (920) for the dairy cows alone, a reduction of 13%.

BEEF

There are numerous systems for producing beef which are heavily influenced by factors such as feed and forage, breeds, housing, sale weights, market outlets, labour availability, enterprise scale and personal choice. Thus, the financial performance of beef enterprises is diverse. The enterprise gross margins shown on these pages represent the 'standard' systems with output prices and costs based on 2022 budgets.

Dairy Cross Calves

The values in the table below are for 2022 dairy bulls or beef cross calves of average quality, less than three weeks old. These values have been used in the budgets for the following beef systems. There is large regional and seasonal variation in calf prices.

Calf values of various beef cattle

	Bulls	Heifers
Holstein Friesians	60	-
Hereford Cross	200	140
HF/Continental Cross	275	230

Calf Rearing
Early Weaning - Bucket Rearing Dairy Beef (per calf)

	3 Months	6 months
	£	£
Value of Calf	355	540
Less Calf Purchase	222	222
Output	**133**	**318**
Variable Costs:		
Milk Substitute	38	38
Concentrates	52	115
Hay	4	19
Vet & Med.	17	22
Bedding	7	14
Miscellaneous	4	11
Total Variable Costs	**122**	**219**
Gross Margin per Calf Reared	**11**	**99**

1. *Calf Purchase*: Equal number of male and female calves (Hereford Cross/ Continental beef cross, 1-2 weeks old). Average = £211 plus 5% mortality, mainly in first 3 weeks = £222.

2. *Milk substitute:* 20 kg @ £1,909/tonne = £38.00. Calves fed on machine or lib milk systems will use more milk powder.

3. *Calf concentrates:* to 3 months, 160 kg @ £324/t and 10% home grown grain = £52
    Rearer Feed to 6 months, additional 290kg @ 290/t and 30% home grown grain = £115

4. *Hay:* 50kg to 3 months, 200kg to 6 months (£75/tonne) See page 44.

5. *Miscellaneous:* Ear Tags etc.

6. *Weights*: at start = 45 to 50 kg; at 3 months = 115 kg; at 6 months = 245kg.

7. *Contract rearing charge* (both 0 to 3 months and 0 to 6 months): £14.50/week. *Direct labour cost:* approximately £30 per head to 3 months, £44 per head to 6 months.

8. *Labour requirements (all beef systems):* see page 172.

Suckler Cows

Single Suckling (per Cow): Lowland

System	Spring Calving		Autumn Calving	
	8 months		12 Months	
Performance Level	Average	High	Average	High
	£	£	£	£
Value of Store Calf Sold	*615*	*695*	*815*	*866*
Calf Sales per year	523	619	693	754
Less Cow and Bull Depreciation	114	114	129	129
Calf Purchases & Bull Maint.	13	13	15	15
Output £/cow/year	**396**	**492**	**548**	**609**
Variable Costs £/cow/yr:				
Concentrate (Cow and Calf)	48	40	82	74
Vet & Med	34	34	36	36
Bedding	42	42	48	48
Miscellaneous	35	36	38	41
Variable Costs (ex. forage)	**159**	**152**	**204**	**199**
Gross Margin £/Cow/yr				
ex. Forage	237	340	344	410
Forage Variable Costs	97	97	97	97
Purchased Bulk Feeds	14	12	22	18
Gross Margin £/Cow	**126**	**231**	**226**	**296**
Stocking Rate: Cows/Ha. *(Acre)*	1.50 (0.6)	1.50 (0.6)	1.50 (0.6)	1.50 (0.6)
Gross Margin £/Forage Ha *(Acre)*	**189** (76)	**347** (140)	**338** (137)	**443** (179)

1. *System*: Relates to performance per year. Assumed 390 days average calving interval, showing figures per 365-day period. Calves sold at approximately 8-months for spring calvers and 12-months for autumn calvers.

2. *Performance level*: relates to variations in both outputs and inputs.

Calving Period	Spring Calving		Autumn Calving	
Performance Level	Average	High	Average	High
Calf Sale Weights (kg)	280	309	371	385
Sale Age (Days)	250	240	365	340
Sale Prices (£/kg)	£2.20	2.25	£2.20	2.25
Calves reared per 100 cows mated	85	89	85	87

3. *Cow & Bull Depreciation:*

	Spring C.	Autumn C.	Bull
Purchase Price - £	£1,600	£1,600	£2,000
Cull Price - £	£750	£750	£850
Animal Life (Years)	8	7	5
Depreciation £/cow	£106	£121	£8

4. *Calf Purchases:* £211 each, 3 per 100 cows mated (spring calving) 4 per 100 cows mated (autumn calving). Bull maintenance £192/year per 30 cows.

Dairy cross beef cows have better fertility performance than continental pure-bred cows, but lower cull sale prices.

5.   *Concentrate feed:*

	Spring Calving		Autumn Calving	
Concentrates	Average	High	Average	High
Cow kg's	120	100	190	165
Cow - £/t	275	275	275	275
Calf kg's	60	50	120	115
Calf - £/t	250	250	250	250
Total Concentrate	£48	£40	£82	£74

6.   *Straw:* where yarded in winter, straw requirements average 0.7 tonnes per cow for spring calvers and 0.8 tonnes for autumn calvers at £65/tonne.

7.   *Forage Area:* includes grazing and conserved grass (silage and hay). Higher stocking rates imply better use of grassland or achieved by buying in more winter fodder, or feeding more arable by-products, including straw. Purchased bulk fodder and/or straw balancer concentrates will reduce gross margin per cow but increase gross margin per hectare. Forage cost from Improved Permanent Pasture in Forage at £145/ha page 42.

8.   *Headage Payment:* A payment is made in Scotland on three-quarter bred beef calves from Suckler Cows. This is a flat rate payment, on all eligible calves, in the region of €100 per calf on the mainland and €160 per calf on the islands. Actual rates depend on the number of calves claimed on each year. See Top-up Schemes in Chapter III.

9.   *Multiple calves:* In lowland conditions rearing two or more calves per cow is an option but needs substantially greater labour input. Output is raised by fostering a second purchased calf onto a cow soon after calving, with little impact on costs of keeping the cow. The cow breed needs to be of a quiet temperament and have enough milk to rear two calves.

Single Suckling (per Cow): Upland

System	Spring Calving 8 months		Autumn Calving 12 Months	
Performance Level	Average	High	Average	High
	£	£	£	£
Value of Store Calf Sold	600	630	800	833
Calf Sales per year	504	567	672	716
Less Cow and Bull Depreciation	116	116	131	131
Calf Purchases & Bull Maint.	13	13	15	15
Output £/cow/year	**374**	**438**	**525**	**570**
Variable Costs £/cow/yr:				
Concentrate (Cow and Calf)	51	43	84	76
Vet & Med	33	33	35	35
Bedding	47	47	53	53
Miscellaneous	35	36	38	41
Variable Costs (ex. forage)	**165**	**158**	**209**	**204**
Gross Margin £/Cow/yr				
ex. Forage	209	280	316	365
Forage Variable Costs	87	79	87	79
Purchased Bulk Feeds	14	12	22	18
Gross Margin £/Cow	**108**	**189**	**207**	**268**
Stocking Rate: Cows/Ha. (*Acre*)	1.00 (0.4)	1.10 (0.4)	1.00 (0.4)	1.10 (0.4)
Gross Margin £/Forage Ha *(Acre)*	**108** (44)	**208** (84)	**207** (84)	**295** (119)

1. *System:* Relates to performance per year, i.e. for the production period. Assumed 390 days average calving interval. Performance level: relates to variations in both outputs and inputs.

2. *Performance Level*

Calving Period	Spring Calving		Autumn Calving	
Performance Level	Average	High	Average	High
Calf Sale Weights (kg)	273	280	364	370
Sale Age (Days)	250	240	365	330
Sale Prices (£/kg)	£2.20	2.25	£2.20	2.25
Calves reared per 100 cows mated	84	90	84	86

3. *Cow & Bull Depreciation:*

	Spring C.	Autumn C.	Bull
Purchase Price - £	£1,600	£1,600	£2,000
Cull Price - £	£750	£750	£850
Animal Life (Years)	8	7	4
Depreciation £/cow	£106	£121	£10

4. *Calf Purchases*: £211 each, 3 per 100 cows mated (spring calving) 4 per 100 cows mated (autumn calving). Bull maintenance = £197 per 30 cows.

Dairy cross beef cows have better fertility performance than continental pure-bred cows, but lower cull sale prices.

5. *Concentrate Feed:*

	Spring Calving		Autumn Calving	
Concentrates	Average	High	Average	High
Cow kg's	130	110	195	170
Cow - £/t	275	275	275	275
Calf kg's	60	50	120	115
Calf - £/t	250	250	250	250
Total Concentrate	£51	£43	£84	£76

6. *Straw:* where yarded in winter, straw requirements average 0.75 tonnes per cow for spring calvers and 0.85 tonnes for autumn calvers at £65/tonne.

7. *Forage Area:* includes grazing and conserved grass (silage and hay). Higher stocking rates imply better use of grassland or higher can be achieved by buying more winter bulk fodder, or by winter feeding more arable by-products, including straw. Purchased bulk fodder and/or straw balancer concentrates will reduce gross margin per cow but increase gross margin per hectare. Forage cost from Low Input Permanent Pasture in Forage page at £133/ha on page 42.

8. *Headage Payment:* A payment is made in Scotland on three-quarter bred beef calves from Suckler Cows. This is a flat rate payment, on all eligible calves, in the region of €100 per calf on the mainland and €160 per calf on the islands. Actual rates will depend on the number of calves claimed on each year. See Top-up Schemes in Chapter III.

Store Cattle

Maintenance / Keeping of Young Dairy Store Cattle (per head)

	Summer Keeping		Winter Keeping	
	Average	High	Average	High
	£	£	£	£
Store Sales £/head	884	916	876	904
Less Purchased Store (incl. mortality)	551	551	551	551
Output £/Head	**334**	**365**	**325**	**353**
Variable Costs £/Head:				
Concentrates	7	5	74	64
Vet & Med	14	13	16	14
Bedding	0	0	48	42
Miscellaneous	13	9	15	12
Variable Costs £/head ex. Forage	**34**	**27**	**153**	**132**
Gross Margin £/Head, (ex. Forage)	**299**	**338**	**172**	**220**
Forage Variable Costs	48	45	77	77
Gross Margin per Head	**251**	**293**	**94**	**143**
Stocking Rate Head/Ha.	3.00	3.25	n/a	
Gross Margin £/Forage Ha	**753**	**954**		
Gross Margin £/Forage Acre	305	386		

1. *System:* Buying dairy cross steers and heifers at 6 months old (245kg) for keeping / rearing. Animals spend 6 months in system before sale / transfer to a finishing enterprise. This is a 6-month enterprise.

2. *Sales:* at 402kg summer, 398kg winter (liveweight), both at £2.20/kg for "average" and £2.25/kg for "high".

3. *Purchases:* Both systems 245kg purchase weight (6-month calves from calf gross margin plus, 2% mortality.

4. *Concentrates:* Winter 270kg concentrates (1.5kg/day for 180 days) @ £210 per tonne. Summer, 150g/day.

5. *Forage Costs:* Summer Keep based on 'Improved Permanent Pasture' in forage section (page 42) at £145/ha gross margin. Winter Keep: 2.9 tonnes per head grass silage consumption (2.8t/cow for "high"). Full costs of grass and ensiling are included here at contract rates making £26.71/tonne silage. Similarly, bought in silage will increase the forage costs over those shown.

This means that the two gross margins are not comparable as different levels of overheads are included in the calculation. Be sure what is included in the forage calculation when working out the costs.

Finishing Cattle

Finishing of Dairy Bred Store Cattle (per head)

| | Summer Finishing | | Winter Finishing | |
| | Average | High | Average | High |
	6 months		8 months	
	£	£	£	£
Finished Sales	1,315	1,328	1,330	1,344
Less Purchased Store (incl. mortality)	893	884	902	893
Output	**421**	**444**	**428**	**451**
Variable Costs:				
Concentrates	87	81	165	179
Vet & Med	16	13	23	18
Bedding	0	0	42	36
Miscellaneous	25	20	26	22
Variable Costs (ex. forage)	**128**	**114**	**256**	**255**
Gross Margin £/Head, (ex. Forage)	**294**	**330**	**172**	**196**
Stock per Ha.	2.00	2.25		
Forage Variable Costs	72	64	99	99
Gross Margin per Head	**221**	**266**	**73**	**97**
Gross Margin £/Forage Ha	**443**	**598**		
Gross Margin £/Forage Acre	179	242		

1. *System*: Finishing of dairy bred store cattle (as shown in previous margin – summer finishing cattle will have been winter stores and *vice versa*). Purchased / transferred in at 12 months old and finished over 7 months (210 days for summer finishing, 220 days winter finishing). Summer finishing takes place entirely at pasture whilst winter finishing is a housed system for the production period. These gross margins are for less than 12-months.

2. *Sales*: Finished sale liveweights of 598kg for summer finishing and 604kg for winter finishing. Sale price £2.20/kg in both systems.

3. *Purchases*: Purchase / transfer-in weight of 398kg (402kg for high) and 402kg (407kg high) for summer and winter finishing respectively. Cost in both cases £2.20/kg plus 1% mortality allowance.

4. *Concentrates*: Summer finishing 1.5kg/day (= 315kg); winter finishing, 3.5kg/day (=770kg) at £210 per tonne for summer and £185 for winter.

5. *Forage Costs*:

   Summer finishing based on 'Improved Permanent Pasture' in forage section (page 42) at £145/ha.

   Winter Finishing is housed. Uses 3.7 tonnes per head grass silage consumption. Silage production costs are full production costs (£26.71/t fresh wt. on page 42) so relevant overheads are included in this calculation. Similarly, bought in silage increases forage costs.

   This means that the two gross margins are not comparable as different levels of overheads are included in the calculation. Be sure what is included in the forage calculation when working out the costs.

Finishing of Suckler Bred Store Cattle (per head)

	Summer Finishing		Winter Finishing	
	Average	High	Average	High
	10.5 months		6 months	
	£	£	£	£
Finished Sales	1,308	1,387	1,231	1,278
Less Purchased Store (incl. mortality)	627	621	831	823
Output	**681**	**766**	**399**	**455**
Variable Costs:				
Concentrates	99	86	173	141
Vet & Med	15	14	23	21
Bedding	0	0	47	42
Miscellaneous	37	33	41	40
Variable Costs (ex. forage)	**151**	**133**	**284**	**244**
Gross Margin £/Head, (ex. Forage)	**530**	**633**	**115**	**211**
Stock per Ha.	2.00	2.25		
Forage Variable Costs	199	176	91	80
Gross Margin per Head	**331**	**457**	**24**	**131**
Gross Margin £/Forage Ha	**662**	**1,028**		
Gross Margin £/Forage Acre	*268*	*416*		

1. *System*: Beef suckler progeny purchased / transferred in at 8 months old for summer finishing and 12 months old for winter finishing (summer finishing cattle will be from spring calving suckler cows, with winter finishers from autumn calving suckler cows). Summer finishers = 300 days in system, winter finishers = 180 days in system. These margins are therefore 10-month and 6-month systems, not full year systems.

2. *Sales*: Summer finishing 595kg liveweight, winter finishing 560kg liveweight. Sale price of £2.20/kg in both systems.

3. *Purchase Price*: Summer and winter bought in at 280 and 371kg respectively, both at £2.20/kg and allowing 2% mortality for average and 1% for high performance.

4. *Concentrates*:

	Summer		**Winter**	
	Average	High	Average	High
Concentrates - kg/day	1.20	1.10	3.50	3.00
Concentrates - £/t	£275	£261	£275	£261
Total Concentrates Kg	360	330	630	540

5. *Forage Costs*:

Summer Finishing based on 'Long term ley' in forage section (page 42) at £216/ha and 3t silage per head.

Winter Finishing: Housed so uses 3.4 tonnes per head preserved forage. Silage production costs are full production costs (£26.71/t fresh weight on page 42) so relevant overheads are included in this calculation. Similarly, bought in silage increases forage costs.

This means that the two gross margins are not comparable as different levels of overheads are included in the calculation. Be sure what is included in the forage calculation when working out the costs.

Maize & Grass Silage Beef Finishing (per Head Produced)

System	Dairy X Progeny 12 months		Suckler Progeny 10 months	
Performance Level	Average	High	Average	High
	£	£	£	£
Finished Sales	1,422	1,503	1,420	1,552
Less Purchased Store (incl. mortality)	535	535	615	695
Output	**888**	**968**	**805**	**857**
Variable Costs:				
Concentrates	181	171	117	109
Vet & Med.	20	18	19	17
Misc Variable Costs	79	78	101	100
Variable Costs (ex. forage)	**279**	**266**	**238**	**226**
Gross Margin £/Head, (ex. Forage)	**609**	**702**	**568**	**631**
Forage Cost	103	93	96	87
Gross Margin per Head	**505**	**609**	**471**	**544**

1. *System*: An intensive finishing system utilising a housed forage-based system of grass silage and maize silage with heavy finished weights. Dairy cross progeny bought or transferred in at 6 months and suckler progeny at 8 months. Dairy-cross finishing period of 365 days and suckler progeny at 305 days. The gross margins are higher than in other finishing enterprises but overhead costs (fixed costs) will also be high in comparison.

	Dairy Cross		Suckler Progeny	
	Average	High	Average	High
Age at purchase	6 months	6 months	8 months	8 months
Days in System	365	365	305	305
DLWG Kg	1.10	1.20	1.20	1.30
Sale Weight - kg	647	683	646	706
Sale Price - £/kg	£2.20	£2.20	£2.25	£2.25
Purchase Weight - kg	245	245	280	309
Purchase Price - £/kg	£2.20	£2.20	£1.92	£1.92
Mortality - %	1%	1%	1%	1%
Concentrates				
Concentrates - kg/day	1.80	1.70	1.40	1.30
Concentrates - £/t	£275	£275	£275	£275

2. *Miscellaneous* Variable Costs: assumed to be proportionally higher than the store and suckler finishing enterprises shown previously. Assumed 8% premium for average performance and 5% for high performance.

3. *Forage Costs:*

Maize Cattle per head	Dairy Cross		Suckler	
	Average	High	Average	High
Tonnes Maize Silage	1.90	1.71	1.80	1.62
Maize Silage Cost £/t	£27	£27	£27	£27
Tonnes Grass Silage	1.85	1.7	1.70	1.5
Grass Silage Cost £/t	£28	£28	£28	£28
Total Per Cow	**£103**	**£93**	**£96**	**£87**
Total Silage Tonnes	3.75	3.38	3.50	3.15

The silage costs relate to the total operational cost of growing and harvesting the forage, but not the costs incurred in preparing/mixing rations as shown in page 42.

Cereal Bull Beef (per Head)

Performance Level	Continental Cross Holstein/Friesian Bulls 14.5 months		Holstein Friesian Bulls 14.5 months	
	Average	High	Average	High
	£	£	£	£
Finished Sales	1140	1193	974	1056
Less Calf Purchase	281	279	61	61
Output	**859**	**914**	**913**	**995**
Variable Costs:				
Concentrates	516	500	516	500
Other Feed	24	22	24	22
Vet & Med	23	21	23	21
Bedding	54	54	54	54
Miscellaneous	41	38	41	38
Total Variable Costs	**658**	**635**	**658**	**635**
Gross Margin per Head	**201**	**279**	**254**	**360**

1. A traditional cereal based system for finishing cattle. Animals are housed throughout the production period and fed on a barley concentrate and straw based ration. Production period typically from 2 weeks to 14 months old. This system is highly exposed to swings in cereal commodity prices. A £10 per tonne feed price movement equates to a margin change of £20 per head.

2. *Sales:*

   Cont. cross bulls = average 530kg, high 555kg; average at £2.20/kg liveweight;

   Holstein Friesian, average 475kg, high 515kg average, at £2.10/kg

   All year-round production is assumed. Average slaughter age is 15 months, with killing out percentages ranging from 54% to 59%, with the better conformation continental cross bulls achieving higher percentages.

3. *Purchases:* £275 for continental cross male calves at 3 weeks of age plus mortality; £60 for dairy bulls plus mortality. Mortality, average 2%, high 1.5%.

4. *Concentrates:* £90 calf rearing (to 12 weeks including milk powder: see page 60) + finishing ration. Finishing ration: 17 parts barley @ £151 per tonne, 3 parts concentrate supplement at £275 per tonne; plus £22 per tonne milling and mixing cost. Total, £192 per tonne.

   Barley ration quantity; average 2,225kg, high 2,140kg (excluding calf feed to 12 weeks – see page 60).

5. *Bedding:* 0.9 tonnes at £65 per tonne

SHEEP

Spring Lambing Flocks

Lowland Spring Lambing per Ewe (selling lambs off grass)

Performance Level	Low	Average	High
Value of Lamb £/Lamb	87	92	97
£/Ewe	£	£	£
Lamb Sales	112	138	164
Wool	0.40	0.40	0.40
Less Ewe and Ram Depreciation	20	20	20
Output	**92**	**118**	**144**
Variable Costs:			
Concentrate (Ewe and Lamb)	18	17	16
Vet & Med	9	10	12
Miscellaneous	13	13	13
Variable Costs (ex. forage)	**40**	**40**	**41**
Gross Margin £/Ewe, (ex. Forage)	**52**	**78**	**103**
Number of Ewes with lambs per Ha.	8	9	10
Forage Variable Costs £/Ewe	27	24	22
Gross Margin £/Ewe	**25**	**54**	**81**
Gross Margin £/Forage Ha (Acre)	**200**	**486**	**810**
	(81)	*(197)*	*(328)*

1. *Rearing Performance Data:*

Lambing Stats	Low	Average	High
Ewes in Lamb	92%	95%	97%
Lambing Percentage	160%	175%	190%
Lambs born per 100 ewes	147	166	184
Young Lamb Deaths	8%	6%	5%
Older Lamb Deaths	4.5%	4.0%	3.5%
Total Lamb Losses	13%	10%	9%
Lambs sold per 100 ewes put to ram	129	150	169

These performance figures are assumed for flocks of mature ewes, i.e. shearlings and older. Where ewe-lambs or mainly shearlings are included in flock performance adjustment needs to be made. The breed will have a large effect on performance data.

2. *Lamb Sales.* Prices for lambs sold for slaughter are based on the projection for the 2022 season. Average sale liveweight of 40kg, averaging £2.30/kg making £92 per average lamb

3. *Wool:* 2kg/ewe at £0.20/kg

4. *Depreciation:*

	Ewes	Ram	Per Ewe
Purchase Price - £	£145	£500	
Cull Price - £	£65	£85	
Animal Life (Years)	5.0	3.5	
Mortality	5%	5%	
Ewes per Ram		45	
Depreciation £/ewe	£17.45	£2.79	£20.24

5. *Concentrate Feeding:* Concentrate finishing of late season lambs has been common, but there has been a swing to sell as stores (for finishing on winter forage crops) rather than finish on high-cost concentrates. Late season grass availability influences the store trade.

Feeding Schedule	Low	Average	High
Ewe Feed Kg	51	48	45
Ewe Feed £/t	£255	£255	£255
Ewe Feed £/Ewe	£13	£12	£11
Lamb Feed Kg/ Lamb	13	11	10
Lamb Feed £/t	£285	£285	£285
Lamb Feed £/Lamb	£3.71	£3.14	£2.85
Lamb Feed £/Ewe	£4.77	£4.69	£4.81
Total Feed Cost £/Ewe	**£18**	**£17**	**£16**

6. *Veterinary and Medicine:* includes allowance for wormer (ewes and lambs), vaccines, fly strike chemicals and foot treatments.

7. *Miscellaneous Costs:* include contract shearing at £1.20/ewe, scanning £1.08/ewe and ewe and lamb tags £1.50/ewe (assuming slaughter batch tags are used), carcase disposal £0.75/ewe, straw £1.30/ewe, minerals and licks etc. £2.10/ewe, marketing, levy and transport £5.25/ewe.

8. *Forage Costs:* Based on Low Input Permanent Pasture (£145/ha) refer to forage section, page 42. Only variable costs are included and therefore overhead costs of forage production need to be considered. Similarly, bought in grass keep and forage may increase the forage costs over those shown.

9. *Other Costs:*

   a. *Prices of Specialised Equipment*
Troughs (2.75 m)	£35 to £48
Racks (2 to 3 m)......................	£230 to £270
Foot Baths (3 m)	£110 to £200
Shearing Machines..................	£530 to £1,250
Lamb Creep Feeders	£410 to £870
Weigh Crate...........................	£560 to £820
Mobile Handling System	£3,000 to £9,000

   b. *Fencing: Refer to page 271.*

   c. *Labour:* see page 161.

Upland Spring Lambing per Ewe (selling lambs off grass)

Performance Level	Low	Average	High
Value of Lamb £/Lamb	*83*	*87*	*91*
£/Ewe	**£**	**£**	**£**
Lamb Sales	99	124	144
Wool	0.28	0.28	0.28
Less Ewe and Ram Depreciation	18	18	18
Output	**81**	**106**	**126**
Variable Costs:			
Concentrate (Ewe and Lamb)	19	13	7
Vet & Med	9	10	12
Miscellaneous	12	12	12
Variable Costs (ex. forage)	**41**	**35**	**31**
Gross Margin £/Ewe, (ex. Forage)	**40**	**71**	**95**
Number of Ewes with lambs per Ha.	4	9	10
Forage Variable Costs £/Ewe	22	10	9
Gross Margin £/Ewe	**19**	**61**	**86**
Gross Margin £/Forage Ha (Acre)	**74**	**551**	**861**
	(30)	*(223)*	*(349)*

1. *Rearing Performance Data:*

Lambing Stats	Low	Average	High
Ewes in Lamb	92%	95%	97%
Lambing Percentage	150%	170%	185%
Lambs born per 100 ewes	138	162	179
Young Lamb Deaths	9%	7%	7%
Older Lamb Deaths	5.0%	5.0%	5.0%
Total Lamb Losses	14%	12%	12%
Lambs sold per 100 ewes put to ram	119	142	158

These performance figures are assumed for flocks of mature ewes, i.e. shearlings and older. Where ewe lambs or mainly shearlings are included in flock performance adjustment needs to be made. The breed will obviously have a large effect on lambing percentage, liveweight gains and carcase grades.

2. *Lamb Prices.* Average market price of £2.30/kg liveweight (equivalent to £5.00/kg deadweight) has been assumed giving £87.40 per finished lamb at an average liveweight of 38kg. Performance variation is 5% each way caused by differences in weights, time of marketing and proportion sold finished or retained as stores.

3. *Wool:* Wool price assumed for upland flocks is £0.28 per ewe, based on a price of £0.17/kg at 1.7kg/ewe. Upland sheep wool is harsher than lowland which is softer and therefore dearer. Variations between breeds affect wool quality and ewe size affecting weight of wool produced.

4. *Depreciation*

	Ewes	Ram	Per Ewe
Purchase Price - £	£125	£490	
Cull Price - £	£55	£85	
Animal Life (Years)	5.0	3.5	
Mortality	5%	5%	
Ewes per Ram		45	
Depreciation £/ewe	£15	£3	£18

5. *Concentrate Feeding*: Concentrate finishing of late season lambs has been common, but there has been a swing to sell as stores (for finishing on winter forage crops) rather than finish on high-cost concentrates. Late season grass availability influences the store trade.

Feeding Schedule	Low	Average	High
Ewe Feed Kg	59	40	24
Ewe Feed £/t	£265	£265	£265
Ewe Feed £/Ewe	£16	£11	£6
Lamb Feed Kg/ Lamb	10	6	2
Lamb Feed £/t	£290	£290	£290
Lamb Feed £/Lamb	£2.90	£1.74	£0.58
Lamb Feed £/Ewe	£3.44	£2.47	£0.92
Total Feed Cost £/Ewe	**£19**	**£13**	**£7**

6. *Veterinary and Medicine*: includes allowance for wormer (ewes and lambs), vaccines, fly strike chemicals and foot treatments.

7. *Miscellaneous Costs:* include contract shearing at £1.20/ewe, scanning £1.08/ewe and ewe and lamb tags £1.50/ewe (assuming slaughter batch tags are used), carcase disposal £0.84/ewe, straw £0.80/ewe, minerals and licks etc. £1.60/ewe, marketing, levy and transport £5.25/ewe.

8. *Forage Costs:* Based on Low Input Permanent Pasture (£87/ha) refer to forage section, page 42. Only variable costs are included and therefore overhead costs of forage production need to be considered. Similarly, bought in grass keep and forage may increase the forage costs over those shown here.

Rearing Ewe Lambs

Purchasing ewe lambs and rearing over winter & summer for breeding

Sales:	£ Per Ewe Lamb Sold
Sale Price / Transfer Out Value	145
Wool	0.28
Culls for Meat, 3% at £87 per head	2.61
Less Purchase Price / Transfer In Value	101
Output per Ewe	**42**
Variable Costs:	
Concentrate	3.71
Vet and Med	6.95
Miscellaneous	9.33
Variable Costs (ex. forage)	**20**
Gross Margin £/Ewe Lamb, (ex. Forage)	**22**
Stocking Rate (Ewe lambs per forage Hectare	15.0
Forage Variable Costs (inc bought-in)	5.78
Gross Margin per Ewe	**16**
Gross Margin £/Forage Ha. (Ac.)	240 (97)

1. *System*: Involves rearing or purchasing ewe lambs for further breeding. Animals are purchased / transferred in late summer / autumn, grazed and outwintered, grazed on in the following summer before sale / transfer out in the autumn (i.e. 12-month system). The terminology for this system varies between regions; gimmers, thieves, shearlings and tegs all relate to the same age of female sheep.

2. *Sales*: wool, 1.4kg at £0.20/kg

3. *Purchase Price*: Assumes best quality ewe lambs are acquired at £94 per lamb than sold to market. Includes 4% mortality charge.

4. *Concentrate*: 14kg each at £265/tonne

5. *Veterinary and Medicine*: includes wormer, fly strike chemicals, vaccines and miscellaneous treatments.

6. *Miscellaneous Costs*: Shearing at £0.94/head, minerals at £1.60/head, carcase disposal at £0.34/head. Marketing and haulage costs are included at 3% sale price and £2.10 per lamb respectively, but not payable if for home use.

7. *Forage Costs:* Based on Low Input Permanent Pasture (£87/ha) refer to forage section, page 42. Only variable costs are included and therefore overhead costs of forage production need to be considered. Similarly, bought in grass keep and forage may increase the forage costs over those shown here.

Finishing Store Lambs

Purchasing store lambs and finishing late autumn & winter

Sales:	£ Per Lamb Finished
Sale Price	108
Less Purchase Price / Transfer In Value	55
Losses	2
Output per Lamb	**50**
Variable Costs:	
Concentrates	4
Vet and Med	3
Miscellaneous	7
Variable Costs (ex. forage)	**14**
Gross Margin per Lamb, (Ex. Forage)	**36**
Stocking Rate (lambs per forage Hectare	28
Forage Variable Costs (inc bought-in)	5
Gross Margin per Lamb	**32**
Gross Margin £/Forage Ha. (Ac.)	885 (358)

1. *System:* lambs are batch bought in the autumn at or shortly after weaning in September or October, then drawn out and sold as they are ready in smaller groups from then through to March the following year.

2. *Sales:* Assumes 43kg liveweight at £2.50/kg, a higher lamb price than other margins as out of season.

3. *Losses:* assumed at 4% of transfer price

4. *Concentrates:* 14kg per lamb at £265 per tonne

5. *Veterinary and Medicine:* Allows for wormer and scab injection, clostridial vaccines and miscellaneous treatments.

6. *Miscellaneous:* Including transport, marketing, minerals, carcase disposal.

7. *Forage Costs:* Based on Low Input Permanent Pasture (£87/ha) and Stubble Turnips (£151/ha) refer to forage section, page 42. Only variable costs are included and therefore overhead costs of forage production need to be considered. Similarly, bought in grass keep and forage may increase the forage costs over those shown.

8. This is a gross margin covering only a few months of the year, but it is also worth remembering that the stubble turnips will be growing for 6 months. Fitting the enterprise into the other farm enterprises can add value to the business if carefully planned.

GRAZING AND REARING CHARGES: CATTLE AND SHEEP

Grazing charges vary greatly according to the quality of the pasture, access, fencing and infrastructure. Local supply and demand also affect the value of grazing charges. Grass is more available in 2-19 than it was in 2-18 (thanks to more rain this year). The following figures are estimated for 2020:

Summer Grazing (per head per week)

Store cattle and in-calf heifers >21 months,	£2.00 - £3.00
dry cows, and fattening bullocks >18 months	£2.00 - £3.00
Heifers and steers, 12-21 months	£2.00 - £3.00
6-12 months cattle	£1.00 - £2.25
Cattle of mixed ages	£1.00 - £2.50
Ewes (with lambs)	£0.45 - £0.70

Winter Grazing (per head per week)

'Strong' Cattle (including Bulk feed).	£1.75 - £3.00
Heifers	£1.50 - £2.50
Sheep	£0.30 - £0.50

Note: the above figures assume the farmer on whose land the livestock are present does all the fencing. The livestock owner remains their keeper, else the landowner would become liable for all the livestock based cross compliance such as tagging. If the stock owner does the fencing, the figures may be much less. Prices vary on local demand.

Grass Keep

Most typically around £100-£175 per ha (£40-£70/acre), with a high range of £62-£275 per ha (£25-£110/acre), depending on grass quality and location.

These figures are highly variable, especially between parts of the country and levels of local demand. Good fencing, electricity supply, mains water etc. add a premium to grass keep as does the quality of grassland and any licensor fertiliser applications. Grazing may be offered to livestock keepers at very little or no charge where the need for maintenance of grassland is the driving factor (e.g. amenity value, requirement to cross comply or meet agri-environment scheme agreements, value of cattle and sheep to 'clean-up' pasture or to provide beneficial mixed grazing). The length of grazing period offered will also influence the premium of grass keep (e.g. grazing until 30th September or until 31st December) as will permission to take a grass crop from the land (hay, haylage, silage).

The Nitrate Vulnerable Zone (NVZ) rules in England mean that demand for grass keep is high in some areas, especially where dairy enterprises are commonplace. The additional acreage helps some producers to keep within their livestock manure loading limit.

Winter Keep (Cattle per head per week)

Grazing + 9 kg hay and some straw	£10.00
Full winter housing in yards	£9.50 - £12.50
Calf bucket rearing for beef	£12.00 - £15.00

These figures would include bulk feed and straw. A typical rental for labour, buildings and maintenance diet would be £9.50 per head per week. These rates apply where feed to achieve maintenance plus some growth is supplied plus labour and buildings and bedding where applicable. A typical rental for labour, buildings and a maintenance diet would be £7.50 per head per week. In recent years the cost of bedding (usually straw) has influenced the final values of winter keeping cattle.

Heifer Rearing Charges

There have historically been two types of arrangement:

1. Farmer X sells calf to a Rearer at agreed price; the calf is then Rearer's responsibility and he pays for all expenses and bears any losses. Farmer X has first option on heifers, which he buys back two months before calving. Approximate price: £1,200 above cost of calf for Holstein Friesians. Rearer fetches calf; Farmer X supplies transport for heifer. *This system is now less common due to the increasing popularity and general transparency of option 2 below.*

2. Farmer X retains ownership of calf but sends it to a specialist rearer. Approximate rearer charges range from £0.60 to £1.20 per head per day for winter rearing and £1.00 to £1.30 per head per day for summer rearing. Charges vary depending upon cattle, system and location. Newer agreements often include a fixed incentive payment to the Rearer if the cattle have met specification at the end of the rearing period. This is usually defined in terms of final liveweight and the level of in-calf heifers. A typical fixed fee incentive payment would be £50 per head.

   Usually the owner of the cattle is responsible for transport costs and the choice and cost of vaccine programmes. The cost of semen for artificial insemination of the heifers is also usually incurred by the owner and paid for over and above the standard rearing charge. The rearer is responsible for all standard rearing costs including for normal veterinary services and worming etc. and any animal losses over an agreed tolerance level. *Model agreements are available from industry associations and advisors.*

Contract rearing on behalf of a third party may appeal to some producers who wish to reduce borrowing exposure and / or lower capital investment in a business. A well laid out contract rearing arrangement will also provide greater cost and income clarity to both the rearer and owner and therefore reduce the risk exposure to both businesses. It also enables each business to focus and specialise to achieve optimum performance without being distracted by other enterprises. Biosecurity issues are becoming increasingly paramount where an agreement is set up. In many cases the owner of heifers will require exclusive occupancy of a rearer's farm without cattle owned by the rearer or others being present. The Bovine TB movement rules must be considered by parties entering into heifer rearing agreements including the need for pre-movement TB testing between holdings.

RED DEER

System (per 100 breeding hind)	Breeding & Finishing	Breeding & Selling Stores	Deer Park
Sales:	£	£	£
Stags	13,200	6,750	8,360
Hinds (for meat)	7,875	10,500	6,967
Hinds (for breeding) ⑤	3,990		
Less Breeding Stock Depreciation	2,600	2,600	1,525
Output	**22,465**	**14,650**	**13,802**
Variable Costs:			
Concentrate (Hinds)	1,080	312	960
Concentrate (Calves)	1,723		
Vet & Med	900	405	340
Miscellaneous	408	204	102
Variable Costs (ex. forage)	**4,111**	**921**	**1,402**
Gross Margin £/100 head	18,354	13,729	12,400
Hinds per Ha.	4.50	6.50	3.00
Forage Variable Costs	4,797	2,230	2,892
Gross Margin (Inc. Forage)	**13,558**	**11,499**	**9,507**
Gross Margin £/Ha	**610**	**747**	**285**
Gross Margin £/Acre	247	303	116

Assumptions	Breeding & Finishing		Breeding & Selling Stores		Deer Park	
Calves	**Hinds**	**Stags**	**Hinds**	**Stags**	**Hinds**	**Stags**
Deer Sale Weight - kg	50	60	£/head		50	55
Sale Price £/Kg	£3.50	£4.00	£250	£150	£3.80	£3.80
Breeding £/head	£450					
Animal Sales	42	44	42	45	37	40

Breeding Depreciation	Hinds	Stags	Hinds	Stags	Hinds	Stags
Purchase Price - £	£350	£1,500	£350	£1,500	£350	£1,500
Cull Price - £	£200	£500	£200	£500	£200	£1,000
Number Bought	8	1	8	1	8	0.75
Number Sold	7	1	7	1	7	1
£/100 head	**£1,400**	**£1,000**	**£1,400**	**£1,000**	**£1,400**	**£125**

Notes:

1. System: Lowland systems assumed. Replacements bought in.

2. *Concentrates:* 4.5t per 100 breeding hinds for Breeding & Finishing systems and Deer Park; 1.3t per 100 breeding hinds for Breeding and Selling Store systems a cost of £240/t. Many are now outwintering calves on forage crops such as kale, stubble turnips and swedes with a grass runoff area.

3. *Forage costs*: Refer to Forage Variable Cost section. Breeding and Finishing system is based on Long Term Ley variable costs and includes hind plus finishing progeny; Selling Stores is based on Improved Permanent Pasture costs; Deer Park forage costs are based on Low Input Pasture.

4. *Price*: The venison price reflects projected sales for 2022 to wholesale buyers and the higher prices being paid for farmed venison by supermarkets. Higher prices will be obtained for direct sales to consumers (e.g. farm shops and farmers' markets) and caterers, but extra costs will normally be incurred. Demand is expected to pick up from the restaurant trade as venues start to open back up.

5. *Hinds for breeding*: Following a rapid period of expansion in deer farming, demand for breeding hinds has fallen due to a decline in demand from new herds.

Finishing Stag Calves

Per 100 Stags	Average	High
	£	£
Stag Sales	26,813	29,250
Less Purchased Store (incl. mortality)	15,000	15,000
Output	**11,813**	**14,250**
Variable Costs:		
Concentrates	2,210	1,920
Vet & Med	306	306
Miscellaneous	498	498
Variable Costs (ex. forage)	**3,014**	**2,724**
Gross Margin (ex. Forage)	**8,799**	**11,527**
Stock per Ha.	11	13
Forage Variable Costs	1,962	1,660
Gross Margin per 100 Head	**6,837**	**9,866**
Gross Margin £/Forage Ha	**752**	**1,283**
Gross Margin £/Forage Acre	*305*	*519*

Assumptions	Finishing Stags	
	Averag	High
Deer Sale Weight - kg	55	60
Sale Price - £/kg	£5.00	£5.00
Animal Sales	98	98

Sources of further information: The British Deer Farms and Parks Association; Venison Advisory Service Ltd

Acknowledgement: Thanks to – Dr. John Fletcher and the Venison Advisory Service Ltd

HORSES: LIVERY

The British Equestrian Trade Association's (BETA) National Equestrian Survey 2019 found the economic value of the equestrian sector was £4.7 billion, an increase of £0.4 billion since 2015. Although the number of horse owners has fallen to 374,000 (16%), the number of regular riders has risen from 1.3m in 2015 to 1.8m in 2019. LANTRA estimates that there are over 19,000 equine-related businesses employing more than 41,000 people. These statistics indicate the UK equine industry is substantial and possibly still growing. Covid-19 may have stopped this growth although being an outdoor pursuit, may survive the virus. It is anticipated that there may be a shift to the lower cost DIY yards.

The most common equine enterprises that farm businesses can operate is providing accommodation for horses, i.e., livery. There are many different forms of livery and the charges therefore vary widely. This is in addition to the effects of local supply and demand, which lead to large price differences from one area to another. However, three fairly standard forms are offered on farms:

Grass Livery. Keep at grass, preferably with shelter, water supply and secure area to keep tack and store feed. Some grass livery will provide an exercise arena and off-road riding. Charges range from £15-£50 per week.

DIY Livery. The owner still has full care of the horse but has the facilities of a stable, grazing, and in some cases an all-weather exercise arena. The owner is responsible for mucking out, turning out, grooming, exercising and all vet/med care and the cost of all feed and bedding. Charges range from £35-£90 per week.

Part Livery. The yard manager is responsible for the majority of tasks, such as turning out, feeding, rugging up, all fodder and bedding costs, but not exercising. Charges range from £75-£200.

There is also *Full Livery*. The yard supplies a complete service to the horse owner including tasks such as grooming and exercise. Services provided by the yard may be fitted to the needs of a horse/owner. Equine expertise is required. Full livery charges range from £100-£250.

The above are guidelines. There is a wide variation both within, and between regions and are dependent on the location of the yard, proximity to conurbations and other attractions including cross country centres, beaches and a good network of bridal paths. The largest demand is for lower cost DIY or grass livery, but owners are increasingly looking for minimum facilities of a surfaced riding arena, parking for vehicles and safe off-road riding.

Other Costs:

Grazing. Variable costs average £86 per horse per year. Average stocking rates are 0·4 ha (1 acre) per horse.

Hay. Average price £4.00 per conventional good quality bale (approximately 20kg) (range £2.5-£6.00), depending on the season. Consumption is one to two bales per horse per week; less in the summer depending on the grass quality/quantity and the work of the horse. Some horses have haylage; more expensive, dust free and higher fibre and energy/protein levels; less required per head (£7.50 - £9.00/bale).

Concentrate Feed. Ranges from almost nil to 4.0kg per day depending, amongst other factors, on breed, size and intensity of work. Compound feed 35 to 65p per kg. Only supplied in part or full-time livery.

Bedding. Averages around £12 per stabled horse per week stabled. Some horses are stabled year-round, others have significant turnout in the summer. Typical cost £300-£400 per year. Straw costs only half as much; however, more expensive, but preferable, alternatives such as wood shavings, shredded paper and hemp fibre are increasingly used.

Vet. and Med. Average £220 per horse per year. Some yards include worming in the livery cost, all other vet & med costs are payable by the horse owner.

Rates. Livery is a non-agricultural use, and therefore any buildings being used for the enterprise were historically liable to business rates. Currently livery yards are not rateable.

Filling a yard has become more difficult in recent years, with a good reputation paramount- 80-90% occupation 48-52 weeks per year is typical. The level of service and facilities expected by customers has increased. There is a trend towards greater professionalism in the running and management of livery yards. Livery contracts should be exchanged showing the responsibilities of each party. Comprehensive third-party insurance is also important.

To be successful, a livery enterprise needs higher quality facilities than farm livestock. Good customer relations and a good security system (burglar and fire) are crucial to success, as is good market research and effective advertising. Ensuring prompt payment of livery fees is another issue, this can be helped by payment in advance or by direct debit.

A full livery yard requires stables, a secure room to store tack, a vermin-proof hard feed store, storage for hay and bedding, a muck heap, a riding arena and parking provision with room for horse boxes. Planning permission is required for the conversion of an existing building to stabling or the erection of purpose-built stables. Permission is also required for construction of an all-weather arena. Hay and straw should be stored away from the stables and downwind of them to minimise the fire risk. A hard standing area with a water supply and good drainage should be provided for grooming and washing down the horses.

Fences must be sound and free of protruding nails, wire etc. Ideally fields should be fenced using post and rail. Barbed wire should be avoided wherever possible or should be 'protected' with an offset electrified fence. Fields should be divided into smaller paddocks to reduce the possibility of fighting between incompatible horses and to separate mares and geldings. Paddocks may be divided using two or more strands of electrified tape or rope.

Off-road riding opportunities on the farm are a real asset. The farmer may provide riding trails, a jumping paddock, or a cross country course. An all-weather manège possibly with floodlighting, is highly desirable, and some livery yards have horse walkers too. Good facilities can be rented out to individuals or organisations such as pony clubs.

Construction Costs. The cost of conversion of existing buildings depends on their quality; prefabricated hardwood and steel internal stable partitions can be purchased from upwards of £1,500 per stable, depending on size and specification. Free standing timber stables cost between £2,000 and £3,000 (plus base), depending on size and quality. All weather arenas (20m x 40m) cost between £20,000 and £50,000; construction is a specialist job as good drainage is essential; a badly constructed arena is worthless. A specialist waxed surface is preferred to plain sand or shavings.

Contact*:* Further financial information on horse enterprises, including riding schools and equestrian centres, is available in the 'Equine Business Guide', 7th Edition, 2019. www.abcbooks.co.uk

WILD BOAR

Wild Boar is farmed in the UK on about 50 farms, with a population of 1,750 sows. Wild Boar come under the Dangerous Wild Animals Act and farms must be licensed by the Local Authority. The cost of a licence varies greatly between authorities and ranges anywhere from £150 - £700 plus veterinary inspection fees. These are annual costs following a farm inspection with renewal fees at a lower rate. Enclosures must be secure with strong fencing: at least 1.8 metres high and most authorities require 30-80cm below ground plus an additional strand of electric fence inside the main fence. The minimum cost of fencing using approved contractors is £13.50 per metre plus the hire of a digger.

Wild Boar live outdoors in groups of up to 10 sows per boar. Large arcs are suitable for a group of gestating sows, or sows running with maturing boarlets. About a hectare would be needed for 5 sows and a boar. They forage but need feeding concentrate and root crops. Gilts mature at 18 months. Farmed sows can give two litters in most years. Young sows produce 2 to 3 boarlets and mature sows 6 to 9. A well-run enterprise should average 7 boarlets per sow per year raised to maturity. Wild boar can live from 12 to 15 years, but in a commercial herd the sows are usually culled at 7 to 8 years. Wild boar take 9 to 18 months to reach a slaughter weight of 75-85 kg. This produces a 45-50 kg carcase.

Capital costs include housing and fencing at £4,200 per hectare (*£1,700 per acre*); pure-bred adult boar £500-£700; pure-bred in pig sow £350-£500. Labour requirements are low, owing to the 'hands off' nature of wild boar management. One person should manage a herd of 30-40 sows plus fatteners. There is no organised marketing system and producers develop their own outlets. There are some wholesale butchers and game dealers who will take whole carcases, but many producers organise their own processing and arrange their own retailing. Customers are often high-end restaurants.

Performance Level	Low	Average	High
Finished Boarlets per Sow per Year	6	7	9
Finished Carcase Weight (over 15 months)	45	48	50
Price per kg deadweight	4.50	5.50	6.50
Sales:		£	
Meat sales per Sow per Year	1,215	1,848	2,925
Less Depreciation per Sow per Year	41	41	41
Output per Sow	**1,174**	**1,807**	**2,884**
Variable Costs:			
Concentrates sow		300	
fatteners (0.15t each at £250/t)	270	263	338
Other Feed		180	
Bedding		40	
Vet, Med and Licence		100	
Miscellaneous (inc. Water and Electricity)		30	
Total Variable Costs per Sow	**920**	**913**	**988**
Gross Margin per Sow	**254**	**895**	**1,897**
Gross Margin per Hectare (5 Sows/Ha)	**1,270**	**4,473**	**9,483**

1. *Depreciation:* Cost of sow £350, cull value £200, active herd life 5 years, plus share of boar and 5% mortality.

2. *Concentrates:* Sow includes share of boar. Sow 1.1t at £250/t. Fatteners 0.15t (0.18t for low) at £250/t.

3. *Other feed:* Includes bought-in waste vegetables, these are necessary for wild boar.

GOAT DAIRYING

Performance Level	Low	Average	High
Milk Yield (litres) per Goat	700	900	1,100
Sales:	£	£	£
Milk Value	371	477	583
Value of Kids	2.8	3.6	3.6
Less Livestock Depreciation	68	68	68
Output per doe	**306**	**413**	**519**
Variable Costs:			
Concentrates	116	168	230
Miscellaneous (inc. Vet and Med)	95	95	95
Total Variable Costs	**211**	**263**	**325**
Gross Margin per Doe, before Forage	**96**	**150**	**194**
Forage Variable Costs	22	28	34
Gross Margin per Doe	**74**	**122**	**160**

1. *Yield:* Per annum. Extended lactations and out of season breeding often used to improve seasonality.

2. *Price:* 53p per litre; 40p to 65p (+) with the higher prices being in the winter months (November to February) and the lower end of the range in the summer. 12.0% solids delivered. Those retailing direct should achieve higher prices but will have higher costs.

3. *Kid(s):* Prolificacy relates to age, breed, seasonality and feed level. Assumptions: low 140%; average and high 180%. There is very little trade in kids for meat (£2 per kid assumed).

4. *Culls and Replacements:* Replacements does at £250-300/head, bucks at £400-600/head; culls £50 to £80, average productive life 3 – 4 years. Bucks: 1 per 40-50 does. Young goats can be mated from 6 months.

5. *Concentrates:* Average 0.85kg concentrate per litre, at £200 per tonne.

6. *Forage:* Average 0.5 kg DM forage per litre at £164 per tonne DM plus 20% wastage (Refer to Forage Section). Goats can be grazed but are normally storage fed to avoid problems with worms, fencing, milk taints and pneumonia. Farmers able to produce maize silage will have a better forage conversion ratio.

7. *Miscellaneous:* Bedding £50, vet and med. £25 (includes treatment for out-of-season breeding, vaccination against Johnes), sundries £20.

8. *Labour:* 1 full-time person per 150 to 200 goats, dependent on technology employed.

9. *Markets:* Herd sizes in the UK range from 50 to 4,000 milking does. Securing a reliable milk contract is critical as bulk purchasers of goats' milk are few and far between and oversupply has affected the market over recent years. Prolificacy and technical improvements allow higher annual growth than the market and there is a cycle in milk and stock prices.

SHEEP DAIRYING

Performance Level	Low	Average	High
Milk Yield (litres per ewe per year)	150	400	650
Sales:	£	£	£
Milk Value at £1.15 /l	173	460	748
Value of Lambs	62	62	62
Cull sales (less ram depreciation)	8	8	8
Output per Ewe	**227**	**514**	**802**
Variable Costs:			
Concentrates	97	141	203
Miscellaneous (inc. Vet and Med)	25	25	25
Total Variable Costs (excluding forage)	**122**	**166**	**228**
Gross Margin per Ewe, (Exc. Forage)	**105**	**349**	**574**
Stocking Rate (Ewes per Ha)	11	11	11
Forage Variable Costs	26	26	26
Gross Margin per Ewe	**80**	**323**	**549**
Gross Margin per Hectare	**877**	**3,553**	**6,034**

1. *Price*: 115p per litre at farm gate (range from 100p-120p per litre). Most sheep milk is sold to cheesemakers. It is important to find a market prior to setting up an enterprise.

2. *Lambing %*: 175%. Assume a 300 Friesland ewe flock. Retain 75 ewe lambs for flock replacements (25%). Sell 371 finished lambs reared from 2 days old (including 15% mortality) at £50. If meat-type terminal sires used, then cross-bred lamb values increase to £65.

3. *Cull ewes:* Assumed 25% culled at £60 per head (average, including 5% mortality). Average herd life 5 years. Home-grown replacements are put to the ram at 17months, rearing cost of £200. Ram depreciation based on average ram cost of £1,000, cull value £60, life expectancy 3 years. Ram to ewe ration 1:50.

4. *Concentrates:* Milking ewes: Low, 180 days at 0.5kg/day; Average, 240 days at 1.0kg/day; High, 300 days at 1.5kg/day; 200 days at 1.5 kg/head/day, 100 days at 0.5 kg/head/day; cost £295/tonne. Ewe lamb replacements and artificially reared finished lambs at £70/ewe.

5. *Forage costs:* Quality silage: 1 tonne per milking ewe (or hay equivalent). Grazing: early grass in March/April; good grazing on leys or pasture; similar for dry stock and lambs. Refer to Forage Variable Cost Section, based on Intensive 3-5 year ley.

   Fixed Costs per Ewe: Labour (paid) £84; Power and Machinery £36; Property Costs £25; Other £15; Total, excluding Finance and Rent, £140.

   Capital Costs of Equipment: Complete milking unit for 300 ewes (including yokes, bulk tank, dairy equipment, installation): £45,000; cost of sheep £300-350 each £90,000-£105,000; cost of rams (3) £3,000; add contingency 10%, total set-up cost: £152,000. Any building works would be additional.

Acknowledgements: thanks to – The British Sheep Dairying Association (BSDA).

ANGORA GOATS

Angora goats produce mohair; angora rabbits produce angora; cashgora is produced by angora cross dairy goats; cashmere is produced by improved feral goats (valuable 'down' has to be separated from guard hairs; thus, with cashmere production, 'yield of down' must not be confused with 'weight of clip' as percentage of down is low and can vary widely). Goat meat is sometimes called 'chevon'.

The UK angora goat population is thought to be about 1100 animals which produce and estimated 6 tonnes per year. The figures below are for a commercial enterprise. There is a strong demand for angora goats from smallholders and smaller farmers which is making stock sales buoyant. Many UK angora flocks are kept on a semi-commercial or hobby basis, in which case different criteria may apply – does retained longer, mortality rates lower, doe/buck ratio different.

Performance:	Per Doe
Kids per Doe per Year	1.4
Fibre: Doe/Buck, 2 clips, 3 & 4.5kg/clip respectively	6.4 kg
Kids (1.4), first and second clips	5.0 kg
Wethers/Replacement Does (0.9), third clip	3.2 kg
Fibre Sales per doe:	£
Doe/Buck: 6.4kg @ £12.00/kg	76
Kids: 5.0kg @ £21.9/kg	110
Wethers/Replacements: 3.2kg @ £18.0/kg	57
Stock Sales:	
0.5 female kids sold for breeding @ £200 each	100
Wethers: 0.7 males sold for meat @ £40 each	28
Culls: 0.17 does @ £50 each	9
Skin Sales:	9
Less Replacements buck only	2.6
Output per Doe	**386**
Variable Costs:	
Concentrates	55
Vet and Med	22
Miscellaneous	22
Total Variable Costs per Doe	**99**
Gross Margin per Doe before Forage Costs	**287**
Forage Variable Costs	22
Gross Margin per Doe	**265**
Gross Margin per Forage hectare	2,652
Gross Margin per Forage acre	1,074

Over the last 5 years, the world price of mohair has risen but has fluctuated due to political uncertainty in South Africa (SA) affecting the Rand. A world shortage has increased sale price by 54% in 2021. The figures used in the calculations are based on prices in June 2021. The producers' co-operative, British Mohair Marketing, organises a national collection and sale of mohair. In recent years the entire clip has been exported to SA where it was graded and sold through the Cape Mohair auctions. Currently BMM is arranging sales in the UK for the 2021 clip. The rest of the annual clip is processed for other enterprises in UK and for hand spinning where higher prices can be achieved.

Angora goats require more management than sheep. Fencing requirements are similar but housing costs higher. Margins are sensitive to the value and number of breeding stock sold, yield and value of fibre, kidding percentage and meat values. There is a market for meat from older animals, but no reliable market has yet been developed specifically for younger animals. Angoras are usually more successful as a subsidiary enterprise on a farm rather than a stand-alone operation.

1. 1.9 kids born alive per mated doe; 2% mortality. Of 0.9 surviving doe kids, the majority (0.6) are sold for breeding, the remainder (0.3) are retained for replacements. Culls (0.15) and casualties equal replacements (unless the flock size is changing). Progeny are sold after 2 clips for breeding or after 3 clips for meat. Stock may be retained for further shearing. This has become more common, as the demand for breeding stock is small, fibre quality has improved and there is little market for meat. There is increasing demand for wethers from hobbyist spinners.

2. The data for Breeding Does includes output and inputs for breeding bucks. Assumes 25 does to one buck.

3. Angora goats are usually clipped twice a year. Yield increases over first six clips, but quality decreases with age. Prices are dependent on fashion. World market is dominated by South Africa and Texas. Demand and prices are highest for the high-quality kid fibre <25 microns in diameter.

    The following yields and prices have been used:

    Clip 1 = 1.35 kg at £25.00 per kg; clip 2 = 2.25 kg at £20.00 per kg; clip 3 = 3.5 kg at £18.00 per kg. Adult doe: 3.0 kg, adult buck 4.5 kg at £12.00 per kg.

    British Mohair Marketing arranges a collection once a year, currently in September. Membership of BMM costs £30 and there is a handling/marketing levy of £1.10/kg. (Some producers process and use the fibre themselves or sell to local spinners. Commercial processing costs are significant: combing about £6.50 per kg and spinning about £50 per kg).

4. *Stock sales*. Breeding stock in commercial flocks are culled after seven years on average. Subsequent shearing stock culled after a further 4 clips. Value of all cull stock: £50 each. Depending on quality, the skin can be worth £10 before curing or up to £150 after curing. Replacement costs: does, £250; bucks, £450. Shearing stock, £20 (as transfer from breeding enterprise). Show quality stock command a premium.

5. *Skin Sales:* From cull does and males sold for meat @ £10.00/skin

6. *Concentrates*. Quantities: Kids - 50 kg to clip 2, 15 kg to clip 3; Adults - breeding adults 90 kg per year, shearlings 40 kg per year.

7. *Veterinary* costs can be high and include vaccinations, worming & foot trimming. Membership of disease control schemes (MV/CAE) or Scrapie monitoring is extra.

8. *Miscellaneous* costs include £2.50 to £3.50 per shearing per head (it may be more) and bedding materials.

9. *Forage:* 10 does/ha, refer to Forage Variable Cost Section, based on Long Term Ley.

Contact: *British Angora Goat Society*: https://angoragoats-mohair.org.uk   British Mohair Marketing: https://angoragoats-mohair.org.uk/british-mohair-marketing

Acknowledgements: thanks to - Stephen Whitley, Corrymoor Angoras, Stockland, Honiton, Devon EX14 9DY socks@corrymoor.com www.corrymoor.com

4. NON-GRAZING LIVESTOCK

PIGS

Breeding and Rearing *(to 35kg liveweight)*

Performance Level	*Average*		*High*	
	per sow	per pig	per sow	per pig
	£	£	£	£
Weaners: (ave) 26.4 (1) @ £55	1452	55.0		
(high) 30.1 (2) @ £55			1654	55.0
Less Livestock Depreciation	108	3.9	125	4.0
Output	1344	51.1	1529	51.0
Variable Costs:				
Food	785	28.5	723	23.3
Miscellaneous	111	4.0	105	3.4
Total Variable Costs	896	32.6	828	26.7
Gross Margin (per year)	**449**	**18.5**	**701**	**24.2**

1. *Weaners per sow:* - average: 12.2 weaned per litter, 2.25 litters per year, 4% rearing losses = 26.4 weaners sold per sow per year. Productivity has improved markedly in the UK pig sector over the last few years.

2. *Weaners per sow:* - high: 13.2 weaned per litter, 2.35 litters per year, 3% rearing losses = 30.1 weaners sold per sow per year. For Outdoor Breeding performance figures see page 90.

3. *Weaner Price:* assumed price for the next 6-12 months. (See General Prices on page 89). Prices for 35kg weaners have varied from £15 to £65 during the past decade. Prices are forecast to improve marginally in line with the finished pig price.

4. *Average livestock depreciation* assumes an in-pig gilt purchase price of £250, a cull value per sow of £88.40 and a 54% replacement rate (i.e. approximately 4.2 litters per sow life). Sow mortality 6%. Boars (1 per 24 sows) purchased at £1,250 (40% a year replacement), sold at £80. 'High' compared with 'Average': higher gilt and boar purchase prices, higher replacement rate and slightly fewer sows per boar assumed.

5. *Food:*

Food:	*Average*			*High*		
	Tonnes	Value £/t	Total Cost	Tonnes	Value £/t	Total Cost
Sow	1.4	270	378	1.4	270	378
Boar	0.05	270	14	0.06	270	15
Weaner feed	1.31	300	393	1.10	300	330
Total	*2.76*	*284*	*785*	*2.56*	*283*	*723*

High performance: lower sow feed but extra piglet rearing feed for additional weaners. Piglets weaned at average 3.75 weeks, 7.5kg weight.

6. *Miscellaneous Average:* vet. and med. £38, transport £12, straw and bedding £24, miscellaneous £12, electricity and gas £15, and water £10.

7. *Direct Labour Cost* per sow: average £243, good £194; per weaner: average £8.84, good £6.27. This figure does not include labour used for 'overhead' activities – repairs etc. More pig fixed costs on page 209. *Building Costs:* see page 223.

Feeding (from 35 kg liveweight): per pig

Gross Margin	Pork		Cutter		Bacon	
	Average	High	Average	High	Average	High
	£	£	£	£	£	£
Sale Value	106	105	120	119	133	131
Less Weaner Cost	55	55	55	55	55	55
Mortality Charge	1.50	1.40	1.60	1.50	1.70	1.50
Output	49.1	48.4	63.3	62.6	76.1	74.7
Variable Costs:						
Feed	36	30	47	37	55	44
Miscellaneous	6.5	6.5	6.9	6.9	7.3	7.3
Total Variable Costs	**43**	**36**	**53**	**44**	**62**	**51**
Gross Margin	**6.2**	**12.4**	**9.9**	**19**	**13.8**	**24**

Physical Data						
Liveweight (kg)	87	86	100	98	112	110
Deadweight (kg)	64	63.5	74	73.5	83	82
Killing Out %	74%	74%	74%	75%	74%	75%
Price per Deadweight (p)	165		162		160	
Price per Liveweight (p)	122		120		118	
Feed Conversion Rate	2.50	2.10	2.60	2.15	2.65	2.20
Feed per Pig (kg)	130	107	169	135	204	165
Average Cost of feed £/tonne	£280	£275	£275	£270	£270	£265
Food Cost per Kg l/w Gain (p)	70	58	72	58	72	58
Liveweight Gain per Day (kg)	0.77	0.78	0.79	0.81	0.83	0.85
Feeding period (days)	68	65	82	78	93	88
Mortality (%)	2.8	2.6	2.9	2.7	3.1	2.8
Direct labour costs per pig (£)	5.2	4.0	6.3	4.9	7.2	5.5

Sensitivity in Gross Margin (£)	Pork		Cutter		Bacon	
Price: 5p/kg dw difference	3.20	3.18	3.70	3.68	4.15	4.10
Food Cost £/t: £10 difference	1.30	1.07	1.69	1.35	2.04	1.65
FCR: 0.1 difference	1.46	1.40	1.79	1.70	2.08	1.99

1. *Weaner cost* assumes on farm transfer. If purchased (i.e., feeding only) transport and purchasing costs have to be added: these are very variable but average about £2.00 per weaner.

2. *Average of home-mixed and purchased compounds:* There can be big variations in feed costs per tonne between farms, according to whether the food is purchased as compounds or home-mixed, bought in bulk or in bags, size of unit, etc.

3. *Labour:* see page 161.

4. *Building Costs:* see page 223.

Combined Breeding, Rearing, and Feeding: per pig

This schedule is a combination of the two previous gross margins brought together as a single management system.

	Pork £		Cutter £		Bacon £	
Performance Level*	Ave.	High	Ave.	High	Ave.	High
Sale Value	106	105	120	119	133	131
Sow and Boar Depren	3.92	4.04	3.92	4.04	3.92	4.04
Mortality Charge	1.50	1.40	1.60	1.50	1.70	1.50
Output	**100**	**99**	**114**	**114**	**127**	**126**
Food	65	53	75	60	84	67
Miscellaneous	11	10	11	10	11	11
Total Variable Costs	**75**	**63**	**86**	**70**	**95**	**78**
Gross Margin per Pig	**25**	**37**	**28**	**43**	**32**	**48**
Gross Margin per Sow	**679**	**1136**	**781**	**1343**	**887**	**1488**
Labour Costs per Pig	14	10	15	11	16	12
Labour Costs per Sow	386	318	416	346	441	365

* Performance levels refer to breeding and rearing differences as on the previous 2 pages and, for feeding, differences in food conversion rate, food costs and labour cost only.

Prices - General

Pig prices are notoriously difficult to predict. Over the last five years the GB average pig price (SPP GB average DAPP beforehand) has ranged from 170ppkg down to 115ppkg. The vast majority of UK pigs are taken to baconer weight. The level shown in the finisher margins for baconers above, of 160p, is an estimated average for late 2021 through into 2022. In practice there is likely to be considerable variation around this level. The price shown is somewhat above the prevailing price at the time of writing (summer 2021) as it is believed UK (and EU) pig prices will firm slightly after being at low levels during the early part of the year due to over-supply in the market.

Further Performance Data

Source: AHDB Performance Data – 12 months to March 2021

Indoor Breeding	Average	Top Third*	Top 10%*
Replacement rate (%)	53.1	56.4	58.6
Sow and gilt mortality (%)	7.5	7.2	7.5
Litters per sow per year	2.24	2.32	2.36
Pigs weaned per litter	12.4	13.3	14.0
Pigs wened per sow per year	27.7	30.9	33.1
Weight of pigs produced (kg)	7.4	7.4	7.1
Average weaning age (days)	26.7	27.1	25.6
Sow feed per sow per year (tonnes)	1.42	1.44	1.40

* selected on basis of pigs reared per sow per year.

Pig Performance data by Level

Rearing	Average	Top Third*	Top 10%*
Weight of pigs at start (kg)............................	7.4	7.1	7.7
Weight of pigs produced (kg)........................	39.3	36.8	32.7
Mortality (%)..	3.7	4.1	3.5
Feed conversion ratio....................................	1.77	1.54	1.40
Daily Gain (g)..	508	514	541
Feeding period (days)....................................	61	57	48

Feeding/Finishing	Average	Top Third*	Top 10%*
Weight of pigs at start (kg)............................	38.4	35.5	35.0
Weight of pigs produced (kg)........................	113.4	114.1	114.6
Carcass weight of pigs produced (kg)...........	82.5	86.1	86.5
Killing-out %	73%	75%	75%
Mortality (%)..	3.5	3.4	2.8
Feed conversion ratio....................................	2.17	2.37	2.72
Daily Gain (g)..	865	905	922
Feeding period (days)....................................	84	88	89

* selected on basis of feed cost per kg liveweight gain.

Outdoor v Indoor Performance

Breeding	Outdoor	Indoor
Replacement rate (%)......................................	49.5	53.1
Sow and gilt mortality (%)..............................	4.8	7.5
Litters per sow per year..................................	2.25	2.24
Pigs weaned per litter.....................................	10.9	12.4
Pigs weaned per sow per year.........................	24.5	27.7
Weight of pigs produced (kg).........................	7.4	7.4
Average weaning age (days)............................	26.7	26.7
Sow feed per sow per year (tonnes).................	1.50	1.42

1. *Stocking Rate for outdoor pigs* is mainly between 12 and 25 per hectare (5 and 10 per acre), 20 (8) being the most common. Good drainage is essential. A low rainfall and mild climate are also highly desirable. It is estimated that the cost of establishing a sow herd (selling weaners) would by £2,500 to £3,000 per sow place for an indoor system and £750 to £1,500 per sow for an outdoor system.

2. *Data on the split* of indoor and outdoor herds is hard to come by. However, it is thought that more than half of the UK breeding sow herd is now kept outdoors. A somewhat smaller proportion (probably <10%) of pigs are finished outdoors.

Further costing information can be found in 'Pig Production in England 2019-20' produced by Askham Bryan College, York on behalf of Rural Business Research.

Acknowledgement: The main data source for the margins within the Pigs section is the AHDB Pork performance data, but the pig and feed prices are the author's responsibility.

EGG PRODUCTION

Brown egg layers; Pullets arrive on farm at 16 weeks, kept for a 60 week laying period, 4-week changeover period. This reflects current commercial practice.

These figures reflect costs per 64-week cycle, not per year. To reach annual figures, multiply by 0.8125 (52/64).

Level of Performance	*Enriched Cages*				*Free Range*	
	Average		High		Average	
	per bird	per doz eggs	per bird	per doz eggs	per bird	per doz eggs
	£	p	£	p	£	p
Egg Returns	18.43	66.0	18.98	66.0	24.00	96.0
Less: Bird Depreciation	4.36	15.6	4.27	14.8	4.31	17.2
Output	**14.07**	**50.4**	**14.71**	**51.2**	**19.69**	**78.8**
Variable Costs:						
Food	12.10	43.3	12.10	42.1	13.30	53.2
Vet & Med	0.20	0.7	0.20	0.7	0.30	1.2
Electricity	0.50	1.8	0.50	1.7	0.50	2.0
Miscellaneous & Clean	1.00	3.6	1.00	3.6	1.20	4.3
Total Variable Costs	**13.80**	**49.4**	**13.80**	**48.1**	**15.30**	**60.7**
Gross Margin	**0.27**	**0.9**	**0.91**	**3.1**	**4.39**	**18.1**

1. *Hen-housed data* are used throughout, i.e. the costs and returns are divided by the number of birds housed at the start of the laying period. Large variations in input costs and returns occur.

2. *Yields, Depreciation and Feeding* costs as detailed below:

	Average	*High*	*Free Range*
Eggs per 64-week Cycle	**335**	**345**	**300**
Dozens per cycle	27.92	28.75	25.00
Egg Price - p per doz	**66.0**	**66.0**	**96.0**
Pullet Purchase Price - £	4.20	4.20	4.20
Cull Hens Sales - £ per bird	0.05	0.10	0.10
Mortality	5.0%	4.0%	5.0%
Total Depreciation	**4.36**	**4.27**	**4.31**
Feed Use - g/day	115	115	127
Feed Use - kg/64 week cycle	48.3	48.3	53.3
Feed Cost - £ per tonne	250	250	250
Total Feed Cost per Bird/cycle	**12.10**	**12.10**	**13.30**

3. *Egg price:* If sold direct (to local shop, add 40p/doz., if sold to consumers (farm-gate) add 70p/doz. Retail margins imply a secondary enterprise.

4. *Feed* cost is dependent on breed, housing and environmental conditions, quantity purchased and type of ration.

5. *Direct Labour Costs:* average £1.60 per bird (double for free range) dependant on level of automation. See page 173.

6. *Housing Costs:* see page 224. Building at £30.00/place depreciate at about £1.50 per housed bird place (over 20 placings *(25 years)*). Building maintenance also required.

7. *Other overhead costs* not included; vehicle costs, administration, bird and general insurance and clean-down between batches.

8. *Housed Stocking density:* 750cm²/bird (13.3 birds/m²) in enriched cage systems.

9. *Free Range Stocking density in house:* 1,111 cm² /bird (9 birds per m²), stocking in multi-tier systems can be higher, if appropriate use is made of the height of the building. *Stocking density outside the house*; regulations allow 2,500 birds/ha (1,000/acre). Freedom Foods and the Lion Code allow 2,000 birds/ha (810/acre).

POULTRY MEAT & PULLETS

Notes on Table Poultry and Pullets

1. *Pullet Miscellaneous:* Excluding transport (30p) but includes full vaccination costs.

2. *Pullet Labour (50p);* deadstock depreciation (45p).

3. Broilers Building depreciation cost approximately 8.4p per bird sold. For capital costs of housing: see page 224.

4. Labour: 8p, excluding catching and cleaning out (5.7p) but includes management; see page 173.

5. Stocking density: 38kg/m², 263cm²/kg

6. O.R. = Oven Ready

7. Rearing turkeys all the year round is in the hands of a few large and vertically integrated companies. Imports have outcompeted many small operators.

8. Miscellaneous Turkey costs include processing (including plucking and eviscerating) and marketing

9. Christmas Turkeys reflect smaller, seasonal enterprises using bagged feed, and otherwise redundant barns etc.

Note: With both turkey enterprises, considerable variations will occur between individual strains and because of different production systems and feeding regimes. Free range systems for example will show higher costs and returns. The figures should therefore be used only as rough guidelines.

10. There are very few indoor duck farmers left in the UK operating to this system, but they are large-scale.

11. Goose 16.5kg feed wheat at £150/t and 40kg goose concentrate at £307/t

12. Goose Farm gate output values used

13. Goose *Miscellaneous* costs include processing / marketing

POULTRY

£/Bird	Rearing Pullets	Table Poultry Broilers	All Year Turkey	Christmas Turkey Light	Christmas Turkey Medium	Christmas Turkey Heavy	Large Roaster Chicken	Pekin Duck	Goose
Sale Price £/Bird	4.20	2.18	39.20	59.40	64.00	84.00	15.36	9.20	57.20
Less Cost of Chick & Mort.	0.76	0.36	3.21	5.78	5.83	4.97	0.92	0.70	7.02
Output	**3.44**	**1.81**	**36.0**	**53.63**	**58.17**	**79.03**	**14.44**	**8.50**	**50.18**
Variable Costs:									
Feed	1.84	1.10	16.5	8.93	11.45	16.91	4.93	3.73	17.36
Miscellaneous	1.25	0.21	6.8	14.70	15.50	16.00	1.95	2.70	15.50
Total Variable Costs	**3.09**	**1.31**	**23.3**	**23.63**	**26.95**	**32.91**	**6.88**	**6.43**	**32.86**
Gross Margin	**0.35**	**0.50**	**12.7**	**29.99**	**31.22**	**46.12**	**7.56**	**2.07**	**17.32**
Sale Weight Kg		2.2	14.0	6.6	8.0	12.0	4.8	2.3	5.2
Oven Ready Weight (kg)				5.4	6.6	10.2			
Sale price £/Kg L.Wt.		£0.99	£2.80	£9.00	£8.00	£7.00	£3.20	£4.00	£11.00
Chick Cost - p	0.74	0.35	3.00	5.50	5.50	4.60	0.85	0.65	6.75
Chick /Poult Weight				0.30	0.30	0.30			
Feed Use - kg	6.35	3.20	50	20.8	27.0	40.4	14.3	11.3	56.0
Feed Cost - £ per tonne	£290	£345	£330	£429	£424	£419	£345	£330	£310
Food Conversion Ratio		1.5	3.6	3.2	3.4	3.4	3.0	5.0	10.8
Sale Age (Weeks unless stated)	16	41 days	20	22	22	22	12	7	
Total Mortality - %	3%	4%	7%	5%	6%	8%	8%	8%	4%
			Sexed Stags	Slow growing sexed hens	Indoor Reared	Stags	Christmas Market		free range, dry plucked

93

RAINBOW TROUT (FRESHWATER)

	£ per tonne of fish
Returns: 1 tonne of fish @ £2.25 per kg	2,250
Less 4000 fingerlings @ 8.0p each	320
Output	**1,930**
Variable Costs:	
Food: 1 tonne @ £1200 per tonne	1,200
Vet and med	150
Miscellaneous	80
Total Variable Costs	**1,430**
Gross Margin	**500**

1. Fish growing to 350g from fingerlings at 4.5g.

2. Prices are estimated ex-farm to processor or wholesaler for portion sized (c.500g) freshwater rainbow trout. Higher prices of up to £4.20 per kg can be achieved by selling direct to retailers, caterers and consumers at, say farmers markets, but significant additional costs are associated with such sales.

3. Fingerlings price: varies according to quantity ordered and time of year.

4. Average feeding period, 10 months. Mortality, from fingerling to market size, 15%. Food conversion ratio 1.1:1, having a very low maintenance requirement. The price for fish food is for a pigmented high oil expanded pellet. It is a guide price, as different diets and formulations will retail at different prices and at different economies of scale depending upon volume purchased.

5. Current capital costs for construction of earth pond unit approximately £90 per cubic metre, to include buildings, holding systems and installation of water supply and services, but excluding land.

6. Labour requirement: the basic norm has in the past been 1 man per 50 tonnes of fish produced per annum on a table fish farm, but to remain competitive farmers now need to produce at least 150 tonnes per annum of table fish per man.

The figures given are illustrative and do not reflect the complexities of trout farming. Trout farming varies in the UK from Cage Farming in Scottish lochs (freshwater and marine) to 'traditional' flow through earth/pond/concrete raceway river farming. Trout farming also encompasses both the table and restocking sectors, prices given above relate to the sale of fish for the table market. As such feed costs, conversion rates etc. do vary which obviously has an effect on the costings for the enterprise. Differences in water temperature will also impact significantly on food conversion ratios, growth rates etc.

Acknowledgement: thanks to - British Trout Association

MEAT RABBITS

Rabbit rearing for meat within the UK is at an all-time low but is increasing year-on-year. The meat is starting to be 'championed' for its health benefits plus its mild taste lending itself to a range of recipe options. Since Brexit many Smithfield wholesalers have stopped importing European rabbit opening a strong market for UK producers. There are 33 routes to market with rabbit, which include, meat sold for human consumption, fresh pet food and fallen stock can be sold as reptile food. There is also a growing demand for the pelts both home and abroad for furniture making, glove manufacture, glues and artist products. If processed at the unit this aspect alone can help profit margins considerably. Demand for rabbit meat is seasonal. Sales should be concentrated between January and mid-June and from September to the end of December.

There are several varieties of rabbit suitable for meat production, the most popular UK meat rabbits are The New Zealand White, with other varieties including the American chinchillas, English and Flemish Giants. The Rex, Californians, Silver Foxes, and Satines are also suitable for both meat and pelts. All but the Silver Foxes are highly suitable for grazing pasture. Expect to pay up to £60 for a good breeding buck and £40 each for good breeding does. Not all does are natural at raising their progeny. It is essential that the stockman should select the best natured from an early stage.

Meat rabbits require a safe environment in order to protect them from foxes, stoats, rats and other predators. A high fence (min. 1.65m) with maximum gaps of 25mm square is recommended set deeply (min. 450mm) into the ground. Three strands of electric fence set at varying distances from the fence will deter climbing predators. Adequate shelter from wind, rain and the heat of the sun is essential for a successful breeding herd. Accommodation should conform to Defra guidelines. Hutches should be a minimum of 0.75sq metres per single doe or buck and 0.75sq metres for doe and litter up to 5 weeks of age, increasing to 0.93sq metres for doe and litter up to 12 weeks of age. All hutches should be a minimum of 450mm in head height. Arrangements need to be in place to cool stock down in high temperatures during the summer months.

Growing rabbits can run together and require 0.09sq metres per rabbit. Breeding Does should be given individual accommodation particularly towards and post kindling. Barren Does can run together, progeny can also mix irrespective of sex from between 6 and 16 weeks. One Buck can run freely within the same colony, but additional bucks should be kept isolated to prevent fighting. Rabbits can be raised indoors or out, with ventilation important for the former and good hygiene essential with the latter. The progeny is raised on a free range type system from 6 to 16 weeks. The biggest risk to a rabbit herd are myxomatosis; the stockman should routinely search for evidence of mosquito larvae. Rabbit haemorrhaging disease (RHD), is also a major problem and precautions need to be taken to separate the herd from the wild reservoir.

Rabbits can be fed on fresh grass, grazed or freshly cut, plus herbs during summer months. Lactating does should receive a good dry matter supplement such as pellets, seasonal treats can be added from time to time such as fruit and vegetables. During winter months the fresh grass is substituted for hay. It is possible to make a balanced ration on the farm which saves purchasing dry feed. There is however a cost in additional labour. Hydroponically grown wheat grass has proved successful as a cheap feed solution.

An outdoor rabbit unit of 150 does is a full-time job, this includes 15% allowance for managerial duties, breakdowns and maintenance. A 100-doe unit is considered a full time job, if a significant amount of enhanced product is undertaken, such as processing of pelts and producing pies and pâtés etc.

Meat Rabbit Gross Margin Schedule

	£	£
	Per Doe	Per 150 Does
Finished Young per Doe per Year	45	6,750
Live Weight Each (at 16 weeks)	2.9	435
Price per kg to processor	2.71	407
Sales:	£	
Meat sales per Doe per Year	354	53,048
Other sales	126	18,900
Less Depreciation per Doe (incl.Buck) per Year (2)	15.5	2,326
Output	**464**	**69,622**
Variable Costs:		
Feed (Doe, progeny & share of buck)	46	6,825
Bedding	3	400
Vet and Med	13	2,000
Miscellaneous	3	500
Total Variable Costs	**65**	**9,724**
Gross Margin	**399**	**59,898**

1. *Sales:* The prices quoted are based on the wholesale environment, however, many purchasers of rabbit meat have high end restaurants. There is growing demand from the London independent restaurants. Further profits can be achieved by selling retail to the public and enhancing the value of product. A major income stream can be achieved by selling pelts. Fallen stock can be sold for reptile food and waste products as raw pet food. Demand for BARF is growing very quickly and in some cases meat rabbit barf products are selling for more than those for human consumption.

2. *Depreciation* – Doe £14.40 (incl.15% mortality), Buck £1.10 per doe (incl. 15% mortality) Average 1 buck per 10 does. Does are kept for 2 years, bucks for 6 years. Does purchased at £40 each (15% mortality), culled at £15; buck purchased at £60 (15% mortality) negligible residual value.

3. *Feed conversion:* 4:1 includes doe, progeny and 10% of buck. Food conversion rate is compatible with poultry. The feed cost assumes the availability of fresh grass/herbs on a daily basis, carrots or other vegetables and home-grown hay in the winter.

4. *Vet & Med:* Includes vaccination for Rabbit Viral Haemorrgic Disease (RVHD). It is advisable that at least half the breeding stock are vaccinated. RVHD 2 has no symptoms and can wipe out a Herd in just a few hours.

5. Young does are bought in at between 10 and 12 weeks old, mated at 20 weeks. A ratio of one buck to 10 does is recommended. Gestation is 31 days. Average litter size is 8 to 9 of which 6 to 7 should be successfully fattened. Re mating can be immediately post-partum or up to 6 weeks afterwards. A doe can have a useful life of 10 to 12 litters over a 2 year period. A mortality rate of 15% can be expected

Acknowledgements: Thanks to – T & S Rabbits, part of T & S Nurseries and the Abbey Vineyard Group.

5. RENEWABLE ENERGY

GENERAL

The Renewable Energy industry is a response to incentives to cut emissions of climate changing greenhouse gases (GHGs) as a result of human activities. Renewable energy enterprises are commonplace across the UK. Returns vary as with any enterprise, but most investors have been pleased with the result. As with any diversification or capital investment project, due diligence and sensible planning is necessary ahead of renewable energy projects, particularly since prices paid for renewable energy have fallen. Renewable energy requires space, is capital intensive and requires an entrepreneurial mind to embrace it. Agriculture, which has all these resources is therefore a natural partner for the sector.

Renewable energy is subsidised, but this support has fallen sharply in recent years. Projects in the future will need to be viable without long term subsidy. This is a status most other types of energy provision have not achieved. Renewable energy technologies in several locations are now viable without support at all.

The generation of UK renewable electricity reached 43% in 2020, fossil fuels provided 38.5%. This was the first-year renewables have outperformed fossil fuels in the UK generating over 300TWh (Terra Watt hours) (offshorewind.biz). However, electricity still accounts for a minority proportion of UK energy usage compared with gas for heating and petroleum, mainly for transport.

RENEWABLE ENERGY POLICY

In 2019, the UK Government committed to become carbon neutral (no net greenhouse gas emissions) by 2050. This is laid out in an amendment of the 2008 Carbon Change Act of 2008. The EU has set out ambitions (and legal obligations) to become carbon neutral by 2050. UK Government's energy policy is focussed on three objectives of security, affordability, and decarbonisation. They refer to it as the energy trilemma. Energy policy for the last 4 years has been to meet the Government's Clean Growth Strategy.

The statutory body whose purpose it to monitor and advise Government on the UK's climate targets is the Climate Change Committee (CCC). The CCC recommends 5-year carbon budgets (targets). It has made 5 which the Government accepted. A sixth budget, for the years 2033-2037, published in December 2020 recommended a 78% reduction in UK emissions (1990 levels) by 2035. This is their first budget since the net zero target was set.

Total GHG emissions fell by 45% from 1990 to 2019, largely from the transition from coal and gas to renewables, but also as we manufacture far less than we did before, having become a service sector economy.

At least 14% of road fuel must be from renewable sources by 2030. The proportion of fuel from '1st generation' biofuels (biodiesel and bioethanol) is 7% – the same as now. This underpins both bioethanol demand for wheat, and the oilseed rape market through the EU biodiesel industry. It had been thought that these 1st generation fuels would be phased-out in favour of fuel-from-waste technologies that can have a greater environmental benefit and do not compete for land with food production. Energy use, the primary release of GHGs, is divided into three categories; electricity, heat and transport. The renewable generation of each is incentivised by government policy.

The Renewables Obligation (RO)

From 2002 to 2017, the RO was the primary mechanism for encouraging electricity supply from large renewable sources in the UK. In April 2017, the RO closed to new applicants in place of Contracts For Difference (CfD). The RO remains operational for existing renewable electricity suppliers until their terms of agreements expire.

Contracts For Difference (CfD)

Contracts for Difference (CfDs) is a contract between a renewable electricity generator and the Low Carbon Contracts Company (LCCC), a government-owned company. The generator firm is paid the difference between the 'strike price' – a price for renewable electricity and the 'reference price'– the average wholesale price for electricity for 15 years. Generators therefore supply electricity at the agreed strike price, receiving support when wholesale prices are lower than the strike price and paying back any surplus when wholesale prices are higher than the strike price.

Feed-in Tariffs (FIT)

The Feed in Tariff scheme was the key policy for encouraging small scale renewable electricity generation from 2010 to 2019 when it ended. Existing agreements will run their course. This policy is being replaced by the Smart Export Guarantee which is discussed below.

Feed-in Tariffs encouraged the production of renewable electricity at levels up to 5MW capacity, equivalent to a large offshore turbine or a very large anaerobic digestion plant. Almost all farm-scale renewable energy schemes therefore fitted into the FIT scheme.

The FIT programme provided a renewable electricity generator a fixed payment for each kWh electricity generated; the 'Generation Tariff' set at different levels depending on technology type, installation size and start date. An 'Export Tariff' was payable as a market payment for the export to the wider market about 5.5p/kWh for installations since late 2012 or 3.9p/kWh for earlier installations. Generators could forego the export tariff and use the electricity themselves. Generation Tariff rates for new installations fell as government objectives have changed and targets were met. Generation and Export Tariffs are index linked once commissioned. Tariffs are guaranteed for 20 years (25 for solar PV if installed before 1 August 2012).

Smart Export Guarantee (SEG)

SEGs, introduced in January 2020 replaced FITS (above). They pay households for renewable electricity they generate but do not use. SEGs must be provided by all energy supplier companies with over 150,000 customers. Standard renewable facilities are eligible to receive SEG payments including Solar PV, wind, anaerobic digestion and hydro power, up to 5MW capacity, subject to certification from the Microgeneration Certification Scheme (MCS). The concept of this is that the market decides what renewable electricity is worth, not Government so major power suppliers will set prices for SEGs making it beneficial to shop around each year. SEG rates range from less than 1p/kWh to 5.5p/kWh. Households or farms would also expect to pay less for electricity as they would use their home generated electricity first. Recipients of FIT cannot participate in SEG but can switch from one to the other.

The Renewable Heat Incentive (RHI)

Heat accounts for a third of energy used in the UK. The value of heat is low (possibly 1-3p/kWh thermal energy depending on local market) which rarely justifies the capital expenditure of harnessing it or generating it from a renewable source. The RHI addresses this. The scheme is divided into domestic and non-domestic installations. RHI recipients need to meet sustainability requirements on the feedstock. This applies to all RHI payments so, for example, those using biomass boilers need to prove where their woodchip comes from. The domestic RHI has been extended until 2022. It will be replaced with the two schemes:

- The Clean Heat Grant offering a proposed £4000 installation grant for all eligible technologies.
- The Green Gas Support Scheme is planned to support the biomethane production from anaerobic digestion through a tariff-based system.

Domestic RHI

Payments are based on estimates of heat demand and generators efficiency irrespective of installation capacity and are available for new installations. The RHI is administered by OFGEM. Metering is required for some technologies. The Domestic RHI pays tariffs quarterly per unit of heat generated for seven years. Rates for existing recipients rise by inflation:

Levels of support for the Domestic Renewable Heat Incentive

Generation Technology	Domestic Tariff p/kWh Rates from April 2020
Air-source heat pumps	10.71
Ground source heat pumps	20.89
Biomass boilers and stoves	6.88
Solar thermal	21.09

Non-Domestic RHI

Once a RHI rate is agreed, payments are index linked but not exposed to renegotiations of the policy for the 20-year term. Payments (index linked) are made quarterly based on the heat generated.

Levels of Support for RHI for Non-Domestic Installations

Tariff name	Eligible technology	Eligible sizes	Tariff rate (p/kWh)*
Biomass	Solid biomass; including waste	all sizes	Tier 1: 3.15 Tier 2: 2.21
Air Source	Heat Pumps	all sizes	2.89
Deep Geothermal			5.56
Ground source	Ground and Water-source heat pumps;		Tier 1: 9.68 Tier 2: 2.89
Solar thermal		< 200 kWth	11.12
Biomethane	Injection	1st 40,000 mWh	4.92
		next 40,000 mWh	2.90
		remaining mWh	2.24
Biogas	Biogas combustion	under 200 kWth	4.80
		200-600kWth	3.77
		Over 600kWth	1.20

* *Tier Break is: installed capacity x 1,314 peak load hours (15% rating), i.e.: kWth x 1,314*

The Renewable Transport Fuel Obligation (RTFO) and Fuel Excise Duty

For every litre of biofuel that excise duty is paid on, a Renewable Transport Fuel Certificate (RTFC) is issued. For biogas 1.9 certificates are issued per kilogram supplied (1.75 RTFCs/kg biobutane or biopropane). Fuel generated from feedstocks classed as 'wastes' or 'residues' receive double certificates.

Companies supplying at least 450,000 litres of any fuel for road vehicles and (since 2013) 'non-road mobile machinery' (NRMM) to the UK market annually (about 14 companies) must participate by incorporating a proportion of biofuel into their sales, buying

RTFCs from another biofuel provider or paying a 'buy-out' penalty (fine) of 30p/l (index linked to 2008). As a compelling incentive, the 'buy-out fund' generated is redistributed equally to every RTFC issued by the year-end. This means that the further away the UK is from hitting the annual target, the greater the incentive to incorporate as RTFC values rise. These subsidies make the industry viable; without them there would be no biofuel industry.

The required proportion of biofuels to incorporate is 9.75% in 2020 and is set to rise to 12.4% by 2032. The RTFO includes sustainability criteria of the Renewable Energy Directive. The criteria include minimum carbon savings requirements. Biofuels have the same duty payable as mineral fuels for most producers. A 100% duty exemption for small scale biofuel producers of up to 2,500l biofuel per year (notionally sufficient for home use) is in place.

Fuel Excise Duty:	Since April 2016 ongoing
Petrol, Diesel *ppl*	57.95
Bioethanol and biodiesel *ppl*	57.95
Rebated gas oil (red diesel) *ppl*	11.14
Biodiesel for non-road use *ppl*	11.14
Natural gas (*inc.* biogas) *p/kg*	24.70
Liquefied petroleum gas *p/kg*	31.61
Fuel oil used for heating *ppl*	10.70

These figures are before VAT. Pump prices include VAT (20%)

PERENNIAL ENERGY CROPS FOR HEAT AND POWER

Biomass includes crops grown to be burnt to produce heat and/or electricity. Plant material is chipped or baled and is generally used in boilers in dedicated biomass power stations. Biomass includes short rotation coppice, Miscanthus, straw, canary reed grass and switch grass. The Basic Payment can be claimed on eligible land with these crops.

Short Rotation Coppice

Short Rotation Coppice (SRC) is a fast-growing willow (occasionally poplar) that when chipped and dried is used as a fuel for heat or power generation. SRC willow needs ample moisture but grows on any cultivated land. Planting is in the spring using un-rooted cuttings at 15,000/ha. Rabbit fencing may be necessary. Crops are usually harvested on a 3-year cycle (2 or 4-year cycles depending on conditions). At this stage, the crop can be up to 7-8 metres tall. Crops should last 22 years (7 harvests). Most growers apply some fertiliser post-harvest, 60 kg/ha N is sufficient. Sewage sludge is commonly used as are animal manures.

There is one market of high volume for SRC willow – Iggesund Paperboard Mill in Cumbria - who offers long-term contracts for willow grown in the north of England and the south of Scotland. The grower pays for the establishment of the crop but receives free advice and access to low price materials (cuttings etc), meaning establishment costs are significantly lower than when growing for own use. Iggesund harvests and transports the crop meaning the price paid varies depending on the distance that the grower is from the plant. A grower in Cumbria could achieve a price of £55 per oven dry tonne (ODT), lower elsewhere.

SRC Gross Margin

Production level	Low	Average	High
Yield: T/ha (tons/acre)	7.00 (2.8)	8.00 (3.2)	9.00 (3.6)
	£	£	£
Output at £53 per T	371 (150)	424 (172)	477 (193)
Variable Costs:			
Establishment		83 (33)	
Fertiliser/spray		25 (10)	
Total Variable Costs	108 (44)	108 (44)	108 (44)
Gross Margin per ha (acre)	**263** (107)	**316** (128)	**369** (150)

1. *Yield:* Based on 25ODT/hectare harvested every third year.

2. *Establishment costs:* of £1817/ha (£714/ac) excluding fencing over 22 years.

3. *Harvest and Haulage* costs are netted from contracted price of £53/delivered ODT

SRC can be used for heating projects especially self-supplying private boilers. In these situations, establishment costs will be higher, and they will need to manage their own harvesting and woodchip drying. There are four harvesting contractors (based in Cumbria, North Yorkshire, Nottinghamshire, and Warwickshire); the further the grower is from one of these contractors the higher the cost is likely to be.

Traders and self-suppliers need to consider additional costs associated with the heat market, such as Biomass Suppliers List registration and annual fees. However, greater value may be harnessed from the crop especially when RHI payments are received. Guideline areas required to provide sufficient energy are 2.7-3.5 hectares for a large farmhouse or 3.3 – 4.25 hectares for a 40,000-bird poultry shed (based on a 10.4 and 8.0 ODT/Ha). Other costs such as harvest, drying, storage etc, will be incurred.

SRC provides additional fringe benefits such as:

- Providing a means of flood mitigation (due to the dense planting and coppice nature of the crop slowing water flow)
- Reducing soil erosion
- Potential for use as a biofilter (particularly if farmers have effluents they wish to dispose of cheaply and gain a yield benefit at the same time)
- Willows provide abundant pollen and nectar in Jan-March providing fodder for pollinators at a time of year when there are few other sources in the countryside – this could benefit growers with insect pollinated crops such as WOSR, orchards, soft fruits, vegetables)

Miscanthus (Elephant Grass)

Miscanthus is a perennial grass crop lasting 20 years grown for energy and fibre. It is harvested annually with conventional farm machinery. Aside from biomass, it can be used as animal bedding, paper making biopolymer or to produce bio-degradable products, such as plant pots. It is usually propagated from rhizomes. A mature crop suppresses weeds but weed control is very important during establishment of the crop. Wireworms can be a problem if Miscanthus is planted on former grassland without a break crop in between, but otherwise there are no significant pathogens or pests in the UK meaning agrochemical use is minimal.

There is a single major buyer for Miscanthus, Terravesta, who offers ten-year contracts. The current price for delivered tonne (at under 16% moisture) is £74 per tonne, although there are penalties if the crop is out of specification and bonuses available of £2/tonne if bales have been stored in a barn.

Miscanthus Gross Margin

Production level	Low	Average	High
Yield: tonnes/ha (tons/acre)	11 (4.5)	13 (5.3)	15 (6.1)
	£	£	£
Output at £74/t	814 (330)	962 (390)	1110 (450)
Variable Costs:			
Establishment		86 (35)	
Fertiliser/spray/top		23 (9)	
Harvest		80 (32)	
Bale	134 (54)	159 (64)	183 (74)
Transport	137 (55)	161 (65)	186 (75)
Total Variable Costs	460 (186)	509 (206)	558 (226)
Gross Margin £/ha (ac)	**354** (133)	**453** (183)	**552** (234)

Yield accounts for average over 21 years

The crop shoots in April and grows to 4 metres by September. The canes are harvested in February-March by which time the moisture content is below 20%. Harvest method depends on end use. For energy, the crop is cut with a mower conditioner or modified forage harvester and then baled 10 days later into Hesston bales. Contract specifications require a moisture content of 16% when sold (although they may be baled when wetter than this) and a bale weight of 525kg. For other uses, a maize harvester is used.

1. *Establishment costs:* of £1805/ha (£730/ac) including land cultivations and weed topping at the end of the first year but excluding fencing shared between 21 years. There are likely to be economies of scale for fencing larger areas but is not often considered cost effective. Establishment costs for crops for own use are likely to be significantly higher in the region of £3,000/ha.

2. *Fertiliser and agrochemicals:* Requirements are low. Whilst the harvest will remove P and K, the plant is deep rooted so accesses minerals from deeper than most crops. Sewage sludge is an ideal fertiliser. The Miscanthus gross margin has a small cost for imported slurry, biosolids or other organic manure. Some agrochemicals will probably be required in the first 2 years.

3. *Harvest:* contracted. *Baling costs:* £7.50/bale (of 615kg) making £12.20/t

4. *Transport:* to Lincolnshire need to be included and are likely to be in the region of £11.50-£20/tonne (included at £12.40/tonne in this example)

In year 2 it is possible to achieve 8 tonnes per hectare for a very good crop, but peak yields tend to be achieved from year 4 onwards. Recent precision planting machinery improvements facilitate evenly established crops, offering greater fresh weight yields on light land 9 – 12t/ha and on medium to heavy land 12 – 18 t/ha.

Small on-farm boilers have been developed to produce heat and energy which offer potential for Miscanthus growers who can benefit from the Renewable Heat Incentive (see page 98). Emissions certificates are required as well as evidence of fuel sustainability which can be registered on the Sustainable Fuel Register.

Acknowledgement ~ Thanks to Kevin Lindegaard of Crops for Energy Ltd
(www.crops4energy.co.uk) and Terravesta

ANAEROBIC DIGESTION

Anaerobic Digestion (AD) is the digestion of non-woody organic material in the absence of oxygen by micro-organisms to produce biogas (a mixture of 40:60 carbon dioxide CO_2 and methane CH_4) and digestate (a soil conditioner). It works in the same way as a very large rumen. The biogas is collected and normally used in a combined heat and power (CHP) generator to produce heat and electricity for use or sale. The biogas can also be purified by removing the CO_2 and contaminant gasses (less than 1%) making biomethane and compressed for use as road fuel or in place of natural gas.

Most organic materials can be used as feedstock. Livestock manure is cheap with lots of micro-organisms but has a low biogas yield and is not commercially viable as the sole feedstock. Energy crops such as maize silage offer high yields and are commonly used in AD plants. They are expensive feedstocks so add substantially to operating costs but are predictable and supply is easily managed. Non-farm waste streams from food processing companies or separated kitchen wastes offer a high return, with potential to earn revenue from gate fees. Regulatory controls (such as Animal By-Product Regulations) and 'front-end' processing requirements (e.g. separators, stores, weighbridges, shredders) are far greater when importing others' wastes though, especially if animal by-products are included pushing up capital costs substantially. These tend to have unpredictable supply.

The rate of turnover of digestate is controlled by the rate at which feedstock enters the digester less the small (usually 3-10%) fall in volume from the production of biogas (most of the bulk is water which remains as water). Depending on feedstock and system used, digestion can take as little as a week up to 2 months in some circumstances.

Example On-Farm Feedstocks for Anaerobic Digestion

Feedstock	Biogas Yield m³/t feedstock	Value of Biogas £/t feedstock*
Cattle/pig slurry	15 – 25	3.25 – 5.40
Poultry manure	30 – 100	6. 50 – 21.70
Maize silage	190 – 220	41.30 – 47.70
Grass silage	150 – 200	32.50 – 43.40
Whole crop wheat	185	40
Maize grain	560	121
Rolled wheat grain	600	130
Crude glycerine	580 – 1,000	126 – 216
Rape meal	620	135
Fats	Up to 1,200	up to 260

* 4.3p/kWh Generation Tariff, 5.38p/kWh Export Tariff, 1p/kWh heat based on FIT support

Policy

When biogas is used to generate electricity, it can be sold with a Smart Export Guarantee or Feed in Tariffs for older installations. Biomethane for road transport is technically eligible for RTFCs (see Biofuels section above) or the RHI. AD also benefits indirectly from the Landfill Directive by diverting waste from landfill to uses such as AD. AD does not facilitate NVZ implementation regulations.

Economics

The two major costs associated with AD are usually the capital set up and feedstock (if home grown or purchased feed is used). Operating and maintenance costs such as insurance, labour and utilities are usually comparatively low. A relatively small plant (2,500m³ digester and 490kW CHP generator) would cost in the region of £2.5 million to build and commission. Depending on feedstock, temperature and other settings, this size plant could digest in the region of 20,000 tonnes of feedstock per year with a 45-day retention time (spent in the digester) or 30,000t with a 30-day retention period.

Revenue from this system digesting 20,000 tonnes using the assumptions from the table above, an average gas yield per tonne of feedstock of 100m³/tonne and an efficiency of 90% gas conversion would return income before costs and without gate fees of about £430,000 with FITs per annum.

SOLAR POWER

In England and Scotland, most private solar installations do not require planning permission unless the building is of conservation status, is in a designated area or is a large free-standing system. Installers in Wales and Northern Ireland need planning permission from their local planning authority.

Solar Photovoltaic (PV)

Solar PV panels generate electricity through the direct conversion of daylight. Panels can either be roof mounted, free-standing or integrated as a form of building material though solar slates, tiles or glass laminates.

Installation rates for anything above 20kW tend to be about £900 per kW. For example, a 30kW roof mounted array with high specification panels would cost in the region of £27,000 to install, depending on connection fees, cabling, etc. a comparable 20kW system would currently cost nearer to £19,000 (£950/kW) to install. Smaller arrays are dearer per kW, at £1,200 to £1,500 per kW installed. Little maintenance is required.

The standard solar panel has an input rate of around 1kW per square meter, and the majority of solar panels available absorb around 15-20% power. Therefore, if your solar panel was 1 square meter in size, then it would likely only produce around 150-200W in good sunlight. Approximately 6m² of PV panels is therefore required to generate 1kW of electricity.

A typical panel weighs 10kg per m² so additional roof support may be required. Panels should last for 25 years although electricity inverters will need replacing after 5 -10 years. Panels should be south facing at an angle of 30-40 degrees and un-shadowed. Productivity varies across the UK with levels between 1100 kWh per m² in the South West, to 800 kWh per m² in Scotland.

Solar Thermal

Solar thermal systems use the sun's energy to warm water through using either evacuated tubes or flat plate collectors fitted to a roof. A conventional boiler is then used to heat the water further. Costs are typically £3,000 to £7,000 and require little maintenance. Savings are modest; the average system provides one third of water needs, reducing heating bills by approximately £85-£180 per year.

LIQUID BIOFUELS

Liquid biofuels are road transport fuels produced from organic materials, including crops. *Biodiesel* is produced from oilseeds such as oilseed rape and is a replacement for diesel. *Bioethanol* is a petrol replacement, produced from starch-based crops including wheat, maize and sugar beet or cane.

Biofuels from cellulosic (woody) feedstock are referred to as 'second generation' biofuels. They enable a higher energy return per hectare and the opportunity to process household, manufacturing and agricultural organic 'wastes'. However, their production is not financially viable and requires more energy to process the cellulose than the energy released.

Supply

In 2019 in the UK, 46.5 billion litres of road fuel was used, approximately 38 million tonnes (diesel exceeding petrol use by about 68:32). To meet the RTFO target, about 3.7m tonnes of biofuel are required (9.75%). The RTFO does not differentiate between biofuels so one may dominate the market. Splitting the market proportionally would require roughly 2.5 million tonnes of biodiesel and 1.1 million tonnes bioethanol. This would need 3.25m tonnes OSR or equivalent feedstock (at 42% extraction) covering 1.8 million hectares (at 3.25t/ha about 4 times the UK area grown) and 4m tonnes of wheat (or equivalent feedstock) covering 450,000 hectares (at 8.5t/ha).

Farmers' options on whether to grow a crop for biofuel manufacture are determined simply by price and contractual terms. Crops used in biofuel production are, in the most part, mainstream crops. There are therefore no farm-level gross margins for biofuel crops. Despite considerable investment and funding, the biofuel industry has only ever reached operating levels of about a third of capacity. It seems unlikely it will ever grow further.

BATTERY ELECTRICITY STORAGE

Renewable energy is usually generated intermittently rather than on demand so does not match consumer requirements. Modern demands for electricity are rising with the advent of the electric car, in many cases going beyond the capacity of the electricity network system, leading to local opportunities for electricity provision or storage. The facility to store and regulate the release of electricity is therefore becoming valuable.

Electricity storage has, until recently been uneconomic for most large-scale situations. Lithium-ion batteries though, are becoming increasingly capable of storing electricity profitably. Costs are still high, but falling and likely to become viable for greater numbers of locations in coming years. This creates an opportunity for landowners and occupiers with accessible land near to substations or renewable electricity facilities, to either rent to electricity network companies or to use for their own requirements.

The largest battery storage facility is 50MW. It is next to Whitelee onshore 540MW capacity, 215-turbine wind farm (also the largest in Britain). This very large site is 3,500 square metres (60m x 60m). Whilst this example exceeds all farm-scale renewable electricity generation, the United Kingdom overall, there is already 700MW of large-scale battery storage and it is rising quickly, expected to more than double within 2 years.

Land rents on 25-year leases on small parcels of land (typically 0.5-1.5 acres) can be secured for figures in the region of £2,000-£5,000 per MW per year for electricity storage capacity of 2-50MW. There is a large number of developments that are between 10-20MW, typically being built to work in conjunction with pre-existing renewable energy sources.

Acknowledgement ~ Thanks to Darren Edwards of Fisher German

HYDRO POWER

The UK has about 4,600MW hydro-electricity capacity including pumped storage. Most of the 5200GWhr (Giga Watt hours) generated each year is from large (10-100MW) schemes. Viable sites vary from around 5kW to a few MW. Typically, power output is more constant (and manageable) for hydro than wind or solar power.

Hydro, like other renewable energy projects is capital loaded, expensive to install but cheap to operate and can have a very long life. Installation costs of around £3,000 to £6,000 per kWe for small hydroelectric systems are typical but are site dependant. Operational costs are low, generally 1-2% of capital setup. Capital cost and electrical capacity depend on the following:

- *The head (maximum vertical fall) of water:* The higher the head, the smaller the flow required to generate the same amount of electricity. Smaller flow means smaller pipe and turbine. High head is over 50 metres drop, less than 10m is low head.

- *The flow rate of water* is determined by the catchment size, amount of rainfall and the proportion of flow abstracted. The latter is determined by the environmental sensitivity of the river. Flow for small schemes is measured in litres per second.

- *Project size:* The cost of construction per kW falls as capacity rises; smallest projects take longest to repay the investment. Access affects costs. Costs for obtaining planning permission, abstraction and impoundment licenses and detailed design and specification of the equipment are similar for a 5kW scheme or a 30kW scheme.

- *Construction management:* Projects can be contracted to a single contractor to undertake design, specification, procurement and construction work, requiring little input from the landowner but is dearer. Many landowners oversee the project management which with some specialist input, costs can be greatly reduced.

- *Grid connection:* The capacity of the grid can be a major limitation, with upgrade of grid connection lines being expensive, particularly so in more rural or remote areas.

- *Development companies* take on a complete project and pay a rent to the landowner, typically 5% to 20% of income. Schemes of interest to such companies are usually at least 100kW. There is significant competition for larger schemes.

Typical costs of example projects:

- 5kW medium to low head scheme, by civil contractors with specialist hydro input. Annual generation 20 MWh. Cost around £50,000 (£10,000/kW)

- 15kW very high head. Landowner undertook project management and most civils and pipe-laying works. Annual generation 65 MWh. Cost around £120,000 (£10,000/kW)

- 30kW high head scheme. Managed by landowners using local contractors. Annual generation around 130 MWh. Cost around £200,000 (£6,700/kW)

- 100kW scheme medium head, managed by the landowner with significant time input. Annual generation around 450 MWh. Cost around £500,000 (£5,000/kW)

- 300kW scheme high head. Contractors led constructor with specialists. Annual generation around 1,200 MWh. Cost around £1,200,000 (£4,000/kW)

WIND TURBINES

There are 8,670 operational large onshore wind turbines (over 100kW) spread across 2,580 wind farms throughout the UK with 13,700MW electrical generation capacity (July 2021) (renewableuk.com). Small scale turbines have capacities of as little as 100 watts (W) up to models of 4 megawatts (MW). Wind farms are becoming larger; the average size of a new installation a decade ago was 7MW and is now 20MW, albeit with considerable offshore wind farm growth. The average onshore turbine has 1.6MW capacity.

Wind turbines in good locations produce energy equivalent to their rated capacity for around 30% of the time. For example: for a turbine rated at 40kW this calculates as 40kW x 30% x 8760 (hours in a year) = 105,120 kWh per year (105.12MWh). If this electricity is sold at 13.62p/kWh (8.24p Generation Tariff + 5.38p Export Tariff – 2019 figures) with FITs, then a return of £14,300 per year is achieved.

Typical costs for a range of turbine capacities are in the region of the following table. Good quality constructions should have an operational life of 20 years.

Guideline Figures for Capital and Revenue of Wind Turbines

Capacity kW	Capital Cost	Annual Output (kWh)	Revenue/yr using ET*
5.0	20,000	13,100	£530
10	50,000	26,280	£1,050
100	340,000	263,000	£10,500
250	680,000	657,000	£26,300
800	1,000,000	2,100,000	£84,000
1,000	1,250,000	2,628,000	£105,000

* ET Export Tariff 4p/kWh. Offset own electricity usage would add to these figures

The land surrounding a wind turbine is usually un-affected, apart from access required up to the base of the tower. A minimum average wind speed of 5 metres per second (m/s) is required; they operate at their rated capacity at 11-15m/s. Many turbines have automatic shut-down mechanisms when wind speeds exceed about 25m/s to avoid damage. Selection of the correct turbine technology and size is important.

Planning permission is required and consultation with neighbours and stakeholders for all scale turbines. Many schemes are operated by developers with land rented to them by the landowner for 20 years. In this situation, a rent will be payable to the landowner, usually at about 2-4% of income. Access to the turbines must be possible, but land between the turbines can be farmed normally. Other benefits like road improvements may also be included. An option to develop a site could be worth £1,000 to £5,000 per year.

An 11kW turbine will have a hub (mast) height of 15 to 18 metres, blade diameter of 9 metres and a 63m³ swept area. Tip height will be up to 22.5m. A large (800kW) wind turbine has a standard hub height of 76m, a height at the maximum blade position of 102m, and a blade diameter of 53m. The area of wind captured by this size blade is 0.88ha.

6.   OTHER ENTERPRISES

TURF

The turf market is now almost exclusively supplied with seed sown turf or cultivated lawn turf. The use of pasture turf has declined to an insignificant share of the market - suitable pasture for turf lifting is scarce and it is usually cheaper to grow cultivated turf than treat and prepare existing pasture. Special seed mixtures and cultivation techniques produce a range of types of turfgrass that can be matched to particular sites and uses. The Turfgrass Growers Association (TGA) has quality standards (*to be a member, growers must produce cultivated turf rather than pasture turf*). It is estimated that there are around 16,000 ha (*40,000 acres*) of turfgrass grown in the UK. Although several turfgrass companies were originally set up by farmers, the production is now in the hands of specialist turf growers but there are also farmers who use turf as part of their agricultural rotation.

Selling existing pasture turf to a turf company or the farmer cutting their own pasture

The cutting of existing pasture for turf is no longer a production system that is practised in the current market.

Renting land to a turf company for production of cultivated turf

Turf companies rent land for turfgrass production. Typically, land is rented on a per crop basis and one or two crops grown. A turf crop usually takes 12 to 18 months from preparation to harvest but autumn sown crops may be harvested within 12 months. Rent levels depend on the quality of the land, the provision of irrigation and the profitability of competing agricultural enterprises. Currently rents are in the order of £600-£925 per hectare per crop (£240-£375 per acre) or £480-£740 per ha per year (£195-£300 per acre).

The effect on the land of cultivated turf production is not detrimental, the amount of topsoil removal is not much greater than other root crops; some say there are benefits (removal of accumulated pests, etc. in the top half inch of grass, roots and topsoil).

Cultivated turf production

Important features when choosing fields: good root structure, number and type of weeds, level, well-drained, stone-free land; good access. Access to irrigation is becoming increasingly important to allow cutting during dryer periods. Turf has a short life once cut and stacked - a maximum 1 to 2 days in summer, 3 to 4 days in winter, depending on temperature. On their own land turf producers can grow turf continuously, taking a crop every 18 months to two years on average. On rented land they take one or two crops and move on. Usually they produce a quick growing turf on rented land and cultivate more specialist and slower growing turf on their own.

A high level of agronomic expertise and considerable investment in machinery are needed and labour requirements are heavy. A high degree of marketing expertise is essential. Whilst the bulk of the trade goes into general landscaping or garden centres there is an increase in the number of contracts where the quality and type of turf is specified. It is estimated that a turf farm would need to be 150-200 hectares (400-500 acres) or more in size to be viable – in order to justify the machinery and equipment necessary and to produce a succession of turf for the market. There are significant economies of scale. The cost of specialist machinery for turf production can be £350,000. A new one-man harvesting machine costs in the order of £200,000-£400,000 but significantly reduces labour costs.

Costs and Returns

Variable Costs plus Rent:	£/ha	(£/ac)
Seed	750-1,100	(300-445)
Fertiliser	700-1,400	(280-565)
Herbicide	100-150	(40-60)
Fungicide	100-210	(40-85)
Rent (for 15 months)	600-925	(240-375)
Total Costs	2,250-3,785	(910-1,530)

It may be necessary to irrigate and on occasions use netting to grow the grass for certain sites.

Labour: Special seed bed preparation (including subsoiling and stone burying), regular mowing (twice a week May/June), picking up clippings, harvesting (2 men on harvester plus one loading lorry) between 0.2-0.4 hectares per day (0.5-1.0 acre). The new one-man harvester can do 2 ha (5 acres) a day.

Total costs of the order of £5,000-£7,500 per ha (£2,000-£3,035 per acre), approximately 50-75p per square metre.

Value of Turf (on the field)

	per m²	per sq. yd.	per ha*	per acre*
Hardwearing, domestic general contract	70-95p	58-79p	£6,300-£8,550	£2,550-£3,460
Football, hockey, prestige landscape	115-145p	95-120p	£10,260-£12,825	£4,150-£5,200
High quality/specialist**	190-475p	160-405p	£17,100-£42,750	£6,910-£17,290

* assuming 90% recovery, but some producers work on 85%.

** for some contracts the price may be higher – up to £8m² (£72,000 per ha) for specific uses.

Delivery charges 45-55p per m² for a full lorry load. Higher for smaller deliveries.

Acknowledgements: Turfgrass Growers Association, www.turfgrass.co.uk. *Robert Laycock Turf Consultant,* www.robertlaycock.co.uk.

GOLF

Most golf courses in the UK have been struggling with an aging golfing population, pressure on leisure time, and a squeeze on discretionary spending. Against this background, any new course development, costing many millions of pounds on top of the land value, has reached an all-time low. Any golf construction work is in the reconstruction of older courses or on courses affected by major construction projects such as HS2.

New stand-alone golf courses are not a viable investment, with the value of a completed course being significantly less than the cost of construction or even agricultural value. There are a few projects where developers are offering new courses to existing clubs where they believe the existing course can be closed and redeveloped as residential. Values of land for this purpose have ranged from £20,000 to £35,000 per acre.

Some developers try to get consent for landfill and build new courses on top of the fill. However, legislation on landfill has changed and the number of such new developments has decreased significantly. There are also a few situations, particularly associated with existing hotels, where courses are being added.

There are no areas of the UK where there is unsatisfied demand for golf – the market continues to age and whilst various attempts have been made to interest youngsters, other sources of entertainment appear to hold a greater attraction.

Driving range development has also virtually stopped with a declining marketplace for golf, less spend on golf equipment and less practice taking place. The rising agricultural land prices have seen development finance become extremely difficult to obtain meaning few sales and even fewer new projects. Local Authorities have been struggling with unviable municipal facilities and are attempting to obtain private interest. They are therefore not in the market for further golf development.

It is highly unlikely that there will be many new courses in the UK in the near future. Some developments may occur as enabling developments – for instance supporting large housing schemes – but the provision is often regarded by developers as 'infrastructure' and may not even be viable once constructed.

It is crucial to obtain professional advice at the outset for investment appraisal, feasibility study and a business plan. In the current situation, it would be wise to seriously consider whether even the £10-£15,000 needed for a feasibility study is worth the investment. The chances of a viable study are really very low.

Type of business organisation

To sell land with planning permission: There is currently no premium over agricultural value (indeed agricultural values often exceed golf development site values) unless the situation or planning consent offers something exceptional. The cost of obtaining permission can vary enormously depending on the sensitivity of the site but it would seldom cost less than £300,000 including design, environment impact study and Local Authority fees. The demand from Local Authorities for an ever-increasing amount of supporting information and studies to accompany an application means that few developers are prepared to take the associated risks.

To let land to a developer/operator: Assuming the latter pays for constructing the course, a long lease will be required. Rental levels will depend on the expected profitability of the facility but currently, in our experience, leases remain around £20-£65,000 for an 18-hole course. This figure has continued to drop over the last couple of years as clubs struggle to survive and leaseholders surrender leases.

To form a joint company with a developer/operator: This obviously means the farmer shares in the success or failure. The land would be all or part of the farmer's equity. There are no known active developers in this market at present.

To develop and operate the course himself: The farmer would need good knowledge of golf and exceptional management ability besides access to substantial capital. Any such decision in today's market would be bizarre. If a framer wishes to stop farming our advice would be to consider selling land before considering the risks associated with building a new golf course.

Returns

It will cost considerably more to build and fit out a course than it will be worth for resale.

Bankable rates of return on new courses are extremely rare. Associated residential or other development could make developments profitable but planning permission for such developments is very difficult.

Acknowledgement: *International Design Group*

CHRISTMAS TREES

About 7 million real Christmas trees a year are sold in the UK; this figure has reduced as the quality of artificial trees has improved. Around 70-80% of real trees sold are UK-produced, with the balance from imports, chiefly from Denmark. Two decades ago 80% were Norway Spruce, but this is now around 15%, with Nordman Fir, which retains its needles longer, accounting for around 75%. Other firs and spruces such as Fraser Fir, Noble Fir and Blue Spruce make up the remainder. The most popular sizes are between 1.75 and 2.25m (5 to 7 feet).

There are some 400 British growers, with plantations ranging from less than one hectare to over 100 ha. It is estimated that there are around 50 million trees being grown, covering up to 7,000 ha. Most sales are through garden centres, which require a uniform tree, netted and palletised, but there are many successful 'choose and cut' operations, an enterprise which works well on a farm with a farm shop. Internet sales are growing.

The enterprise is slow to make a return. Nordman Firs are typically harvested in years 7 to 9, while the quicker-growing Norway Spruce takes 5 to 7 years. This extended period from planting to marketing makes the enterprise vulnerable to changing market conditions. Typically, about 20% of the crop is harvested in the first harvesting year, 50% in the second, 30% in the third. All species need a well-drained site free from late frosts, with good access. As with any crop, the better the land, the better the crop. The margin calculation below is for an eight-year rotation and assumes first quality trees only. A well-managed plantation has the capability to produce 80% of the crop as first quality.

	Nordman Fir	
	£/ha	(£/ac)
5000 5 to 7 foot trees per ha @ price of . .	£3.00 - 3.50 / ft	
Output (average)	97,500	(39,458)
Variable Costs:		
Plants	4,305	(1,742)
Planting	1,107	(448)
Fertiliser	723	(293)
Weed control	483	(195)
Plant protection	900	(364)
Pruning and shaping	5,369	(2,173)
Harvesting	5,310	(2,149)
Marketing	9,750	(3,946)
Total Variable Costs	27,947	(11,310)
Gross Margin (whole period)	69,553	(28,148)
Gross Margin per year over 8 years	**8,694**	**(3,518)**

1. *Output:* Sale number of 5,000 trees per ha is based on approx. 80% saleable from a population of 6,000 per ha (see below). Price shown is for sales to local garden centres and shops. Prices are likely to be 20-30% lower if selling to wholesalers, national garden chains or DIY stores. Prices can be 50% more for retailing direct to the public. There is little market now for second quality trees.

2. *Establishment:* Rabbit fencing (£5 per m) is necessary and possibly deer fencing (£6-£8 per m). Spacing is now standardised at 1.2m x 1.2m which gives 6,000 plants per ha allowing for 15% land loss for headlands, access, etc. Losses of up to 5% in the first year means around 250 replacements are needed in second year. Norway Spruce

transplants 25p-40p each, Nordman Fir 50-90p (*70p used in the margin*). Planting, by hand or machine, 15-20p per plant (*18p used in margin*).

3. *Quality*: The above costings are only relevant to the sale of first quality trees. The market for second quality trees has become hugely oversupplied due to the increased availability of poorly managed trees. Second quality trees are no longer profitable, and even if a market is found, will be at heavily discounted prices, so may not even cover the costs of growing. It is therefore essential to adhere consistently to best management practice if the crop is to be profitable.

4. *Variable Inputs:*

   NPK, typically 18:14:14 (depending on soil analysis) is applied in late March with a further light nitrogen application applied in late July or early August after crop hardening.

   Weed control through residual herbicide in March at £70/ha and glyphosate at £10/ha in October/November plus spot weeding of perennial weeds until the canopy closes over.

   Insect control will require aphicide at £10-£50/ha and spider mite control £5-£100/ha commencing in the year of planting and subsequently in January for Spruce and April for Firs. A number of diseases can affect Firs, with these treated on an as-needed basis.

   In years 5 - 7 Nordmann Fir will require leading shoot suppression through treatment with cutters and growth regulators. Required over 3 - 4 years at a cost of 10p/tree per treatment. Fraser Fir and Noble Fir will also require 4-6 week applications to suppress phytophthora at £30-£50/ha/application.

5. *Pruning and Shaping*: This is essential to produce the shape of tree the market demands. Nordmann Fir: basal pruning in year 3 or 4 at 20p per tree plus shaping in the same year at 16p per tree and bud-rubbing every year except harvest at 5-10p per tree per year. Norway Spruce: shaping 17p per tree per year from year 3 or 4.

6. *Harvesting:* Undertaken from early November. Minimum of one full-time person per 3,000 trees sold, or one person per week per 400-500 trees. Cost: Norway Spruce 70-90p per tree, Nordmann Fir 80-105p (*90p used in margin*). Marketing costs around 10% of output.

7. *Machinery:* Inter-row plantation tractors £15,000-£65,000; stump clearing machines £7,000-£25,000; palletiser £13,000-£14,000; mist blowers £8,000-£10,000; hydraulic netting funnel £8,000-£10,000; manual netting funnel £175; guillotine tree cutter £4,000.

8. *Labour:* Required for planting from mid September to mid April, pruning / shearing over winter, and tagging for height and quality from August to November. A number of specialist contractors are available to assist. Generally fits in well with combinable cropping operations. Casual help is likely to be required for harvest and sales.

9. Further information: A guide to Christmas tree growing "Christmas Trees. A Growers Guide" is available from www.ruralservice.info.

   The gross margins given are high, but these will only be achieved through a high level of expertise and commitment. The long period before any return is obtained must also be stressed, together with the risk this entails.

Acknowledgement: Thanks to - British Christmas Tree Growers Association, www.bctga.co.uk. Colin Palmer, Rural Services, www.ruralservices.info

BED AND BREAKFAST

The person running bed and breakfast should enjoy meeting people, have good social skills and be prepared to work unusual hours. In a crowded market, and with rising customer expectations, the standard of the product and service is critical. Farms must provide a standard of accommodation equal to that found in hotels. This will involve some refurbishment; both before starting the enterprise, to upgrade existing B&B to rising standards and ongoing repair of wear and tear.

It is vital to know the planning, legislative and financial requirements involved in B&B. Details are available from VisitBritain in the *'The Pink Booklet' - a practical guide to legislation for accommodation providers'*. This is available online at https://www.visitbritain.org/business-advice/know-your-legal-obligations. Advice is also provided by National Tourist Boards of England, Scotland and Wales and Regional Tourist Boards.

Marketing is important. Some establishments produce a brochure or card giving details of the B&B, its location, facilities, and quality standards rating. New routes to customers have opened up through 'peer-to-peer' renting websites such as Airbnb. To join a marketing organisation the B&B should have a Quality Assurance Standard rating. These are awarded either by the official National Tourist Board inspectorate (which in England is Quality in Tourism), or the AA. The rating is at one of five levels, expressed as stars.

As there is considerable competition, it is useful for the enterprise to offer something special or different such as accommodation for visitors' horses, a welcome for pets, or access to view the working farm. Establishments that can accommodate bigger parties are also popular. The number of B&Bs offering an evening meal has declined in recent years but providing locally grown produce can be a draw.

Prices that can be charged reflect the quality of accommodation and location but cannot be far out of line with other local B&Bs and hotels. Prices can also vary depending on length of stay and time of year. The price range for one person per night ranges from £25 to over £100 on the basis of two adults sharing a room. A higher rate per person usually applies for single occupancy. There are regional differences with higher prices generally being charged in the south and east.

The range of B&B facilities has become enormous in the last decade. Decide the marketplace that suits you by identifying your selling point. Is it low-cost, luxury, access to a working farm, family comfort etc.? Prepare the B&B enterprise, target your marketing and price the rooms accordingly to meet that marketplace.

Receipts from the enterprise can be calculated as follows: If the B&B is open for 40 weeks of the year at £50 per person per night, given a 60% occupancy rate the gross return per bed place will be around £8,400. Most farmhouse B&Bs have 4-6 bed spaces, which would generate a gross return of between £33,000 to £50,000 p.a.

Costs vary considerably: As every farmhouse B&B is different and some costs are difficult to apportion between guests and family, the following provides some pointers. Variable costs are food, electricity, heating, laundry, cleaning materials and additional help. There will also be regular redecoration costs, repairs, and replacement and renewal of glassware, china, cutlery, towels and bed linen. Variable costs if no non-family labour is used average about 20% of the nightly charge. If casual labour has to be included variable costs rise to 30-35% of the nightly charge.

Fixed costs include insurance, business rates (if they apply), membership of marketing organisations, regular advertising, repayments on loans taken out for building and equipment and regular labour; they are likely to average 30-35% of charges.

Contact: Farm Stay UK, VisitBritain, Quality in Tourism,

CAMPING AND CARAVAN SITES

Camp sites and caravan parks can appear an easy way to increase farm profit with its revenue divorced from the vagaries of agricultural markets and largely unaffected or even boosted by economic downturns. To run a successful site requires some capital investment, a suitable location and time to maintain it, collect fees and market your site. A tourist area, away from busy roads, a good view, a well-drained stone-less field (at least a half hectare), with flat areas is necessary. Water and electricity are required (most also have Wi-Fi). The site needs to be licenced by the local authority (not Scotland). Exemptions apply for some camping and caravanning organisations. They also require planning permission.

Initial Capital

Infrastructure includes; toilets and hot showers with disabled access, refuse collection, electrical hook-ups for caravans, compressed gas storage and landscaping including recreational space, road and footpath improvements, land levelling (at the pitches), and screening (hedges and fences). Capital spend will vary according to existing facilities and what level of camping experience is required as suggested here for just camping.

Capital	Low Intensity	High Intensity
Planning & Licencing	1,100	1,100
Landscaping	1,700	3,500
Small toilet and shower block	10,000	25,000
Mower	2,000	3,000
Business Development	600	3,000
Other - e.g. Drainage		1,300
Total Ex-Land	**15,400**	**36,900**
Depreciate over 10 Years	1,540	3,690

Gross Margin	Low Intensity		High Intensity	
	Per hectare	Per pitch	Per hectare	Per pitch
Pitches per hectare	25		70	
Occupancy per year (1)	650	26	2,940	42
Price £/pitch/night		15		25
Output	**9,750**	**390**	**73,500**	**1,050**
Costs				
Depreciation; 10 years	1,540	62	3,690	53
Ground maintenance (2)	840	34	2,954	42
Utilities (3)	1,080	43	2,675	38
Insurance	1,080	43	2,200	31
Staff & Management (4)	2,330	93	11,960	171
Attributable Costs	**6,870**	**275**	**23,479**	**335**
Net Margin	**2,880**	**115**	**50,021**	**715**

(1) 26 = 75% occupancy for 5 weeks, 42 = 85% occupancy for 7 weeks

(2) includes lawn cutting, hedge trimming, site repairs & general maintenance

(3) water, drainage, electricity, possibly Wifi

(4) receiving bookings and payment & general management

These two gross margins demonstrate differences in pitches per hectare, occupancy rates and fees paid according to location, desirability of site and level of management. The impact on output is dramatic.

LOG CABINS AND GLAMPING

An interest in British short breaks (which might be compounded by the virus) and holidays has led to a popularity surge of 'alternative' accommodation as well as the more traditional cottage rentals or caravan and camping. This might be accelerated by Brexit. As with any tourism and leisure-based enterprise, location is key and can determine the success or failure of the proposal as much as good management. It will also determine the rental income and occupancy that can be achieved. There may also be potential for using log cabins as a substitute for 'permanent', traditional buildings for office, storage facilities etc.

Log cabins range from unglorified cladded caravans on bricks to opulent, luxurious and spacious living spaces. Some have hot tubs, access to pools and sports facilities. *Full planning permission* is required for any log cabin. Professional support should be sought prior to any expenditure on equipment / groundwork.

Build Costs

Prices for cabins vary considerably, primarily linked to the size and finish (quality) of the final build and the cost of routing mains services which will depend on remoteness, topography, environmental restrictions etc. and the extent of supplies required (bottled gas and septic tanks can be used in place of mains gas and sewage). The figures below are a guide to log cabin purchase and build costs but exclude fixtures and fittings which may add £85.00 to £125.00 of additional cost per m²:

Log Cabin Capital Costs

Fishing Cabin	30m² floor space plus sleeping 'loft'	£10,000 - £43,000
Holiday Let Cabin	60m² floor space with 2 bedrooms	£23,000 - £57,000

For cabins larger than the examples above, add £280 to £330 per m² for every m² over and above the sizes stated

Rental Potential

Good occupancy rates will be paramount to the viability of any investment. Annual occupancy rates will vary depending on location, seasonality of local attractions and level of discount given in the 'off' season. Rental incomes vary, from £260 to £1,200 per week, with the higher incomes being achieved where the cabins are in more desirable locations i.e. near to areas popular for fly and course fishing, mountain biking, walking, coastal activities, tourist attractions etc. Single night stays and short breaks often command a higher income *pro-rata* than weekly lets but more work, including administration and cleaning, as well.

Other Accommodation

Yurts, tipis and other 'high specification' camping can also be lucrative if the resources are in place and high occupancy achieved, although these may not have a long a life as the cabins. Weekly rents of £220 to £650 per week are possible with the right locations and glamping specification. Capital cost for a furnished yurt can be £5,000 to £10,000 depending on size and specification. Ground and site maintenance as well as yurt preparation and booking administration should also be accounted for.

COARSE FISHING

Over 1.5 million people regularly coarse fish in the UK. It is a freshwater method of line fishing usually from the banks of a watercourse. Coarse fish species include Rudd, Roach, Bream, Barbel, Tench, Chub, Perch, Pike, Carp, exclude sea species and 'game' fish like salmon and trout (usually 'fly fished'). Coarse fish are returned to the water after catching and weighing. Facilities can be rivers, streams, canals, lakes, ponds and even drains. The close season for coarse fishing is 15th March to 15th June although most canals and still waters are exempt. Anyone fishing must have a rod licence (from the Environment Agency). Take advice before starting a fishing enterprise.

Fishing permit prices vary depending on the location, quality of the fishing, species etc. They will be higher if the water is actively managed to attract more or certain fish species. Maintenance and landscaping of the water banks will add a premium to a facility as will secure car parking and easy access to fishing pegs (platforms). Typically permits cost (concessions usually apply):

	Per Rod	*Multiple Rods*	*24-hour*
Half-Day	£4 to £7	£6 (2-rods) £8 (3-rods)	
Full-Day	£5 to £13	£8 (2-rods) £10 (3-rods)	£20 (2) £25 (3)
Season	£50 to £180		

Typical Net Margin for Coarse Fishing Lake, Labour excluded

1 Hectare (2.4 acre) Lake	**per peg**	**per lake**
	£	**£**
Fishing Permits	776	12,416
Fish Sales	80	1,280
Output	856	13,696
Costs		
Setup Capital	104	1,656
Peg Maintenance	8	120
Fish Restocking	6	100
Feed Feed	100	1,600
Plants and Ground Maint.	27	430
Staff & Management	250	4,000
Total Variable Costs	494	7,906
Gross Margin per ha (acre)	282	4,510

The figures above are a guide based on 20 half-day tickets per peg per year (£6.20 each), 20 full days (£9 each), and 4 season tickets (at £118). There are 16 pegs on this lake. It takes time and commitment to build up a good reputation. Pegs should be spaced at least 25m apart (dictating income potential). A 2-acre carp lake would cost around £5,200 to initially stock but should then self-replenish. Plants and other costs would total around £3,200 initially and will then need maintaining. Peg capital price is £510, depreciated over 10 years.

The larger the fish, the higher the price that can be charged therefore the smaller fish can be routinely removed and sold. The total income from a two-acre well-managed lake should be £12,000 (more for popular sites). Further diversifying into accommodation (log cabins) could charge £1,000 per week for 4 anglers. Labour could become significant to manage the permits and landscape. Generating this return might take some building up of regular fishers, managing the layout and facilities and so on and requires an existing suitable lake.

GAME SHOOTING

Game shooting is the shooting of game species which include birds and mammals. The most common birds shot in the UK include pheasant, partridge, duck, woodcock, snipe and grouse. Most feathered game are reared in captivity and then released but wild populations can be enhanced by different management techniques. There are strict and differing shooting seasons for different species, both game and pests.

'Driven' game shooting is the most popular method in the UK where game birds are 'flighted' towards a standing line of guns. The quality and type of driven shoot varies according to landscape and management as well as the number of birds present. These variances also have a major impact on the cost of partaking in a shoot.

	Per Placing	per bird Shot	per Gun	per Shoot Day	per Season
		3 placings	22 birds	8 guns	8 shoots
		£	£	£	£
Charge for Gun		32.00	704	5,632	45,056
Other Income (poults etc.)					2,000
Output		32	704	5,632	47,056
Costs					
Bird Placing	1.35	4.05	89	713	5,702
Bird Feed	1.47	4.41	97	776	6,209
Game Cover Seed	0.12	0.36	8	63	507
Veterinary and medicines	0.05	0.15	3	26	211
Gas, pens & misc.	0.30	0.90	20	158	1,267
Hospitality			75	600	4,800
Beaters & Pickers			63	504	4,032
Ground Maint. Costs					5,200
Capital Depreciation					4,100
Gamekeeper					8,500
Directly Attributable Costs	3.29	9.87	355	2,841	40,529
Net Margin					6,527

1. *Bird Placings:* More are placed than shot; this example is 3-fold.
2. *Beaters and Pickers:* 15 beaters and pickers per shoot
3. *Capital Depreciation: Bird pens, feeders, water, etc.*
4. *Gamekeeper: Part time wage included here. May include imputed costs.*
5. *Overheads: Vehicles often shared with farm or dedicated. Excluded here.*

Gamekeeper costs vary depending on the scale of the shoot. Owners may game-keep in small-scale shoots, but the opportunity cost of the owner's time should still be considered (unless treated as a hobby). Excluded from above is the cost of land used for rearing and game cover which may have an opportunity cost even if the land is owned, but there may be other benefits from this too, such as income from environmental schemes.

As a rough guide, a 200-bird day driven shoot will cost in the range of £800 per gun (participant), at £32 per bird. A driven shoot normally has 7 to 9 guns with up to 8 'drives' in a day. The expensive nature of most driven game shoots is required by the amount of work and cost involved in running a shoot (buying birds, feeding, structural equipment costs, game plot establishment, game keeper and beater's costs, shoot day hospitality etc.). Margins may be small. Many shoots are not run for profit but sport.

Further information: British Association for Shooting and Conservation

OTHER DIVERSIFICATION

A farm is a remarkable place to diversify from, with land-based resources, spare labour, excellent local social connections and collateral. 'Non-commodity' enterprises, managed with the farming operation, offer business benefits spreading risk, using redundant resources such as buildings or labour, and offering more profit.

Any new enterprise will have its own risks and 'unknowns' associated with it. These must be calculated (especially if borrowed money is necessary). Resources employed have opportunity costs. Capital is easier to calculate but labour is less straight forward. For example, a B&B might require minimal capital investment, but tie somebody to the house at key times of the day, restricting other employment opportunities.

Before changing a business to incorporate new diversifications, generate a business plan and undertake market research to assess the income potential. Most new enterprises require new skills (such as different production systems, marketing and sales techniques). These may take time and dedication to acquire. Developing new ideas and expanding a novel business venture can be exciting and time consuming; maintaining sufficient management time on the existing farm business is a common problem. Also check plans with your accountancy professional.

Two thirds of UK farms have diversifications generating £1.2 billion, and it is rising. Let buildings is the most common non-farming activity, but if lettings are stripped out, the percentage of diversified farms falls to 48%. Arable farms are more diversified than livestock and farms in the South East are more than elsewhere in the UK. Diversified enterprises might have different VAT and taxation treatment. Check in advance with your accountant. Some 'diversification' enterprises have been included above. There are many others, such as;

Novel crops / livestock

- Herbs
- Carp and crayfish
- Quails
- Ostrich
- Lammas
- Alpacas
- Snails & worms
- Maggots
- Insect farming

Building conversions

- Business lets
- Dwelling let
- Wedding/party venues

Tourism

- Holiday cottages
- Public open farm

Sporting

- Fisheries
- Stalking
- Clay pigeon shooting
- Riding school
- Trekking (horse, other)
- Motor sports
- Go-karting

Vertical integration

- Yoghurt / ice cream
- Farm shop
- Meat sales
- Brewing
- Distilling

Many of these have been taken to new levels in recent years. For example, the farm shop in some cases has adopted the 'garden centre' model and is now a vibrant and growing industry for high-end shoppers in market towns, even motorway service stations. Camping has given rise to Glamping, again focussing at the more affluent end of the market keen on luxury and service, one that is covered in this book now.

Many of these enterprises are covered in more detail in the Agro Business Consultants' Agricultural Budgeting and Costings Guide found at https://abcbooks.co.uk/

FORESTRY

ESTABLISHMENT COSTS (BEFORE GRANT)

Unit Cost of Operations

Year	Operation	Cost (£)
1.	Trees for planting[1]	
	Conifers	400-500 per 1,000
	Broadleaves	400-650 per 1,000
1.	Tree Protection	
	(i) Fencing (materials and erection)	
	Rabbit	4.40-6.30 per metre
	Stock	4.35-5.40 per metre
	Deer ....6.80-8.90 per metre	
	Deer and Rabbit..	8.40-11.00 per metre
	Split post and rail..	5.70-8.90 per metre
	(ii) Tree guards/shelters	
	Spiral and canes (750mm)	40-45 per 100
	Plastic tubes (1,200mm)	140-190 per 100
	Softwood stakes 1.5mx32mm	75-100 per 100
1.	Spot spraying	60-90 per 1,000 trees
1.	Hand planting and installing guard	
	Conifers..	600-900 per 1,000 trees
	Broadleaves[2]..	600-900 per 1,000 trees
	Machine planting tree only (loams and sand only) ...	110 -215 per 1,000 trees
2-3.	Replacing dead trees[3]	
	Operation...	115-210 per ha
	Plant supply..	95-160 per ha
1-4.	Weeding per operation	
	Herbicide[4]..	75-135 per ha weeded
2.	Inter-row mowing...	75-210 per ha

Costs specific to location in Year 1		Upland	Lowland
Ground Preparation:	ploughing	140-220 per ha	70- 105 per ha
	mounding	290-405 per ha	290-405 per ha
Drainage (mole)...............................		90-115 per ha	—
Scrub Clearance...............................		300-400 per ha	250-350 per ha
Fertilising		132-297 per ha	—

Notes:

1. Price dependent on size and species.

2. Includes cost of erecting 0.75m spiral guards/shelters.

3. Replacing dead trees (beating up) may be necessary, once in the second year and again in the third year. Costs depend on number of trees.

4. Up to two weeding operations may be necessary in each of the first four years in extreme situations. Costs are inclusive of materials.

Access roads may need to be constructed and can typically cost between £13,500 and £33,000 per kilometre run (£21,700 to £53,000 per mile) depending on availability of road stone and the number of culverts and bridges required.

Total Establishment Costs up to Year 3

1. *Conifer—Lowland Sites:* On a fairly typical lowland site, requiring little or no clearing or draining, the approximate cost before grant of establishing a conifer plantation at **2500 trees per hectare** would be in the range of £4,500-£6,800 per hectare. Up to 8 separate weeding operations may be required.

2. *Conifer—Upland Sites:* Establishing a similar conifer plantation on an upland site could cost £4,000 to £6,500 per hectare. Normally some form of site preparation and drainage is required but only one weeding operation may be necessary. Overall costs tend to be £500 per hectare less than on lowland sites.

3. *Broadleaves:* Costs of establishing broadleaf plantations are highly dependent on the fencing and/or tree protection required and density of trees planted. If tubes are needed, the overall costs will be influenced by the number of trees per hectare. Costs could be in the range of £4,500-£8,500 per hectare. Site conditions normally mean that trees being grown for timber production are restricted to lowland sites.

4. *Farm Woodlands:* Establishment costs for farm woodlands may be lower than those indicated for broadleaves in (3) above if lower planting densities are used at between 1,100 to 1,800 trees/ha; costs of about £6,800 per ha for woods under 3 ha and £5,500 per ha for woods of 3 to 10ha would be typical. However, it should be noted planting at lower densities may increase maintenance cost and will lead to production of lower-quality material.

5. *Size Factor:* Savings in fencing and other economies of scale may reduce average costs per hectare by 10 to 20% where large plantations are being established.

6. *Method of Establishment:* A range of organisations and individuals undertake forestry contracting work and competitive tendering can help to control costs.

The costs of establishment given above, and those for maintenance given below, are estimates for England. Costs in Scotland tend to be lower.

Re-Stocking Costs

Once trees on a site have been felled, the Forestry Commission usually requires the site to be restocked as a condition of awarding a felling licence. This can be done by replanting or through natural regeneration, leaving a proportion of the trees standing and using seed from these trees to re-stock. Site preparation is usually required for natural regeneration through scarification and ongoing maintenance will be required to encourage a viable crop. Re-stocking a clear-felled area would incur similar costs to those above.

MAINTENANCE COSTS

Once trees have been established, they normally require some maintenance and management work each year. For trees being grown primarily for timber production on a large scale, operations required may include ride and fence maintenance, pest control, fire protection, management fee and insurance premiums. Costs are normally £600-£900 per hectare per annum depending on the size of the plantation and the complexity of management. In upland areas, fertiliser is occasionally applied once or more times in the first 20 years of the tree's life, depending on the quality of the site. The estimated cost of this is £110-£275 per hectare, depending on elements applied. For trees being grown for sporting and amenity purposes, annual maintenance costs are likely to be less and may range up to about £30 per hectare.

Brashing is no longer practised on large-scale conifer plantations as a result of mechanical harvesting techniques.

TIMBER PRODUCTION

Production is usually measured in terms of cubic metres (m^3) of marketable timber per hectare and will vary according to the quality of the site, species planted and thinning policy.

Sites in lowland Britain planted to conifers typically produce an average of 12 to 18 m³ of timber per hectare per year over the rotation as a whole and would accordingly be assessed as falling in yield classes 12 to 18. Under traditional management systems, thinning begins 18 to 25 years after planting and is repeated at intervals of approximately 5-7 years until a conifer wood is clear-felled at between 40 and 60 years, or a broadleaf wood at 80 to120 years. Approximately 40-45% of total production will be from thinnings. Broadleaves typically produce an average of between 4 and 8 m³ of timber per hectare per year and fall in yield classes 4 to 8.

Prior to a thinning sale, the trees normally have to be marked and measured at an estimated cost of 75p - £1 per m³. For a clear-felling sale the cost can range from £300 to £400 per hectare, or about £1.50 per m³ where a full tariff applies. These costs associated with mensuration and marking can vary significantly and will correlate to the value of the crop to be harvested.

Felling permission is required when more than 5m³ is to be removed in any one calendar quarter or more than 2m³ per calendar quarter if the timber is sold. This requires an application to the Forestry Commission for a Felling Licence either in paper format or online. The complexity of the application will depend on the size and variety of the woodland. A felling licence must be obtained from the Forestry Commission before any felling takes place, unless a Woodland Management Plan detailing operation to be undertaken has already been approved by them. Grants are available for preparing a Woodland Management Plan under Countryside Stewardship in England. Similar provisions operate in other parts of the UK.

TIMBER PRICES

Prices for standing timber are extremely variable, depending on species, tree size and quality; ease of extraction from site; geographical location (nearness to end user); quantity being sold; world market prices and effectiveness of marketing method used. The use of wood for energy generation continues to provide a market for poorer quality hardwood, conifer logs and forest residues.

Conifers/Softwood

Coniferous Standing Sales Price for Great Britain from the Forestry Enterprise Estate

Average Price (per m³ overbark)	Nominal terms	Real terms (2016 prices)
31ˢᵗ March 2021	31.03	26.88

Source: Forestry Commission: Timber Price Indices. May 2021.

Hardwoods

The hardwood trade is complex. Merchants normally assess and value all but the smallest trees by stem. Actual prices achieved, vary depending on species, size, form, quality and marketing expertise of the seller. Felling usually takes place in the winter.

Some indicative prices for hardwoods are given below but actual prices vary widely. Wood quality is important in determining prices and is relevant when considering selling into the UK's developing export markets. Ash for internal joinery and poplar for plywood are in demand but size specification and seasonality of felling are crucial.

Product	Price per Unit at roadside
Poplar for the domestic market	£25-£40 per tonne
Quality poplar for the export market......................	£60-£80 per tonne
Ash logs..	£3-£5 per hoppus foot[1]
Oak logs – milling timber	£3-£15 per hoppus foot[1]
Firewood	£20-£24 per tonne
Softwood sawlogs	£38-£50 per tonne

| Cricket bat willow | £300-£450 per tree |
| Ash Hurley stick butts | £180-£200 per m^3 |

1. A hoppus foot is an imperial measurement that is still used in the hardwood trade (not softwood). It estimates what volume of a round log would be usable timber after processing (allowing for wastage). Because of the wastage factor a hoppus foot is larger than a cubic foot. $1m^3 = 27.736$ hoppus feet.

2. $1m^3 = 35.31$ cubic feet (normal feet).

TIMBER MARKETING

In-house marketing by the owner or agent can be cost effective but only if they have good knowledge of timber buyers in the marketplace. The alternative is marketing through a forestry manager or management company. Sales can take place of either standing timber or felled timber at roadside. Standing sales place felling and extraction costs onto the purchaser who will usually pay for the timber on an outturn basis, whether by weight (tonne) or volume (m^3). These types of sales suit thinning and lower quality material. Roadside sales require the owner to pay for trees to be felled and extracted to a collection point where they can be accurately measured and inspected by potential purchasers. These types of sales are generally suitable for higher value timber. Nationwide electronic sales of timber by auction and tender are now available for all types and quantities of timber.

MARKET VALUE OF ESTABLISHED PLANTATIONS AND WOODS

The value of woods depends on many factors such as location, access, species, age and soil type. From years 20 to 25 onwards, prices of commercial woods will also be increasingly influenced by the quantity of merchantable timber they contain. Depending on the time of clear-felling, the timber may be worth up to £18,000 per hectare standing.

The UK Forest Market Report published by Tilhill and John Clegg and Co quoted an increase in commercial forestry of 39% year on year on to 2019 with a price of £15,962 per stocked hectare (£6,460 per acre).

Relatively small woods or those with high amenity or Ancient Woodland status often command a premium over prices for commercial woodlands as can those that are freehold with minerals or sporting rights; this is particularly true in southern England. Conversely, conservation designation can restrict value due to a perception of preventing economic forest management; however, this need not be the case. Recent sales of predominately broadleaved, amenity woodlands range from £12,000 per hectare to £25,000 per hectare with exceptional woodlands exceeding this by over 20%. The value of woods containing mature hardwoods will depend on the quality and value of the timber they contain and the quality of access.

WOODLAND GRANTS

Each part of the UK has its own woodland grant scheme administered by the Forestry Commission. Details of all the schemes are on the Forestry Commission's website.

Countryside Stewardship - England

The main priority of Countryside Stewardship (CS) is to protect and enhance the natural environment, in particular the diversity of wildlife (biodiversity). Water quality is another important priority as are flood management, the historic environment, landscape, genetic conservation and educational access.

The scheme is jointly run by Natural England (NE), Forestry Commission England (FC) and the Rural Payments Agency on behalf of Defra. Applications are competitively scored and must demonstrate that they meet the specific scheme priorities/statement of priorities.

CS provides both capital grants and funding for ongoing management. Capital grants are available for; Woodland Creation; Tree Health measures; and The creation of a Woodland Management Plan.

A Management Plan must be in place for any woodland that is to be entered into an ongoing Higher Tier management agreement for Woodland Improvement (WD2).

1. *Woodland Creation:* From 2019 woodland creation grants are open all year round but applications must be submitted by July if an agreement is to be guaranteed for the following planting season. Woodland Creation Planning Grant is also available to help support the initial design and research required for woodlands over 10ha in size:

   - Woodland creation £1.28/tree with spiral guard + various supplements for enhanced protection measures – maximum £6,800 per hectare;

   - Maintenance £200 per hectare per year for 10 years.

2. *Woodland Tree Health:* Grants are available for restoration and improvement but only available for trees infected by ash dieback (widely referred to as *Chalara* dieback of ash, scientifically called *Hymenoscyphus fraxineus*) or *Phytophthora ramorum*. Official confirmation of infection by Forestry Commission Plant Health is required to be eligible for this grant.

3. *Woodland Management Plans:* Capital grants are available for the production of Woodland Management Plans on a rolling basis (no application window). They can secure 10 years' felling permission by the creation of a Plan of Operations.

   - Minimum grant is £1,000 for three hectares and over of woodland;

   - First 100 hectares is paid at £20 per hectare; £10 per hectare thereafter with no further limit.

4. *Woodland Improvement Grant (WD2 £100/ha per year):* This is a competitive multi-year scheme (five years) offering annual payments to undertake practices that will benefit the environment including thinning, ride management and deer/squirrel control. It falls under the 'higher tier' of CS. Infrastructure grants and Capital grants to support the management objectives are also available under this scheme.

Some example capital items that can be applied for under the WIG are as follows:

Option	Funding
Rhododendron Control	£2,800-£4,400 per hectare
Deer High Seats	£300 per unit
Deer fencing	£7.20 per metre

England Woodland Creation Offer

A new grant has been introduced in 2021. The England Woodland Creation Offer (EWCO) is available in addition to the grants offered under the Countryside Stewardship (CS) scheme (see above). The EWCO has more emphasis on public and environmental benefits that woodlands bring, with 'Additional Contributions' to ensure the 'right tree is planted in the right place, and for the right reason'. It supports the creation of a range of woodland types, but particularly incentivises new native woodland, especially where it extends existing woodland and for woodland creation alongside watercourses which lack shade and where woodland can provide public access. Sizes range from a minimum of 1 hectare per application with blocks as small as 0.1 hectare allowed.

Capital grants covering the standard costs of buying and planting a tree, up to a maximum cap of £8,500 per hectare is available. In addition, there will be a £200 per hectare per year maintenance payment for 10 years.

The EWCO also has optional Additional Contributions to encourage woodland creation for environmental and public access benefits these are;

- Between £1,100-£2,800 per hectare is available where woodland creation will help woodland-dependent priority species to recover.

- £1,600 per hectare is available for the creation of native broadland woodland along watercourses.

- £500 per hectare for woodland creation that can reduce flood risk.

- £2,200 per hectare for improved public access and £500 per hectare where located close to settlements.

- £400 per hectare for woodland creation that will improve water quality.

Applicants will also be encouraged to register their planting under the Woodland Carbon Code (see below). This allows carbon credits to be sold to private buyers or to the Government if successful in a Woodland Carbon Guarantee auction, providing extra revenue from the woodland.

CARBON FUNDING

The Forestry Commission will not fund applications for new woodland creation that include carbon co-funding if there is any link between the proposals and use of the term 'offsetting'. It will, however, allow co-funding provided certain criteria are met and appropriate language is used. This has been formalised within the Forestry Commission's Woodland Carbon Code under which new plantations can be registered to verify their CO_2 sequestration and allow it to be marketed as a potentially valuable asset to be sold or reported in the short or longer term. Carbon is currently being traded valued at between £5-14 per tonne. A typical broadleaved planting on a no-thin option may sequester over 500 tonnes of carbon per hectare over 60 years).

The Government's Woodland Carbon Guarantee (WCaG) is a £50 million scheme that aims to help accelerate woodland planting rates and develop the domestic voluntary market for woodland carbon. It was launched in the 2018 budget and the first auction was held in January 2020.

The WCaG provides an option to sell captured carbon in the form of verified carbon credits, called Woodland Carbon Units (WCUs), to the government for a guaranteed price every 5 or 10 years up to 2055/56. Prices are agreed through a reverse auction which is currently held twice a year in January and June. This provides an additional long-term income for woodland. If values increase in the future it is still possible to sell onto the open market rather than the government. WCUs are generated through verification checks carried out under the Woodland Carbon Code as detailed above.

WOODLAND TAXATION

Income from commercial woodlands is not subject to income tax and tax relief cannot be claimed for the cost of establishing new woodlands. In general, grants are tax free but annual Farm Woodland Payments are regarded as compensation for agricultural income foregone and are liable to income tax. The sale of timber does not attract capital gains tax, although the disposal of the underlying land may give rise to an assessment.

Woodlands which are managed commercially, or which are ancillary to a farming business, may be eligible for business property relief or agricultural property relief respectively, for inheritance tax purposes, if owned for more than two years.

Acknowledgement: The above estimates are based on information supplied by Justin Mumford of Lockhart Garratt Ltd.

7.   ORGANIC FARMING

THE ORGANIC SECTOR:

Land area registered as organic rose in 2020 by 0.8%. The largest rise was in the Cereals sector. The number of registered organic producers and processors fell 6% to 5,754. In 2020, 2.4% of UK agricultural land (excluding common land) was registered as organic and is summarised as follows:

Area in '000 Hectares	Fully Organic	In conversion	Total	% of Agric. Area	% of UK Organic Area	Number of Organic Producers
England	281	20	302	3.3	62	2,043
Wales	83	2	83	4.9	17	608
Scotland	87	7	96	1.7	20	399
N. Ireland	8	0	8	0.8	1	168
UK 2020	458	31.3	489	2.8	100	3,604
UK 2019	281.6	19.0	485.2	3.3		3,617
UK 2018	441.1	32.9	474.0	2.7		3,619
2017	484.4	32.6	517.4	2.9		3,609
2016	482.7	25.2	507.9	2.9		3,552
2015	500.8	20.6	521.4	3.0		3,602
2010	667.6	50.8	718.3	4.0		
2008	594.4	149.1	743.5	3.6		

Whilst the area of organic farming is two thirds of a decade ago, the interest by consumers in organic food remains strong. Nearly 80% organic land is grassland, mostly permanent pasture (the easiest land to convert being mostly low-input farming in any system). The average area per organic producer is 136 hectares.

ORGANIC PRICES

The table below gives an indication of prices comparing organic with conventional. Note it is not possible to simply change the prices or even gross margins in a farm system, the overhead structure would also change, probably considerably. These are not the current spot commodity prices, but typical values based on trend differences to non-organic values, more suited for projecting values a year ahead.

Organic Farmgate Prices

	Unit	Organic	Conventional	Difference	
Feed Wheat	£/t	£288	£160	£128	80%
Milling Wheat*	£/t	£330	£171	£159	90%
Feed Barley	£/t	£260	£142	£118	80%
Milling Oats	£/t	£280	£142	£138	100%
Beans (human spring)	£/t	£360	£205	£155	76%
Finished Beef (R4L Steer)	£/kg dw	£5.00	£4.17	£0.83	20%
Stores (lowland Suckler)	£/kg lw	£2.60	£2.20	£0.40	20%
Finished Lamb	£/kg dw	£5.60	£5.11	£0.49	10%
Finished Pig (pork)	£/kg dw	£2.70	£1.62	£1.08	67%
Milk (ppl)	p/l	40	29	11	38%
Free Range Eggs (med.)	£/doz	£1.60	£0.96	£0.64	65%

*   *Organic milling wheat specification tends to be 12.0% protein as opposed to 13.0% for conventional*

Organic crop types rose in area in 2020 apart from herbaceous and ornamental plants which fell 6.9% and permanent pasture which fell 0.3%. Below are the land use statistics of producers of organic and in-conversion crop areas and livestock numbers for the applicable years. *The data is supplied to Defra from the Certification Bodies. In 2019 data issues were identified with the detailed split of crops for 2017 and 2018. The overall totals for 2017 and 2018 remain unaffected but the breakdowns are subject to a degree of error and therefore should be treated with caution:*

| *Organic Land Use according to Crop Type (UK)* | | | | | | *year on year* |
'000 ha	*2015*	*2017*	*2018*	*2019*	*2020*	*% change*
Cereals	39.6	37.4	37.1	39.7	42.7	7.5
Other arable crops	6.9	7.4	7.4	8.9	9.2	3.2
Fruit & Nut	1.9	1.8	1.7	2.0	2.0	2.0
Vegetables & Pots	10.4	9.6	9.3	9.4	9.5	1.2
Herbs & Ornam's	6.2	5.9	6.7	0.4	0.4	-6.9
Temporary pasture	92.2	92.3	61.8	95.1	97.1	2.0
Permanent pasture	347	333	330	305	305	-0.3
Woodland	6.9	9.0	7.6	15.2	16.0	5.0
Unused Land	10.0	20.7	4.0	4.5	2.8	-38.7
Total area ha	*521*	*517*	*474*	*485*	*489*	*0.8*

| *Organic Livestock Numbers (UK)* | | | | | | *year on year* |
'000 head	*2015*	*2017*	*2018*	*2019*	*2020*	*% change*
Cattle	292	274	324	301	304	1.0
Sheep	845	887	827	782	731	-6.5
Pigs	30	59	38	34	27	-19.8
Poultry	2,560	3,060	3,381	3,464	3,837	10.8
Other Livestock	4.3	2.6	6.0	6.0	6.5	8.8

ECONOMICS OF ORGANIC FARMING

Different resources are needed to produce each unit of organic produce to non-organic produce. These resources tend to be dearer (seed, feed) or more is required (labour, land) per unit of output, so organic goods are more expensive. For example, yields per hectare or per unit of labour tend to be lower, meaning more land and labour is used per unit of product. Higher sale prices (or greater subsidisation) are therefore necessary to make organic farming as financially viable.

In its Organic Farming in England Report for 2017/18, Rural Business Research reports cropping, horticulture and LFA grazing farms as more profitable than their non-organic counterparts, particularly on a per hectare basis (non-organic farms tend to be larger).

Organic food is an added value good. This means the consumer is wealthier than average and therefore more inclined to eat the higher value products. For livestock, this means that capturing the organic premium for the entire livestock carcass can be a challenge, especially when consumption habits change for example when people feel richer or poorer. Some fifth and fore-quarter (lower value) meats do not find organic homes and are sold as non-organic.

Organic livestock farming is usually easier in the summer when forage is available, but costs of keeping stock rise in winter and this is exaggerated in the organic sector with high cost feeds.

Aid for Organic Farmers:

Organic farming receives support under the Countryside Stewardship Scheme in England, which grants an agreement to all those organic farmers who apply (i.e. it is not competitive). This provides support for the two-year conversion period of £50-£450/ha/year depending on land use. Rates then drop to a 'maintenance' level thereafter at £8-£300/ha. There are also specific organic related options. The Welsh organic farming Glastir Organic has not been open for some years Existing applications continue and may even been offered extensions. In Scotland, support under the Agri-environment Climate Scheme did not open in 2020 but did open in 2021 for certain types of applications including organic conversion and maintenance agreements. See Chapter 3 for details.

Further Information:

No gross margin data for organic enterprises are included in this section because a specialist publication is available on the subject: the '2017 Organic Farm Management Handbook', (11th Edition) by Nic Lampkin, Mark Measures and Susanne Padel, Organic Research Centre, Elm Farm, Newbury. Tel: 01488 658 298.

8. SUMMARY OF GROSS MARGINS

This page summarises the key figures of the gross margins over the previous pages. There are well in excess of 100 gross margins in the Pocketbook and additional data for other enterprises too. They cannot all be directly compared on a like for like basis, as different resources are required in order to produce each one and some offer whole farm benefits beyond the gross margin. Some, for example require different resources such as higher quality land, more overheads in terms of machinery, labour, buildings or working capital than others. Management requirement varies from one enterprise to another. Others are subject to having a supply contract with the processor.

SUMMARY OF ARABLE CROP GROSS MARGINS

Crop	Price £/t	Yield t/ha	Output £/ha	Variable Costs £/ha	Gross Margin £/ha	Gross Margin £/t
Winter feed wheat	£160	8.58	£1,372	£544	£828	£97
Winter milling wheat	£171	7.90	£1,353	£599	£753	£95
Spring milling wheat	£171	6.18	£1,057	£432	£624	£101
First feed wheat	£160	8.71	£1,394	£546	£848	£97
Second feed wheat	£160	7.90	£1,263	£591	£673	£85
Winter feed barley	£142	7.27	£1,033	£471	£562	£77
Winter malting barley	£156	6.75	£1,049	£422	£627	£93
Spring malting barley	£157	5.75	£901	£354	£547	£95
Winter oats	£142	6.13	£870	£361	£509	£83
Spring oats	£142	5.57	£791	£275	£516	£93
Naked oats	£200	5.07	£1,014	£347	£667	£132
Winter OSR	£380	3.50	£1,330	£508	£822	£235
Spring OSR	£380	2.28	£865	£322	£543	£239
Spring linseed	£430	1.75	£753	£229	£524	£299
Winter linseed	£430	2.01	£865	£280	£585	£291
Winter beans	£195	4.29	£836	£293	£543	£127
Spring beans	£205	3.90	£800	£290	£509	£131
Blue peas	£230	4.00	£920	£296	£624	£156
Marofats	£325	3.60	£1,170	£402	£768	£213
Herbage seed ryegrass	£1,140	1.30	£1,482	£628	£854	£657
Late perennial	£1,200	1.10	£1,320	£604	£716	£651
Rye	£170	5.50	£935	£418	£517	£94
Triticale	£155	4.50	£698	£311	£387	£86
Borage	£2,900	0.40	£1,160	£334	£826	£2,065

Summary of Arable Crop Gross Margins (Continued)

Crop	Price £/t	Yield t/ha	Output £/ha	Variable Costs £/ha	Gross Margin £/ha	Gross Margin £/t
Lupins	£300	3.00	£900	£301	£599	£200
Durum wheat	£210	6.20	£1,302	£350	£952	£154
Crambe	£180	2.50	£450	£300	£150	£60
Hemp	£160	7.50	£1,200	£457	£743	£99
Grain maize	£175	7.50	£1,313	£360	£952	£127
Millet	£250	3.00	£750	£286	£464	£155
Poppies	£650	2.00	£1,300	£376	£924	£462
Soya	£400	2.20	£880	£304	£576	£262
Vining peas	£270	4.80	£1,296	£419	£877	£183
Maincrop potatoes	£160	50.4	£8,062	£3,669	£4,394	£87
Early potatoes	£240	26.0	£6,240	£3,229	£3,011	£116
Sugarbeet	£26	77.0	£1,967	£904	£1,063	£14
Dessert apples	£790	40.0	31,600	25,221	£6,379	£159
Culinary apples	£553	42.5	23,481	21,650	£1,832	£43
Pears	£805	32.5	26,163	19,953	£6,209	£191
Raised bed strawb.s	£3,215	20.5	65,908	59,727	£6,180	£301
Everbearer strawb.s	£3,215	36.0	115,740	96,822	18,918	£526
Raspberries	£6,755	11.5	77,683	63,271	14,412	£1,253
Cider apples	£125	35.0	£4,375	£3,364	£1,011	£29
Blackcurrants	£713	6.50	£4,631	£2,130	£2,501	£385
Dry bulb onions	£170	41.0	£6,970	£1,935	£5,035	£123
Cauliflower	£440	13.0	£5,720	£3,960	£1,760	£135
Calabrese	£500	10.0	£5,000	£3,672	£1,328	£133
SRC /year	£53	8.0	£424	£108	£316	£40
Miscanthus	£74	13.0	£962	£453	£509	£39
Christmas trees	£3.25/ft		£12,188	£3,308	£8,879	

SUMMARY OF LIVESTOCK GROSS MARGINS

Livestock		Output	Variable Costs	Gross Margin /Head	Gross margin £/Ha
Bovine Dairy					
All-Year-Round calving Holstein	per Cow	£2,213	£1,131	£1,082	£2,273
Autumn calving Fries./Hol.	per Cow	£1,664	£755	£909	£2,000
Spring calving Friesians	per Cow	£1,447	£514	£932	£2,238
Once a day milking	per Cow	£1,115	£312	£802	£1,926
Three times a day milking	per Cow	£2,675	£1,486	£1,189	£2,378
Channel Island *autumn calving*	per Cow	£1,733	£690	£1,042	£2,606
Friesian followers *AYR*	per Head	£1,333	£586	£746	£1,066
Channel followers *autumn c.*	per Head	£1,074	£331	£743	£1,143
Beef Cattle					
Bucket reared calf 6 month	per Calf	£318	£219	£99	
Spring calving lowland sucklers	per Cow	£396	£270	£126	£189
Autumn calving lowland suckler	per Cow	£548	£323	£226	£338
Spring calving upland suckler	per Cow	£374	£266	£108	£108
Autumn calving upland sucklers	per Cow	£525	£318	£207	£207
Store cattle keeping summer	per Head	£334	£83	£251	£753
Store cattle keeping winter	per Head	£325	£231	£94	
Summer store finishers	per Head	£421	£200	£221	£443
Winter store finishers	per Head	£428	£355	£73	
Summer finished sucklers	per Head	£710	£314	£396	£792
Winter finished sucklers	per Head	£427	£375	£52	
Maize finishing (dairy)	per Head	£888	£382	£505	
Maize finishing (suckler)	per Head	£837	£334	£504	
Cereal bull beef (continental)	per Head	£886	£658	£227	
Cereal bull beef (dairy)	per Head	£936	£658	£278	
Sheep					
Lowland spring lamb	per Ewe	£118	£56	£62	£557
Upland spring lamb	per Ewe	£106	£45	£61	£551
Rearing ewe lambs	per Head	£42	£26	£16	£240
Finishing store lambs	per Head	£50	£18	£32	£885

Summary of Livestock Gross Margins (Continued)

Livestock		Output	Variable Costs	Gross Margin /Head	Gross margin £/Ha
Pigs					
Weaners	per Sow	£1,344	£896	£449	
Pork	per Pig	£49	£43	£6.20	
Cutter	per Pig	£63	£53	£9.90	
Bacon	per Pig	£76	£62	£13.8	
Combined pork	per Pig	£100	£75	£25	
Combined cutter	per Pig	£114	£86	£28	
Combined bacon	per Pig	£127	£95	£32	
Poultry					
Enriched caged eggs	per Bird	£14.07	£13.80	£0.27	
Free range eggs	per Bird	£19.69	£15.30	£4.39	
Pullets	Bird Reared	£3.44	£3.09	£0.35	
Broilers	£/Bird	£1.81	£1.31	£0.50	
All year turkey	£/Bird	£35.99	£23.30	£12.69	
Christmas turkey	£/Bird	£58.17	£26.95	£31.22	
Large roaster chickens	£/Bird	£14.44	£6.88	£7.56	
Ducks	£/Bird	£8.50	£6.43	£2.07	
Geese	£/Bird	£50.18	£32.86	£17.32	
Other Livestock					
Breeding & finishing deer	/100 Hinds	£22,465	£8,907	£13,558	£610
Breeding and selling stores	/100 Hinds	£14,650	£3,151	£11,499	£747
Deer park	/100 Hinds	£13,802	£4,294	£9,507	£285
Finishing stag calves	/100 Stags	£11,813	£4,976	£6,837	£752
Wild boar	per Sow	£1,807	£913	£895	£4,473
Dairy goats	per Doe	£413	£291	£122	
Dairy sheep	per Ewe	£514	£191	£323	£3,553
Angora goats	per Doe	£386	£121	£265	£2,652
Ostriches ~ laying trios	per Trio	£1,024	£928	£96	£479
Ostriches ~ fatteners	per bird	£408	£355	£53	£264
Alpacas	Per head	£147	£161	-£14	-£145
Rabbits	/200 Does	£69,622	£9,724	£59,898	
Trout	/tonne Fish	£1,930	£1,430	£500	

III. GOVERNMENT SUPPORT

1. INTRODUCTION

Since the UK joined the EEC in 1973 until 2020, farm support was largely provided through the European Union's Common Agricultural Policy (CAP). Since 2021, agricultural policy will be set through the devolved Governments of England, Wales, Scotland and Northern Ireland. Changes from funding via the CAP to new domestic support will take time to implement, meaning farm support will still resemble that of the CAP for 2022 and in the short term afterwards as policy transitions from old EU schemes to new domestic ones. As agricultural is devolved, policy will gradually diverge between each UK nation from now on; England is moving the quickest.

The CAP has two main budgets (or Pillars). Pillar 1 includes the Basic Payment Scheme (BPS), which provides direct aid to farm businesses and also market support for agricultural produce. Pillar 2 is support through Rural Development and provides direct support to farmers for environmental protection, improvement of the countryside, and encourages sustainable enterprises and thriving rural communities. In 2019, Pillar 1 accounted for approximately 75% of support paid to UK Farmers and 24% for Pillar 2. Market support (which is not paid direct to farmers) was just 1%. The Rural Development Programme for each devolved region ran for the period 2014 to 2020. Going forward, there will not be a two Pillar structure. Funding for the environment, increasing productivity and sustainability will be provided through the main agricultural budget.

Some of the 'old' Rural Development schemes will continue whilst new policy is being drawn-up, but the devolved regions have closed others to new applications. Multiannual schemes will continue until their Agreement end date. Some may even be rolled over for further years until schemes under the new farm policies are ready. The Sections below for each country of the UK outlines the schemes availability at the time of writing (July 2021).

The UK will no longer receive money via the Common Agricultural Policy (CAP). Support for the agricultural industry will be from the UK budget. The UK Government has pledged to keep spending on farm support at current levels (current or real is unclear) until the end of the next Parliament. The current Parliament is planned to run until 2024. The way spending is delivered will change, meaning some recipients receive less, others more.

The Agriculture Act 2020 received Royal Assent in November 2020. This legislation primarily provides the framework for future support in England. It does contain some UK-wide measures such as dealing with the WTO and setting standards. But devolution of most powers, to allow farm policy to be set by Scotland, Wales and Northern Ireland has been maintained and specific legislation has been enacted in each part of the UK.

The devolved regions of the UK have held consultations on post-Brexit policy. New domestic support systems are being drawn-up, with each devolved region following their own policy. In the short term, new policies will be based on the existing Basic Payment Scheme (BPS see below). It is likely the BPS scheme will then be phased out whilst new schemes are being developed, this has already commenced in England (See English Support Section later).

As the BPS will continue in all the devolved regions in the short term, details are included below. The sections after are split into each country of the UK, giving an update on the progress of future support for each region and the schemes that are currently available.

2. THE BASIC PAYMENT SCHEME

The Basic Payment Scheme (BPS) was introduced in 2015. Following Brexit, the devolved regions of the UK have been running their own domestic agricultural policies, but in the short term these will continue to include the BPS. *Details are included here but are not exhaustive; always check with the latest legislation and the devolved administrations' publications for individual situations regarding specific farms.*

ENTITLEMENTS AND REDISTRIBUTION

To receive the BPS, entitlements must be matched against eligible land which generates a yearly payment if certain conditions are followed (cross-compliance). Top-up payments are available which are discussed below. The total funds allocated to a region remains unchanged, so top-ups simply reallocate funds.

- **Entitlements.** These were issued to farmers in 2015. At least once in every two years a farmer must activate (use) all of their entitlements in a single year, otherwise the excess is removed. This requirement has been removed in England from the 2021 scheme onwards.

- **Regions.** Since 2019, the BPS payment is equal throughout the region the land is in. In England, there are three regions; Lowland, Severely Disadvantaged Areas (SDA) and Moorland. Entitlements are not tradable across these regions.

  Scotland has three regions. Better land (arable and grassland) is one payment region (approximately 1.8m ha) – Region 1. Rough grazing is split into 2 regions using the Less Favoured Area Support Scheme (LFASS) classification (see Scotland Section later).

  Wales has one flat rate payment system. However, a Redistributive Payment (see below) applies to the first 54 hectares (133 acres) of any claim, rising to the estimated rate of €127.50 per hectare in 2019.

GREENING

Greening required farmers to provide environmental benefits in return for their direct payments. Greening payments accounted for 30% of the BPS. The three basic EU measures of Greening were crop diversification, Ecological Focus Areas (EFAs), and permanent pasture retention. Claimants are exempt from greening on organic land although the greening payment is still made.

As of 2021, none of the Greening requirements apply in England or Wales. Although, in Wales Environmentally Sensitive Grass (ESPG) is now protected as part of cross compliance. Scotland decided to retain the EFA requirements and the permanent pasture retention in 2021 but not crop diversification. It is assumed this will be the same for 2022 but has not been confirmed at the time of writing and applicants should ensure they read the relevant guidance.

Although Greening is not being followed in England and Wales and only partly in Scotland, there will be no loss of payment (apart from the planned deductions in England - See England Section later). The Greening element (30%) will be subsumed into the 'main' BPS payment.

As the change to the rules is not retrospective, we have included all of them in this edition in case of ongoing or future inspection/penalty cases.

- **Land Definitions.** Under greening there are three types of land, all three categories added together are known as the claimant's eligible area;

  ➢ Permanent Pasture – land that has been in grass for five years or longer. The sixth time it is entered as grass on the subsidy claim form it becomes permanent pasture. It doesn't matter if it has been reseeded, it is the length of time the land has been out of the arable rotation.

> ➢ Permanent Crops – land in crops that are in place for five years or more without replanting and that yield repeated harvests e.g. vines, orchards, short rotation coppice, Miscanthus, nurseries.

> ➢ Arable Land – any eligible land that is not permanent pasture or permanent crops, including fallow land and temporary grass.

- **Crop Diversification**. Where a claimant's arable land area (defined above) is between 10-30 hectares a minimum of two crops are required. Three crops will be needed when the arable land area is above 30 hectares. No crop should cover more than 75% of the farm area. Where three crops are required, the two main crops together should not exceed 95% of the area. The crop diversification requirement does not apply where;

> ➢ more than 75% of the *arable land* is used for temporary grass or left fallow

> ➢ more than 75% of the *eligible land* is in permanent or temporary grass

> ➢ there is less than 10 hectares of *arable land*

A crop is defined by its genus and species. Wheat, barley, oats, oilseed rape, linseed, potatoes, sugar beet etc. are all separate crops. Spring and winter crops are also separate crops. Fallow is a 'crop type', as is temporary grass. Crop Diversification rules were suspended for 2020 due to the wet weather.

- **Permanent Pasture**. Permanent pasture area has to be maintained at member state level. The overall percentage of permanent grassland in each country compared to the total agricultural area must not fall by more than 5%. In the UK it has not making this a non-issue for UK farming.

- **Ecological Focus Areas (EFAs)**. Claimants must put 5% of their eligible *arable* land into EFAs. Countries can choose from a list of features to offer to farmers as eligible EFAs. This includes landscape features (hedges and trees), buffer strips, fallow land, protein-fixing crops, agro-forestry and short-rotation coppice. A matrix system converts linear features (e.g. hedges) into EFA area equivalents and gives some features extra value. E.g. in England a 1m stretch of hedge can be worth $10m^2$ of EFA. Some claimants are exempt; EFAs are not required on farms where;

> ➢ more than 75% of the *arable land* is used for temporary grass, legumes or left fallow

> ➢ more than 75% of the *eligible land* is in permanent or temporary grass

> ➢ there is less than 15 hectares of arable land

The table below shows the features that are available in Scotland to fulfil the requirements and those most recently available in England and Wales (2020).

TOP-UPS AND OTHER POINTS CONCERNING THE UK

The Basic Payment Scheme and Greening form the 'foundation' of direct support, but a system of top-up payments was available and has been retained by the devolved administrations as outlined below.

- *Young Farmers Payment*. This provides a 25% (17.5% from 2021 in England as now includes the 'old' Greening payment) top-up to the value of entitlements for 5 years to those under 40 years old. This is capped at 90 hectares in England & Scotland and 25 hectares in Wales. At the maximum 90 hectares the extra payment is worth around £3,500 per year. Rules apply regarding having at least 50% of business accountability and dates since that began.

- **Coupled Support.** There are no coupled payments in England or Wales. Scotland has coupled support for beef and sheep enterprises. Cattle with 75% beef genetics receive an annual payment, dependant on the number of animals claimed each year but is approximately €100 per calf. There is also a coupled top-up for beef producers on the islands in the region of €160 per calf. There is coupled support for sheep producers who farm in Scotland's rough grazing areas (80% of BPS area in region 3 and less than 200ha in region 1). Payment rates vary annually depending on the number of animals claimed but is around €100 per eligible yearling ewe.

- **Redistributive payment.** This is a 'top-up' to the first 54 entitlements held by claimants. Only Wales has taken up this measure in the UK.

- **Minimum Claim size.** The minimum BPS claim in each of the GB regions is;

  ➢ England – 5 hectares

  ➢ Scotland – 3 hectares

  ➢ Wales – 5 hectares

- **Historic and Flat Rate Payments.** Wales and Scotland retained an historic method of calculating farmer payments until 2019, based on their farming practices of 2000 to 2003. This ended in 2014 with a transition to a flat rate payment (similar to England) which was completed in 2019. Thus, before 2019, all farmers in Wales and Scotland had unique payment amounts per hectare.

- **Conversion Rate.** BPS entitlements have historically been denominated in Euros and payment could have been received in Euros or converted to Sterling using the average exchange rate for each working day throughout September. Now that the UK has left the EU, payments are made in Sterling only. For 2020 and 2021 Euro denominated entitlements will be converted into Sterling using the 2019 exchange rate (see below). This exchange rate is forecast to be used going forward, it is expected entitlements will be converted permanently into Sterling at some point in the future.

- **Financial Discipline.** Under this mechanism all direct payments were reduced pro-rata to remain within the budget and fund a 'Crisis Reserve'. Deductions were only made to amounts over €2,000. If funds were not all used it was refunded to those who made a BPS claim in the following year. The rate deducted in 2019 was 1.4327%. From the 2020 BP scheme Financial Discipline will not apply.

- **Capping and Degessivity.** Under the CAP, all member states had to levy a minimum 5% reduction to aid rates above €150,000. The greening element is not affected. Member states could raise levels of degressivity up to 100 per cent and reductions could be 'banded'. England levied the minimum EU degressivity requirement, but from 2021 this has been superseded by the Agricultural Transition deductions – See England Section. Scotland still applies the 5% to payments above €150,000 and also a 100% cap on payments above €600,000. Wales has also retained its banded policy:

  ➢ 100% cap on payments above €300,000 (excluding greening);

  ➢ 55% on payments between €250,000 and €300,000,

  ➢ 30% on payments between €200,000 and €250,000 and

  ➢ 15% on payments between €150,000 and €200,000.

BPS PAYMENT RATES

The rates below are estimated by The Andersons Centre for illustrative purposes. In the tables below the following exchange rates are used. These are the official conversion rates from Euros into Sterling.

Exchange Rate	2017	2018	2019	2020	2021	2022
€ = £	0.8947	0.8928	0.8909	0.8909	0.8909	0.8909

In 2021 there was a conversion from euro denominated entitlements to Sterling. The rate for this was the same as 2019, this will be used going forward.

All the figures represent the rates received by farmers.

England

Flat Rate Area Payments for England (forecast figures for 2021 onwards)

£/ha (acre)	2019	2020	2021	2022	2023	2024
Lowland	230 (93)	233 (94)	222 (90)	187 (76)	152 (62)	117 (47)
SDA	228 (92)	232 (94)	220 (89)	185 (75)	151 (61)	116 (47)
Moorland SDA	63 (25)	64 (26)	61 (25)	51 (21)	42 (17)	32 (13)

2019 includes Financial Discipline levy at 1.4327%
2021 – 2024 Includes the deductions under the Agricultural Transition phasing. Payments over £30,000 will receive larger deductions – See England Support Section.

Wales

Rates for Wales converged per hectare for the entire region in 2019.

Flat Rate Area Payments for Wales (forecast figures for 2021 onwards)

£/ha (acre)	2019	2020	2021	2022	2023	2024
BPS & Greening	119 (48)	121(49)	121(49)	121 (49)	121 (49)	121 (49)
Redistrib ①	112 (45)	114 (46)	114 (46)	114 (46)	114 (46)	114 (46)

2019 includes Financial Discipline levy at 1.4327%
① redistributive payment made on the first 54ha

Scotland

Rates for Scotland converged per hectare from 2019 in each of the three regions; Arable & Grassland (Region 1), Rough Grazing (Region 2) and Poor Rough Grazing (Region 3) respectively.

Flat Rate Area Payments for Scotland (forecast figures for 2021 onwards)

£/ha (acre)	2019	2020	2021	2022	2023	2024
Region 1	215 (87)	221 (89)	221 (89)	221 (89)	221 (89)	221 (89)
Region 2	43 (17)	45 (18)	45 (18)	45 (18)	45 (18)	45 (18)
Region 3	13 (5)	14 (6)	14 (6)	14 (6)	14 (6)	14 (6)

2019 includes Financial Discipline levy at 1.4327%

In 2019 Scotland was awarded £160m from the UK Government for money that had previously been given to the UK under CAP convergence rules. This money was used to top-up BPS as follows:

Convergence Uplift Payments

£/ha (acre)	2019	2020
Region 1	16 (6)	10 (4)
Region 2	29 (12)	18 (7)
Region 3	12 (5)	10 (4)

3. MARKET SUPPORT

In the past market support measures in the UK have been available via the second part of Pillar 1 funding in the CAP architecture. It includes intervention buying, export subsidies, tariff barriers and tariff rate quotas (TRQs). Tariffs are now the main measures. Until the end of 2020, tariffs that applied to UK imports were agreed by the WTO on behalf of the entire EU. They (invisibly) provided considerable support to UK farm-gate prices by charging importers a fee for each unit of good brought into the 'Single Market' of the EU, thereby making competition to domestic goods more expensive, allowing 'internal' domestic prices to rise. Conversely, if a UK exporter wanted to export to a country with a tariff, they had to pay for that as well, making our exports less competitive.

Now the UK has left the EU, it is responsible for setting its own trade policy including the tariff schedule to apply to imports from countries we do not have a specific trade deal with. The UK Government has announced its new Most-Favoured Nation (MFN) tariff regime, the UK Global Tariff (UKGT). This sets the tariffs to be paid on imports entering the UK from any country in the world. It started after the end of the Transition Period (31 December 2020) when it replaced the EU Common External Tariff (CET).

The table below summarises tariffs of the main agricultural commodities for 2021. Most of the tariffs under the CET have been maintained at similar levels but converted from Euros into Sterling. In most cases, the currency conversion rate is €1 = £0.83, but there are some variations due to rounding and simplifications. Effectively, the protection around the UK market will be kept at the same level as it was around the EU Single Market.

Little information is available regarding Tariff Rate Quotas (TRQs) - these allow specified volumes of agricultural commodities to be imported either tariff-free or at much lower tariff levels. Any new TRQ that the UK introduces could change commodity prices noticeably. For instance, the UK Government may decide to continue the TRQ for beef that the UK has used in previous years. It has proposed 230,000 tonnes would be able to enter the UK tariff-free. Similarly, non- EU feed wheat has been imported into the EU at €12/tonne and a similar arrangement might be implemented. This section of the Pocketbook will be developed in future Editions as more information becomes available.

UK Global Trade Tariffs – source Dept for International Trade

% or €/£ per tonne	EU Common External Tariff	UK Global Trade Tariff	*Reason for Change*
Feed Wheat	€95	£79	*currency*
Feed Barley	€93	£77	*currency*
Oilseeds	none	none	*n/a*
Maize	€10.4	£0	*liberalisation*
Sugar (raw cane)	€339	£280	*currency*
Butter	€1,896	£1,580	*currency*

Cheese (Cheddar)	€1,671	£1,390	*currency*
Beef Carcases①	12.8%+€1,768	12%+£1,470	*currency*
Lamb Carcases①	12.8%+€1,713	12%+£1,430	*currency*
Pig Carcases①	€536	£440	*currency*
Chickens①	€262	£210	*currency*
Potatoes	14.4%	14%	*simplification*
Oranges	12%/16%	12%	*simplification*

① fresh/chilled

Source: UK Government (Department for International Trade)

UK-EU Free Trade Agreement

The UK-EU Trade and Co-operation Agreement (TCA) was agreed in December 2020. This allows trade in goods, including agricultural products, to continue to be traded between the EU and UK without tariffs or quotas being applied. However, trade between the UK and the EU is more difficult than before due to paperwork, checks, delays etc (Non-Tariff Measures) that are imposed on the UK now it is not part of the Single Market.

4. ENGLISH FARM SUPPORT

AGRICULTURAL TRANSITION

From 2021 there will be a seven year 'agricultural transition' period to 2027. All BPS payments will gradually reduce to zero. The highest payments will have bigger initial reductions as the table below sets out. The bands work like Income Tax, i.e. a £40,000 BPS payment would have the first £30,000 reduced by 5% and the remaining £10,000 would be cut by 10% as follows:

Reduction in Direct Payments for 2021- 2024

Payment Bands	2021	2022	2023	2024
Up to £30,000	5%	20%	35%	50%
£30,000-£50,000	10%	25%	40%	55%
£50,000-£150,000	20%	35%	50%	65%
£150,000 or above	25%	40%	55%	70%

Defra has only the published the deductions to 2024 but BPS payments will continue to be phased out, with 2027 being the last year of the scheme in England. The money saved will be put towards piloting new schemes including Environmental Land Management (ELM) (see below).

- **Delinking** - Payments made during the Agricultural Transition will be 'delinked' from the 'requirement to occupy farmland' this is expected to be introduced in 2024 (originally expected in 2022). It will not be optional. Amounts will be calculated according to the money received in a 'base year or years'. Once support is delinked a recipient will continue to receive the last of their BPS payments throughout the tapering period, regardless of farmed area. Details are being consulted on at the time of writing (July 2021).

- **Lump-Sum Payments** - A lump-sum payment is being proposed which would mean recipients can receive their full BPS tapering money up-front. Here, the future stream of income from BPS payments would be rolled into one single payment. Such payments are only expected to be offered in 2022 to those exiting or retiring from the industry. A £100,000 cap is being proposed. At the time of writing the details were being consulted on and the tax treatment was under consideration with HMRC. Full rules are expected by the end of October 2021.

NEW SCHEMES

The current system of support will largely be replaced by Environmental Land Management (ELM), but a number of other programmes will also be available, especially during the early years of the Agricultural Transition. This section gives an overview of what is known at the time of writing about each of the new schemes and when they are expected to be available.

Environmental Land Management (ELM)

The flagship scheme of England's new agricultural policy will be Environmental Land Management (ELM). This is the idea that land managers will be paid for providing 'public goods' such as;

- better air and water quality
- improved soil health
- higher animal welfare standards
- measures to reduce flooding and hazard protection
- public access to the countryside, heritage
- societal engagement and education
- climate change management

The public benefits in this list could not be recouped from the market. Whilst they are valuable to society, no individual is likely to purchase them. Thus, the concept of 'public goods', which will be payable for using 'public money'. Natural Capital is also likely to come into agricultural policy. Natural Capital is the amount of natural assets within a holding of value to society. This might include bird counts, soil quality, water cleanliness and so on. Defra intends to pay recipients according to outputs rather than actions.

ELM will consist of three components:

- ***Sustainable Farming Incentive (SFI)*** - This will be the 'entry-level' component of ELM. It is intended to be a scheme that is relatively easy to get into and thus replaces (some) of farmers' lost BPS income. The scheme will focus on reducing the 'negative externalities' produced by land management, particularly around air, soil, and water pollution. See below for more information on the SFI.

- ***Local Nature Recovery (LNR)*** – This will pay for actions that support local nature recovery and deliver local environmental priorities; making sure the right things are delivered in the right places. The scheme will also encourage collaboration between farmers, helping them work together to improve their local environment. This component may have elements that are competitive. Pilots will commence in 2022 with the component expected to launch fully in 2024.

- ***Landscape Recovery (LR)*** - This will support the delivery of landscape and ecosystem recovery through long-term, land use change projects, including projects to restore wilder landscapes in places where that is appropriate, large-scale tree planting and peatland restoration projects. The aim is to deliver a wide variety of environmental outcomes and support local environmental priorities while making an important contribution to national targets. This component is expected to be competitive. Ten projects will be piloted between 2022-2024.

Sustainable Farming Incentive (SFI)

The SFI will be made up of 'Standards'. Each Standard will have three ambition levels – Introductory, Intermediate and Advanced. The payments will rise for the higher levels, but a greater intervention is expected. Applications and administration of the scheme is likely to be carried out online. The SFI will be launched in stages. The SFI Pilot will run from 2021 to 2024. The first phase, SFI 2022, will commence next year and concentrate on soils (see below). The scheme will be expanded over the next few years, with full launch from 2024. Between 2022 and 2024, the SFI will run alongside existing schemes (e.g. Countryside Stewardship). Farmers will be able to choose which schemes to participate in and can participate in multiple schemes if they wish, but they will not be paid twice for the same action.

SFI Pilot

The SFI Pilot opened for expressions of interest in Spring 2021. Over 2,000 land managers have been invited to take part. This will include:

- Implementing the pilot version of the SFI on their own farm

- Taking part in learning activities based on their experiences

- Providing regular, comprehensive feedback on what is working and what is not

Those who have been invited to take part have until 1ˢᵗ September 2021 to make an application. Defra wants to learn from applicants' experiences thus they will be paid £5,000 per annum for taking part in the learning activities. It is envisaged these will take up to 15 hours per month. Pilot agreements will commence in October 2021 and run until 2024. Payments will be made monthly in arrears. A summary of the payment rates is shown in the table below. But these are subject to change, they are not expected to be reduced, but if rates increase as the scheme rolls out, those taking part in the pilot will not lose out.

Sustainable Farming Incentive Pilot – Standards and Payment rates. – Source: Defra

Standard	Introductory	Intermediate	Advanced
Arable & Horticultural Land	£28/Ha	£54/Ha	£74/ha
Arable & Horticultural Soils	£26/ha	£41/Ha	£60/ha
Improved Grassland	£27/Ha	£62/Ha	£97/ha
Improved Grassland Soils	£26/Ha	£44/Ha	£70/Ha
Low & No Input Grassland	£22/ha	£89/Ha	£110/Ha
Hedgerows	£16/100m	£21/100m	£24/100m
Farm Woodland	£49/Ha	None	None
Buffering of Watercourses	£16/Ha	£29/ha	£34/Ha

SFI 2022

SFI 2022 will concentrate on soils, it will also introduce the first element of the Animal Health and Welfare Pathway which will be available under SFI. There will just be four Standards within SFI 2022, these are:

- Arable and Horticultural Soils Standard

- Improved Grassland Soils Standard

- Moorland and Rough Grazing Standard

- Annual Health and Welfare Review

At the time of writing only the rates for the Arable and Horticultural Soils and Improved Grassland Soils Standards had been released - See SFI Pilot rates for Soils above. But even these are subject to change. The final versions will be available by November 2021 following further refinements and feedback from farmers and stakeholders. Under these Standards farmers will be rewarded for management practices which improve the soil structure and soil organic matter. With the aim of promoting clean water, improving climate resilience, biodiversity and food production.

Under the Moorland and Rough Grazing Standard, farmers will be rewarded for assessing the range of habitats and features present on their moorlands. This has the aim of identifying the pressures on them and also the risks posed by wildfires. For 2022 there will only be an Introductory level; higher levels of ambitions are planned later in the Agricultural Transition. No indicative payment rate has been announced for this Standard. The plan is for this Standard to be developed further during the summer of 2021 with farmers and stakeholders. It will be finalised by November 2021 along with a payment rate. This Standard will be available to all Moorland farmers, including those already taking part in Countryside Stewardship.

The Annual Health and Welfare Review is the initial phase of the Animal Health and Welfare Pathway. It will involve a Defra-funded yearly visit from a vet. It is initially planned to be available for three years. The review will include;

- Data collection to benchmark against the national herd/flock and to track progress on the holding

- Actions to improve biosecurity, including training, capital investment, changes to farm management practices

- A review of medicine usage. Including uploading medicines to an e-medicines recording hub

- Recommendations to improve health and welfare and signposts for further support to help make changes.

- Diagnostic testing for priority diseases – Bovine Viral Diarrhoea (BVD), Porcine Reproductive and Respiratory Syndrome Virus (PRRS) and for sheep, parasitic resistance to anthelmintic treatments.

Payments are expected to range from £269-£775. The main difference in the rate is due to the costs of the diagnostic tests which vary across the species.

SFI 2022 will open for applications in spring 2022. Full scheme literature should be available from November 2021.

Capital Grants

To increase productivity in the sector, capital grants will be available.

Farming Investment Fund (FiF)

The FiF is expected to be similar to the previous Countryside Productivity Scheme (See Rural Development Schemes later). It will offer grants (likely to be 40%) for investment in items of equipment deemed to improve productivity. Like the CPS, there will be two tiers;

- Farming Equipment and Technology Fund - a fixed rate of grant for equipment that has been pre-identified for increasing farm productivity. Application is expected to be relatively straight forward via an online portal.

- Farming Transformation Fund - for high-value items or projects. A two-stage process with an EOI and then full application is expected.

The FIF is expected to open in rounds. The first is due in October 2021. The scheme will run until 2026.

Slurry Investment Scheme (SiS)

The SiS will help farmers invest in new slurry stores that exceed current regulatory requirements (6 months storage is expected). The scheme may focus on locations where environmental impact of slurry is greatest. The scheme will open for applications in autumn 2022.

Skills and Training

There will be help and advice for farmers to cope with the loss of BPS payments and also training offered as part of an overall effort to 'upskill' the farming sector.

Future Farm Resilience Fund (FFRS)

The first round of the Future Farm Resilience Fund opened in August 2021and will run until March 2022. It is designed to provide business support to farmers during the early years of the Agricultural Transition. Nineteen organisations have been awarded funding to deliver a variety of business support, which will be free of charge including; one-to-one farm resilience reviews, resilience planning webinars, access to online skills & training and workshops. This initial phase will be fed-in to design the final scheme which will run from 2022 to 2024.

Institute for Agriculture and Horticulture

A new professional body, the Institute for Agriculture and Horticulture, will be set up in 2022. The AHDB is to draw up a set of Standard Key Performance Indicators (KPIs) to facilitate benchmarking.

Other Support

Farming in Protected Landscapes (FiPL)

FiPL will support farmers and the wider community in National Parks, Areas of Outstanding Natural Beauty (AONB) and the Broads. Land outside of protected landscapes may be eligible but the project must benefit the protected landscape, or the protected landscape body's objectives or partnership initiatives.

FiPL is not an agri-environment scheme. It will fund one-off projects that;

- Support nature recovery
- Mitigate the impacts of climate change
- Provide opportunities for people to enjoy the landscape and its cultural heritage
- Suport nature-friendly, sustainable farm businesses

The programme will run from July 2021 to March 2024. Applications for the first year of funding need to be made between 1st July 2021 and 31st January 2022. Application forms can be obtained from the protected landscape body where the project will take place. Projects will be assessed, they need to provide value for money and meet at least one of the outcomes in the 4 themes; Climate, Nature, People or Place.

Payment rates will vary depending on whether a commercial gain can be made through the project. If no commercial gain is identified, then up to 100% of the costs could be available in support. Land can still be entered into ELM and CS as long as the same work is not being paid for twice. Those interested are advised to contact their local protected landscape body.

New Entrants

The New Entrants Scheme is expected to open from 2022-2024. However, it does not look like there will be any direct funding for new entrants. It appears grants will be aimed more towards 'programmes' such as matching schemes and hubs to support new entrants.

ENGLISH RURAL DEVELOPMENT

The Rural Development Programme ran from 2014-2020 funded through the second Pillar of the CAP. Some of the schemes are now closed to new applications as we move to a new domestic agricultural policy but as many of the previous scheme contracts are for more than one year and will carry on for many years until the agreements end, brief details of these schemes are included in the sections below. There are a few instances of even older Rural Development schemes continuing from legacy schemes that are not included in this Edition. For information on these, refer to back copies of this book. *The UK Government has confirmed all structural and investment projects, including agri-environmental schemes, signed before 31st December 2020, will be fully funded for the life of the Agreement.*

The Environment – Countryside Stewardship (CS)

Countryside Stewardship (CS) is the existing agri-environmental scheme for England and continues into 2022. It will remain open until the new Environmental Land Management (ELM) scheme is fully launched in 2024. The last application date will be in 2023 for a 1st January 2024 start. Those who enter a CS agreement from 2021 onwards will be able to end their agreement, at agreed points, where they have secured a place in ELM.

The aim of the scheme is to support measures to 'restore, preserve and enhance the natural environment'. The scheme is open to farmers, foresters and land managers mostly through competitive application. It is run jointly by Natural England, Forestry Commission England and the Rural Payments Agency (RPA); it provides three tiers of funding:

- **Higher-Tier.** Multi-year agreements for environmentally significant sites, commons and woodlands where complex management requires one-to-one support from Natural England or the Forestry Commission to help build an application. Applicants select from 244 options and capital grants. Most agreements are by invitation. See Forestry Section for Woodland Grants.

- **Mid-Tier.** Multi-year agreements for environmental improvements in the wider countryside. Applicants choose from 120 management options and capital items. The minimum annual value must exceed £1,000. 'Priorities' for different areas have been identified. Agreements are scored against these and only those offering the best outcomes are given an agreement. There are four simplified, non-competitive *Wildlife Offers;* Arable, Lowland Grazing, Mixed Farming and Upland. Each offer a reduced set of options with minimum requirements aimed at providing winter food for seed-eating birds.

- **Stand-alone Capital Grants.** Capital items are available in Mid and Higher-Tier applications, but it is also possible to have a stand-alone Capital Agreement for 1 to 2 years. From 2021 the stand-alone capital grants have been expanded. The previous 12 options under the Hedgerows and Boundaries Grant and Water Capital Grants have been expanded to 67 capital items grouped under 3 headings: Boundaries, Trees and Orchards; Water Quality and Air Quality. The maximum spend has also increased from £10,000 to £60,000 (£20,000 under each heading).

Further funding is available for improving water quality via the Catchment Sensitive Farming project which from 2021 has been increased to cover all farm land, and also for historic buildings and planning for more complex Higher Tier agreements. There is also support for woodland management plans, woodland creation (establishment), woodland improvement and tree health.

Higher & Mid-Tier agreements normally run for five years (starting 1 January), although ten years may be offered if benefits will take longer to achieve (typically for woodland). There is a menu of management options and capital items to choose from depending on the agreement. One agreement per holding is allowed, with no separate 'strands' for uplands or organics, although there are specific options for these types of land:

- **Organic** – The CS provides 16 options exclusive to organic farmers and land managers including options for conversion and maintenance. These options can be used alone through the Mid-Tier process or with other options within the Mid or Higher Tier as long as they are compatible with organic status. Conversion payments are paid for 2 years, except for permanent crops (3 years). For the duration of the agreement applicants must be registered with an Organic Control Body. Organic only applications are non-competitive.

- **Uplands** – There are 6 specific upland grants available, including management of enclosed rough grazing, managing grazing for birds, management of moorland and supplements for moorland re-wetting, introducing or reintroducing shepherding. Other options within the Mid or Higher Tier can be selected as long as they are compatible with upland management such as capital payments for Historic Building Restoration.

- **Facilitation Funds** – deliver the CS on a landscape scale for organisations/people with environmental land management skills to help groups of land managers work together. The 'group' must manage at least 2,000 hectares (unless there is a smaller more obvious environmental boundary) and spread over at least four neighbouring holdings. After a long period of closure, £2.5 million has been made available and this fund opened briefly in autumn 2019. No further dates had been announced at the time of writing, but a further round was expected.

- **Scoring** – Applications are scored against criteria. Applicants should use 'Statements of Priorities' and supporting maps for their area to identify the priority features and issues being targeted to help select options as part of an application. To enhance the chances of an offer, applicants can choose options from the '**wild pollinator and farm wildlife package** (WPFWP). These are designed to benefit wild pollinators, farmland birds and other farm wildlife. Applications which select these options and meet the minimum area thresholds; 3% for Mid-Tier and 5% for Higher-Tier, will enhance their score. The Mid- Tier Wildlife Offers and applications to the organic conversion and maintenance options are non-competitive. Eligible applications are subject to the availability of budget.

- **Application window** – There are different application windows, the dates for 2021 are shown here; although not guaranteed, similar application windows are likely in 2022.

Mid-Tier ①	9 Feb to 31 July 2021
Higher Tier ②	9 Feb to 30 April 2021
Capital Grant Scheme	9 Feb to 30 April 2021
Woodland Management Plans and Tree Health	All year
Woodland Creation	All Year
Woodland Improvement ②	9 Feb to 30 April 2021

① Paper Application Packs must be requested by 28 May 2021. Online packs by 30th June. No deadline to request an online Wildlife Offer Application Pack.

② Application Packs must be requested by 31 March 2021

Increasing Productivity – The Countryside Productivity Scheme
This scheme is closed to new applications, with the change to domestic policy following Brexit, it is not expected to re-open again. Funding for this type of support is being replaced by the Farming Investment Fund – see earlier under New Schemes.

This scheme aimed to improve the competitiveness of farming and forestry businesses. Its total budget was £140 million. Applicants bid for funds for projects which were innovative, used new technology and the latest research and improved skills & training in the business. Co-operation and collaboration with others in land-based sectors together with projects which benefit the environment in a number of ways i.e. tackle environmental problems whilst increasing productivity have been encouraged to bid for a share of the funds. Grants cover up to 40% of total eligible costs. The scheme opened in rounds. Funds were available in the areas below,

- Water resource management and reservoirs
- Improving forestry productivity
- Adding value to Agri-food
- Improving farm productivity

The minimum grant under the last round was £35,000.

The Countryside Productivity Small Grant Scheme

This was introduced in 2018. Farmers chose from a set list of capital items identified to improve the productivity of businesses. It made grants of £3,000 to £12,000 with a fixed grant for each item.

Rural Economic Growth

The last round for Expressions of Interest closed in February 2020. Projects should be finished, paid for and grant claims submitted by 30th September 2021.

Funding for Rural Growth has been available through Local Enterprise Partnerships (LEPs) or LEADER Local Action Groups (LAGs). LEPs are partnerships between public bodies and businesses whose role is to award grants to maximise local benefit. Each LEP has its own strategy and local priorities. There are three types of grants:

1. Business Development – to develop new or existing businesses
2. Food Processing – for agricultural & horticultural processors
3. Rural Tourism Infrastructure – to attract more visitors & prolong their stay

Applications were competitive, focussing on business growth, job creation and development of the rural economy, worth up to 40%, usually from £35,000 to €200,000 (£170,000).

A LEADER scheme fund programmes run by local community partnerships called Local Action Groups (LAGs) gives grants for projects which improve the rural economy and create jobs. Potential applicants need to make contact with their local LAG to ascertain if any funding is still available.

Funding for projects which would have fallen under the Growth Programme or LEADER are likely to be funded through the new Shared Prosperity Fund.

5.   WELSH FARM SUPPORT

WELSH FUTURE AGRICULTURAL POLICY

The BPS will remain in place for 2022, subject to minor amendments to Greening (see earlier). A new Sustainable Farming Scheme (SFS) is being designed. The BPS will be phased out and the SFS will be introduced at some point. The Welsh Government has suggested the new support scheme should start in 2024 (although this is not 100% certain). At the time of writing, there is no indication of how long it will take to be phased in. A new Welsh Agriculture Bill is to be laid before the Senedd in autumn 2021. This will contain the powers to enact the new Sustainable Farming Scheme (SFS). The Bill is unlikely to give details of how the SFS will work in practice. Instead it will set the legal framework under which the scheme will operate, so may give an indication of start date and phase in times.

Sustainable Farming Scheme

Details of the SFS are still being designed, but it is expected that a Sustainable Farming Payment will effectively replace the BPS and Glastir. This will be an annual payment to land managers that rewards 'sustainable farming practices'. This will be based on four principles;

- *providing a meaningful and stable income stream* - Payment rates will not be constrained by the 'income foregone' calculation.

- *rewarding outcomes in a fair way* - It is clear that the support will not simply be available 'as of right' like the BPS and will be made for the provision of public goods

- *paying for both new and existing sustainable practices*

- *flexibly applied to every type of farm*

There will also be additional business support. This will focus on advice, capital investment and skills development although, again, no details are available. It is likely that a Farm Sustainability Review will be required to enter the scheme.

WELSH RURAL DEVELOPMENT

The Welsh Rural Development Programme ran from 2014-2020 and was funded by the second Pillar of the CAP. Most Welsh RDP schemes continue for existing recipients but some are now closed to new applications as the new domestic policy is designed. The section below outlines the schemes that are currently open and those where agreements will still be running.

Area-based Measures - Glastir

Most funding has been available for the Area-based schemes through Glastir which has run for the last two Rural Development Programmes in Wales, but some of the elements are now closed to new applications. The Welsh Government confirmed all Glastir Advanced agreements, including underlying Glastir Entry, Glastir Commons and Glastir Organic agreements coming to an end in 2020 would be extended until 2021. At the time of writing it was unclear if there would be a further one year extension to these agreements and an extension to those ending in 2021. No new agreements are expected to be offered for these elements. The only elements expected to open for new applications in 2021 and 2022 are the Glastir Woodlands and Glastir Small Grant Scheme.

Glastir has six elements;

- Glastir Entry (GE)
- Glastir Advanced (GA)
- Glastir Commons (GC)
- Glastir Woodlands (GW)
- Glastir Organic (GO)
- Glastir Small Grant Scheme

Glastir Entry; has not opened since 2015 and is closed to new applications, but as contracts are still running details of the scheme are given here. Applicants have to obtain a points threshold through selecting options for their farm. Payment for Glastir Entry is £17 or £34 per hectare for all land in the scheme depending on threshold achieved. Payment is made annually on the SAF. Producers need to comply with the Whole Farm Code; 13 standards of environmental practice. This attracts an additional payment of:

0 – 20 hectares £15/ha

| 21 – 50 hectares | £8/ha |
| 51 - 100 hectares | £2.75/ha |

Glastir Advanced (GA); Further application windows are not expected but will be publicised in the Gwlad e-newsletter and the Welsh Government website if there is a change to this. GA addresses soil carbon management, water quality, water quantity management, biodiversity, the historic environment and improving access. It is a competitive scheme and applications are assessed against the objectives on target maps (Geographical Information System (GIS) maps). At this level management is of a prescribed nature, payments consist of both capital and non-capital items. Glastir Advanced contracts are for 5 years and are whole farm commitments. Farmers are not required to enter GE before they apply to the GA. Contracts start on 1st January. The value depends on the Management Options undertaken.

Glastir Commons is for those with rights on Common Land and have established a Grazing Association. It is unlikely this strand will re-open to new applications but potential applicants are advised to check the Gwlad e-newsletter for details.

Glastir Woodlands (GW). funds woodlands under the Glastir Woodland Creation Grant (GWC), the Glastir Woodland Restoration Grant (GWR) and the Glastir Woodland Management Grant (WMG).

GWC has four funding streams; Establishment, Maintenance, Premium and Fencing grants. There are four categories of woodland, Establishment grants vary from £1,600/ha for the agroforestry category to £4,500/ha for trees planted in the mixed woodland-carbon category. Maintenance payments are available for 12 years at £60/ha/annum (5 years and £30/ha for agroforestry). A premium payment pays £350/ha for 12 years to compensate for the income foregone for stock exclusion of agricultural land. Fencing grants, of £3.48/m are available. The last window for Expressions of Interest ran from 16th November 2020 to 15th January 2021. Further rounds are expected in 2021 and 2022, potential applicants are advised to check the Gwlad e-newsletter for details.

The GWR funds replanting areas of Larch that were felled to help prevent the spread of phytophthora ramorum disease affecting trees. Payment rates from £1,900/ha to £2,770/ha. This last opened from 18th May to 25th June 2021. Further rounds are expected and those interested are advised to check the Gwlad e-newsletter or the government website for details.

WMG**s** have not opened for some years. It seems unlikely it will re-open. Payments were available for managing existing woodlands from £54 to £120/ha. A Timber Business Investment Scheme was introduced to provide funds for existing woodlands. A grant for small woodland planting is potentially available through the Glastir Small Grant Scheme.

Funding may also be available via the ***Co-operative Forest Planning Scheme*** which offers support to new collaborations to develop project proposals which will encourage planning for the creation of broadleaved and conifer woodland. At the time of writing future application dates had not been released.

Glastir Organic *Payment Rates*

| £/Ha | Conversion | | Maintenance | Certification* |
	Years 1-2	Years 3-5	Years 1-5	
Horticultural	600	400	400	80
Enclosed Land	130	65	65	10
Rough Grazing	15	15	15	3

* Certification costs are capped at £500 per contract

Glastir Organic (GO) supports organic farming in Wales. GO has been closed to new applications since 2016 and there is no evidence it will reopen. Those agreements coming to an end may be eligible to be extended.

Farmers joining GO remained eligible for other parts of Glastir. Conversion and maintenance contracts are for five years. Support for ongoing training and skills development is available. The table below summarises the payment rates;

Glastir Small Grant Scheme is a stand-alone scheme. It is competitive and grants up to £7,500 per theme towards capital works which help tackle climate change, improve water management, restore traditional landscape features and increase Wales' native biodiversity. There are 3 themes under Glastir Small Grants; Carbon, Water and Landscape & Pollinators. Each has its own separate Expression of Interest window. Both Carbon and Landscape & Pollinators have been available during 2021. All are expected to have further rounds, Water may be available in autumn 2021. Those interested are advised to check the Gwlad e-newsletter or the government website for details

Investment Measures; Schemes under this element include:

The Farm Business Grant scheme provides support to farmers to improve both the economic and environmental performance of their agricultural holdings. It provides a 40% contribution towards capital investments in equipment and machinery that benefit farm enterprises. Applicants 'choose' from a list of capital items with standard costs, centred on five themes:

- Animal Health, Performance and Genetics
- Crop Management
- Resource Efficiency
- Energy Efficiency
- ICT

The scheme is competitive, applications are scored and ranked in order to the scoring criteria. The grant is from £3,000 to £12,000. There have been nine application windows, the last was in spring 2021. In addition, there has been two windows specifically for Yard Coverings in 2020 and 2021. A further round is expected in Spring 2022. Future dates will be announced on the Welsh Government website and in the Gwlad e-newsletter.

The Sustainable Production Grant funds capital works to improve the resource efficiency of farms. In the latest round, which was open from 1st February to 12th March 2021, funds of up to 40% worth £12,000 to £50,000 were available to assist farm businesses to meet the requirements of The Water Resources (Control of Agricultural Pollution) (Wales) Regulations 2020. A set list of capital investments is available for applicants. Future dates will be announced on the Welsh Government website and in the Gwlad e-newsletter.

The Food Business Investment Scheme (FBIS) is a discretionary scheme designed to help farmers add value to their outputs that do first and/or second stage processing activities. It improves the performance and competitiveness of their businesses; to respond to consumer demand; encouraging diversification and to identify, exploit and service new emerging and existing markets. FBIS covers capital investments in processing equipment. Priority is given to Micro, Small or Medium Enterprises (SME's). Applicants must demonstrate that a viable market has been identified for their product(s) and the project would not proceed without the grant. The grant is from £2,400 to £5,000,000 and is 20% to 40% of the investment.

The last round closed at the end of October 2020. At the time of writing no application dates had been announced for 2021. Any future application dates will be published on the Welsh Government website and in the Gwlad e-newsletter.

The Timber Business Investment Scheme; a capital fund to add value to forests and woodlands by supporting woodland management activities, timber harvesting and/or in-forest or small scale timber processing. The last round closed in April 2021. Further rounds will be published on the Welsh Government website.

The Sustainable Management Scheme offers grants to groups looking to improve the resilience of businesses and communities to climate change, reducing greenhouse gas emissions or are improving the natural resources. Grants range from £10,000 to £5,000,000, up to 100% of costs. The SMS is part of the Co-operation and Supply Chain Development Scheme (See below). The scheme is currently closed to new applications. Future application dates will be published on the Welsh Government website.

The *Sustainable Management Scheme – Supporting Natura 2000 Restoration,* provided funds of £10,000 to £4m to support landscape-scale investment delivering action to improve the condition of Natura 2000 sites. The scheme closed in August 2020, with work to be completed by 31ˢᵗ March 2021.

Other funding available may include support for entry into *Quality schemes; Risk Management* – subsidising insurance that will extend to losses incurred due to bad weather; *Restoration of Forestry Potential* – support for woodland and habitat restoration to mitigate natural disasters.

Human & Social Capital Measures

The main interventions available under this element include:

Knowledge Transfer & Innovation and Advisory Services – Farming Connect is a programme of knowledge transfer, innovation and advisory services targeting farming and forestry businesses. It is being delivered by Menter a Busnes and Lantra.. Many services are fully funded or subsidised up to 80%. Services include; subsidised business support tailored to the business needs, professional development and training, demonstrations, coaching, workshops, specialist events. In addition the *Farm Liaison Service* provides free help with scheme rules, record keeping and form filling via telephone support, events and evening meetings.

Co-operation and Supply Chain Development Scheme supports the development of new products or processes in agriculture, forestry and food. It aids short supply chains and local markets including those for biomass production. Also support for new and emerging Producer Groups falls under this funding stream building on the Supply Chain Efficiencies Scheme and previous provisions for this kind of work under Farming Connect. Recently there has been a number of new initiatives falling under this heading including Pilot Actions for Community Cohesion & Green Recovery & Support, Anti-microbial Resistance, Food Tourism, Food-Covid Recovery Plan and Pilot Action for Green Growth. Future application dates will be published on the Welsh Government website.

LEADER & Local Development - LEADER Local Action Groups (LAGs) encourage innovation and achieve rural development. Under the Rural Community Development Fund (RCDF) the Welsh Government offers grants, primarily aimed at LEADER Local Action Groups (LAGs) and other community-Based organisations for investment funding across interventions designed to mitigate the impact of poverty in the countryside, improving conditions which can lead to future jobs and growth. Application dates are published on the Welsh Government website however funding via LEADER is currently limited. In the future rural economic development is expected to be through the new Shared Prosperity Fund, details of which are not currently available.

Other funding for diversification projects may be available through the *Tourism Amenity Investment Support Scheme (TAIS)* and the *Micro Small Business Fund*, both providing grants for projects in the tourism sector. *Wales Rural Network* helping to communicate the opportunities available under the WRDP.

6. SCOTTISH FARM SUPPORT

SCOTTISH FUTURE AGRICULTURAL POLICY

The 'Agriculture (Retained EU Law and Data) (Scotland) Bill' was passed by the Scottish Parliament in the summer of 2020 but it was specifically designed to make minimal change to the previous EU support schemes. This is in line with the Stability and Simplicity consultation from 2018 which foresaw no major change to the BPS and only tweaks to the Less Favoured Area Support Scheme (LFASS) before 2024. The implication is the BPS and LFASS will be available in a similar format for at least 2022 with any changes being made only to improve the application process, mapping system and perhaps a simplification of the greening rules (see earlier).

One important inclusion in the legislation is effectively a 'sunset clause' that means a replacement for the current legislation has to be put forward before the end of the next Scottish Parliament in May 2026. The Government could put forward plans before this date, which the industry is pushing for, but it means that the current schemes cannot carry-on indefinitely. However, at the time of writing, the Scottish Government had not released any proposals for future farm policy. It is likely that there will be some transition to payment for 'public goods' but with an element of coupled support retained. Sector-led climate groups have each produced reports giving advice and proposals on how to cut emissions and tackle climate change within their industry and it seems Scottish farm policy will be, to a large extent, framed by the need to address climate change.

SCOTTISH RURAL DEVELOPMENT

The Scottish Rural Development Programme ran from 2014-2020 and was funded by the second Pillar of the CAP. Scottish RDP schemes continue for existing agreement holders and contracts will be honoured to their end dates, but some are now closed to new applications. There is likely to be a funding gap whilst Scotland draws up its new agricultural support policy. The section below outlines the schemes that are currently open and those where agreements are still running.

Less Favoured Area Support Scheme (LFASS)

The LFASS has been running for many years and the Scottish Government has announced it will continue to be available until 2024. Furthermore, payment rates will revert back to 2018 levels. Under EU rules the rates for 2019 and 2020 were paid at 80% and 40% respectively of the 2018 rate.

The LFASS is calculated as follows; eligible hectares are adjusted for non-ring fenced dairy land, variable minimum or maximum stocking density restrictions, grazing category and an enterprise mix multiplier. The adjusted hectares are then paid at the payment rates below depending on the grazing category and location of the land. There is a minimum payment of £385.

LFASS Payment Rates 2021-2024	Grazing Category	
£ per adjusted Hectare (acre)	A & B	C & D
Very Fragile	71.35 (28.88)	63.00 (25.50)
Fragile	62.10 (25.13	54.51 (22.06)
Standard	52.16 (21.11)	32.14 (13.01)

Agri-environment Climate Scheme (AECS) – This subsidises management and capital work for environmental purposes. The AECS is a competitive scheme that promotes land management practices which protect and enhance Scotland's natural heritage, improve water quality, manage flood risks and mitigate and adapt to climate change. It will also help to

improve public access and preserve historic sites. Support for organic conversion and maintenance is provided.

Most applications need a Farm Environment Assessment (FEA) which records key environmental features on farm and helps plan what to include in the application. Funding is available for the FEA. This grant is geographically targeted. The scheme usually opens for applications from January to April each year. However, in 2020 it did not to open for new applications, but a one year extension was made available for AECS contracts which expired in 2020. In 2021 the AECS only opened for applications which; benefitted designated sites, for organic farming, for priority bird species, for slurry storage or improved public access. It is currently unclear what will happen in 2022.

Forestry Grant Scheme - The Forestry Grant Scheme (FGS) supports the creation of new woodlands, contributing towards the Scottish Government's target of 10,000 hectares of new woodlands per year and the sustainable management of existing woodlands. Support is available under eight categories;

- Woodland creation that brings economic, environmental and social benefits. An initial planting payment is from £560/ha to £3,600/ha. Annual maintenance payments are for five years (from £96/ha to £624/ha). There is a range of capital grants for example for fencing and tree protection. There is no Farm Woodland Premium payment, but land remains eligible for BPS.
- Agroforestry for the creation of small scale woodlands (0.25-5ha) on agricultural pasture or forage land which will allow for a mix of trees and sheep grazing. An initial planting grant; £1,860/ha at 200 trees/ha or £3,600/ha for 400 trees/ha and an annual maintenance grant for 5 years; £48/£84/ha/year at a stocking rate of 200/400 trees/ha.
- Woodland Improvement Grant options provide capital grants to improve existing woodlands. These support forest management to enhance the environment and the public's enjoyment of existing woodlands (Woodlands in and Around Towns (WIAT).
- Sustainable Management of Forests options support the management of existing woodlands with a high environmental value. Includes control of grey squirrel & deer, predator control for Capercaillie and Black Grouse, public access, livestock exclusion, woodland grazing and low impact silvicultural systems.
- Tree Health prevents the spread of *Phytophthora ramorum (P. ramorum)* and restores affected woodlands.
- Harvesting and Processing develops the small-scale premium softwood and hardwood processing sector. Funding for equipment in small, undermanaged woods.
- Forest Infrastructure – support for access into undermanaged or small woodlands.
- Forestry Co-operation funds projects involving multiple landowners

This scheme is being delivered by SRDP and Forestry Commission Scotland, applications are online only and can be made throughout the year.

Sustainable Agricultural Capital Grants Scheme – this is a new pilot scheme being offered through the government's Agricultural Transformation Programme. The scheme offers grants of up to £20,000 to farmers and crofters towards the capital cost of specific items which have been identified to reduce Greenhouse Gas (GHG) emissions and improve land and livestock management on Scottish farms and crofts. Grants of 50% (60% in the Highlands and Islands) will be paid on the standard costs of agricultural equipment. The pilot scheme opened on 7th September and closed on 11th October 2020, with claims to be submitted by 30th September 2021 (originally 31st March 2021) A further round is expected, but no dates had been announced at the time of writing.

New Entrants Support (£20m) - This provides start-up grants for new and young entrants. At the time of writing these are closed and it is unlikely they will re-open, although support for new and young entrants is expected to be available again in the future under the new domestic policies being drawn up for post Brexit.

- New Entrants Capital Grant Scheme - for farmers and crofters who have been head of an agricultural business for up to five years before the application for support. Funding can be used for capital projects, such as the construction or improvement of agricultural buildings. The total amount of grant aid available in any two-year period is individuals; up to £25,000 and groups; up to £125,000.
- Young Farmers Start-Up Grant Scheme - Young farmers or crofters (between 16 and 41 years) starting an agricultural business for the first time or taking over an existing agricultural business. Applicants must have at least an NVQ level 2 or equivalent in agriculture or five years agricultural experience. The grant is €70,000. An initial payment of €63,000 with the remaining paid once business milestones are reached.
- New Entrants' Start-Up Grant – those who have started their business within 12 months. There is no upper age limit. The total grant is €15,000. There is an initial payment of €12,000 and the remaining payable on reaching business plan milestones.

Crofting Agricultural Grant Scheme pays crofters to improve their crofts and sustain their business. Capital funding for construction and renovation of agricultural buildings or the establishment of Common Grazing Committees. The total grant available in any two-year period is £25,000 for individual crofters and £125,000 for groups. Applications can be made to this scheme at any time. The scheme is competitive and once the annual fund of £2m has been used, the scheme will close for the year. In addition, the *Croft House Grant Scheme* provides grants to crofters to improve and maintain standards of crofter housing.

Small Farms Grant Scheme supports small farms for capital projects, such as construction or improvement of farm buildings, including the cost of materials, contractor costs and own labour. The holding must be 3 to 30 hectares. The total grant available in any two year period is £25,000 for individual small farmers and up to £125,000 for groups of small farmers. Applications can be made to this scheme at any time, but the scheme is competitive and once the annual fund of £1m has been used, the scheme closes for the year.

Farm Advisory Service provides information and resources for increasing the profitability and sustainability of farms and crofts. Grants for Integrated Land Management Plans (ILMP) including specialist advice, mentoring new entrants and carbon audits. Events include workshops, farm meetings, conferences and training courses. There is a subscription service specifically for crofts and small farms, providing access to advice and information. An advice line is available covering topics including cross compliance, the water framework directive, climate change etc. The service is being delivered by SAC Consulting and Ricardo Energy and Environment on behalf of the Scottish Government. The scheme is contracted to run until the end of December 2021, unless a further extension is granted.

Knowledge Transfer and Innovation Fund (KTIF) provides funding to cover the running costs of 'operational groups' to provide training, workshops, farm visits etc. which deliver improvements in competitiveness, resource efficiency, environmental and sustainability in the farming and forestry sector. Projects are assessed in rounds by a Project Assessment Committee (PAC). The last round was in autumn 2020 and all projects had to be completed by 31st March 2021. The budget has been used up and the programme did not open in 2021.

LEADER – supports individuals, communities and businesses to design and implement Local Development Strategies across Scotland. Available through Local Action Groups (LAGs). In Scotland 21 LAGs implement Local Development Strategies. £20 million has been allocated for specific support for small business growth, including £10 million for farm and croft diversification, which is also available through LEADER. Any type of organisation can apply for LEADER funding, as long as the idea can support the aims of the Local Development Strategy in the area. The LEADER 2014-2020 Programme is now closed to new projects. All approved projects need to be completed by 31st December 2020. Funding for rural economic development in the future is likely to be through the UK Shared Prosperity Funding. No details were available at the time of writing.

Food Processing, Marketing and Co-operation. This scheme provides support for SMEs with start-up grants for new enterprises, and business development grants for existing businesses. This scheme is delivered through the Scottish Government's Food and Drink Division. A new funding round ran from 4th August to 12th September 2021. The FPMC now operates as a single year scheme, which means all projects need to be completed and claimed for by 31st March 2022. A further round may run from 2022 to 2023.

Broadband. Support for communities to join together to deliver a broadband solution for their rural area. The scheme is delivered by Community Broadband Scotland.

7.   NORTHERN IRELAND FARM SUPPORT

NORTHERN IRELAND FUTURE AGRICULTURAL POLICY

There has been little announced on the progress of future farm policy in Northern Ireland. It is recognised by the Government that the current decoupled area-based payment does not deliver the outcomes and the agricultural industry that Northern Ireland wants. An area-based resilience payment that provides a safety net, but that does not stop producers from trying to become more productive or from delivering better environmental outcomes is being explored. Furthermore, as part of the resilience package, a proportion of the agricultural budget would be used to fund coupled payments targeting for example, suckler cow and breeding ewe producers. However, they would need to achieve the goals of increased productivity and environmental sustainability.

A new part of the agricultural framework will be the environment programme. The objective is to create a regime that properly incentivises and rewards the protection of existing environmental assets and the creation of new ones. With the aim to create an approach whereby management of the environment becomes a profit centre within a farm business rather than a cost centre. Future policy is also expected to include support for, capital support schemes, new entrants, upskilling and professional development, opportunities to develop the horticultural sector, supply chain efficiencies. There has been no indication when the new schemes will commence and whether there will be a transition period.

NORTHERN IRELAND RURAL DEVELOPMENT

The main components of the Northern Ireland Rural Development Plan are set out below. Some of these will continue until new agricultural policy is introduced:

- *Competitiveness of Agriculture* – The Farm Business Improvement Scheme is a set of measures for improving the competitiveness and sustainability of farming in Northern Ireland. It offers up to 40% of the cost of equipment and machinery that will improve efficiency, environmental practice, animal health & welfare and health & safety. Within the FBIS is the Farm Family Key Skills initiative to help families adapt to the changing needs of the industry. The Business Development Groups scheme is closed to new applications but paid to set up discussion groups. There are 150 groups in operation, delivering on-farm meetings, demonstrations and skills training. There is an Agri-food Processing Investment Scheme (AfPIS), providing capital to improve the agri-food sector and an Agri-food Co-operation scheme providing funds to reduce fragmentation and improve competitiveness and sustainability.

- *Protecting the Rural Environment* – Most funding through the Environmental Farming Scheme over five-year agreements. There are three levels, 'Higher Level' is mainly for designated sites or priority habitats. 'Wider Level' is for land outside these areas. 'Group Level' facilitates collaboration between landowners to offer landscape agreements, such as for river catchment areas. Group Level facilitation was introduced in 2017. Refer to the Daera website for application dates. The Forestry Grant Schemes provide grants to encourage the creation of new woodlands and the management of existing ones via the Forest Expansion Scheme, the Forest Protection Scheme and the Woodland Investment Grant.

○ **Developing Rural Economies** - Funds have previously been available for measures to encourage economic development of rural areas through the LEADER Local Action Groups (LAGs) and the Rural Tourism Scheme. Funding for rural economic development in the future is likely to be through the UK Shared Prosperity Funding. No details were available at the time of writing.

8.   ENVIRONMENTAL SCHEME PAYMENTS

There are many agri-environment schemes across the UK providing annual payments. The table below summarises the latest payments made for environmental schemes.

£ Million

Environmental Scheme Payments, 2019 and 2020 (provisional)

		2019	2020
England:	Environmental Stewardship (c)	193	164
	Countryside Stewardship Scheme – Environment	89	136
	Countryside Stewardship Scheme – Organic	6	5
Wales:	Glastir	52	44
	Environmentally Sensitive Areas Scheme	3	-
Scotland:	Less Favoured Area Support Scheme	51	30
	Land Managers Options (c)/ Rural Priorities (c)	4	2
	Agri-environment Climate Scheme	14	12
	New Entrants Scheme	4	2
N. Ireland	Countryside Management Scheme	1	-
	Areas of Natural Constraint	-	-
	Environmental Farming Scheme (new from 2017)	4	4

Source: DEFRA, SGRPID, DAERA, WGDEPRA. Agriculture in the UK 2020
(c) Schemes that are now closed to new entrants.

IV.   LABOUR

1.   LABOUR COST

There are 9 National (UK) Bank Holidays in 2022, 1 more than usual; New Year's Day (Monday 3 January), Good Friday 15 April, Easter Monday 18 April, May Bank Holiday Monday 2 May, Spring Bank Holiday Thursday 2 June, Platinum Jubilee Bank Holiday Friday 3 June, Summer Bank Holiday Monday 29 August, Boxing Day (Monday 26 December) and Christmas Day (Tuesday 27 December). An employer is not obliged to give a day's holiday on bank holiday.

NATIONAL LIVING AND MINIMUM WAGES

Agricultural workers are subject to the National Minimum Wage (NMW) as follows:

Minimum Wage from April 2021	£/hour
23 Years and over *	**£8.91**
21 – 22 years	£8.36
18 – 20 years	£6.56
16 – 17 years	£4.62
1st year apprentice under 19	£4.30

* This is projected to rise to £9.42/hour in April 2022 by the Low Wage Commission

The rates above apply from 1 April 2021 and are reviewed annually by the Low Wage Commission. Most farmers pay a higher wage than legally necessary to attract greater calibre staff (as shown on page 158). More qualified workers such as machinery operators and livestock handlers command a premium. There are some occasions when the minimum wage is applicable in agriculture.

STATUTORY LIVING AND MINIMUM WAGE RATES - ENGLAND

The Agricultural Wages Board (England & Wales) ended in 2013 (Scotland, which has its own AWB is not affected). No changes can be made to existing agricultural workers employment contracts without mutual consent.

For workers Employed before 30th September 2013, Terms and Conditions under the Agricultural Wages Order (AWO) remain in place (unless there is a variation to the employee's terms and conditions of employment). For workers classified as Initial Grade under the 2012 AWO and employed before the 30th September 2013, the minimum wage increases in line with the National Living Wage.

For workers Employed after 30th September 2013, employers can decide on the rate of pay increases and other employment related benefits, with no standard increases dependent on skill level, responsibilities or qualifications.

STATUTORY MINIMUM WAGE RATES - SCOTLAND

The Scottish Agricultural Wages Board (SAWB) continues to operate, setting wages at the same level as the UK Living Wage. The following rates applied from the 1ˢᵗ April 2021;

	39 Hr Weekly Rate	Hourly Rate*	Overtime per Hour (2)
	£	£	£
All Workers (1)...	347.49	8.91	13.37
SCQF Level 4 or 5 apprentices *	217.62	5.58	8.37

1. *Hourly Rate.* This is a single rate irrespective of worker age, full or part time or what work is done.

2. *Overtime.* This is 1.5 times the normal rate when worked over 8 hours on any day or starting after 48 hours have been worked in the week for those in their first 26 weeks of employment and after 39 hours for others.

3. *For* appropriately qualified workers add £1.32 per hour

4. Those owning dogs as part of their work 6.57/dog/week (up to 4 dogs)

5. Accommodation provision (other than a house) £8.36/day off-set

6. * SCQF = Scottish Credit and Qualifications Framework or equivalent.

STATUTORY MINIMUM WAGE RATES - WALES

The abolition of the Agricultural Wages Board applied to England and Wales but the Welsh Government established its own Wages Board for Wales and operates, setting wages at the same level as the UK Living Wage ever since. The Agriculture Wages Order (Wales) 2021 is still 'under consideration' when this book went to press:

Normal Hours (Standard Rates) Agriculture Order 2020 still most recent

	39 Hr Weekly	Weekly Rate	Per Hour	Overtime Rate*
		£	£	£
Grade 1.	**23 and Over**	347.49	**8.91**	13.37
Grade 1.	21 - 22 years	326.04	8.36	12.54
Grade 1.	16 -20 years	305.76	7.84	11.76
Grade 2.	23 and Over	347.49	8.91	13.37
Grade 3.	Lead Worker	347.49	8.91	13.37
Grade 4.	Craft Grade	371.67	9.53	14.30
Grade 5.	Supervisory Grade	392.34	10.06	15.09
Grade 6.	Farm Management Grade	422.37	10.83	16.25
Apprentice:	Year 1 (all ages)	161.85	4.15	6.23
	Year 2 ~ 16-17 years	170.43	4.37	6.56
	Year 2 ~ 18-20 years	251.55	6.45	9.68
	Year 2 ~ 21-24 years	326.04	8.36	12.54
	Year 25 years and over	347.49	8.91	13.37

1. *Overtime rates are 1.5 times basic pay for all grades of worker*

2. *On-call allowance is set as the sum of two hours of overtime pay.*

3. *Night work supplement is specified at £1.58 per hour.*

4. *Dog allowance is £8.32 per dog.*

WORKPLACE PENSION SCHEMES

All employers in the UK must offer a workplace pension scheme. Unless they actively opt-out, all workers must be automatically enrolled into a scheme if they are:

- Employed as a worker
- Aged between 22 and state pension age (varies according to age and gender) although workers between 16 and 74 have a right to *opt in*
- Earning at least £10,000 per year (although those earning £6,240 per year have a right to *opt in*).

The employer is obliged to pay a minimum contribution into the pension as shown below, and the employee has to make up to at least the total minimum contribution (either employer or employee could pay more).

Employer Contribution	Employee Contribution	Total Minimum Contribution
3%	5%	8%

FARM MANAGERS SURVEY 2020

The average pre-tax cash earnings (average basic salary plus average bonus/profit share) for 2020 was £46,527 plus £3,016 bonusses with non-cash benefits of £8,368 giving a total of £57,911. Factors such as age, experience, farm size and number of employees managed all influence pay levels.

Over half of farm managers now have a full degree and have done post-graduation management training. Older and more experienced managers tend to earn more, averages rising from £37,000 for under 30-year olds to over £67,000 for those 60 or over. Unfortunately, still only 2% are female.

Farm managers are mostly paid under fixed salary schemes (60%), although often with bonuses or profit share arrangements alongside and some on a purely profit share basis. Holiday entitlements tend to be 21-30 days per year excluding public holidays. Earning go up with age (and therefore presumably experience). Members of the Institute of Farm Management are paid more than those who are not.

Farm managers are usually employed by private individuals and after that, increasingly land management companies. Almost all (94%) have either an agricultural degree or diploma. Typical responsibilities on top of manual duties include day-to-day organisation, staff management, stock and machinery sales and purchases, and farm system decisions and can often include at least partial responsibility for investment decisions and financial control.

Reference: IAgrM Survey of Farm Managers in 2020; Their Jobs and Their Pay. Crane R.T., Redman G.P., Bywater, V.A., Pub; Institute of Agricultural Management, 2020.

TYPICAL ANNUAL LABOUR COST

Estimated for 2021/22 (from 1st April 2021), based on a minimum wage (Standard) Worker and ASHE Median Labour costs.

Minimum Wage Labour Costs (1)		Hourly rate	Weekly	Annual	Cost per hour worked
			(39 hours)	(52 weeks)	(1755 hrs/yr)
		£	£	£	£
Standard worker Gross Basic Salary		8.91	347.49	18,132	10.33
National Insurance Contribution (NI)	13.8%	1.23	47.95	2,502	
Employers Liability Insurance (ELI)	1.0%	0.09	3.47	181	
Workplace Pension Employers Contribution	3.0%	0.27	10.42	544	
Minimum Cost to Employer		**10.50**	**409.34**	**21,359**	**12.17**
Overtime					(450 hrs/yr)
Typical additional hours/working week	10				
Number of weeks overtime worked	45				
Standard Overtime Rate		13.37	133.65	6,014	
NI & ELI		1.98	19.78	890	
Workplace Pension Employers Contribution		0.40	4.01	180	
Total Cost to employer for overtime hours		**15.74**	**157.44**	**7,085**	
Total Cost to employer for all hours		**11.57**	**566.78**	**28,444**	**12.90**
Employers Gross Earnings			481.14	24,146	10.95

Median Labour Costs (2)		Hourly rate	Weekly	Annual	Cost per hour worked
			(40 hours)	(52 weeks)	(1800 hrs/yr)
		£	£	£	£
Median worker Gross Basic Salary		11.19	447.43	23,346	13.30
National Insurance Contribution	13.8%	1.54	61.75	3,222	
Employers Liability Insurance	1.0%	0.11	4.47	233	
Workplace Pension Employers Contribution	3.0%	0.34	13.42	700	
Minimum Cost to Employer		**13.18**	**527.08**	**27,502**	**15.67**
Overtime					(108.1 hrs/yr)
Typical additional hours/working week	2.3				
Number of weeks overtime worked	47				
Standard Overtime Rate		16.78	38.59	1,814	
NI & ELI		2.48	5.71	268	
Workplace Pension Employers Contribution		0.50	1.16	54	
Total Cost to employer for overtime hours		**19.77**	**45.46**	**2,137**	
Total Cost to employer for all hours			**572.54**	**29,639**	**15.91**
Employers Gross Earnings		13.19	486.03	25,160	11.41

1. **Standard Labour Costs** are based on the 'Standard Worker', as set by the UK Minimum Wage 2021 (and Welsh & Scottish Standard Agricultural Worker).

2. *Per Hours worked: Average basic hours per* year = 1,755 hours, i.e. statutory holidays (23 days), public holidays (8 days) and illness (3 days), have been deducted from 52 weeks x 39 hours = 2028.

3. **Median Labour Costs** are based on the average farm worker earnings and hours according to the Annual Survey of Hours and Earnings.

LABOUR HOURS AVAILABLE FOR FIELD WORK

This section calculates the theoretical maximum time a single worker could spend on fieldwork per month in 2022.

Hours available for fieldwork per worker per month in 2022

	Total Ordinary Hours (1)	Adjusted Ordinary Hours (2)	Per cent workable (3)	Available Hours (4,5,6)		Total Available Hours (7)		percent o/t at w-ends (8)
				Ordinary	Overtime			
Jan	160	148	50%	74	33 (60)	106	(134)	100%
Feb	160	148	50%	74	31 (60)	105	(134)	76%
Mar	184	171	60%	102	63 (69)	165	(171)	45%
Apr	152	141	65%	92	91 (57)	183	(149)	46%
May	168	156	70%	109	107 (84)	216	(193)	45%
Jun	160	148	75%	111	111 (80)	223	(191)	47%
Jul	168	156	75%	117	114 (84)	231	(201)	45%
Aug	176	163	75%	122	112 (88)	235	(210)	42%
Sep	176	163	70%	114	100 (88)	214	(202)	39%
Oct	168	156	65%	101	79 (63)	180	(164)	49%
Nov	176	162	50%	81	34 (66)	116	(147)	69%
Dec	160	148	50%	74	33 (60)	106	(134)	100%

1. *Ordinary Hours:* 8 hours per working day (less 8 bank holidays). No deductions have been made for other holidays because they may be taken at various times of the year.

2. *After deducting* for illness (1.5% Nov. to Feb., 1% March to Oct.), and for contingencies and non-delayable maintenance (½ hour/day).

3. *Per cent Workable:* estimates severe weather, soil conditions e.g. waterlogging etc.

4. *Available Ordinary Hours:* Adjusted Ordinary Hours x Percentage Workable.

5. *Available Overtime Hours: Daylight hours above working day (8 hours)* to a maximum of 4 hours per day and 12 to 14 hours at weekends according to season. Same adjustments for illness and percentage workable.

6. Available Hours in brackets indicate hours available if headlights used, up to 4 hours/day (summer) and 3 hours/day (winter).

7. *Total Available Hours:* Time potentially to undertake fieldwork in daylight and (in brackets) with headlights.

8. *Overtime at Weekends.* Out of hours fieldwork that is undertaken in daylight.

Additional Notes

9. *Figures relate to medium land.* The percentage workability will be higher with light soils, less with heavy soils. On heavy soils, land may be almost 100% unworkable from late November to early March (or later, according to the season), particularly if un-drained. A rough estimate of variations in workability according to soil type (compared with the figures above) is as follows.

   Heavy land - March, October, November: 30% less; April: 20% less; September: 10% less; May to August: no difference. Light land — October to April: 15% more; May and September: 10% more; June to August: no difference.

10. *Indoor work,* e.g. livestock tending or potato riddling, continues over the full working week Also, some handwork in the field has to continue even in rain, e.g. sprout picking.

11. *Percentage workability* varies according to the particular operation, e.g. compare ploughing and harvesting.

2.   SEASONAL LABOUR REQUIREMENTS

CROP TIMINGS IN A NORMAL SEASON:

Winter Wheat

Drilling mid-September to 3rd week October.
Harvesting mid-August to approx. 10th September.

Winter Barley

As for winter wheat, except that:

- Ploughing unlikely to start before cereal harvest, as usually follows a cereal crop.
- Harvesting some weeks earlier: mid-July to approx. 10th August.

Winter Oats

As for winter wheat, except that:

- Drilling usually first half of October.
- Harvesting earlier (late July or first half of August).

Spring Barley

Drilling end of February to very early April
Harvesting last half of August to early September

Spring Wheat

As for spring barley, except that:

- Drilling on average 1-2 weeks earlier (should finish in March) - lose more if later than barley.
- Harvesting, on average, 2 weeks later: last week August/first half of September (two-thirds in September).

Spring Oats

As for spring barley, except that:

- Drilling usually a little earlier.
- Harvesting is later than spring barley, earlier than spring wheat: end of August/beginning of September.

Critical Questions affecting Timing for Spring-sown Cereals

1. What was the previous crop?
2. Will the crop be ploughed traditionally, chisel ploughed, subsoiled, minimally cultivated, or direct drilled?
3. Months when winter ploughing is possible, on average (where relevant).
4. Is spring ploughing satisfactory (where relevant)?
5. Average period of cultivations and drilling.
6. Earliest dates for starting and finishing spring cultivations/drilling and latest dates for starting and finishing cultivations/drilling, ignoring extreme seasons (1 year in 10).
7. Effect on yield if drilling is delayed.
8. Is the crop rolled (a) within a few days of drilling or (b) later?
9. (a) Average period of harvesting.
   (b) Earliest dates for starting and finishing harvest, and latest dates for starting and finishing harvest, ignoring extreme seasons (one year in ten).

Critical Questions affecting Timing for Autumn-sown Cereals

1. What weed control is required, particularly of herbicide tolerant grasses?
2. What was the previous crop (affects time available and need for deep cultivations)?
3. Will the crop be ploughed traditionally, chisel ploughed, subsoiled, minimally cultivated, or direct drilled?
4. Earliest and latest drilling date, by choice.
5. Effect on yield if drilling is delayed.
6. In the spring: (a) whether crop is rolled, and when,
   (b) whether crop is harrowed, and when,
   (c) time of top dressings,
   (d) number of spray applications.
7. (a) Average period for harvesting.
   (b) Earliest dates for starting and finishing harvest, and latest dates for starting and finishing harvest, ignoring extreme seasons (1 year in 10).

CROPS AND GRASS LABOUR REQUIREMENTS

On the following pages, data on labour requirements for various crops and types of livestock are given. Two levels are shown: average and premium. The average figures relate to the whole range of conditions and commercial farm sizes, i.e. small and medium-sized farms as well as large; the figures give all farms equal weight.

The premium rates do not denote the maximum rates possible, for instance by the use of high-powered tractors under ideal conditions but relate to rates of work estimated to be obtainable over the whole season, averaging good and bad conditions, with the use of wide implements, relatively large tractors (170hp (126kW) to over 200hp (148kW)) and high-capacity equipment in up to 8-hectare fields and over, where no time is wasted. Most farmers with more than 250 hectares (620 acres) of arable land ought to achieve at least the premium levels shown. Those with over 450 hectares (1,110 acres) will have still bigger machines and therefore faster work rates, and thus require 15 to 25% less labour per hectare than even the premium levels given.

The rates of work include:

- preparation,
- travelling to fields,
- minor breakdowns and
- other stoppages
- They relate broadly to medium and medium-heavy land

Some jobs, such as ploughing, may be done more quickly on light soils. Operations such as combine harvesting vary according to factors to do with the topography and other natural features of the farm as well as crop and yield.

The usual times of year when each operation takes place are shown; these relate to lowland conditions. They will vary between seasons, soil types, latitude and altitude. In particular, light land can be ploughed over a longer winter period and a high proportion of cultivations for spring crops may be completed in February in many seasons. All such factors must be allowed for in individual farm planning. Conditions in different seasons also affect, for instance, the number and type of cultivations required in seedbed preparation. Typical monthly breakdowns of requirements are given for various crops.

To illustrate the type of questions that need to be asked for full details of seasonal labour requirements on the individual farm, critical questions affecting timing are listed for cereals.

Note: These data are old and little new research has been completed to replace it with. However, productivity per labour unit has increased since then.

Winter Cereals

Operations	Labour-hours per hectare Average	Premium	Time of Year
Plough (1)	1.4	1.0	July to October (according to previous crop)
Cultivate (often power harrow).	1.0	0.7	September to October (according to previous crop) (½ Aug if ploughed in July)
Drill (often with power harrows followed by roll)	1.1	0.7	Mid-September to 3rd week October (according to previous crop and soil)
Apply Fertiliser	0.3	0.2	
Spray	0.3	0.2	October-November
Top Dress (three times [2])	0.9	0.6	March and April
Spray (three or four [2])	1.0	0.5	March-June
Combine, Cart Grain, Barn Work	2.5	1.9	Mid-Aug to approx. 10th Sept
Later Barn Work (3)	0.7	0.4	September to June
Total	**9.2**	**6.2**	
Straw: Bale	1.3	0.8	Mid-August to end
Cart	3.5	2.6	September

Typical Monthly Breakdown

Month	Average	Premium	Notes
October	2.4	1.7	Approx. 60% of Ploughing,
November	—	—	Cults., Drill, Harrow
December	—	—	
January	—	—	
February	—	—	
March	0.4	0.2	Part Top Dress
April	0.8	0.5	Part Top Dress, Spraying
May	0.3	0.2	Spraying
June	0.3	0.2	Spraying
July	—	—	
August	1.7 (+2.4 Straw)	1.3 (+1.7 Straw)	⅔ of harvesting (4)
September (harvest)	0.9 (+2.4 Straw)	0.6 (+1.7 Straw)	⅓ of harvesting (4)
September (prepn. drill)	1.7	1.1	40% of Ploughing, Cults., Drill, Harrow

1. *Some cereal crops* are direct drilled or drilled after reduced, or minimal, cultivations, i.e. without traditional ploughing. Direct drilling reduces man-hours per hectare by about 2.5 (average) or 1.8 (premium), and minimal cultivations by about 1.2 (average) and 0.9 (premium).

2. *This is for winter wheat;* winter barley will often have one less top dressing and spraying and oats two less. Also see next page for harvest times for winter barley and oats.

3. *Later barn work* is excluded from monthly breakdown.

Spring Cereals

Operations	Labour-Hours per hectare		Time of Year
	Average	Premium	
Plough (1)................................	1.4	1.0	July to October (according to previous crop and soil type)
Cultivate (often power harrow)...	1.0	0.7	March (½ in second half February on light land)
Apply Fertiliser...........................	0.3	0.2	
Drill (often with power harrow), plus roll	1.2	0.8	March (½ at end February on light land)
Top Dress (once, some possibly twice)......................................	0.4	0.2	
Spray (two or three)....................	0.7	0.3	May
Combine, Cart Grain, Barn Work	2.4	1.8	Last ¾ of August (affected by variety and season)
Later Barn Work (2)...................	0.6	0.4	September to June
Total...	**8.0**	**5.4**	
Straw: Bale (unmanned sledge)	1.3	0.8	Mid-August to end
Cart...	3.5	2.6	September

Typical Monthly Breakdown

Month	Average	Premium	Notes
October......................................	0.4	0.3	Ploughing. How much in
November...................................	0.8	0.5	October depends on area
December	0.2	0.2	W. Wheat, Potatoes, etc.
January	—	—	
February	—	—	
March	2.4	1.6	All Cults. Drilling, Rolling, (nearly half in February on light land)
April	—	—	
May	1.1	0.6	Spray and Top dress
June	—	—	
July..	—	—	
August (3)..................................	2.4	1.8	Harvesting
	(+2.6 Straw)	(+1.8 Straw)	
September...................................	—	—	
	(+2.2 Straw)	(+1.6 Straw)	

1. *Autumn drilling* preferable if possible to allow frost to crumble soils
2. *Later barn work* excluded.
3. *This is for spring barley*; spring wheat and oats partly September.

Maincrop Potatoes

	Labour-Hours per hectare		
Operations	Average	Premium	Time of Year
Plough	1.4	1.0	September to December
Cultivating, Ridging, De-stoning/			
Clod Sep. (as required)	6.5	5.0	March, early April
Plant and Apply Fertiliser (1)	4.5	3.5	Last quarter of March, first
Apply Herbicide	0.3	0.2	three-quarters of April
Spray for Blight (av. 6 times)	1.2	0.9	July, first half August
Burn off Haulm	0.3	0.2	End September, early
			October
Harvest, Cart, Clamp (2).............	15.0	10.0	End September, October
Work on Indoor Clamp...............	4.8	3.2	November
Riddle, Bag, Load......................	40.0	30.0	October to May
Total...	**74.0**	**54.0**	

1. *Automatic planter.* Hand-fed planters: approx. 12hrs plus 8 (could be casual labour).

2. *Mechanical harvester,* excluding up to 25 hours for picking off on harvester - usually casual labour. None may be needed on clod and stone-free soils. Hand harvesting: additional approx. 80 hours of casual labour.

Typical Monthly Breakdown

Month	Average	Premium	Notes
March	7.8	6.0	All fert', ½ cults', ¼ plant
April	3.5	2.7	½ cult's, ¾ plant
May	—	—	
June	—	—	
July...	0.9	0.7	3 blight sprays
August...	0.3	0.2	1 blight spray
September.....................................	3.1	2.0	20% harvest, ½ burn off
October...	12.2	8.2	80% of harvest, ½ burn off
November.....................................	5.9	4.0	Clamp work and ¾ plough
December	0.3	0.2	¼ plough
January	—	—	
February	—	—	

These figures exclude casual labour and riddling.

Early Potatoes

Operations	Labour-Hours per hectare		Time of Year
	Average	Premium	
Plough	1.4	1.0	September to December
Cultivating, etc.	6.5	5.0	Late February, early March
Plant and Apply Fertiliser...........	4.5	3.5	Late February, early March
Apply Herbicide	0.3	0.2	1st half March (some in February on light land or in early season)
Further Spraying........................	0.3	0.2	
After-Cultivation/Spray..............	0.3	0.2	April, early May
Harvest, bag, load......................	30.0 (1)	25.0 (2)	2nd week June onwards. All June or till mid-July

1. Excluding 80 hours picking—usually casuals.
2. Excluding 60 hours picking—usually casuals.

Second Early Potatoes

Operations	Labour-Hours per hectare		Time of Year
	Average	Premium	
Plough	1.4 (1)	1.0 (1)	September to December
Cultivating, etc	6.5 (1)	5.0 (1)	March
Plant and Apply Fertiliser...........	4.5 (1)	3.5 (1)	March
Apply Herbicide	0.3 (1)	0.2 (1)	Half 2nd half March, half 1st half April
Further Spraying........................	0.9 (1)	0.7 (1)	End April, May, early June
Harvest	15.0 (1)	10.0 (2)	Mid-July to end August

1. *Spinner or elevator-digger*, excluding picking and riddling—usually casual labour.
2. *Mechanical harvester*, excluding picking off on harvester/riddling - usually casual.

Sugar Beet

Operations	Labour-Hours per hectare		Time of Year
	Average	Premium	
Plough	1.4	1.0	September to December
Seedbed Cults........................	3.2	2.2	Mainly March (some early April. Some late February in good seasons)
Load, Cart, Apply Fertiliser........	0.7	0.4	
Drill (and Flat Roll)...................	1.8	1.1	Between mid-March and mid-April
Spray (herbicide: pre- and post-emergence)	0.6	0.3	Late March/April
Spray (x 2)................................	0.6	0.3	May/June
Spray (aphis).............................	0.3	0.2	July
Harvest (machine)	14.0	9.0	End September, October, November
Load	3.4	2.5	End September to early January
Total........................	**26.0**	**17.0**	

Typical Monthly Breakdown for Sugar Beet

Month	Average	Premium	Notes
October............................	7.2	4.6	45% harvest; + loading
November	8.2	5.3	45% harvest; ¾ ploughing; + loading
December	1.0	0.8	¼ ploughing; + loading
January	0.5	0.4	Loading
February	—	—	
March	3.8	2.3	Fert., most cults., some drilling
April	2.5	1.7	Some cults., most of drilling
May	0.3	0.2	Spray
June	0.3	0.15	Spray
July..................................	0.2	0.15	Spray
August	—	—	
September........................	2.0	1.4	10% harvesting; + loading

Vining Peas

| | Labour-Hours per hectare | | |
Operations	Average	Premium	Time of Year
Plough	1.4	1.0	September to December
Cults, Fert. and Drill..................	2.3	1.6	Mid-Feb. to April
Post Drilling and Spraying..........	1.5	0.8	
Harvesting	19.0	14.0	July and early August
Total..	**24.2**	**17.4**	

Drilling is staggered in small areas through the season, ranging from early varieties to late varieties.

Dried Peas

| | Labour-Hours per hectare | | |
Month	Average	Premium	Notes
October..	1.2	0.8	
November....................................	0.8	0.5	Stubble cult., Plough
December	—	—	
January	—	—	
February	0.2	0.1	Cult. x 2, harrow; drill & fert.
March	2.8	1.9	(80% March); light harrow
April	0.6	0.4	roll; and spray
May	2.5	1.2	
June	0.2	0.2	Scare pigeons; spray
July...	1.8	1.1	Possible spray desiccant;
August..	2.2	1.3	combine and cart, dry
September....................................	0.5	0.3	Stubble cult.

Assumes direct combining.

Field Beans

Winter Beans

Operations	Labour-Hours per hectare		Time of Year
	Average	Premium	
Broadcast Seed	0.6	0.4	
Apply Fertiliser............................	0.3	0.2	
Plough	1.4	1.0	September/October
Power Harrow..............................	1.0	0.8	
Spray (pre-emergence)	0.3	0.15	
Spraying (two or three times)	0.8	0.35	Spring
Combine and cart and			
Barn-work....................................	3.0	2.4	August

Spring Beans

Operations	Labour-Hours per hectare		Time of Year
	Average	Premium	
Plough	1.4	1.0	September to December
Cultivate (often power harrow)...	1.0	0.7	
Apply Fertiliser............................	0.3	0.2	
Drill, Roll	1.2	0.8	End Feb, early March
Spray (two or three times)	0.8	0.4	
Combine and cart and			
Barn-work....................................	3.0	2.4	September

Winter Oilseed Rape (*Desiccated*)

Month	Labour-Hours per hectare		Notes
	Average	Premium	
October............................			
November........................	0.6	0.3	Spray herbicide and
December			insecticide if necessary
January	—	—	
February	—	—	
March			
April	0.8	0.4	Top dress twice
May	—	—	
June	—	—	Desiccate (1st half July);
July..................................	2.4	1.7	combine (½ 2nd half July
August	2.0	1.4	½ 1st half Aug.); dry
August	1.6	0.9	Cults. (x 2), spray, drill, fert.;
September	1.6	0.9	harrow, roll, barn work (0.5)

Herbage Seed *(first production year)*

Undersown

Operations	Labour-Hours per hectare		Time of Year
	Average	Premium	
Undersown	0.6	0.4	March, April
Roll.. {	(0.6	0.4)	Straight after drilling
	0.4	0.3	September
	0.4	0.3	Late February, March
Harvest (by Combine): Mow	1.4	0.9	3 to 4 days before combining
Combine and Cart.......................	4.5	3.5	Ital. Ryegrasses and Early *Perennials: late July.* *Intermed. Perennials: late July/early August.* *Late Perennials/White Clover: mid-August*
	6.0	4.5	Meadow Fescue: early July
	7.0	5.0	Cocksfoot: early July
	10.0	7.0	Timothy: mid-August Red Clover: late September

Direct Drilled in Autumn

Operations	Labour-Hours per hectare		Time of Year
	Average	Premium	
Plough	1.4	1.0	
Seedbed Cults.............................	2.2	1.6	Depends on previous crop—
Load, Cart, Apply Fertiliser........	0.3	0.2	Usually July or August
Drill (with harrows behind)	0.8	0.6	As early as previous crop allows. This may be up to mid-Sept for ryegrass without detriment to the yield.
Roll (soon after drilling).............	0.6	0.4	Meadow fescue and cocksfoot are best sown no later than July and it is risky to sow Timothy much later than this.

Grass

Production

Operations	Labour-Hours per hectare		Time of Year
	Average	Premium	
Plough	1.4	1.0	Autumn drilling. If necessary.
Seedbed Cults.............................	2.2	1.6	
Load, Cart, Apply Fertiliser........	0.3	0.2	
Drill*	0.7	0.5	Mid-March to mid-April (1) or end July to mid-Sept.
Roll..	0.6	0.4	Soon after drilling
Load, Cart, Apply Fertiliser* (three lots)	0.9	0.6	March to mid-August (2)
Top*	1.3	0.8	Mid-June to mid-July; if grazed only.

1. * These operations apply only where the seeds are undersown in a spring cereal crop soon after drilling. One extra harrowing and rolling is needed if undersown in an autumn-sown cereal crop.
2. *Spring drilling* may continue to mid-May to enable extra cleaning cultivations or the application of farmyard manure.
3. *P. and K.* may be applied in September - especially on undersown ley in year sown.

Conservation

Operations	Labour-Hours per hectare		Time of Year
	Average	Premium	
Plough	1.4	1.0	Autumn drilling: If necessary.
Hay (5.5 tonnes per hectare)			
Mow	1.2	0.9	
Turn, etc	2.6	1.9	Two-thirds June, one-third
Bale	1.3	0.9	July
Cart......................................	6.0	4.5	
Total per hectare........................	11.1	8.2	
Total per tonne...........................	2.0	1.5	
Silage (17 tonnes per hectare)			
Mow	1.2	0.9	
Turn, etc	0.7	0.5	Two-thirds May, one-third
Load......................................	2.3	1.7	June
Cart......................................	3.0	2.3	
Clamp...................................	2.3	1.7	
Total per hectare........................	9.5	7.1	
Total per tonne...........................	0.56	0.42	

Specialised Equipment Prices for Grass Conservation: see page 163.

Typical Monthly Breakdown

Production (figures averaged over the life of the ley)

	1-year ley undersown in spring		3-year ley undersown in autumn (1)		1-year ley drilled		3-year ley drilled	
	Ave.	Prem.	Ave.	Prem.	Ave.	Prem.	Ave.	Prem.
March	0.9	0.5	0.7	0.5	0.6	0.3	0.6	0.3
April	0.9	0.5	0.7	0.5	0.6	0.3	0.6	0.3
May	0.6	0.3	0.6	0.3	0.6	0.3	0.6	0.3
June	0.6	0.3	0.6	0.3	0.6	0.3	0.6	0.3
July............	0.6	0.3	0.6	0.3	0.6	0.3	0.6	0.3
August	0.3	0.2	0.3	0.2	5.0	3.4	1.9	1.4
September...	0.6	0.3	0.3	0.2	3.2	2.2	1.4	1.0

1. *If ploughed after a cereal crop,* drilled early August to mid-September.

	1-year ley drilled in autumn (1)		3-year ley drilled in spring		Permanent Pasture	
	Ave.	Prem.	Ave.	Prem.	Ave.	Prem.
March	3.0	2.1	1.4	1.0	0.6	0.3
April	1.8	1.2	0.9	0.7	0.6	0.3
May	0.3	0.3	0.6	0.3	0.6	0.3
June	0.6	0.3	0.6	0.3	0.6	0.3
July	0.6	0.3	0.6	0.3	0.6	0.3
August	0.3	0.2	0.2	0.2	0.3	0.2
September	—	—	—	0.2	0.2	0.2
October	0.9	0.5	0.6	0.3	—	—
November	1.4	1.0	1.0	0.3	—	—
December	0.7	0.5	0.6	0.2	—	—

Conservation

	Hay				Silage			
	per hectare		per tonne		per hectare		per tonne	
	Av.	Prem.	Av.	Prem.	Av.	Prem.	Av.	Prem.
May	—	—	—	—	6.3	4.7	0.37	0.28
June	7.4	5.6	1.3	1.0	3.2	2.4	0.19	0.14
July	3.7	2.6	0.7	0.5	—	—	—	—

Kale

Production

Operations	Labour-Hours per hectare		Time of Year
	Average	Premium	
Plough	1.4	1.0	September onwards
Seedbed Cults	2.2	1.6	March, April, early May
Fertiliser	0.3	0.2	April, early May
Drill	1.3	1.0	May
Roll	0.6	0.4	Straight after drilling
Spray (weed killer)	0.3	0.2	6 weeks after drilling

Catch Crop

Kale may be drilled up to the first week of July; the crop will be smaller but either an early bite or silage crop may have been taken from a ley earlier in the year, or the ground may have been fallowed and thoroughly cleaned during the spring and early summer. The smaller crop is also easier to graze using an electric fence.

The above operations will still apply although the times of the year will obviously be different, but there may be an additional three or so rotavations and two or three heavy cultivations if fallowed for the first half of the year or ploughed after an early bite. This means approximately an extra 10 (average) or 8 (premium) man-hours per hectare in April, May, June.

LABOUR FOR LIVESTOCK

This data is updated for 2022

Dairy Cows

The hours worked by a typical dairy farm worker is falling. In previous pocketbook editions, the dairy farm worker's year was 2,770 hours (a full-time worker plus 10 hours overtime per week). The figures now are for somebody working 2,216 hours a year, equivalent to 8-hours a day for 6 days a week minus standard holidays etc.

Hours Labour Requirement per cow

	Calving:	Spring	Autumn	AYR	
	l/cow	5250	7000	8000	9500
January		0.5	2.5	3.1	3.8
February		1.9	2.4	3.1	3.8
March		2	2.2	3.1	3.8
April		2.2	2.0	3.0	3.8
May		2.2	1.8	2.7	3.5
June		2	1.3	2.6	3.2
July		1.9	1.5	2.6	3.2
August		1.7	2.7	2.6	3.2
September		1.5	2.9	2.8	3.5
October		1.5	2.9	3.1	3.8
November		1.3	2.7	3.1	3.8
December		1.1	2.6	3.1	3.8
Total		**19.8**	**27.5**	**34.9**	**43.2**
Seconds/L		13.6	14.1	15.7	16.4
Cost; p/l		4.9	5.1	5.6	5.9
Thousand litres per worker		588	564	508	487

No time is allocated here for youngstock. This schedule is based on a 200-cow herd for each calving system. Low yielding cows tend to spend more time at grass and less housed. High milk yielders and all-year round calving herds take more management time. The most labour efficient milk producing operations in the UK achieve over 800,000 litres per employed worker.

Hours staff Requirement per Cow per Year.

Calving System	Spring	Autumn	AYR	AYR
Cow Annual Milk Yield (L)	5,500	7,000	8,000	9,000
Cows per Herd				
100..............................	20.5	28.4	36.1	44.7
150..............................	19.8	27.5	34.9	43.2
225..............................	18.9	26.2	33.2	41.1
350..............................	17.5	24.3	30.8	38.1
500..............................	16.1	12.3	28.3	35.0

Labour Cost per Litre

Calving:	Spring	Autumn	AYR	
ppl	5250	7000	8000	9500
100	5.0	5.2	5.8	6.1
150	4.9	5.1	5.6	5.9
225	4.6	4.8	5.4	5.6
350	4.3	4.5	5.0	5.2
500	3.9	4.1	4.6	4.8

Earnings. The average earnings of 'dairy herdsmen' in 2022/23 is estimated at £28,000 working 2,216 hours (8 hours for 277 days). This includes relief milking etc. but no cover for young stock or fieldwork, such as hay and silage making.

Dairy Followers and Beef

No recent survey work has been published on labour requirements for beef animals and dairy followers. The following data is therefore only 'best estimates'. They are for average performance and average conditions, excluding fieldwork. Substantial variations occur, e.g. through differing management styles or economies of scale with differing herd sizes.

Calves *(per head, early weaning)*	**Labour hours per month**	
Age Group	*Average*	*Premium*
0-3 months	2.3	1.6
3-6 months	0.9	0.6
(av. 0-6 months	*1.6*	*1.1)*
6-12 months, yarded	1.1	0.8
6-12 months, summer grazed	0.3	0.2
(av. 0-12 months, during winter *(1)*	1.3	0.9)
(av. 0-12 months, during summer *(1)*	0.9	0.6)

Assuming 6 to 12-month olds housed in winter and grazed in summer, and calvings or calf purchases fairly evenly spaced throughout the year.

Stores *(per head)*		
Yearling, housed	1.0	0.7
2-year olds and over, housed	1.4	0.8
Out-wintered store	0.7	0.5
12 months and over, summer grazed	0.2	0.1

Dairy Followers

(Per 'replacement unit', i.e. calf + yearling + in-calf heifer.) (1)		
During winter	2.9	2.0
During summer	1.2	0.8

Assuming calvings evenly spaced through the year and heifers calve at 2 to 2.5 years

Beef Finishing *(per head)*		
Housed	1.8	1.2
Summer Grazed	0.2	0.1
Intensive Beef (0-12 months)	1.3	1.0

Suckler Herds *(per cow, average whole year)*		
Lowland Single suckling	0.9	0.6
Lowland Multiple suckling	2.9	2.1
Upland/Hill Single suckling	1.1	0.7

Sheep *(per Ewe)*

	Labour hours per month	
	Average	*Premium*
January	0.3	0.2
February	0.3	0.2
March	1.0 *(1)*	0.7
April	0.4	0.25
May	0.3	0.2
June	0.4 *(2)*	0.3
July	0.2	0.15
August	0.2	0.15
Septembe	0.25	0.15
October	0.25	0.15
November	0.2	0.15
December	0.2	0.15
Total	*4.0 (3)*	*2.75*

1. Assuming mainly March lambing.
2. 0.3 if shearing is by contract.
3. A full-time shepherd, i.e. one who did no other work on the farm, would have a flock of 550 ewes for the average 4 hours per ewe per year to be achieved, assuming full-time assistance during lambing time. Some farms achieve 3 times this number of ewes per single worker.

Pigs

	Labour hours per month	
Age Group	*Average*	*Premium*
Breeding and Rearing, per sow	1.5	1.20
(Average 130 sows per worker, Premium 160)		
Feeding only, per 10 pigs	1.6	1.25
No. at a time, per worker:		
Average 1,200 per man, Premium 1,600		
No. per year, per worker:		
Average: 6,000 porkers, 4,800 cutters, 4,450 baconers		
Premium: 8,000 porkers, 6,400 cutters, 5,750 baconers		
Breeding, Rearing and Feeding, per sow (with progeny)		
Porkers, average 90 sows per worker, premium 110	2.4	2.0
Cutters, average 80-85 sows per worker, premium 100-105	2.6	2.1
Baconers, average 75-80 sows per worker, premium 95-100	2.8	2.2

Poultry *(large scale, automated)*   **Labour hours per month**

Laying hens: battery cages (18,000 per full-time worker).   1.1 per 100

free range ....   4 per 100

Broilers: 32,500 at a time per full-time worker*

(225,000 a year) ....   1.0 per 100

* additional help needed for catching and cleaning out (included in labour hours/ month)

3. STANDARD MAN DAYS

Standard Man Days (SMD) is a general estimate of the farm labour requirement per enterprise. A Standard Man Year is 2,200 hours. This is 45 weeks' work of 39 hours (after holidays, illnesses etc. have been deducted), plus an average of 10 hours overtime per week (45 x 49 = 2,205). These total hours are converted into 275 notional 8-hour Standard Man Days. This figure includes an assessment for overtime but can be increased by further overtime working.

Every farm enterprise requires a number of SMDs per unit of key input (per hectare, per cow etc.). The total SMD requirement for each enterprise is therefore calculated by multiplying by the size of the operation. The total labour needed on the holding is the sum of all the individual enterprises. An additional 15% has then traditionally been added to account for general maintenance, repairs and management. The total SMD requirement is then divided by 275 to find the number of full-time employees that will be required. This system can work when the labour requirement is constant during the year – e.g. some livestock enterprises. However, when labour use is seasonal, e.g. most field operations, it does not show the 'peaks and troughs' that are crucial in labour planning. It also fails to reflect that daylight hours, soil conditions, rainfall etc. will alter the amount of time available for fieldwork during the course of the year. SMD does not recognise the efficiency of larger units, so SMD requirements fall per unit as the enterprise grows. Equally, this data is designed to reflect commercial scale agriculture so will be of limited value to smallholder scale production operations.

Livestock (per head) (1)

Dairy Cows	4.00
Bulls	3.50
Beef Cows (single suckler including calf):	
lowland	1.35
upland/hill	1.68
Cereal Beef (0-12 months) (2)	1.90
18-month Beef (2)	1.60
Grass Silage Beef (2)	1.90
Finishing Suckler bred stores:	
Grass	1.10
Winter	1.10
Calves; to 6 months (2)	1.20
Ewes: lowland	0.50
upland	0.45
hill	0.40
Rams	0.50
Winter Finishing Store Lambs	0.30
Sows (including weaners to 30kg)	2.25
Boars	2.00
Other Bacon Pigs	0.25
Laying Birds: battery cages	0.017
free range	0.06
Pullets reared (2)	0.005
Broilers (2)	0.002

Crops (per hectare)	S.M.D.s
Winter Feed Wheat	
Winter Milling Wheat	
Spring Wheat	
Winter Feed Barley	1.15 /
Winter Malting Barley	1.75 (3)
Spring Malting Barley	
Winter Oats	
Spring Oats	
Winter Oilseed Rape	1.10
Spring Oilseed Rape	1.00
Linseed	1.00
Winter Field Beans	0.90
Spring Field Beans	0.95
Dried Peas	1.60
Lupins	1.50
Vining Peas	3.00
Maincrop Potatoes	9.25 (4)
Early Potatoes	5.50 (4)
Sugar Beet	3.00
Herbage Seed (Ryegrass)	1.40
Hops	9.50 (4)
Kale (grazed)	1.40
Silage:~ one cut	1.60 (5)
two cuts	2.80 (5)
Grazing only	0.40 (5)
Hay for sale	1.80 (5)
Let Keep	0.40 (5)
Bare fallow / set-aside	0.20
Rough Grazing	0.20

1. Note that for grazing livestock, the S.M.D.s per head exclude field work, e.g. grass production and silage making, i.e. the labour for these has to be added to give total labour for these enterprises.

2. For these livestock, S.M.D. per annum should be based on numbers produced (sold) during the year. For all other livestock, average numbers on the farm at any one time during the year should be used (i.e. average of numbers at end of each month).

3. 1.15 if straw ploughed in; 1.75 if straw harvested. Highly mechanised larger farms will require no more than 0.75 S.M.D./ha of direct labour for cereals and other combinable crops (assuming straw ploughed in).

4. Excludes casual labour for harvesting.

5. Excludes any reseeding carried out – this is likely to be around 0.6 S.M.D./ha in the year reseeding is carried out.

'Other Cattle' can refer to both beef animals and dairy followers (ref. detail on page 172).

Please note, that whilst this data is widely used, it is rather dated and many commercial enterprises will have more efficient working practices, requiring fewer SMD per unit of output or input (hectare or head).

V. MACHINERY

1. AGRICULTURAL MACHINERY PRICES

This schedule is for 2022 purchase of new machinery, net of discounts and ex. VAT During the early and mid-2000's, machinery price inflation was significant because of dearer raw materials and sterling weakening. Between 2010 and 2013, price changes were minimal. Between 2014 and 2015, general machinery costs increased approximately 5%, although tractors remained static in price. From 2015 to 2017, general machinery price inflation was static and for tractors was small at around 2% per year. Data from 2015 to 2020 demonstrates an average increase in machinery prices (of all types – tractors, implements, equipment) of just under 8% over the five years. This is a result of input price inflation, increasing overseas demand for second-hand machinery, Covid-19 and Brexit delays/impacts on supply. Looking at prices quoted by manufacturers and dealers recently, a further 10% has been assumed for 2022 generally. Machinery price inflation is currently one of the industry's largest input cost challenges but not fully seen yet due to the phased nature of machinery replacement policies. Prices shown are a range as they vary considerably between makes, models and specifications. Machines with a star '*' denote those used in subsequent 'farmer' cost' calculations.

Tractors

		£ Range	
(a)	Two-Wheel Drive		
	80-90 hp	44,627	51,942
	90-100 hp	49,500	52,800
(b)	Four- Wheel Drive		
*	100-120 hp	60,720	75,350
*	125-140 hp	68,035	92,906
*	150-180 hp	97,295	124,366
	180-220 hp	114,125	150,700
	225-270 hp	136,796	185,075
(c)	Crawlers - rubber tracks		
*	230-300 hp	214,335	236,280
	340-400 hp	236,280	272,855
	450-550 hp	294,800	353,320

Cultivating Equipment

(a) Ploughs

		Mechanical Adjustment		Hydraulic Adjustment	
				Variable width	
Reversible:					
	3-furrow	12,705	15,015	—	
	4-furrow	13,860	17,903	20,790	24,255
	5-furrow	20,790	24,255	25,410	28,875
*	6-furrow	23,100	25,988	28,298	36,960
	7-furrow (mounted)	34,650	41,580	41,580	48,510
	8-furrow (mounted)	40,425	48,510	48,510	57,750

Price Range

(b) Furrow Presses

	2.0-2.4 m double row	6,145	7,681
*	2.6-3.0 m double row	8,449	12,289

(c) *Front Presses (excluding linkage)*

	1.5 m single row	4,148	4,916
	3.0 m single row	5,198	8,085
*	4.0 m single row — hydraulic folding	9,240	12,128

(d) *Front Press Linkage*

1.0 to 2.0 tonne	2,310	4,505

(e) *Other Cultivating Equipment*

*	Sub Soiler 2-3 leg		9,240	16,170
	Shakarator (3m)		12,705	19,058
	Low Disturbance Sub-soiler (5 leg 3.5m)		9,818	16,898
	Stubble Cultivator - discs and press (3m)		12,289	16,898
*	(heavy duty)	(4m) hydraulic folding	21,506	29,187
		(6 m): hydraulic folding	26,115	41,476
		(8 m): hydraulic folding	34,650	48,510
		8-12m straw rakes (excl. roller)	14,438	28,875
*	Spring-tine Cultivator	(3-4 m):	10,753	18,434
		(5-6 m): hydraulic fold	15,362	24,578
	Tine / Disc Cultivator Combinations (one-pass type)			
		(3-4 m) mounted	12,705	30,723
*		(5-6 m) trailed	38,404	67,591
*	Disc Harrows	(3.6 - 4.4 m): trailed	18,434	32,271
		(4.4-6.0 m): trailed folding	32,259	53,765
		(8.0-12.0 m): trailed folding	46,200	69,300
*	Harrows (5-6 m): light-medium, hydraulic foldin		12,289	21,506
*	Rotovator		13,825	21,506
	Power Harrow (with packer roller)			
	(3 m)		9,818	12,705
*	(4m)		16,170	23,100
	(4-6m): folding		27,651	43,012
*	Rolls:	Triple gang, hydraulic folding (6 m)	9,217	16,898
		Five gang, hydraulic folding (12m)	26,115	33,795

Fertiliser Distributors, Seed Drills, Sprayers   *Price Range*

(a) *Seed Drills - standalone hydraulic or PTO fan driven*

	4 m Tine coulters	21,506	26,115
*	4.8 m Tine coulters	27,651	30,723
	6 m Tine coulters	30,723	38,404
	12 m Tine coulters	69,127	99,850
	Extra for electric controls and variable rate	3,072	3,840
	4 m Disc coulters	33,795	36,868
	4.8 m Disc coulters	39,940	46,085
	6 m Disc coulters	52,229	61,446
	12 m Disc coulters	84,488	115,211

(b)   Combined Cultivator Drills - trailed heavy duty machines

3 m	38,404	53,765
4 m	58,374	79,880
6 m	69,127	99,850
8 m	99,850	130,573

(c)   Combined Power Harrow and Pneumatic Drill

* 3 m	27,651	38,404
4 m rigid	35,331	44,548
4 m folding	49,157	61,446
6 m folding	69,127	84,488

*(d)   *Direct Drill (4m Disc Coulter)*

Direct Drill (4m Disc Coulter)	64,518	79,880
Direct Drill (6m Disc Coulter)	75,075	98,175
Direct Drill (12m Disc Coulter)	132,825	155,925
Strip Till Drill (3m)	38,404	48,510
Precision Maize Drill (12 row)	34,650	51,975

(e)   Fertiliser Distributors

Mounted Spinners

(700-1,200 litre): twin disc, hydraulic control	4,608	10,753
(1,300-1,700 litre): twin disc, hydraulic control	7,681	13,057
* (1,650-2,300 litre): twin disc, electronic control	12,289	18,434
(3,200 litre): twin disc, electronic control	18,434	24,578
Bag lifter (850-1,000kg)	2,304	3,072
Variable rate and automated headland management	1,536	3,840

(f)   Sprayers

Mounted, 600-800 litre tank, 12 m boom	6,145	15,362
Mounted, 1,000-1,800 l, 20-24 m hydraulic boom	30,723	47,621
Trailed, 2,500-3,000l tank 18-24 m boom	43,012	64,518
Trailed, 3,000-4,500l tank 24-36 m boom	49,157	89,097
Self-propelled sprayers,		
* 2,500-4,000l tank, 24-36 m boom	138,254	207,380
5,000-6,000l tank, 24 - 36m boom	207,900	288,750
Extra for auto-shut-off and boom height control	6,353	10,973

Grass Conservation and Handling Equipment   *Price Range*

(a)   Silage Equipment

* Forage Harvester: trailed, precision chop	46,085	69,127
Self-propelled (3 m pick-up 400-600 hp)	276,507	399,399
Maize attachment, 8 row	61,446	99,850
Silage Trailer, 12 tonne, tandem axle	14,438	19,635
Silage Trailer, 14 - 16 tonne, tandem axle	15,015	24,255
Buckrake (push off)	5,377	10,753

(b) Haymaking Equipment

	Mowers 1.5-1.8 m, 1-2 drum	4,301	5,837
*	Disc Conditioner, mounted (2.4-3.2 m)	9,818	13,860
	trailed (3.2 - 3.8 m)	17,325	23,100
	Rake: single/double rotor, 3.2m-4.5m range	6,145	11,521
*	multiple rotors 8-10m range	23,042	46,085
	multiple rotors 12-15m range	49,157	59,910
	Tedder/swather		
*	5-7 m, 4-6 rotors	9,217	16,898
	8-11m multiple rotors	23,042	46,085
	Balers and Bale Handling: see 5(c) and (d) below		

(c) Silage Handling Equipment

Silage shear bucket	3,072	4,608
Silage grab	2,688	4,224
Big Bale Silage Feeder, mounted	5,198	12,705
Diet-feeder Wagon (6 tonne)	11,550	21,945
Clamped Silage Mixer (10 tonne)	23,100	36,960

Grain and Straw Harvesting and Handling Equipment   ***Price Range***

(a) Combines

Engine size	Cutterbar width		
hp	metres (feet)		
220-249	4.5-5.5 (14-18)	153,615	215,061
250-299	5.4-6.6 (18-22)	184,338	261,146
300-450	6.0-7.7 (20-25)	199,700	307,230
450+	7.7-12.0 (25-40)	306,075	491,568

(b) Yield monitoring/mapping — 10,753 — 15,362
Self-levelling options — 16,898 — 24,578

(b)	*Yield monitoring/mapping*	10,753	15,362
	Self-levelling options	16,898	24,578

(c) Balers

*	Conventional Small Balers	16,130	19,970
*	Round balers, twine tying and net wrap	32,259	43,890
*	Big Square Balers	103,950	150,150

(d) Bale Wrappers

Big Bale Wrapper: trailed	13,825	24,578
Big Square Bale Wrapper: trailed	30,723	43,012
Combined Baler and Wrapper	46,085	76,808
Bale Trailers, 30 ft - 35 ft long	5,377	7,681
Accumulator, flat 8, mechanical	3,840	6,145
Big bale accumulator	15,362	23,042
Big Bale Shredder, silage or straw	9,217	13,825
Big Square Bale Chasers	69,300	86,625

(e) Drying, Handling, Feed Processing Equipment
Grain driers and Grain storage:

Rotary Cleaner, 10-20 tonnes/hour	20,738	26,115
Grain augers 150 mm, 6-8.5 m, with trolley	3,072	4,608
Grain conveyors, (25-50t/hour) (plus £145-185/m)	3,840	6,145
Hammer mill, 7.5-15 kW	5,377	6,913
Roller mill, 4-5.5 kW	3,840	5,377
Mixer, 750-1000 kg	6,913	7,681
Mill and mixer, 1,000-1,300kg, 3.7-5.5 kW	10,753	13,825

Potato, Sugar Beet and Vegetable Machinery   Price Range

(a) Potato Machinery

*	De-stoner	69,127	92,169
*	Bedformer, 1 bed	7,681	12,289
	Bed tiller (1 bed)	13,825	18,434
*	Planter: 2 row mounted	24,578	39,940
	6 row	53,765	72,199
	Haulm pulveriser (2 row):	9,985	12,289
*	Harvesters: 2 row trailed manned/unmanned	184,338	222,742
	2 row, self-propelled	230,423	337,953
	4 row, self-propelled	460,845	583,737
	Store loader (heavy duty)	38,404	46,085
	Self-unloading hopper, 3-5 tonnes	16,898	21,506
	Clod separator	16,898	21,506
	Sizer, 5-30 tonnes/hour	15,362	27,651
	Barrel washer, 8-10 tonnes/hour	33,795	53,765
	Roller inspection table, 1.2 x 2.4 m	4,608	9,217
	Weigher, automatic, 8-10 tonnes/hour	11,521	15,362
	Box tipper with cross conveyor	23,042	38,404
	Box filler, automatic	20,790	27,720
	Bag stitcher (hand held)	768	2,304
	Complete out of store grading line: 20 tonnes/hour	107,531	199,700
	30 tonnes/hour	184,338	276,507

(b) Sugar Beet Machinery

*	Precision Drill: 6 row (pneumatic)	16,898	23,042
	12 row-18 row (pneumatic)	27,651	53,765
*	Hoe: 6 row-12 row (heavy duty)	13,057	21,506
	Harvesters: Trailed, 4 row, tanker	138,254	153,615
	Trailed, 6 row, tanker	145,934	192,019
*	Self-propelled, 6 row, 18 tonne tank	430,122	537,653
	Cleaner-loader, with engine, 1-3 tonnes per minute	30,723	53,765
	6 Row Fodder beet harvester	99,850	153,615

(c)   Vegetable Machinery

Onion windrower	16,898	19,970
Root crop digger: 1 webb	11,521	13,057
2 webbs	13,825	16,898
Top lifting vege single row, bunker	84,488	107,531
twin row, bunker/elevator	145,934	192,019
four row, elevator	199,700	238,103
four row, self-propelled	460,845	553,014
Leek harvester (mounted)	38,404	61,446

Dairy Equipment

Price Range

Water heater	1,229	2,765
Heat recovery unit	3,840	7,681
Plate Cooler	2,304	6,145
Variable speed vacuum pumps	13,825	16,898
Cow collars for heat-time monitoring (£ per cow	108	138
Electronic auto-shedding systems	10,753	16,898
Auto-dipping and flushing system (£ per point)	1,152	1,459

General

Price Range

Trailer, 12 tonne tipping; grain/silage	15,362	19,058
* Trailer, 14t tipping, tandem axle; grain/silage	16,898	23,042
Grain Chaser Bin - 24t	63,525	75,075
* F.Y.M. Spreader, (10 - 12 tonne)	16,898	24,578
(12 - 14 tonne)	23,042	30,723
Self-propelled Slurry / Digestate applicator with 24 boom	491,568	614,460
* Loaders, front mounted	9,217	14,593
* Materials Handler, telescopic boom (2.5-3.0 tonne)	69,127	92,169
Skid steer loader (500-600 kg)	23,042	33,795
Quad Bikes	5,377	9,985
Vacuum Tankers (5,000-6,000 litre)	7,681	10,753
* Low Ground Pressure Tankers (9,000-11,000 litre	18,434	24,578
Slurry pump	6,145	7,681
Slurry separator	43,012	53,765
Cattle crush	1,536	4,608
Cattle crush with weigher	3,072	6,145
Cattle trailer (twin-axle)	4,608	6,913
Yard scrapers	768	1,536
Rotary brush (2-2.5 m)	3,072	3,840
* Flat roll, ballastable (3 m)	1,920	3,072
* Pasture topper (2.0-3.0 m)	1,843	3,840

General	*Price Range*	
Hedge cutter:		
* hydraulic angling; flail head	18,434	27,651
7.6m reach, 1.3m flail head, double sided	43,012	53,765
Ditcher: fully slewing	14,593	18,434
Post hole digger	1,843	3,072
Post hole driver	2,304	5,377
Saw bench	2,304	3,840
Log splitter	1,229	1,843
Welder	384	2,304
Angle Grinder	38	307
Compressor	384	1,229
Farm Security Camera (single basic camera)	154	307
Farm Security Camera System (automatic and wireless)	1,690	2,151
Tractor Guidance System (basic)	461	1,229
Auto-Steer Guidance System	4,608	11,521

For complete milking parlour costs - see building costs on page 222.

2.   CONTRACTORS' CHARGES', FARMERS' COSTS AND WORK RATES

Contractors' charges vary widely according to many factors; these are estimates for 2022. Farmer-contractors may charge less than dedicated contractors, since their overheads and fixed costs are sometimes *considered* partly covered by their own farming operations. However, the service may not always be so complete, including specialist advice or access to new technology.

Farmers' own costs (including the value of the farmers' own manual labour) vary even more widely; those given (for 2022) are averages in every respect as costs vary according to soil types, size of farm, and so on; they are based on accounting cost procedures in that labour, tractor and machinery fuel, repairs and depreciation are included - no allowance has been added for general farm overheads, interest on capital, supervision/management or under-occupied labour during slack times. They assume four-wheel drive 150hp tractors for the majority of operations (these individual tractor costs are shown in the tractor costs schedule on page 189). 185hp tractors are assumed for work with a higher power requirement such as ploughing, cultivations, certain drilling operations, sub-soiling and big square baling. Fuel adjustments have been made (both upwards and downwards) according to light or heavy work (i.e. where different to the average consumption assumed in the tractor costs schedule). The figures should not be used for partial budgeting. The machinery used in the calculations for farmers' costs is identified by a 'star' * adjacent to specific items of equipment in the machinery list in the previous section (an average has been used for the purchase price). In line with increasingly larger machinery on farm, many of the daily work rate assumptions have been reviewed in the farmers' cost calculations in recent years.

The contract charges and average farmers' costs are put side-by-side for tabular convenience, not to facilitate comparisons. Apart from the fact that contractors' charges must cover expenses omitted from the farmers' cost, the advisability or otherwise of hiring a contractor for a particular job depends on many factors (e.g. timeliness), varying widely according to farm circumstances; therefore, there are advantages and disadvantages not reflected in a cost comparison alone. It is apparent at present that contractor rates may not have increased in line with costs incurred (depreciation, labour, fuel etc) as Farmer Costs have increased by a greater percentage on average in the last 12 months.

Assumptions: Contractors' costs are sensitive to factors including fuel costs, capital machinery prices, and local demand versus competition. Contractors' charges are based on red diesel at 50ppl. The farmers' cost calculations are based on fuel at 55ppl. However, many contractors are now making individual arrangements with customers regarding fuel (i.e. prices quoted before fuel – therefore using the farmer's fuel when on site). The contractor charges shown below include fuel. The rates of work include preparation, travelling to and from the fields and allow for minor breakdowns and other stoppages.

Machinery rings: Prices charged by farmers offering services through machinery rings are variable but are generally between farmers' costs and contractors' charges. There are exceptions, which mainly relate to relatively expensive items of machinery (e.g. root harvesters, de-stoners and combine harvesters), where the charges for services offered through machinery rings are close to and often less than farmers' costs. Machinery and Labour rings are great examples of Joint Ventures that can deliver cost savings for all the farming businesses involved. Structures and circumstances often vary between organisations / groups involved. Many farmers are also achieving similar benefits through machinery sharing arrangements often undertaken on a relatively informal basis.

Acknowledgement. The estimates for contractors' charges are partly supplied by the National Association of Agricultural Contractors (as collected through their survey).

* *Costs are per hectare unless stated. The figures represent a national average.*

Average Contractors Charges & Farmers Costs of Performing Mechanical Operations

Operation	Contract Charge £/ha *	Farmer's Average Cost £/ha *	Average Rate of Work (Ha/8hr day)
Cultivations			
Ploughing – light land	63.18	55.73	10.50
– heavy land	67.09	61.60	9.5
Deep ploughing (over 30cm)	76.06	74.92	8.5
– with furrow press	6.70	5.40	9.5
Rotovating - ploughed land	72.75	67.50	8.5
- grass		88.27	8.5
Sub-soiling/Flat lifting	66.40	50.72	11
Mole-ploughing – single leg	88.21	63.05	14
Stubble raking	23.23	17.91	50
Discing: shallow	54.36	37.17	16
Deep	59.92	46.82	13
Power harrowing – deep/on ploughing	59.38	57.97	9.5
Shallow/seedbed prep	53.92	42.95	12.5
Spring-tine harrowing	40.40	25.15	16
Pressing	34.89	29.78	16
One-pass tillage train (Solo/Discordon etc)	63.13	60.44	16
Cultivation (Rexus Twin / Culti-press etc)	37.07	42.46	16
Rolling – flat (grassland)	28.05	18.99	15
– ring (seedbeds)	19.25	10.23	35

Operation	Contract Charge £/ha *	Farmer's Average Cost £/ha *	Average Rate of Work (Ha/8hr day)
Drilling			
Rape drilling with flatlift/subsoiler	67.16	55.79	11
Cereal drilling – conventional	50.66	28.32	24
Combi-drilling	63.83	68.46	12
Cultivator drill (Vaderstad)	51.37	59.02	20
Direct drilling	59.23	56.72	20
Sugar beet drilling	61.28	60.95	11
Carrot/parsnip/onion precision drilling	79.07		
Grass seed (broadcast)	32.35	22.31	14
Grass seeding with harrow (e.g. Opico)	34.35	23.57	14
Cross drilling grass	63.80		
Chain harrowing	25.53	16.84	20
Maize precision drilling	51.00	54.00	20
Maize drilling under plastic	142.50		
Fertilising & Spraying			
Fertiliser distribution	12.40	7.49	70
Extra for variable rate application	4.84		
Lime spreading (per tonne)	8.89/tonne		
Irrigating (excl. water costs) per inch	103.78		
Spraying (based on 200 l/ha & 24m boom)	12.78	8.26	80
Spraying (120-150l/ha 36 boom)		10.54	150
Extra if less than 50 acres (20 ha)	4.32		
Liquid fertiliser	13.39	9.91	68
ATV spraying	42.19/hr or 13.96/ha		
Slug-pelleting	7.93	2.63	70
Weed wiping	55.00/hr		
Avadex spreading	18.29		
Combining			
Combining cereals	93.13	81.44	20.5
Extra for straw chopper on combine	6.80	*Farmer's cost assumes*	
Extra for seeding (Autocast)	10.38	*average of all machine size*	
Extra for yield mapping	2.47	*and harvested areas*	
Combining peas/beans	94.94	81.44	20.5
Combining grain maize	112.11	98	16.4
Swathing OSR	57.01		
Grain carting to barn (per hour)	43.18/hr	45.74 /hr	
Root Crop Operations			
Potato harvesting – harvesting only	803.08	634.80	2.5
- Harvesting and carting	1,055.12	927.53	
De-stoning potato land	285.01	248.97	3.2
Potato ridging	87.72	57.64	9
Potato planting	191.50	158.50	4
Sugar beet harvesting - harvesting only	237.98	200.30	12
- Harvesting and carting	269.44		
Irrigation (25 mm application / ha)	98.00		

Operation	Contract Charge £/ha *	Farmer's Average Cost £/ha *	Average Rate of Work (Ha/8hr day)
Grass & Forage			
Flail topping margins per hour	44.85/hr		
Grass topping	38.18	24.70	15
Grass mowing	30.29	30.86	15
Tedding	17.62	16.69	25
Raking	18.36	23.43	25
Forage harvesting only – first cut	80.09	69.52	20
- other cuts	65.48	55.62	20
Forage harvesting, cart (3 trailers) and clamping (1st cut)	136.97		
Whole Crop forage harvesting, cart (3 trailers) and clamping	181.77		
Complete service – mow, rake, forage harvest, cart (3 trailers) and clamp	166.62		
Maize harvesting incl carting (3 trailers) and clamping	186.93		
Extra forage trailer (per hour)	44.17/hr	45.74 /hr	
Forage box	117.08/hr		
Baling			
Baling (per bale) - 'small'	0.78/bale	0.41 / bale	8
- 80cm × 90cm	4.00/bale		
- 120cm × 70cm	5.04/bale	3.92 / bale	32
- 120cm × 90cm	6.21/bale	4.70 / bale	32
- 120cm × 130cm	7.83/bale		
- Round 120cm	3.35/bale	2.35 / bale	18
- Round 150cm	3.59/bale	2.53 / bale	18
Bale Chasing	2.64/bale		
Bale-wrapping – Round 120cm (6 layers)	6.25/bale		
- Round 120cm (with 4 layers)	5.00/bale		
- Round 120cm (without plastic)	2.66/bale		
- Square 120cm × 70cm (6 layers)	7.62/bale		
- Square 120cm × 70cm (4 layers)	6.62/bale		
- Square120cm × 70cm (without plastic)	3.49/bale		
Bale Chaser (per hour)	60.00/hr		
Manure Handling - _see below for telehandler costs for loading_			
FYM spreading – tractor & rear discharge	54.10/hr	51.89	
- tractor and side discharge spreader	56.00/hr	46.70	
Slurry spreading – tanker	53.54/hr	51.21	
- umbilical	89.00/hr or 2.55/cube		
- extra pump	46.50/hr		
Slurry injection	78.33/hr		

Operation	Contract Charge £/ha *	Farmer's Average Cost £/ha *	Average Rate of Work (Ha/8hr day)
General / Rural Maintenance			
Hedge cutting - flail	40.04/hr	48.00	
- saw-blade	51.00/hr	59.41	
Hedge laying	16.25/metre		
Fence erection (with materials)			
– post and 4 Barb	7.18/metre		
– post, stock net & 2 Barb	8.74/metre		
– post and 3 rails	16.25/metre		
Quad bike (including man)		18.81	
Tractor + Post Knocker + Man	46.22/hr		
Ditching using 360 deg digger	43.89/hr		
Tractor + trailer + man	45.50/hr	45.74	
100 – 150 hp Tractor + man	38.12/hr		
150 – 220 hp Tractor + man	42.32/hr		
220 – 300 hp Tractor + man	55.76/hr		
300 hp + Tractor + man	72.82/hr		
Forklift/Telehandler + man	43.52/hr	42.06	
Livestock Husbandry			
Sheep dipping	1.40/head		
Sheep jetting / showering	0.98/head		
Sheep – shearing ewes	1.65/head		
-- rams	3.17/head		
-- crutching	0.75/head		
Sheep ultrasound scanning	1.05/head		
Cattle ultrasound scanning	2.05/head		
Foot trimming – sheep	14.75/head		
- cattle	13.33/head		
- bulls	24.50/head		
Tractor + Man + Feeder Wagon		38.89	
Livestock husbandry - Sheep & Cattle	19.38/hr		
Crimping (£/t)	11.25/tonne		
Mobile feed mixing and processing (£/t)	19.75/tonne		

Acknowledgement. The above estimates for contractors' charges are based in part on information kindly supplied by the National Association of Agricultural Contractors.

CONTRACT FARMING AGREEMENTS

Contract Farming Agreements are generally formalised with a written agreement setting out the terms for the Farmer (who can be a landowner or tenant) and a Contractor. The Contractor can be a neighbouring farmer or pure contractor. Contractor remuneration includes a guaranteed Basic Fee which is usually between £235 and £295/ha (£95-£120/acre) for combinable crops and should cover the majority of the fixed costs of the operation. It should not offer any margin for the contractor to incentivise him to farm the land to the best of his ability and therefore generate the maximum return to the farmer and contractor through the share of the divisible surplus. The Contractor provides all of the day-to-day labour, machinery and management to run the farming business, including provision of all cross-compliance and assurance scheme paperwork.

Following deduction of running costs (crop variable costs, drying, insurance, interest charges etc.) and the Farmers Basic Return, the surplus is split between the two parties. The split may typically be 70%-80% to the Contractor and 20%-30% to the Farmer. This incentivises good performance and management from the contractor. A second band of payment rate is sometimes introduced e.g. 50:50 split above a set level of surplus to enable the farmer to benefit from further rises in market prices. This is increasingly the case given the large volatility in cereal prices. The flow chart below demonstrates the flow of income and expenditure through a Contract Farming Agreement, applicable to all sectors of agriculture.

Income

Sales

Cull / Calf, Grain / Straw Sales

Basic Payment *

Environmental Scheme income **

↓

Less, Variable Costs

Feed, Fertiliser, Seed, Sprays, Lime, Agronomy

Livestock Sundries, Vet and Med, Bedding, Livestock Purchases

↓

Less, Overheads

Water, Electricity, Repairs, Office & Professional Fees, Interest

↓

Less,

Contractor's Basic Fee

Farmer's Basic Return

Depreciation

↓

Divisible Return

xx% to Farmer   yy% to Contractor

*　　*can be included or excluded and the Farmer's Basic Return adjusted accordingly*
**　　*above caveat can also apply, particularly if the scheme covers a wider area than solely the land available to the contract farming agreement*

CONTRACT CHARGE FOR ALL OPERATIONS

For cereals and combinable break crops, 'stubble to stubble' charges (i.e. up to and including combine harvesting and carting the grain to store) are typically £346 to £420/ha (£140-170/acre). Variations depend on factors such as distance away, area contracted, field sizes, terrain type, soil quality, cultivation/crop establishment methods and which party provides the storage. At the lower end of the prices around £346 to £370 per hectare (£140-150/acre) it would be solely to cover field operations and carting grain to store, whereas higher prices stated above would be a complete management service to include hedge cutting, field infrastructure maintenance, crop walking and agronomy etc. Local competition affects prices, as with all contract charges. Some regions of the UK are very competitive for certain contract operations, for example hedge cutting or 'tractor and man' provision. This leads to a wide range of prices across the country. Arguably, contractor rates have not kept pace with increasing machinery prices in recent years.

When comparing farmers' total power, machinery and labour costs with stubble to stubble contractors' charges, the former includes cost items not included in the latter, e.g. the cost of farm vehicles, fixed plant such as grain stores, general farm maintenance and other down time for full-time labour. Whilst an important comparison these key differences must be borne in mind. For businesses where full-time labour units cannot be matched to work demands/profiles, this provides opportunities for cost savings by utilising contractors for whole farm operations, whether under a formal contract farming arrangement or stubble-to-stubble type basis.

3. TRACTOR HOURS

Crops		Per Hectare Per Annum	
		Average	Premium
Cereals	....	7.1	5.3
Plus, Straw	....	1.5	1.1
Potatoes	....	15.3	11.5
Sugar Beet	....	10.2	7.7
Vining Peas	....	7.5	5.6
Dried Peas	....	5.8	4.3
Field Beans	....	5.8	4.3
Oilseed Rape	....	7.1	5.3
Herbage Seeds:- 3 year crop		4.3	3.2
Hops (machine picked)	....	120.0	90.0
Kale (grazed)	....	3.6	2.7
Turnips/Swedes (Grazed/Lifted)		6/12	5/10
Fallow	....	0.6	0.5
Grass Ley Establishment	....	3.5	2.6
Making Hay	....	4.1	3.1
Making Silage:	1st Cut	3.8	2.8
	2nd Cut	3.0	2.3
Grazing:	Temporary Grass	1.7	1.3
	Permanent Grass	0.9	0.7

Livestock		Average Per Head
Dairy Cows (Grazed / Intensive)	....	4/7
Other Cattle over 2 years	....	5
Other Cattle 1-2 years	....	4
Other cattle 0.5-1 year	....	2.25
Calves 0-0.5 year	....	2.25
Housed Bullocks	....	3
Sheep (per ewe)	....	1.25
Store Lambs	....	0.8
Sows	....	1.75
Other Pigs over 2 months	....	1
Laying Birds	....	0.04

1. *For livestock,* annual requirements are per head requirements above multiplied by average numbers during the year (i.e. average numbers at end of each month).

2. *As with labour,* the number of tractors required by a farm depends more on the seasonal requirements and number required at any one time than on total annual tractor hours. These can be calculated from the seasonal labour data provided earlier in this book. The soil type and size/power of tractors purchased are obviously other relevant factors. However, a farm business does not necessarily have to have tractors available all-year-round if only required for short periods. Hiring / sharing are often more cost-effective options to cover short peak workload requirements. All figures are for 2022. Where reduced tillage and direct drilling practises are operated on arable farms, it is possible to achieve much lower tractor hours per hectare than is shown above.

4.   TRACTOR COSTS

Four-Wheel Drive Tractors

	120 h.p.		150 h.p.	
Initial Cost............................	£76,813		£95,651	
	per year	per hour	per year	per hour
	£	£	£	£
Depreciation.........................	5,377	10.75	6,696	13.39
Insurance............................	874	1.75	1088	2.18
Repairs and Maintenance............	1,152	2.30	1,435	2.87
Fuel and Oil..........................	3,090	6.18	4,012	8.02
Total	10,493	20.99	13,230	26.46

	185 h.p.		250 h.p.	
Initial Cost..........................	£123,998		£160,936	
	per year	per hour	per year	per hour
	£	£	£	£
Depreciation.......................	8,680	17.36	11,265	22.53
Insurance...........................	1410	2.82	1,831	3.66
Repairs and Maintenance...........	1,860	3.72	2,414	4.83
Fuel and Oil.......................	5,497	10.99	8,667	17.33
Total	17,447	34.89	24,177	48.35

	350 h.p.		450 h.p.	
Initial Cost..........................	£254,568		£324,060	
	per year	per hour	per year	per hour
	£	£	£	£
Depreciation.......................	17,820	35.64	22,684	45.37
Insurance...........................	2896	5.79	3,686	7.37
Repairs and Maintenance...........	3,819	7.64	4,861	9.72
Fuel and Oil.......................	11,839	23.68	15,015	30.03
Total	36,373	72.75	46,246	92.49

Figures are estimates for 2022. Depreciation assumes all tractors are sold for 30% of their original value after 10 years, a slight change in assumption from previous years to reflect current markets. The depreciation schedule shown on page 195 demonstrates the average annual fall in value of machinery over its life (the middle columns are applicable to tractors). Annual repair costs are calculated at 1.5% of initial cost for all tractors. This assumes the majority of basic servicing work carried out by the farm's own labour. No interest on capital has been included. Fuel is charged at 55p/litre plus a 5% allowance for oil. Insurance costs vary depending on the policy type. The above assume the most common practise whereby tractor costs incur the majority of the insurance cost, with any implements of value up to circa £80,000-100,000 are automatically covered by the tractor policy.

The hourly figures are based on 500 hours use per year. A greater annual use than this will mean higher annual costs but possibly lower hourly costs. On some larger farms and within many contracting businesses, many tractors do in excess of 1,000 hours per year, and even as high as 2,000 hours for some contractors. Earlier replacement at a given annual use will increase depreciation costs per hour but should reduce repair costs. The hourly figures are averages for all types of work: heavy operations such as ploughing obviously have a higher cost than light work. The variability of fuel usage is significant depending upon the type of work (light work vs. heavy cultivations) and can vary by up to 80%. The figures shown attempt to depict the average consumption from all types of work.

CONTRACT HIRE, PURCHASE OR HIRE PURCHASE OF MACHINERY

The farmer's cost for the various operations shown in the table above assume machinery and equipment is purchased outright. No interest charge is included in the calculations for the capital required to purchase the machinery. However, a farmer may purchase the machinery through a hire purchase (HP) agreement. Here, a deposit is paid up-front followed by a number of monthly or annual payments. The benefits of HP agreements are purely cash flow, allowing a business to spread the cost over say 3 or 4 years. For new equipment, the interest charge may be very low or even 0%, whereas using HP agreements to finance used machines will usually incur an interest rate currently of 3-7%. Once the HP agreement ends (i.e. all payments are complete), the farmer owns the item outright.

Another option is contract hire (CH) agreements. Here, a rental charge is paid for the equipment for a set time period. At the end of the period, the machine is returned to the company (although sometimes opportunities exist to negotiate a price to buy the machine). Contract hire agreements usually include a full service, maintenance and repair plan. The main advantage of these agreements is the ability to plan and budget costs, as the exact cost of operating that machine is known, with no un-expected repair bills or no need to budget what it will be worth upon resale. These are becoming popular with large arable and contracting businesses as it can be very cost-effective where machinery usage is high.

Another option which is increasingly popular is to use short-term hire agreements to hire key items of machinery as and when required. For example, many arable businesses contract hire combines and/or additional tractors at harvest time when extra machinery is needed. This allows them to access new technology without having large sums of capital tied up in machinery that sits idle for much of the year. The most cost-effective option depends on the specific circumstances of the farm business and will be determined by factors such as ability to access capital, annual usage and life expectancy.

Machinery Hire Costs

Typical Contract Hire charges (see above) for a selection of tractors and other machines are shown below (prices exclude insurance but include repairs/maintenance):

	Short-Term (8-10 weeks)	*52 weeks Contract*
110 hp tractor:	£520 - £620 / week	£230 - £275 / week
130 hp tractor:	£650 - £750 / week	£250 – £300 / week
165 hp tractor:	£820 - £950 / week	£330 - £480 / week
215 hp tractor:	£1050 - £1,300 / week	£400 - £480 / week
290 hp tractor (wheeled):	£1,400-£1,600 / week	£495 - £550 / week
370 hp tractor (tracked):	£2,100 - £2,600 / week (or £630/day)	
130 hp telehandler	£535 - £630 / week	£320 - £355 / week
16 tonne Grain Trailer	£290 – £360 / week or £70-£80/day	
3,000g vacuum tanker	£375 - £570 / week or £110-£130/day	
10t rear discharge spreader	£400 - £550 / week or £110-£130/day	
8ft road brush	£180 - £250 / week or £50-£70/day (+ wear charges)	
13 tonne 360 digger	£675/week (or £225/day)	
16 tonne dump trailer	£300/week (or £75/day)	
Combine (30ft cut)	£22-25/acre (2,000 acres per season)	

HIRE OR OWN?

Whether it is best to hire or buy a machine depends on many factors, often specific to the farm's own circumstances. However, a common practise now, particularly on arable farms, is to hire one of the larger tractors only required for a short period of time, for example as used for autumn cultivations. This type of machine, as well as combine harvesters, often sit idle for much of the year.

The tables below show the way a farmer can calculate whether it is most cost effective to hire or to buy for one specific example. Here, a large 250hp tractor is hired/used for 10 weeks of the year. It demonstrates the cost of the machine per hour on both a hired and owned basis excluding labour and fuel, (being the same whether the machine is owned or hired). It includes the cost of finance based on the average capital employed over the life of the asset at 5%; this is not shown in the tractor costs previously in the book. But, this is one of the main considerations between hiring and buying when the capital cost is so significant. The hire cost assumes a fixed charge for the 11-week period of £16,170 for a 60-hour week maximum (based on 50 being achieved) but assumes the overage charge on additional hours is £22.64/clock hour. The excess hours rate varies between suppliers of hired machines. Indeed, some will hire entirely on a per clock hour basis only anyway.

| | £/hour on 500 hrs | |
	Owned	Hired
Depreciation / Hire Charge	22.53	32.34
Finance	5.63	-
Repairs	4.83	-
Insurance	3.66	0.93
Total	36.65	33.27

The table below demonstrates the point at which, in this example for the above set of circumstances, it is more cost effective to buy the machine. This is above 900 hours. However, this relies upon being able to achieve this level of output in the short space of time, which dependent on weather and cropping may not be realistic.

Total Cost Per Hour (£/Hr)

| | Hours per Year | | | | | | |
	400	500	600	700	800	900	1000
Owned	43.20	36.65	36.98	33.19	30.35	28.14	26.37
Hired	41.59	33.27	31.50	30.23	29.28	28.54	27.95

Depreciation rates for low usage of high value machines matter, because depreciation by age rather than use makes the cost of ownership high. Where a business has high usage/demand for this machine in the spring and autumn, long-term hire costs would need to be considered. These are less per week but likely to cost more for the year and so usage is the key determinant.

UK AGRICULTURAL TRACTOR SALES PER YEAR

(Tractors over 50 HP)

Year	Average Tractor Size HP	Number of Units Sold	Per Cent change y/y
2010	141.7	13,347	-11.1%
2011	144.3	14,094	+5.6%
2012	148.0	13,951	-1.0%
2013	150.7	12,498	-10.4%
2014	155.1	12,433	-0.5%
2015	157.0	10,842	-12.8%
2016	158.3	10,602	-2.2%
2017	162.2	12,033	+13.5%
2018	166.6	12,102	+0.6%
2019	164.8	12,040	-0.5%
2020	171.0	10,380	-13.8%
2021 (Jan-June)		6,844	

(data from the Agricultural Engineers Association).

TRACTOR POWER REQUIREMENTS

		hp/acre		hp/ha		kW/ha	
		av.	prem.	av.	prem.	av.	prem.
Combinable crops:	heavy land	1.20	0.70	3.00	1.75	2.24	1.30
	light land	0.90	0.60	2.20	1.50	1.64	1.10
Mixed cropping:	heavy land	1.35	0.95	3.35	2.35	2.50	1.75
	light land	1.00	0.70	2.50	1.75	1.86	1.30
Mixed Farming:	All Types	1.50	0.95	3.70	2.35	2.76	1.75

Includes tractors, telehandlers, self-propelled sprayers and combines

The above highlights the challenge associated with power and machinery costs for those with mixed farms, depending on the scale of each enterprise e.g. beef, sheep and cereals. Specialist producers tend to be more efficient when it comes to the amount of machinery owned and capital employed in the total machinery and equipment on farm.

5. ESTIMATING ANNUAL MACHINERY COSTS

Annual machinery costs consist of depreciation, repairs, fuel and oil, contract charges, and vehicle tax and insurance. These can be budgeted in three ways;

1) using information on past machinery costs on the farm (e.g. management accounts).

2) per hectare, by looking up an average figure according to the size and type of farm. Approximate levels are shown in the tables of whole farm fixed costs (page 209). This is obviously a guide only and masks huge variations between farms. It is essential to understand your own power and machinery costs given that they vary so significantly between businesses. However, averages may be a useful starting point.

3) Fully detailed calculations, costing and depreciating each machine in turn, including tractors, estimating repairs and fuel costs for each, and adding the charges for any contract work. The following tables give, for different types of machinery, estimated life, annual depreciation, and estimated repairs according to annual use (although this can vary considerably between soil types, weather conditions, operator care and the level of maintenance undertaken).

ESTIMATED USEFUL LIFE OF POWERED MACHINERY IN NORMAL USE

Estimated Useful Life (years)	Annual Use (hours)			
Equipment	50	100	200	300
Group 1: Ploughs, cultivators, harrows, rolls, ridgers, potato planting machinery, grain cleaners	15+	12+	12	10
Group 2: Disc harrows, seed drills, grain drying machines, feed mills/mixes	15+	12	10	8
Group 3: Combine harvesters, pick-up balers, rotary cultivators, hydraulic loaders	20+	20+	12+	10
Group 4: Mowers, forage harvesters, swath turners, rakes, tedders, hedge cutting machines, precision drills	15	12	10	8
Group 5: Fertiliser spreaders, combination drills, FYM spreaders, sprayers	15+	10+	8	7
Miscellaneous:				
Beet harvesters	12+	10	8	6
Potato harvesters	10+	10	8	5
Milking machinery	—	—	—	20+

	Annual Use (hours)					
	500	750	1,000	1,500	2,000	2,500
Tractors	18+	12	10	7	6	5
Electric motors	20+	12	10+	10	9	8

CAPITAL EMPLOYED IN MACHINERY

	£/acre		£/ha	
	average	premium	average	premium
Combinable Crops:	630	460	1,555	1,135
Mixed Cropping	905	630	2,235	1,555
Grazing Dairy:	230	160	570	395
Intensive Dairy:	550	380	1,360	940
Grazing Livestock:	270	195	665	480

This includes tractors, telehandlers, self-propelled sprayers and combines. It excludes fixed items such as parlours, livestock handling equipment and grain drying equipment. Large variations exist depending upon the use of contractors vs own equipment, overall management quality/decision-making as well as farm efficiency variations, particularly land distribution.

DEPRECIATION

There are two methods by which to calculate depreciation rates for agricultural machinery. The **straight line** method takes the difference between the estimated trade-in, second-hand or scrap value of a machine, and the purchase price of the machine. The loss in capital value over the period the machine is retained for is then divided by the age of the machine to arrive at the annual depreciation charge. This can then be used to arrive at the annual % depreciation rate to apply to that machine on a straight line basis over its useful life for budgeting purposes.

Example: If a machine costing £10,000 is retained for 8 years, at the end of which the trade-in value is £2,000, the depreciation has been £8,000. Over 8 years this equates to £1,000 per annum (i.e. 10% per year of the new price).

The **diminishing balance** method takes account of the fact that new machines lose a larger proportion of their capital value in the early years even with modest annual usage. Some estimated percentage rates of depreciation for different machine types under a diminishing balance basis are shown in the table below. *Clearly, in addition to the age of the machine, annual usage has an effect upon depreciation rates which is not necessarily accounted for below.*

AVERAGE ANNUAL FALL IN VALUE

Age of Machine	Complex. High depreciation rate		Traditional machines		Simple equipment: Low depreciation rate	
	Annual % Dep'n	Total % Dep'n	Annual % Dep'n	Total % Dep'n	Annual % Dep'n	Total % Dep'n
1	37.5	37.5	28	28	22	22
2	25	50	19	38	16	32
3	20	60	15.3	46	13.7	41
4	16.5*	66	13.3*	53	12	48
5	14.2	71	11.8	59	10.8	54
6	12.5†	75	10.7	64	9.8	59
7	11.3‡	79	9.8	68.5	9.1*	64
8	10.3	82	9.0†	72	8.4	67
9	9.3	84	8.2	74	7.7	69
10	8.5	85	7.5‡	75	7†	70

Complex: Machines such as potato harvesters, pea viners, etc.
Traditional Machines: with many moving parts, e.g. tractors, combines, balers, forage harvesters
Simple Equipment: with few moving parts, e.g. ploughs, cultivators, trailers etc.

* Typical frequency of renewal with heavy use.

† Typical frequency of renewal with average use.

‡Typical frequency of renewal with light use.

These figures have been calculated from a survey of machinery sale prices. Depreciation is calculated from the new price, asking price of the second-hand machine, and its age. The asking price has been discounted by 5% to account for price negotiations. Prices for a variety of machinery and equipment types have been collated and categorised according to complexity.

Example: If a tractor (traditional machine) costing £80,000 is 5 years old, the value of the machine has depreciated on average by 11.8% per year, totalling a 59% fall in value. This means the tractor is now worth £32,800. The chart shows depreciation over the ten-year period.

Depreciation of Machinery Categories over 10 years

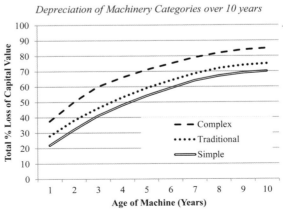

ESTIMATED ANNUAL COST OF SPARES AND REPAIRS

These figures are based on a percentage of purchase price* at various levels of use

Tractors	Annual Use (hours)				Additional 100 hours use add
	500	750	1,000	1,500	
	%	%	%	%	%
	1-2	2-3	4	4-6	0.5

	Annual Use (hours)				Additional 100 hours use add
	50	100	150	200	
Harvesting Machinery:	%	%	%	%	%
Combine harvesters, self-propelled forage harvesters, self-propelled potato harvesters	1.5	2.5	3.5	4.5	2
Trailed forage harvesters, pick-up balers, potato & sugar beet harvesters	3	5	6	7	2
Other Implements and Machines:					
Ploughs, cultivators, harrows	4.5	8	11	14	6
Rotary cultivators, mowers, windrowers	4	7	9.5	12	5
Disc harrows, fertiliser spreaders, farmyard manure spreaders, combination drills, potato planters, sprayers, hedge-cutting machines.	3	5.5	7.5	9.5	4
Tedders, rakes	2.5	4.5	6.5	8.5	4
Seed drills, milking machines, hydraulic loaders	2	4	5.5	7	3
Grain driers, grain cleaners, rollers, hammer mills, feed mixers	1.5	2	2.5	3	0.5

* When it is known that a high purchase price is due to high quality and durability or a low price corresponds to a high rate of wear and tear, adjustments to the figures should be made.

SERVICE PLANS

Most tractor manufacturers now offer extended warranties or comprehensive service plans to cover the cost of all servicing, maintenance and repairs beyond the regular manufacturer warranty. This is usually for a pre-agreed period of time or maximum number of hours (usually this expiry date is determined by which comes first). Costs and offerings vary hugely between manufacturers and tractor models, but the following gives an approximate guide. A 'standard' maintenance and repair plan for a 150hp tractor doing 500 hours per year for 5 years would cost an average of £1,400-£1,600/year. This is for a 'standard' maintenance and repair plan to include all servicing, filters, maintenance fluids and routine labour.

There are 'premium' plans available to go a stage further and protect further parts of the machine. There are, however, always exclusions from these agreements such as tyres, glass and provisions for negligence. Extended warranty agreements to cover all replacement parts and all risks of break-down / major repair works etc can cost up to £4/hour in total in addition. Whilst on the face of it, this may appear expensive, given the rising cost of repairs (and machinery dealer labour costs), such plans can be beneficial for farming businesses, particularly contractors who can fix their repair costs. This therefore helps with budgeting and setting prices to charge customers. However, where annual usage is lower, they may not always be economical. Such agreements are a risk management strategy in protecting against large un-expected repair costs. This also gives peace of mind in the knowledge that the services were carried out by a qualified technician at the correct service intervals, rather than by farm staff who may sometimes lack knowledge and also can be undertaken on a rather ad-hoc basis, particularly during busy times of the year.

TYRES

The length of time a set of tractor tyres lasts before they need to be replaced will vary significantly depending upon a number of factors. These include soil type (stone content is the main determinant of tyre wear), the amount of yard work undertaken (feeding, loading grain etc), and the amount of road travelling undertaken. Many tractors will do in excess of 5,000 hours on a set of tyres assuming the machine does not do excessive road work. Front tyres on loader tractors are likely to require replacement earlier than rear tyres due to the weight of the loader (and items lifted) and the associated increase in wear that this creates when turning on yard areas. Clearly costs vary between tyre sizes but the largest variation can be seen between manufacturer makes due to perceived quality and therefore wear differences. The following table gives a guide for the prices of a range of different tractor tyres:

Size	Price Range	Size	Price Range
320 R24	£195 - £475	540 R38	£640 - £1,780
340 R24	£220 - £475	600 R38	£680 - £1,800
420 R28	£350 - £725	650 R42	£1,000 - £2,550
480 R28	£390 - £975	710 R42	£1,375 - £3,375
520 R38	£580 - £1,525	800 R42	£2,325 - £3,450

As an example, new 520 R38 tyres for the rear and 480 R28 tyres for the front of a 150hp tractor would cost on average approximately £3,500 plus VAT, plus the cost of the fitting and old tyre disposal costs. This could be done on-farm where the correct equipment is held, otherwise most tyre fitters / tractor dealers would fit these. Typical labour charges for technicians vary between £35/hour and £80/hour. Larger dealers' labour charges tend to be much higher. Larger and even flotation tyres are becoming increasingly popular for field-work, and in particular trailers, in an attempt to reduce soil compaction. These will cost significantly more to purchase.

BENCHMARK POWER AND LABOUR COSTS

One of the key areas where significant differences in costs between businesses is apparent is fixed costs. However, whilst many fixed costs such as property expenses, administration, rent and finance differ due to farm circumstances e.g. rented vs owner occupied; power/machinery and labour costs can be easily considered as a method of comparing financial performance and business efficiency. The table below gives some benchmark figures for different businesses in different sectors. For dairy, these costs are presented on a pence-per-litre basis on page 53.

Represents good financial performance

£/Ha	Combinable Cropping		Dairy (120 ha farms)		
	Large	Small-Medium	Spring Calving	All-Year-Round	Autumn Calving
Power & Machinery	*800-2000ha*	*150-500ha*	*5250 l/cow*	*8000 l/cow*	*7000 l/cow*
Fuel	66	62	25	110	50
Light & Heat	15	13	57	71	58
Machinery Repairs	58	42	19	92	47
Contractors	16	13	278	332	324
Hire Costs	5	3	9	15	21
Depreciation	116	150	159	211	176
Total Power Costs	**275**	**283**	**547**	**831**	**676**
Labour					
Paid Labour	68	31	276	391	427
Family Labour	43	104	205	226	142
Total	**112**	**135**	**481**	**617**	**569**
Hectares / FTE	280	220	55	43	46

6.   PRECISION AGRICULTURE

Precision farming is a method of farm management fundamentally centred on responding to very detailed variations in resource capability. The term has been adopted in recent years as a technology to map resource capacity such as land fertility or machinery passes so that each resource unit can be treated individually and precisely to maximise its productive capacity. It is estimated that about two thirds of UK arable land is farmed using some form of precision farming technology, dominated by the larger farms.

The cheapest and most cost-effective piece of precision farming equipment is a tape measure. For example, measuring the 'operating' width of machinery compared with actual width of bouts to identify overlap is a critical starting point. Precision farming is of most benefit to farmers who are least precise in their resource allocation. This might be through considerable variation of in-field nutrient levels or soil types. Larger, more extensive operations that have less management and labour per hectare to examine and treat each small parcel of land (or other resource) individually, will be able to benefit more greatly through automated measurements of resource capacity such as soil fertility or pH in different areas. They can also benefit more by spreading the capital cost over more hectares. Whilst it has taken many years to develop, there are now a wide number of different technologies available. These are covered in the following sections.

Automated / Assisted Steering

This was the first precision farming technology to gather pace in UK agriculture. It ensures that machinery covers precisely the correct area of ground without overlaps or leaving any gaps. Systems vary from GPS controlled in-cab monitors which produce lines at pre-determined bout widths for the operator to follow on the screen (still requiring manual steering) to fully automated systems whereby the in-cab controls result in the tractor steering itself up and down the field at the selected bout widths. With the latter, the operator merely has to turn the tractor round on the headland and re-start it in its new bout before the GPS controls navigate it down the field again. Basic light bar systems cost £400-£1,000, whereas fully automated steering systems cost between £3,500 and £6,500. Costs can be reduced if tractors are purchased with in-built technology readily available, thus requiring the receiver to simply be moved from one tractor unit to the next. Most of these use freely available GPS signals which are generally accurate to between 10cm and 30cm depending on the system. The most sophisticated systems now allow farmers to operate Controlled Traffic Farming (CTF) systems whereby all vehicle types are kept solely on a precise layout of permanent traffic lanes year after year to reduce compaction and soil structure damage. This requires extensive machinery planning to ensure all working widths fit the desired traffic lanes. They also require more accurate GPS signals which are more expensive. For example, RTK (Real Time Kinematic) systems are generally accurate to 2cm, either having base stations on farm or utilising others via an annual subscription fee of £700 - £1,700 depending on requirements.

Variable Rate Fertiliser, Lime and Seed

The application of fertiliser at different variable rates across fields requires those fields to be mapped for nutrients to determine the nutrient balance at a very precise level of field area. This then allows applications to be tailored according to the requirement or yield potential of that precise piece of land. Service providers offer mapping of Phosphate, Potash, soil pH and other micro-nutrients using either grid methods or zoning linked to soil conductivity testing (i.e. soil type variations). These enable variable rate P, K and lime applications, as well as variable seed rates to better target inputs. The aim is to help produce an even crop across varying soil types within fields, whilst ensuring nutrients are only applied where required. Such a comprehensive service costs in the region of £8-£12/ha for all mapping services, often costing more in the early years until all zoning has been completed. Once established, the annual cost could be down to approximately £5.50/ha per annum. The cost of individual soil tests for N, P, K and Mg is circa £9-14 per sample. This can be increased to £18-20 to include organic matter; and in excess of £30 if all trace elements are included. Machine compatibility with control boxes and existing ISOBUS tractor technology is important when considering precision farming techniques/services. When such variable rate nutrient application maps are overlaid with yield monitoring maps, nutrient applications can also be tailored to ensure those high yielding areas receive back the high level of nutrients removed through the high yielding crop.

For the variable application of nitrogen fertilisers, either granular or liquid, growers can choose between satellite-based imagery systems for green leaf area index mapping or Active Light Source (ALS) tractor mounted sensors. The cost of preparing variable rate nitrogen plans using satellite-based mapping services, which convert data into green leaf area/crop biomass maps, is approximately £2 per hectare. A number of images are taken during the growing season and applications adjusted accordingly in line with changes in crop development in different areas of the field. Tractor mounted sensors are also popular due to the arguably more accurate real-time data gathered and processed whilst the machine is driving through the crop. By mapping crop biomass levels, nitrogen and sulphur fertilisers can be applied variably, as well as growth regulators and fungicides. Sensor manufacturers claim from long term trial results, savings of up to 20kgN/ha are possible with yield improvements of circa 3% in cereals. The cost of sensors and software are approximately £25,000 per unit, sufficient for a 1,000 hectare arable unit.

The Future

The variable rate technology is now being applied to spray inputs, in particular fungicides and growth regulator products, utilising the green area index / crop biomass maps to better focus inputs for overall yield benefit and/or resource efficiency. Some growers are also now starting to map problematic weed areas within fields in order to target spray applications, as well as higher seed rates and differing cultivation strategies to better manage weed burdens within crops. The use of drones for visual imagery in order to produce such maps are also becoming more common. Plant tissue tests are also becoming more common now, allowing farmers to identify the precise nutrients and trace elements a crop is short of and therefore adjust applications accordingly. Tissues tests cost between £30-40 per sample.

Economic Benefits

Economic benefits result from better allocated inputs leading to savings of inputs, or higher yields. Inputs saved could include seed, fertilisers, sprays, machinery use, fuel and labour. Faster work-rates achieved can mean achieving more in periods of optimal weather conditions. Environmental benefits can also be achieved through correct input allocations and less wastage/leaching. Many growers report little cost savings actually achieved through variable rate seed and fertiliser applications but do report yield improvements as a result of more even crops through the better targeting of the inputs within each field. Independent data on the economic benefits is difficult to obtain. A HGCA publication 71 (2009) suggests that costs and benefits of automated steering might be in the region of the table below, although this will vary considerably between farms and years.

Table of benefits for Assisted Steer Technology (HGCA Review 71)

Level	Arable area	Accuracy	Machines Adapted	cost £/ha	benefit £/ha	net £/ha
Assisted Manual Steer	300 Ha	+/- 40cm	2	1.25	2.50	1.25
Mid-Level DGPS*	500ha	+/- 10cm	2	12	14	2.00
RTK**	500ha high value crops	+/- 2cm	3	20	22	2.00

* DGPS = Differential Global Positioning System   ** RTK = Real Time Kinematic

Knight S., Miller P. and Orson J. An up to date cost/benefit analysis of precision farming techniques to guide growers of cereals and oilseeds. HGCA Review 71. 2009

Acknowledgement: *thanks to Ian Beecher-Jones 07967 637 985*

7.   OTHER MACHINERY COSTS

IRRIGATION COSTS

Estimated for 2022

Capital Costs

1. Pumps delivering from 30 to 200 cubic metres per hour from a surface water source, complete with monitoring equipment:

Tractor PTO driven (pump only)	£1,600 - £4,700
Diesel engine driven pump unit	£23,000-£26,500 (75-125 m3/hr)
	£23,500-£30,000 *(150-250 m³/hr)*
Electric motor driven pump unit	£42,000 (150 to 250 m3/hr)
Optional remote/wireless monitoring controls	£750 - £1,800
Variable speed drive option – fitted to electric motor	£1,000 - £5,500

Individual pumps for mounting on diesel engines range in price from £3,500 to £20,000 for capacities of between 50 and 250 cubic metres per hour. A sophisticated system, including pump house, pumps and control equipment to feed an irrigation system from a reservoir to cover a total area of approx. 400 ha (as and when required) would cost approximately £37,500 - £55,000 to construct and install.

2. Pipelines (averages £ per metre):

(a)   Portable (excl. valve take-offs):
  50 mm: £3.50   75 mm: £5.75   100 mm: £8.50
  125 mm: £10.50   150 mm: £12.50   250 mm: £18.50-23.00

(b)   Permanent underground PVC pipe 16 bar rating (excludes the cost of laying):
  100 mm: £9.00   160 mm: £13.00   200 mm: £18.00
  Cost of digging, laying and back-filling is £8-£10/metre.

(c)   Hydrants:
  100 mm x 100 mm: £150 (aluminium) £330 (underground)
  150 mm x 125 mm: £180 (aluminium) £400 (underground)

3. Application Systems:-

(a)   Hose reel systems (average cost per machine) complete with rain gun:

	Hose Length	Output	Acre inches/day	Cost
Small	180-250m	30-50m³/hr	4.5-5.5	£18,000 to £23,000
Medium	300-400m	50-80m³/hr	5-10	£22,000 to £33,000
Large	450-650m	80-130m³/hr	12-16	£32,000 to £46,000

To add electric controls would cost an additional £3,500-£4,500.

(b)   Irrigation booms (average cost per unit):

Small	18m boom (24m wetted width)	£7,000 - £9,500
Medium	30m boom (48m wetted width)	£8,000 - £12,500
Large	50m boom (72m wetted width)	£15,000 - £18,500
	64m boom (72m to 90m wetted width)	£16,500 - £22,000

(c)   Pivot and linear systems:

Small Linear	200m width	£45,000 - £58,000
Large pivot	600m radius (100ha approx.)	£62,000 - £88,000

(d)   Solid set sprinkler lines – semi-permanent systems (very specialist and not widely found):

      63mm dia. pipework assemblies at
      18m x 18m triangulated spacing   £1,500 - £1,800/ha
      As above but with infra-red automated
      hand-held controls   £1,700 - £2,100/ha

(e)   Specialist Drip Irrigation systems (excluding the header mains, control valves and filtration equipment) will cost approximately 4.80p per metre for 16mm tape for a one-year life span with 20cm emitter spacing for 1.25L per linear meter (6mm wall thickness). For 20mm 10-year tape with 40cm emitter spacing, emitting 0.65L per emitter (47mm wall thickness), this will cost between 35p and 40p per metre.

4.   Total:

If no source works are needed, as with water from a river, or pond, total capital costs are likely to vary between £1,250 and £2,400 per hectare requiring irrigation at regular intervals, depending on the site layout, levels of sophistication and automation of the system installed. The capital cost of constructing a reservoir to store irrigation water, usually filled during the winter, is typically in excess of £1.50/m^3 for clay-lined reservoirs (although considerable variations will exist depending on precise circumstances). Lining and fencing could double this cost. This cost could be offset partly by the sale of sand / gravel depending upon the location. In some scenarios the sale of aggregates will completely off-set the cost of building the reservoir. This is commonplace as the burden has to be disposed of somewhere and therefore reduces the net capital cost of construction. In addition, there may be a need for pump houses and other infrastructure depending upon the circumstances. New time limited abstraction licences are difficult to obtain, especially for summer abstraction. Hence there is an increasing trend towards constructing reservoirs that can be used to store water abstracted during the winter months.

Acknowledgement: thanks to Briggs Irrigation and Javelin Irrigation Systems

Water Sources

An abstraction licence is required if more than 20m^3 (4,400 gallons) of water per day are taken from surface or underground sources. Once an abstraction licence is obtained, the licence holder must comply with its conditions. *The rules and charges below are based upon the abstraction charges scheme for 2020/21 as at the time of print, the 2021/22 scheme had not been issued.* A temporary abstraction licence is sufficient if more than 20m^3 of water per day is to be taken for less than 28 days, whereas a full abstraction licence is required if more than 20m^3 of water per day is to be taken for more than 28 days. In 2016, there were over 18,000 abstraction licences in place in England. If abstracting more than 10m^3 per day in Scotland, you must obtain authorisation from SEPA. If abstracting less than 10m^3 per day in Scotland and comply with certain General Binding Rules (GBR), you do not require authorisation. Abstraction charges vary widely calculated by a formula combining the following factors together:

- Volume – annual licensed
- the Source Factor; whether the source is Environment Agency unsupported, supported or tidal
- The Season Factor; summer, winter or all year round
- The loss factor – high, medium, low or very low, depending upon what the water is authorised to be used for under the licence
- A minimum annual charge of £25

Annual Charge = Standard Charge + Compensation Charge
= V x A x B x C x SUC + V x B x C x D x EIUC

Where V = annual licensed volume (000 cubic metres)
A = Source factor
B = Season factor
C = Loss factor
D = Adjusted source factor
SUC = Standard Unit Charge (£/1,000 cubic metres)
EIUC = Environmental Improvement Unit Charge (£/1,000 cubic metres)

There are 20 regions 'supported' by the Environment Agency in 2020/21. Abstraction from these rivers is 3 times dearer than 'unsupported' sources. Abstraction from tidal sources costs 20% of 'unsupported' sources.

Winter abstraction charges (authorised for abstraction between 1st November and 31st March) cost 16% of all-year abstraction charges. Summer charges (1st April to 31st October) are 160% of the all-year charge.

An application charge of £135 (a higher application charge of £1,500 is due for those extracting water for use in electricity/power generation) and advertising administration charge of £100 is due, alongside an Annual Charge which is the sum of the Standard Charge and the Compensation Charge which are each calculated from a formula comprising the Standard Unit Charge (SUC) and the Environmental Improvement Unit Charge (EIUC) respectively. The Annual Charge is not payable for temporary licences. The charges for 2020/21 are as follows:

Region (£/1000m^3)	Standard Unit Charges	Environmental Improvement Unit Charge (EIUC)
Anglian	27.51	0.00
Midlands	14.95	0.00
Northumbria	16.66	0.00
Yorkshire	11.63	0.00
North West	12.57	3.86
Southern	19.23	0.00
South West (incl. Wessex)	19.71	12.91
Thames	13.84	5.69
Dee	15.54	0.00
Wye	15.54	0.00

Most abstractors must provide the Environment Agency with accurate records (known as 'returns') of how much water is taken in order to enable them to balance water resources between different users and check compliance with licence conditions. If a licence is in place and you have not extracted any water, a 'nil' return must be submitted. It is a cross-compliance breach to not submit an abstraction return form under GAEC 2.

Water Costs

A typical extraction cost for a non-tidal, non-supported farm in East Anglia for 25mm per hectare (250m³ per hectare) applied through a rain gun (high loss factor) would be as follows:

	£/ha	Pence/m³	£/acre inch
Winter Abstraction only	1.10	0.44	0.45
All-Year Abstraction	6.88	2.75	2.83
Summer Abstraction only	11.00	4.40	4.52
Mains Water	475.00	190.00	195.00

This is clearly just the cost for the water. The capital invested plus the labour and any power requirement should also be accounted for which will vary according to individual circumstances.

Overall Operating Costs

Because of variations in individual farm circumstances in terms of source works and the irrigation system used, the overall cost of applying 25mm per hectare can range widely, from £85 to £155/ha. Very sophisticated systems distributing mains water over intensive specialist crops could be much more expensive.

Conversions and Calculations

The (approximate) imperial equivalents for metric values commonly used in irrigation are as follows:

- 1 cubic metre = 1,000 litres = 220 gallons (1 million gallons = 4,546 cubic metres).

- A pump capacity of 100 cubic metres per hour is equivalent to 22,000 gallons per hour (367 gallons per minute).

- 1,000 cubic metres is sufficient to apply 25 millimetres of water over 4 hectares, which is approximately equivalent to applying 1 inch over 10 acres. An acre inch is therefore 100 cubic meters (22,000 gallons), or a hectare centimetre is 100 cubic meters.

- The cost/volume conversion from a hectare of 25mm depth to an acre-inch is 0.411 or 2.433 from an acre-inch to a hectare 25mm.

GRAIN DRYING AND STORAGE

When reviewing different grain drying systems, consider it alongside existing or new grain storage options. This is because some drying systems necessitate certain storage facilities and vice versa. The tables below outline the cost of grain drying and storage for three options for a 500-hectare arable farm, assuming all grain is dried. Whilst in practical terms, not the entire harvest is necessarily dried, in most cases the vast majority of grain will be dried (or at least cooled) but just to various different extents depending on harvest moisture levels and crop condition.

Grain Drying and Storage Comparison	On Floor Drying & Storage	Continuous Flow Dryer & Concrete Floor Storage	Batch Dryer & Concrete Floor Storage
Capital Costs (per tonne):-			
Store Building	£98	£98	£98
Floor, Tunnels, Fans & Controllers (no stirrers)	£61		
Dryer (16t/hour) + Wet Intake Area		£37	
Dryer (25t/batch system) + Wet Intake Area			£26
Store / Dryer Longevity (years)	35	35 / 25	35 / 25
Interest/Opportunity Cost	4%	4%	4%
Cost per tonne per year			
	£/tonne	**£/tonne**	**£/tonne**
Depreciation	£4.54	£4.28	£3.84
Finance/Opportunity Cost	£3.18	£2.70	£2.48
Fuel & Electricity (per 5% moisture)	£3.75	£4.41	£4.46
Repairs & Insurance	£2.39	£2.58	£2.25
Total *(assuming total tonnage dried)*	**£13.86**	**£13.97**	**£13.03**

Handling costs in terms of elevators, conveyors, telehandlers and trailers to move grain into and out of drying systems are additional to the above figures and vary according to the layout of the buildings and infrastructure.

GRAIN STORAGE

Clearly the capital costs detailed in the table above vary considerably depending on precise requirements and site circumstances. For example, an elaborate plant on a greenfield site, including weighbridge, intake pit, elevator, conveyors, ventilated storage bins, catwalk etc. in a new building could cost well in excess of £300/t. *See page 224.*

Contract Storage: typically, £2.00 - £2.75/t per month with a handling charge of around £2.00 - £2.50 per tonne for loading into store and out of store. Large grain merchants offer storage including haulage for around £10-12/t for the four-month period September to December (giving flexibility on marketing where no on-farm storage is available) with a further charge of £1.50/t per month for every additional month stored prior to sale post-Christmas. Handling charges will be in addition. Alternatively, farmers can choose to buy into farmer owned co-operative grain store operations. Costs vary depending upon membership structures but are in the region of £100-£120/t for membership storage rights (normally partly in the form of a loan/investment), plus annual maintenance and handling charges (including haulage) of typically £10-13/t, plus drying charges of £2-£8/t depending on moisture levels. Normally, the additional drying charges only apply for grain delivered with a moisture content in excess of 16%. The main benefits of membership in a co-operative store are the ability to use own buildings for other uses, as well as take away any on-going store management work, whilst retaining the benefit of flexible marketing. Often, co-operative stores will also allow non-members to store at a premium storage price of circa

£12-15/t and premium handling and drying charges of £4-£12/t according to moisture levels. Retiring farmers can normally choose to sell their storage rights back to the co-operative or to other members, therefore releasing their invested capital.

GRAIN DRYING

Choosing the most appropriate system depends on many factors. The capital cost of installing on-floor drying facilities is significantly greater than a dryer and a concrete floor building to store grain post drying. On-floor drying requires minimal handling of grain post-harvest but time to monitor store moistures and temperatures over 3-6 months post-harvest is needed. On-floor drying is much slower so less suitable for those wishing to sell grain soon after harvest / early autumn.

Continuous flow dryers require good building layout to limit the infrastructure required to convey grain from the dryer into different stores. Labour input for a modern automatic facility is minimal. Continuous flow dryers typically have low resale values being fixed and immobile. Mobile batch dryers are much cheaper but can require more handling of grain (forklift and trailers) unless they are automatic and sited suitably. The capital costs per tonne are therefore often much lower but running costs higher. These machines are popular on many farms, offering flexibility and a viable alternative where a suitable electrical connection is not available (the example above assumes an electrically powered batch dryer, but PTO powered machines are also popular). They also have a better second-hand value. They suit a farm with multiple grain storage sites and where storage does not allow grain to be cooled as each batch is cooled prior to un-loading, unlike continuous flow machines.

There could be a further cost requirement to cool the grain in store after being dried if stored on a concrete floor. This cost varies depending on the system used – pedestals or ducting under the crop are the most common. The costs of suitable fans for duct systems vary between £1,500 and £4,000 depending on requirements. Pedestals are much cheaper at between £150 and £300 per unit depending on type, quality and motor capacity.

The introduction of the Renewable Heat Incentive has offered opportunities to use renewable fuels (woodchip, straw) to reduce drying costs. There is even a market for using drying systems (on-floor facilities) to dry woodchip fuel to utilise grain drying facilities when not required for combinable crops.

There has been considerable investment in grain storage and drying facilities in recent years, which has been much needed, with many businesses having old and often inefficient facilities. Another alternative is Central Grain Stores. These organisations offer grain drying services for about £8.00 to £12.00 per tonne for 5% moisture drying for members and non-members respectively. Contractors' charges vary between £10.00 per tonne and £15.00 per tonne for drying grain by 5% moisture, although often prices quoted are much lower because less drying may be required on average (say 3% average requirement).

Grain cleaning equipment gives flexibility if a crop sample is poor, bushel weights low or admixture high. Cleaning can aid storage, drying and crop value. Superior crop quality, particularly niche crops, attracts premiums. A rotary cleaner with 25 tonne per hour cleaning output and 8-10 tonne per hour very fine cleaning output costs £20,000 - £25,000. Some drying systems enable cleaning systems to be added to their automated controls to enable a fully automated integrated system to be installed. Simpler cleaning systems cost significantly less to purchase but will not enable the same degree of cleaning capability.

LIVESTOCK HAULAGE COSTS

The cost of hauling livestock to market, to field, back to winter housing or other movements between grazing is a cost that is often over-looked. The table below demonstrates the farmers cost of hauling livestock per head per journey, for a number of different journey lengths.

Journey Length	£ Per Head Per Journey		
	Ewe	Finished Lamb	Finished Cattle
1 Mile	0.54	0.36	5.39
5 Miles	0.67	0.45	6.73
10 Miles	0.84	0.56	8.41
15 Miles	1.01	0.67	10.09
20 Miles	1.18	0.78	11.77
30 Miles	1.51	1.01	15.13

The costs calculated above include the cost of running a vehicle (pick-up/Landrover), based upon 12,000 miles annual mileage, attributing this cost on a per mile basis to the livestock transport cost (to reflect the fact that the vehicle is also used for many other purposes). The cost of running a livestock trailer (capital cost and repairs/maintenance) is based upon an average sized farm stock trailer with decks, capable of holding 30 ewes, 45 finished lambs, or 3 finished cattle, assuming it is kept for 10 years and used for 40 journeys per year.

In arriving at a cost per head, the calculations assume that the trailer is always fully occupied with one of the above livestock numbers. The costs per head by journey length assume one journey; therefore, if the journey to market was 30 miles one-way and no return load was bought back (i.e. an empty trailer), the total cost of transporting those livestock to market would in fact be almost double that shown above (although recognising the fact that towing an empty trailer will use less fuel than when fully loaded). The labour costs calculated above exclude time for loading/un-loading but account for time spent driving between destinations averaging 30mph.

Specialist livestock hauliers charge either on a per day basis, cost per section of a lorry, or a cost per head for specific journey lengths. As a result, charges vary widely depending upon the specific circumstances, such as distances and the size of groups etc. As a guide, to move breeding sheep from Yorkshire to the Midlands would cost approximately £2.75-£3.25/ewe assuming the haulier is able to backload. Costs for hauling lambs to market over a distance of more than 40 miles would cost circa £1.75-£2.20/lamb and £22-28/head for finished cattle depending on access and load size etc. An articulated lorry and driver, fully equipped for livestock haulage, would typically cost £640-£800/day or £100-£135/section (approx. 6 sections on an articulated lorry). Charges per section are common for long distances to specialist events or sales e.g. a pedigree breeder taking stock to breeding sales.

GRAIN HAULAGE COSTS

The AHDB's grain haulage survey has now ceased but indicative haulage costs per tonne of grain (and oilseed) in Great Britain for varying journey lengths are shown in the table below. Given that the majority of combinable crops are sold on an ex-farm basis, haulage costs are less relevant to the farmer.

10 miles	20 miles	40 miles	60 miles	100 miles	150 miles
£4.85/t	£5.75/t	£7.35/t	£8.95/t	£12.17/t	£16.15/t

VI.   OTHER FIXED COSTS

1.   WHOLE FARM FIXED COSTS

The following offers a broad indication of the levels of fixed costs per hectare (acre) for various types and sizes of farm, estimated for 2022, including the value of unpaid family manual labour, such as that of the farmer and spouse. The figures are based on Farm Business Survey (FBS) information for 2019-20 (February to February), adjusted for subsequent changes in costs. The FBS is based on a sample of farms which changes over time, so there is not a consistent sample. This emphasises that the costs below should be used as an indication and must be adjusted according to individual situations; see also further notes on the use of this data below. The survey is for England, the figures within this section are broadly applicable to most parts of the UK. Specific regional reports can be accessed via the FBS website. Farm types are standardised across the country based on Defra's standard farm classifications. All of these costs vary considerably according to many factors, especially the intensity of farming, e.g. the number of cows per hectare on dairy farms, the hectares of intensive crops on general cropping farms and level of management.

The figures provided are averages. 'Premium' farms of the same level of intensity can have labour, machinery and general overhead costs at least 20% lower. It is the net amount (Gross Margin – Fixed Costs) that matters. The 'small' farm categories relate only to full-time holdings and do not include very intensive holdings occupying very small areas.

Farms are difficult places to make efficient use of overheads for several reasons:

- Overheads, especially labour and machinery are chunky items; for example, you cannot buy half a tractor.

- Being seasonal businesses, farms are inevitably inefficient at utilising such costs with some machines only used for a few days per year such as ploughs, combine harvesters and even sometimes milking parlours.

- Farmers sometimes prefer to own a piece of machinery rather than hire or contract it, giving them more control of timings and perceived quality of workmanship.

- Farmers are often over-staffed or mechanised to facilitate swift action when short windows of opportunity arise such as between poor weather or lots of harvest to complete in a short period, or business growth if opportunities arise.

- A farm often represents a lifestyle as well as a job meaning the occupier might spend more than necessary time in it. For example, if it is large enough to efficiently employ 80% of a person, it may well have a fulltime owner operating it.

- There are several jobs on a farm that have low returns on investment that owner occupiers in particular spend time doing that a purely profit-centred manager would not entertain.

- Farms often include accommodation for the occupier, meaning resources spent on the house might be considered a business cost.

These factors make typical farm costs considerably higher than efficiently run, well thought out pragmatic farm businesses. The variation between them is enormous.

The term 'fixed costs' is used here as it is in gross margin analysis and planning; a full explanation of the differences between fixed and variable costs in this context is given on pages 3 and 4. Note that all casual labour and contract work has been included under fixed costs. In calculating enterprise gross margins on the individual farm, these costs are normally allocated as variable costs if they are specific to a particular enterprise and vary approximately in proportion to its size, i.e. are approximately constant per hectare of a particular crop or per head of livestock. Otherwise they are included as fixed costs. In both cases, however, they could be regarded as substitutes for regular labour and/or the farmer's machinery - which are both fixed costs. It is therefore simpler if both are included, fully, as fixed costs. If one is comparing results from accounts set out on a gross margin basis, and some or all of the casual labour and contract work have been included as variable costs (especially on cropping farms, e.g. for potato harvesting using casual labour or a contractor's machine), the necessary adjustments need to be made in making the comparisons.

Notes on the Schedules

1. *Unpaid Labour:* Refers to the value of unpaid family manual labour, including that of the farmer and spouse.

2. *Machinery Depreciation:* This is based on current (i.e. replacement) cost. This gives a truer reflection of the real loss of value of machinery (as is apparent when replacement becomes necessary). It also allows easier comparison between different businesses. However, many farm accounts calculate depreciation on the 'historic' (i.e. original) cost of the machinery. This will tend to produce a lower figure. Depending on the age of the machine and bearing in mind recent strong increases in machinery prices, the historic method may underestimate depreciation by 10-20%. Note that both the Depreciation item and Repairs include vehicles.

3. *Leasing Charges:* The capital element, but not the interest, is included in depreciation; the proportion paid as interest varies according to the rate of interest paid and the length of the leasing period but is typically 7%-10%.

4. *Machinery Running Costs:* This includes fuel, oil, repairs, servicing and vehicle tax and insurance. Separate figures for these elements are no longer available. As a general rule, fuel might make up a little over half of all such costs.

5. *General Overheads:* include general farm maintenance and repairs, office expenses, water, insurance, fees, subscriptions, etc.

6. *Rent & Interest:* Rent only relates to the actual rent paid by the average farm in that particular category. It is not an imputed rent for all land farmed by the business; thus, a fully owned-occupied farm will have no rental costs. Only actual interest paid by the average farm in that particular category is shown.

In making comparisons with fixed costs taken from farm accounts it is important to note that in the figures below, unpaid manual labour is included; farm accounts will rarely include this. Also, the figures below include average rent and interest; in farm accounts these will vary widely depending on the farm tenure and borrowing. Very low 'target' figures given in press articles often omit these items and can therefore be misleading; usually, too, they relate only to large, very well-appointed farms. If an 'opportunity cost' for owner-occupied land (often fully paid for many years) is included, then the cost level rises further. Note too that the figures given below do not include management, whether paid or unpaid. The margin after deducting the fixed costs below from the total gross margin plus any other farm receipts represents the total return to management and own capital in the business.

Mainly Dairying

£/ha (£/acre)	Under 75 ha (Under 185 acres)		75 - 125 ha (185 - 310 acres)		Over 125 ha (Over 310 acres)	
Regular Labour (paid)	55	(22)	200	(81)	365	(148)
Regular Labour (unpaid)	640	(259)	460	(186)	210	(85)
Casual Labour	45	(18)	35	(14)	50	(20)
Total Labour	**740**	**(299)**	**695**	**(281)**	**625**	**(253)**
Machinery Depreciation	155	(63)	205	(83)	210	(85)
Machinery Running Costs	160	(65)	210	(85)	230	(93)
Contract	105	(42)	170	(69)	210	(85)
Total Power & Machinery...	**420**	**(170)**	**585**	**(237)**	**650**	**(263)**
Farm Maintenance	60	(24)	90	(36)	110	(45)
Water & Electricity	165	(67)	195	(79)	180	(73)
General Overhead Expenses ...	85	(34)	75	(30)	75	(30)
Total Overheads	**310**	**(125)**	**360**	**(146)**	**365**	**(148)**
Rent & Interest	170	(69)	200	(81)	310	(125)
Total Fixed Costs	**1640**	**(664)**	**1840**	**(745)**	**1950**	**(789)**

Mainly Cereals

£/ha (£/acre)	Under 200 ha (Under 490 acres)		200 - 300 ha (490 - 740 acres)		Over 300 ha (Over 740 acres)	
Regular Labour (paid)	50	(20)	75	(30)	85	(34)
Regular Labour (unpaid)	170	(69)	120	(49)	80	(32)
Casual Labour	15	(6)	15	(6)	10	(4)
Total Labour	**235**	**(95)**	**210**	**(85)**	**175**	**(71)**
Machinery Depreciation	135	(55)	135	(55)	120	(49)
Machinery Running Costs	110	(45)	110	(45)	105	(42)
Contract	105	(42)	80	(32)	95	(38)
Total Power & Machinery...	**350**	**(142)**	**325**	**(132)**	**320**	**(130)**
Farm Maintenance	35	(14)	35	(14)	35	(14)
Water & Electricity	70	(28)	70	(28)	65	(26)
General Overhead Expenses ...	105	(42)	85	(34)	75	(30)
Total Overheads	**210**	**(85)**	**190**	**(77)**	**175**	**(71)**
Rent & Interest	120	(49)	130	(53)	145	(59)
Total Fixed Costs	**915**	**(370)**	**855**	**(346)**	**815**	**(330)**

Large-Scale Cereal Farms (over 800 ha (1,975 acres)

Data from the Farm Business Survey indicates there are further economies of scale for cereals farms at even larger farm sizes. There are likely to be wide variations depending on the precise scale of these businesses (some of which are very large). The following figures may be used as a guide; Labour - £155 per ha (of which paid labour £110); Power & Machinery - £290 per ha; Other Overheads - £190 per ha; Rent & Interest - £110 per ha. This totals £745 per ha (£301 per acre).

Data for larger-scale General Cropping farms (see below) is not so conclusive. Costs on a 'per ha' basis do not necessarily seem to fall as farm size increases. This may be due to the larger proportion of (higher cost) root crops and vegetables seen on larger farm sizes.

General Cropping

£/ha (£/acre)	Under 150 ha (Under 370 acres)		150 - 250 ha (370 - 620 acres)		Over 250 ha (Over 620 acres)	
Regular Labour (paid)	40	(16)	95	(38)	105	(42)
Regular Labour (unpaid)	220	(89)	170	(69)	145	(59)
Casual Labour	10	(4)	25	(10)	30	(12)
Total Labour	**270**	**(109)**	**290**	**(117)**	**280**	**(113)**
Machinery Depreciation	105	(42)	140	(57)	150	(61)
Machinery Running Costs	115	(47)	145	(59)	140	(57)
Contract	170	(69)	130	(53)	110	(45)
Total Power & Machinery...	**390**	**(158)**	**415**	**(168)**	**400**	**(162)**
Farm Maintenance	30	(12)	40	(16)	35	(14)
Water & Electricity	80	(32)	90	(36)	80	(32)
General Overhead Expenses ...	60	(24)	60	(24)	60	(24)
Total Overheads	**170**	**(69)**	**190**	**(77)**	**175**	**(71)**
Rent & Interest	165	(67)	175	(71)	165	(67)
Total Fixed Costs	**995**	**(403)**	**1070**	**(433)**	**1020**	**(413)**

With potatoes and/or sugar beet and/or field vegetables; grade 1 or 2 land.

Mainly Sheep/Cattle (lowland)

	Under 90 ha (Under 220 acres)		90 - 125 ha (220 - 310 acres)		Over 125 ha (Over 310 acres)	
Regular Labour (paid)	25	(10)	40	(16)	65	(26)
Regular Labour (unpaid)	400	(162)	360	(146)	245	(99)
Casual Labour	20	(8)	20	(8)	25	(10)
Total Labour	**445**	**(180)**	**420**	**(170)**	**335**	**(136)**
Machinery Depreciation	105	(42)	120	(49)	115	(47)
Machinery Running Costs	100	(40)	110	(45)	115	(47)
Contract	70	(28)	75	(30)	85	(34)
Total Power & Machinery...	**275**	**(111)**	**305**	**(123)**	**315**	**(127)**
Farm Maintenance	35	(14)	45	(18)	50	(20)
Water & Electricity	75	(30)	80	(32)	70	(28)
General Overhead Expenses ...	60	(24)	60	(24)	65	(26)
Total Overheads	**170**	**(69)**	**185**	**(75)**	**185**	**(75)**
Rent & Interest	95	(38)	110	(45)	125	(51)
Total Fixed Costs	**985**	**(399)**	**1020**	**(413)**	**960**	**(389)**

Mainly Sheep/Cattle (upland)

	Under 130 ha (Under 320 acres)		130 - 200 ha (320 - 490 acres)		Over 200 ha (Over 490 acres)	
Regular Labour (paid)	15	(6)	15	(6)	35	(14)
Regular Labour (unpaid)	300	(121)	235	(95)	155	(63)
Casual Labour	15	(6)	15	(6)	15	(6)
Total Labour	**330**	**(134)**	**265**	**(107)**	**205**	**(83)**
Machinery Depreciation	60	(24)	65	(26)	55	(22)
Machinery Running Costs	60	(24)	55	(22)	50	(20)
Contract	30	(12)	30	(12)	30	(12)
Total Power & Machinery...	**150**	**(61)**	**150**	**(61)**	**135**	**(55)**
Farm Maintenance	20	(8)	20	(8)	15	(6)
Water & Electricity	45	(18)	40	(16)	30	(12)
General Overhead Expenses ...	25	(10)	35	(14)	25	(10)
Total Overheads	**90**	**(36)**	**95**	**(38)**	**70**	**(28)**
Rent & Interest	50	(20)	60	(24)	65	(26)
Total Fixed Costs	**620**	**(251)**	**570**	**(231)**	**475**	**(192)**

Other Farm Types

The other main DEFRA farm types are '*Mixed*', *Pigs*, *Poultry and Horticulture*. As the name suggests, the mixed category includes all farms where one enterprise is not sufficiently dominant for it to be allocated to one of the categories above. As it includes many different mixes of enterprises, the figures are unlikely to be useful for budgeting purposes.

Due to the intensity and variability of the Pig, Poultry and Horticultural farm types, the presentation of average 'per ha' figures would not be useful. Detailed historic FBS data for the different pig, poultry, and horticulture systems found in England are published online at the addresses given on page 5. For pigs, Askham Bryan: for poultry and horticulture, Reading, or go to the FBS website.

2. RENTS

One of the main factors affecting the rental level of agricultural land is the type of tenancy it is let on. There are three main types of agricultural agreements for letting land in England and Wales: Full or Agricultural Holdings Act (AHA) 1986 Tenancies, Farm Business Tenancies (FBTs, under the 1995 Act) and Seasonal Lets of less than 1 year. Since the introduction of the 1995 Act, no new AHA tenancies can be created.

Basic Payment Scheme provisions need to be taken into account when comparing rents. The situation varies from farm to farm and between different regions of the UK. For AHAs & FBTs, the tenant should claim the Basic Payment (BP). In seasonal lets (grazing agreements) the Licensor should claim. In an AHA tenancy agreement the rent is independent of the Basic Payment as the tenant will own the Single Payment entitlements in 2005 which will have been converted to Basic Payment entitlements in 2015 and at the end of the tenancy the tenant retains ownership. With FBTs generally, the tenant claims a 'full' BP, and if land becomes available without BP entitlements then rental levels will be lower than those below.

The BPS structure will be similar in 2022 to 2021. But in England payments continue to be reduced. Furthermore, in England, it is expected that the Basic Payment could be taken as a 'lump-sum' in 2022 for those exiting the industry. In addition direct payments (BPS) will be de-linked from land and entitlements at some time in the future, probably in 2024 – See Government Support Section. This means that a claim for direct support (i.e. BPS) will no longer be dependent on occupying land. How de-linking is to occur is important. The BPS claimant in a 'reference year(s)' is likely to get the future income stream during the 7 year transition. At the time of writing the reference year is unknown. 'Where' support ends up after de-linking will complicate the rental market. Further ahead, the introduction of ELM in England raises questions, as these payments will be variable between farms and who enters the scheme, the Landlord or Tenant, will matter.

Land rents have increased over recent years. The tables below show rents up to 2018 and do not pick up current trends. They include lettings which may not be at full value for one reason or another e.g. lets to other family members and therefore do not correspond to some of the headline rates often seen. Recently, uncertainty over Brexit and farm policy together with challenging weather the rental market has slowed. However, tender rents, especially in the cropping sector, are often above levels that can be justified. As the BPS reduces in England, we may see rents decline.

Unless otherwise stated, the figures in this section relate to farms let with a combination of crops, grass and rough grazing in England; they include housing and buildings.

Agricultural Holdings Act Tenancies:

The average rent for lowland, excluding woodland and rough grazing for farms under full Agricultural Tenancies is approximately £185 per ha, *£75 per acre*, in 2020/2021. The levels on large mixed arable farms (i.e. including potatoes, sugar beet and/or vegetables) on very good soil, or well-equipped dairy farms, will tend to average £175 to £225 per hectare (*£70 to £90 per acre*). Rents on moderate, below average, quality farms, with full repairing and insuring leases are likely to average £125 to £150 per hectare (*£50 to £60 per acre*).

Farm Business Tenancies:

FBT rents are generally higher than AHA tenancies, although this is not always the case especially for lowland cattle and sheep land. When reviewing AHA rents the scarcity value is ignored, but FBT rents (unless they have an agreed alternative rent review formula) reflect an open market and therefore the gap is wider. For cereals land of reasonable quality, offers used to approximate to a tonne of wheat per acre. 2020 was not a good year for most cereals businesses, but 2021 is likely to be better, even so with new farm policies starting to kick-in, good farm managers are assessing their businesses. Nevertheless, high rents for maize land

and other alternatives destined for anaerobic digesters put a base in the market. Local markets for potato land can also command high values and even cause agents to try and increase 3-5 year agreements on the back of this, but there has to be a rotation. A sensible rent for new agreements throughout 2021/2022 for arable land would be £310 to £370 per hectare (£125 to £150 per acre) for FBTs for less than five years. Fixed rents for the next five years are likely to be less, £270 to £300 per hectare (£110 to £120/acre) as the deductions under the Agricultural Transition 'kick-in'.

Farm Business Survey 2019-20:

The following figures are the latest National Statistics produced by Defra showing the estimates of farm rents in England from the 2019/20 Farm Business Survey (FBS). Results from the 2019/20 Survey (Feb-Feb) mainly cover 2019 so are referred to as the 2019 results. Rough grazing may be included in the figures given in the table below. The results from the survey show actual amounts being paid by farm businesses and some land is likely to be let at below competitive rates, for various reasons i.e., to family and are also historic in nature. For this reason, they tend to be lower than rents being struck for newly let or reviewed land.

Average Rent by Type of Agreement:	£/ha	(acre)
Full Agricultural Tenancies	177	(72)
Farm Business Tenancies for 1 year and over......................	222	(90)
Seasonal Lets of less than one year.......................................	150	(61)

Full Agricultural Tenancies in England

Farm Average Rent by Farm Type:

£ per ha (acre)	2015	2016	2017	2018	2019
Cereals	194 (79)	197 (80)	204 (83)	205 (83)	204 (83)
General Cropping	204 (83)	216 (87)	212 (86)	220 (89)	224 (91)
Dairy	193 (78)	193 (78)	197 (80)	206 (83)	205 (83)
Cattle & Sheep (LFA)	79 (32)	69 (28)	56 (23)	54 (22)	63 (25)
Cattle and Sheep (Lowland)	160 (65)	169 (68)	176 (71)	187 (76)	181 (73)
All	179 (73)	181 (73)	170 (69)	170 (69)	177 (72)

Farm Business Tenancies – One year and over:

Average Rent by Farm Type:

£ per ha (acre)	2015	2016	2017	2018	2019
Cereals	234 (95)	259(105)	267(108)	279(113)	263 (106)
General Cropping	277(112)	280(113)	331(134)	329(133)	298 (121)
Dairy	231 (93)	238 (96)	242 (98)	255(103)	271 (110)
Cattle & Sheep (LFA)	78 (32)	69 (28)	67 (27)	71 (29)	79 (32)
Cattle and Sheep (Lowland)	142 (57)	157 (64)	177 (72)	190 (77)	128 (52)
All	210 (85)	219 (89)	227 (92)	231 (93)	222 (90)

Source of Data

The FBS is an annual survey conducted by trained Interviewers. The FBS collects data at business level and collects data for up to 15 agreements per business, with a sample of around 1,900 farm businesses. The 2020-21 Survey is due to be published in March 2022.

3. LAND PRICES

SALE VALUE OF FARMLAND, ENGLAND AND WALES

Current Agricultural Land Prices (CALP)/RICS/RAU

A CALP/RICS Farmland Price Index (England and Wales) began in 1995. It covers sales of vacant possession land in England and Wales. It is calculated by dividing total value of sales by total area sold. Figures for the most recent half-yearly periods are subject to revision as further information becomes available. More recently the survey has been undertaken by the RICS and the RAU (Royal Agricultural University).

As can be seen from the table below, the volume of land traded in any year, and included in the Index, is low – probably only between 0.1%-0.2% of the total agricultural area of England and Wales. The relative scarcity of land for sale has contributed to the increases in prices seen since the early 2000's. Such a 'thin' market can also make prices sensitive to a small number of large transactions. For this reason, in recent years, RICS moved away from the transaction-based figures, to using opinion-based data as its headline land price figures. Both are presented in the table below. The 'transaction' based measure uses actual sales and includes a residential component (where that component is estimated to be worth less than 50% of the total value of the land). The 'opinion' based measure, is an estimate of bare land only, no residential component is included and therefore it tends to be less than the transaction-based figure.

However RICS reports it is becoming increasingly difficult to gain sufficient responses for the Opinion Based Survey to be reliable and RICS/RAU have suspended this element of the survey from 2018. The RICS/RAU Farmland Market Survey is no longer produced but the Transaction Based Weighted Average Price is available in the RICS/RAU Farmland Market Directory of Land Sales and is shown in the table below. The figure is usually reported twice yearly, but data was only collected once in 2020.

CALP/RICS Farmland Price Index 2009-2020

| | | No. of Sales | Area sold '000 | | Weighted Average Price £ | | | |
| | | | | | Transaction Based | | Opinion Based | |
			Ha	acres	Ha	acres	Ha	Acres
2009	H1	181	6.3	15.6	15,204	6,153	12,172	4,926
2010	H1	162	6.6	16.3	15,948	6,454	13,529	5,475
2011	H1	154	4.2	10.6	18,631	7,540	15,110	6,115
2012	H1	166	4.69	11.6	20,586	8,331	16,378	6,628
2013	H1	188	5.02	12.4	21,656	8,764	18,387	7,441
2014	H1	213	6.15	15.2	24,137	9,768	19,934	8,067
2015	H1	149	4.90	12.1	22,921	9,276	20,828	8,429
	H2	388	12.0	29.6	27,302	11,049	20,524	8,306
2016	H1	196	6.60	16.3	27,062	10,952	19,706	7,975
	H2	254	12.6	31.1	25,286	10,509	19,921	8,062
2017	H1	235	12.5	30.9	24,952	10,098	18,634	7,541
	H2	331	14.3	35.3	25,711	10,405	18,369	7,434
2018	H1	192	7.9	19.5	28,332	11,466	18,636	7,542
	H2	356	10.6	26.3	23,641	9,571	18,873	7,638
2019	H1	251	13.0	32.0	24,414	9,880	n/a	n/a
2019	H2	253	5.9	14.5	23,151	9,369	n/a	n/a
2020*		503	12.0	29.7	25,674	10,390	n/a	n/a
2021	Estimate				25,945	10,500		

* = Provisional

Farmland prices weathered the economic downturn of 2008-2013 far better than other asset classes. 'Lifestyle' purchasers were replaced by investors and farmers keeping the demand and the price of land high as the economy faltered. Since 2009, very low rates of borrowing money and negligible returns for cash investments has fuelled farmland values. This has been coupled with tight supply of land and improved farm commodity prices. But the fall in commodity prices in 2016/17 and an increase in supply saw an easing of land values, but not a significant decline.

Demand for land, particularly good land in the right location is strong and there has been a strengthening in values. Lifestyle buyers looking to relocate out of the cities due to the pandemic have strengthened amenity property values. The biggest challenge seems to have been delays in taking a sale to completion due to the pandemic restrictions. Furthermore, the temporary change to Stamp Duty Land Tax rates and 'rollover' buyers helped to keep demand for land high.

The fundamentals driving farmland values such as low supply, tax advantages of owning land and the competition from a variety of land uses remain. Looking further ahead an increase in demand for properties which offer diversified income streams and natural capita may arise due to the introduction of Environmental Land Management and the decline of the BPS. Land prices could drop back (along with other asset classes) when base rates rise, leading to higher costs of borrowing money and fixed interest investments start to generate a return. As always there is a wide variation in prices; location and soil quality remain the key drivers for commercial land. Farmland prices for the period 1995 to 2008 are in previous editions of the Pocketbook.

Other Land Price Series

In past editions of the Pocketbook, Inland Revenue and Valuation Office (VO) land price returns have been published, covering 30 years up to 1996/97 and 1993-2004 respectively. These series contained detailed splits between vacant possession and tenanted land, farms (including houses and buildings) and bare land, and also by size, land class and region. This information is still available from past editions of the Pocketbook. Data in the VO series does not continue beyond 2004, although limited information is available on the website, www.voa.gov.uk. Previous editions also include the Oxford Institute/Savills (1) Series, 1937-2000. Much of the data included in this section is available from the RICS website – www.rics.org

SALE VALUE OF FORESTS AND WOODLANDS

Forests

The figures in this section relate to planted land sold (over 20 hectares) so that values include the value of the property (land) and the timber. They focus on properties that are predominantly conifer.

During 2020, unexpectedly the market for forest properties has grown significantly, in total £200.18 million worth of forestry properties were traded throughout GB. This is an increase of 58% compared to 2019. Properties in Scotland continue to dominate the market, with around 69% of total sales, England recorded lower than usual sales at 5% with Wales higher than normal at 26%, due to the sale of one very large property. In total 16,595 hectares were sold, compared to 14,235 hectares in 2019. The average size of property sold in 2020 was 206 hectares, up from 136 hectares in the previous year, with the average sale price of a property £3.282m (£1.56 million in 2019).

The UK forestry market has been very competitive, experiencing a strong performance through 2020 producing record results. Forestry remains one of the highest performing assets. It continues to be attractive to investors especially due to the tax benefits available to owning woodland. Income tax is not payable on timber sales. There is potentially 100% relief on Inheritance Tax and any gains attributable to standing or felled timber are exempt from Capital Gains Tax. The main factors influencing the increase in forestry property values are:

- Low interest rates that are forecast to remain so for some time
- Uncertain prospects for other asset classes such as retail and office
- Moves to decarbonise the economy backed by Government policy
- Emphasis on renewable/sustainable raw materials
- Corporate reporting to meet obligations under Environmental, Social and Governance (ESG) headings.

Sale Price

The figures below are for predominantly upland with at least 50% coniferous content. Values vary with many factors; only age is recorded here but size of block and yield class are also important. Previous editions of the Pocketbook have included prices by age band and size of block.

Average Sale Price of UK Forestland 2018 - 2020: £ per stocked ha (acre):

By Age Band (approx.)	2018	2019	2020
	£/ha *(£/acre)*	£/ha *(£/acre)*	£/ha *(£/acre)*
1-10 Years	10,500 *(4,249)*	11,000 *(4,452)*	27,500 *(11,129)*
11-20 Years	11,000 *(4,452)*	5,500 *(2,226)*	21,500 *(8,701)*
21-30 Years	7,500 *(3,035)*	11,000 *(4,452)*	16,500 *(6,677)*
31-40 Years	7,500 *(3,035)*	14,000 *(5,666)*	14,000 *(5,666)*
Over 40 Years	10,500 *(4,249)*	11,000 *(4,452)*	12,500 *(5,059)*

Mixed Woodlands

The UK Forest Market Report includes a section on Mixed Woodlands. These are woodlands that are greater than 10 hectares (25 acres) but are managed with 'mixed objectives'. In 2020 the report recorded the sale of 750 hectares (1,853 acres), down from 910 hectares in 2019, across the UK realising a total of £6.68 million (9.25m in 2019). Engl

and achieved the highest average price at £13,170 per hectare (£5,330/acre); Wales £9,662 per hectare (£3,910/acre) and Scotland £3,707 per hectare (£1,500/acre).

The main driver for price, unsurprisingly is location. Values remain the highest adjacent to centres of population and for properties of high amenity value, with investors increasing the latter through attention to good management, improving public access, sporting capacity and adding environmental improvements such as ponds. Woodlands which offer privacy and seclusion for weekend enjoyment are sought after. Likewise, self-contained, attractive small woods where the sporting rights are owned continue to be in demand and make the highest sale price. Most purchasers are looking to combine personal enjoyment with financial considerations, such as family tax planning. It is estimated that 50% of woodland in England is 'undermanaged' meaning there is an investment opportunity in this market. *Note: in order to qualify for the tax advantages of owning woodland, the woodland must meet the criteria of 'commercial management'*

Source: UK Forest Market Report (2020) – John Clegg & Co/Tilhill Forestry

4.   PUBLIC LIABILITY INSURANCE

Public liability insurance is not a legal obligation. However, it is necessary if the general public is interacting with your business in any way, whether deliveries, visitors, etc. With a rising emphasis on encouraging the public to understand farming including visiting farms, this should be a necessity for all farms.

These figures are per year, per farm. Prices of some providers are the same for each band, as they calculate their quotes differently. Often public liability comes with product and environmental liability. These figures are solely for farming, and not other activities that might take place on a farm such a contract farming, other diversifications such as a shoot, livery or a farm shop.

	Mixed Farm (130 ha)	Dairy (130 ha)	Arable (250 ha)
£5m	£400	£400	£360
£10m	£500	£500	£480

5.   BUILDINGS

BUILDING COSTS

Building costs are notoriously variable. Many factors influence a contractor's price, including distance from his yard, size of contract, site access, site conditions, complexity of work, familiarity with the type of work and his current workload. There will also be differences in efficiency and standard of work between contractors and, as is often the case with farm buildings, the absence of detailed specification by the client may mean different contractors will not have quoted for identical buildings. The number of extras that are found to be required after a contract has been agreed will also vary.

The costs given below are an approximate guide. They refer to new buildings, erected by contractor on a clear level site and exclude VAT and grants that may be available. *The cost of raw materials for buildings (steel, timbe concrete etc.) has risen sharply in the last 12 months. It is recommended that up-to-date quotes are gathered for any building project.*

There is now little up-to-date cost information specifically available on agricultural buildings. The Central Association of Agricultural Valuers produce a publication 'Building Reinstatement Cost Assessments For Farms And Estates' based on survey data from 2018. The Rural and Industrial Design and Building Association (RIDBA) publish The Farm Buildings Handbook (3rd Edition – 2019).

There are books or online resources providing general building cost information – for example Laxton's, Spon's, BCIS etc. These will contain some data which is relevant to agriculture but are targeted more at the general building market.

Constituent Parts

Frame, Roof and Foundations   *per m² floor area*

1.   Open-sided timber framed pole barn with round pole uprights on concrete bases, sawn timber rafters and purlins, high-tensile galvanised steel cladding to roof and gable ends above eaves, hardcore floor, eaves height 4.8 m, 9 m span, no side cladding, rainwater drainage to soakaways.   £95

2.   Open-sided steel portal-framed building with fibre-cement or plastic coated steel cladding to roof and gables above eaves, hardcore floor, eaves height 4.8 m, no side cladding, rainwater drainage to soakaways.
     9 m span   £155
     13.2 m span   £145

	18 m span		£135

3. Cost breakdown of 2 above;

Materials:	portal frame and purlins		26%
	foundations		3%
	roofing		16%
	rainwater and drainage		3%
	hardcore and blinding		2%
	Total Materials		50%
Erection:	portal frame and purlins		19%
	foundations		2%
	roofing		19%
	rainwater and drainage		5%
	hardcore and blinding		5%
	Total Erection		50%

Roof cladding

per m²

1. Natural grey fibre-cement, 146 mm corrugations fixed with drive screws

Materials	£16.00	
Fixing	£16.00	
Total		£32.00

2. Extra for coloured sheet — £2.50
3. Deduct for translucent sheets — £0.55
4. Deduct for PVC-coated steel — £3.50
5. Deduct for high-tensile corrugated galvanised steel sheeting — £4.50

per m run

6. PVC 150 mm half-round gutter on fascia brackets, including stop-ends and outlets — £30.00
7. PVC 100 mm rainwater pipe with fixings, swan-neck and shoe — £45.00
8. Fibre-cement close-fitting ridge — £40.00
9. Fibre-cement ventilating ridge — £45.00

Walls and Cladding

per m²

1. Concrete blockwork, fair faced and pointed both sides

150 mm thick	£60.00
215 mm thick	£74.00
215 mm thick hollow blocks	£80.00
215 mm thick hollow blocks, filled and reinforced	£95.00

2. Extra for rendering or roughcast to blockwork on one side — £25.00
3. Vertical spaced boarding 21x 145 mm with 19 mm gaps including horizontal rails, all pressure treated — £32.00
4. Fibre-cement vertical cladding, including rails — £45.00
5. Corrugated high-tensile steel side cladding, including rails — £40.00

6. Wall element: 215 mm thick blockwork, including strip
foundation (base 750 mm below ground level),
2.5 m height above ground level   £195 per m run

Floors

per m²

1. Concrete floor 100 mm thick, Gen 3 mix, on 150 mm hardcore,
including excavation: £39.00

   Breakdown:
(a)	excavate, level and compact	£4.00
(b)	hardcore	£5.50
(c)	blinding	£2.50
(d)	damp-proof membrane	£2.50
(e)	premixed concrete spread and compacted	£20.00
(f)	float finish	£4.50

2. Extra to above for
(a)	150 mm instead of 100 mm	£6.50
(b)	laying concrete to falls	£2.00
(c)	broom or textured finish	£2.00
(d)	Carborundum dust non-slip finish	£3.50
(e)	insulating concrete	£12.50

3. Reinforced concrete slatted floors for cattle
(a)	cattle loading	£80.00
(b)	tractor loading	£95.00

4. Reinforced concrete slats for pigs   £65.00

5. Insulating floor, including excavation and base
(a)	27 mm expanded polystyrene, 38 mm screed	£55.00
(b)	insulating concrete with lightweight aggregate	£45.00
(c)	as (b) with 20 mm screed	£55.00

6. Form channel in concrete   £5.00 per m run

7. Excavate for cast 1 m3 in-situ concrete bases for stanchions   £140.00 each

Services and Fittings

per m²

1. Drainage: 100 mm PVC pipe laid in trench, including 750 mm
deep excavation and backfill   £30.00 per m run

   Breakdown:
(a)	excavate and backfill	£20.00
(b)	100 mm PVC pipe laid	£10.00

   Extras:
(c)	add to (a) for 1 m deep	£4.00
(d)	add to (b) for 150 mm pipe	£7.00

2. Excavate soakaway and fill with stones   £120 each

3. Trap and grid top, 100 mm PVC   £30.00 each

4. Yard gully with heavy duty road grating 400 x 300 mm   £200 each

5. Inspection chamber 900 mm deep, 450 x 600 mm opening and
medium duty cast iron cover   £400 each

6. Slurry reception pit, 20 m³   £6,500 each

7. Slurry channel beneath (not including) slats, 1.8 m deep,
3m wide   £500 per m run

8.	Lighting: 1.5 m 60W single fluorescent unit, including wiring and switch	£135 each
	Extras:	
	(a) PVC conduit	£6.50
	(b) screwed steel conduit	£12.00
9.	Power: 13A switched outlet	£25.00 each
10.	Diagonal feed fence, fixed, including posts (painted)	£140 per m run
11.	Tombstone feed fence, fixed, including posts (painted)	£150 per m run
12.	Feed bunker	£85 per m run
13.	Hay rack, wall fixing	£90 per m run
14.	Cubicle division, galvanised, fixed in place	£115 each
15.	Fencing: three-rail timber with posts, all pressure treated	£32.00 per m run
16.	Gate, 3 m wide, galvanised steel, including posts set in concrete	
	(a) medium duty	£250 each
	(b) heavy duty	£325 each
	Deduct for painted instead of galvanised finish	£30

Complete Buildings

Fully Covered and Enclosed Barn

Portal frame, 18 m span, 6 m bays, 6 m to eaves, 3 m high blockwork walls with sheet cladding above, 6 m sliding doors at either end, 150mm thick concrete floor	£230 per m^2 floor area

Cows and Cattle Housing

1.	Covered strawed yard, enclosed with ventilated cladding, concrete floor, pens only, with 4.0 m^2 per head floor area	£825 per head
2.	Extra to 1 for 4.0 m wide double-sided feeding passage, barrier and troughs	£325 per head
3.	Kennel building	£500 per head
4.	Portal framed building with cubicles	£1,650 per head
5.	Extra to 4 for feed stance, feeding passage, barriers and troughs	£675 per head
6.	Extra to 4 for slatting of cubicle passages	£700 per head
7.	Covered collecting yard, 1.1 m^2 per cow	£250 per head
8.	Milking parlour building, example: 5.5 x 11.5 m for 8/16 parlour	£22,000
9.	Parlour equipment, herringbone parlours:	
	(a) low level, 1 stall per point	£4,250 per point
	(b) pipeline	£3,500 per point
	(c) extra for meter and auto cluster removal	£2,500 per point
	(d) auto feed dispenser	£1,200 per point
10.	Dairy building	£375 per m^2 floor area
11.	Bulk tank and washer	£9.00 per litre
12.	Loose box, 16 m^2 floor area laid to falls, rendered walls	£375 per m^2 floor area
13.	Bull pen and open run	£14,000

14.	Cattle crush and 20 m race	£7,000
15.	Slatted floor cattle building for 120 growing cattle (1.7 m² pen space per head) with drive-through feed passage/troughs	£1,650 per head

Silage   *per tonne stored*

1.	Precast concrete panel clamp with effluent tank	£120
2.	Glass-lined forage tower and unloader	£275

Slurry Storage   *per m³ stored*

1.	Lined lagoon with safety fence	£50.00
2.	Glass-lined steel slurry silo	
	small (400 m³)	£65.00
	medium (1,200 m³)	£60.00
	large (3,600 m³)	£55.00
3.	GRP below-ground effluent tank, encased in concrete	
	small (12 m³)	£550
	large (36 m³)	£500

Sheep Housing

1.	Penning, troughs, feed barriers and drinkers installed in suitable existing building	£37.50 per ewe
2.	Purpose-built sheep shed with 1.35 m² pen space per ewe concentrate troughs, feed passage and barrier for forage feeding	£250 per ewe
	Extras:	
	(a) softwood slatted floor panels, materials only	£11.50 per m²
	(b) slatted panels as (a), made up, plus supports	£35.00 per m²

Pig Housing   *per sow and litter*

1.	Farrowing and rearing	
	(a) Prefabricated farrowing pens with crates, side creep areas, part-slatted floors, including foundations, electrical and plumbing work	£3,750
	(b) Steel-framed farrowing house with insulated blockwork walls, part-slatted pens with side creeps in rooms of eight with off main passage	£4,250
	(c) Flat deck rearing house 3-6 weeks with fully perforated floors to pens, 0.25 m² per pig pen area	£165 per weaner
	(d) Prefabricated veranda house including foundations, electrical and plumbing work, 0.3m² per pig internal lying area	£135 per weaner

2.	Finishing	*per baconer*
	(a) Prefabricated fattening house with part-slatted floors, trough feeding	£290
	(b) Prefabricated fattening house with part-slatted floors, floor fed	£280
	(c) Steel framed building with insulated blockwork walls, part-slatted floors, trough fed	£125
	(d) Automatic feeding systems for items (a), (b) and (c) above:	
	dry-feed system with ad-lib hoppers	£725
	dry on-floor feeding	£17.50
	wet feeding	£25

3.	Dry sows and boars	*per sow*
	(a) Yards with floor feeding	£410
	(b) Sow cubicle system	£650
	(c) Yards with electronic feeders	£1,150
	(d) Yards with individual feeders	£1,375
	(e) Two-yard system with flat-rate feeding	£1,475
	(f) Boar pens as part of sow house	£3,000 each

4. Complete pig unit

Building costs calculated on basis of three-week weaning, 23 pigs per sow per year to bacon, excl. external slurry or dung storage, feed storage and handling/weighing facilities:

	(a) Breeding and rearing only	£2,300 per sow
	(b) Breeding with progeny to bacon	£4,150 per sow

Poultry Housing and Equipment — *per bird*

1.	Intensive enriched cages with automatic feeding and egg collection; (complete with nest box, perches and scratching area as required)	£25.00-£30.00
2.	Perchery/barn	£24.00-£28.00
3.	Free Range: new sites stocked at 9 birds per m², smaller mobile units will cost	£30.00-£36.00 £37.50 plus
4.	Broiler Breeders, deep litter, 0.167 m² per bird	£32.00
5.	Pullets (cage and floor reared)	£18.00
6.	Broilers, deep litter, 0.05 m² per bird	£10.50-£12.00
7.	Turkeys, 20,000 pole barn fattening unit (cost varies with size of unit and degree of automation)	£23.00-£30.00

Grain Storage and Drying — *per tonne stored*

1.	Intake pit, conveyor, elevator, overhead conveyor and catwalk, storage bins within existing building	£265
	extra for low volume ventilation of bins	£100
2.	As 1 in new building	£380
3.	Portable grain walling for on-floor storage in existing building	£60

4. On floor grain storage in purpose-built building   £150
Extras:
  (a) low volume ventilation   £10-£12
  (b) on-floor drying with above-ground main duct and laterals   £140
  (c) add to (b) for below-ground laterals   £18

5. Sealed towers for moist grain, including loading and unloading
equipment   £175-£240

Potato Storage   *per tonne stored*

1. Pallet-box store with recirculation fans   £275
Pallet boxes, 1 tonne   £95

2. Bulk store, building only   £250
Ventilation system: fans, main duct, below-floor lateral ducts   £60

Roads and Fences   *per m length*

3.2 m wide hardcore road with drainage ditches using locally
excavated material   £40.00

using imported hardcore (£6.15/m³)   £55.00

extra for bitumen macadam surfacing, two coats   £60.00

Traditional 7-wire stock fence   £8.50

High tensile 7-wire stock fence   £6.50

Construction Equipment Hire   *hourly rate, with driver*

Excavator   £30.00-£40.00

Tipping lorry   £40.00-£55.00

10-tonne crane   £50.00-£70.00

    weekly rate

Concrete mixer, 100 litre (5/3)   £50

Compressor and heavy breaker   £140

STORAGE REQUIREMENTS

Bulk (cubic metres (feet) per tonne):

		m³/tonne	ft³/tonne
Beans		1.2	(43)
Wheat, peas		1.3	(46)
Barley, rye, oilseed rape, linseed, fodder beet		1.4	(50)
Oats		1.9	(68)
Potatoes		1.6	(57)
Dry bulb onions		2.0	(71)
Concentrates:	meal	2.0	(71)
	cubes	1.6	(57)
Grass silage:	18% DM	1.3	(46)
	30% DM	1.6	(57)
Maize silage		1.3	(46)
Silage: large round bales		2.5	(88)
Wheat straw ⎤		13.0	(464)
Barley straw ⎬ small bales		11.5	(411)
Hay ⎦		6.0	(214)
Wheat straw ⎤		20.0	(714)
Barley straw ⎬ large round bales		18.0	(643)
Hay ⎦		8.0	(286)
Brewers' grains		0.9	(32)

(With straw and hay the storage requirement clearly depends on the packing density; the above are simply typical averages).

Boxes (floor area in square metres (feet) per tonne):

Potatoes:	0.5 tonne boxes, 5 boxes high	0.52	(5.6)
	1.0 tonne boxes, 4 boxes high	0.52	(5.6)
	1.0 tonne boxes, 5 boxes high	0.45	(4.8)

Bags (floor area in square metres (feet) per tonne):

Feedstuffs:	2 bags high	1.6	(17)
Fertiliser:	6 bags high	1.1	(12)
	10 bags high	0.7	(8)

VII. TAXATION

Note: no responsibility can be taken for any errors or omissions in the information presented in this section or for any action taken on the basis of the information provided. Professional advice should always be sought before taking any decision that may affect your tax position.

1. INCOME TAX

RATES OF INCOME TAX

	Rest of the UK			Scotland	
	Tax Rate %	Income Band 2021-22		Tax Rate %	Income Band 2021-22
Basic rate	20	£0 - £37,700	*Starter rate*	19	*£0 - £2,097*
Higher rate	40	£37,701 - £150,000	*Basic rate*	20	*£2,098 - £12,726*
Additional rate	45	over £150,000	*Intermediate rate*	21	*£12,727 - £31,092*
			Higher rate	41	*£31,093 - £150K*
			Additional rate	46	*over £150,000*

Rates for 2022-23 had not been set at the time of writing

A Dividend Tax Allowance exempts the first £2,000 of dividend income from tax for the 2021-22 year and then rates of 7.5%, 32.5% and 38.1% apply for Basic, Higher and Additional rate taxpayers respectively.

Under the Savings Starting Rate up to £5,000 of savings income (primarily bank and building society interest) is potentially exempt from tax for 2021-22. Every £1 of income above the Personal Allowance (see below) reduces the starting rate for savings by £1, thus it reduces to zero for those with incomes over £17,570. In addition, there is a Personal Savings Allowance that allows Basic Rate and Higher Rate taxpayers to earn £1,000 and £500 respectively per year before tax. Any savings incomes are otherwise taxed at the marginal tax rates set out in the table above.

ALLOWANCES AND RELIEFS

Personal Allowance

This is £12,570 for 2021-22. The basic Personal Allowance for income tax is gradually reduced to nil for individuals with adjusted net incomes in excess of £100,000. The reduction is £1 for every £2 over the limit. The previous (higher) age related allowances have now been aligned with the basic Personal Allowance.

Married Couples Allowance

This was abolished from the tax year ended 6th April 2001 except for couples where at least one spouse was born before 6th April 1935. From 2005-06 the allowance has been available to couples in a civil partnership where at least one partner was born before 6th April 1935. The relief is given as a reduction in income tax restricted to the lower of 10% of the allowance (£912.50 for 2021-22) or the total tax liability.

Personal Pension Schemes

Tax relief is obtainable for contributions to a pension. There are limits on how much of the contribution is eligible for relief – both yearly and lifetime. The annual allowance is £40,000 for 2021-22. The £40,000 annual limit is progressively reduced for those earning above £150,000 per year, so that a maximum of £10,000 of contributions qualify for reliefs. The lifetime allowance is £1,073,100 for 2021-22.

2.   PRIVATE COMPANY TAXATION

RATES OF CORPORATION TAX

The rates set out in the table below apply to profits made in any financial year (FY) from 1st April to 31st March. FY21 therefore covers 1st April 2021 to 31st March 2022.

It has been announced that the rate of Corporation Tax will rise to 25% for FY23. At the same time a Small Companies Rate and Marginal Relief will be reintroduced.

	Annual Profits	FY21 and FY22	FY23
Small Companies Rate	£0 - £50,000	n/a	19
Marginal Relief	*£50,000 - £250,000*	*n/a*	*26.5*
Standard Corporation Tax Rate	over £250,000	19	25

COMPANY TAXATION – OTHER ISSUES

Capital Gains

Capital gains of companies are charged at the appropriate rate of Corporation Tax. The indexation allowance is still available to reduce capital gains made by Companies.

Distributions

Dividends are not deductible in arriving at the amount of Corporation Tax profit. However, the recipient of distributions will be exempt from paying Income Tax on the first £2,000 of dividend income received (see Income Tax section). Above that, basic rate taxpayers will pay a rate of 7.5% on dividend income. Higher rate taxpayers are liable to pay tax at 32.5% on that part of their dividend income falling above the higher rate limit. Taxpayers with income in excess of £150,000 will be liable to tax on dividends at 38.1%.

Losses

Carry back of losses not set against other income is restricted to one year. Losses can be carried forward and offset against profits of the same trade.

3.   AGRICULTURAL BUSINESSES: OTHER ITEMS

ASSESSING SELF-EMPLOYED PROFITS

Self-employed people are assessed for tax in any tax year on the basis of the profits recorded in the annual accounts which end in that tax year, i.e. on a 'current year basis'.

LIVESTOCK

Dairy cows or breeding livestock may be treated on the herd basis or on a trading stock basis;

Herd Basis

Under the herd basis valuation changes are not included in the trading account, nor are additions to the herd, but sales from the herd and replacements are. On the sale of all or a substantial proportion (normally taken as 20% or more) of the herd, no tax is paid on any profit over the original cost price, nor is there any relief for loss.

Trading Stock Basis

Purchases, sales and valuation changes are all included in the trading account. Under this method stock should be valued at the lower of cost (or cost of production) and net realisable value. Where animals are home-produced and it is not possible to ascertain actual costs from farm records the 'deemed' cost may be used. This is 60% of market value for cattle and 75% for sheep and pigs.

STOCK VALUATION: CROPS

Crops should generally be valued at the cost of production (or net realisable value, if lower). Costs which are directly attributable to buying, producing and growing the crops should be included. The deemed cost method allows 75% of market value to be used although this method should only be used where it is not possible to ascertain actual costs.

ALLOWANCES FOR CAPITAL EXPENDITURE

Machinery and Plant

1. The same rules apply whether the machinery and plant is new or second hand. An annual writing down allowance of 18% p.a. is available on a reducing balance basis on capital expenditure incurred on the provision of plant and machinery. Qualifying expenditure is added to the asset 'pool' and the writing down allowances are given on the residue of expenditure in that pool.

2. The Annual Investment Allowance ('AIA') gives 100% relief for a set amount of qualifying expenditure per accounting period. The allowance was increased from the previous £200,000 to £1m from 1st January 2019. It will remain at this level until at least April 2022. The limit is proportionally increased or decreased where the chargeable period is longer or shorter than a year. A group of companies can only receive a single allowance. Expenditure on cars does not qualify, although expenditure on long life assets, or on 'integral features' can be claimed. *A 'Super Deduction' of 130% was introduced from the 1st April 2021 to run to the end of March 2023. This provides a tax relief of 130%. It is only available to Limited Companies (for Corporation Tax) and does not apply to Income Tax.*

3. A 6% rate applies to expenditure incurred on certain listed 'integral features' in a building and on long life assets.

4. 100% first year allowances can be claimed for expenditure incurred by any business on designated energy-saving plant and machinery and environmentally beneficial technologies and products. The lists of items which qualify can be found on the Government's Energy Technology Product lists, which is at www.eca.gov.uk.

Cars

For expenditure on motor cars the regime is based on CO_2 emissions;
*   less than 51gm CO_2 /km (including electric) - 100% rate
*   51 – 110 gm CO_2 /km - 18%
*   over 110 gm CO_2 /km - 8%

For unincorporated businesses, cars have their own separate pools where there is an element of private use.

Machinery Leasing

Tax allowances for rental payments on financial leases are spread to reflect the commercial depreciation of the asset. This may mean that full tax relief for rental payments may not be gained in the years in which the payments are made.

Buildings

A Structures and Buildings Allowance was introduced for any commercial building (including farm buildings) from 29th October 2018. This is a 2% flat rate allowance calculated on the original building cost. The relief is available for 50 years and can be transferred to new owners if the building is subsequently sold. The rate was increased to 3% from April 2020 (applies to all qualifying assets, not only construction from this date).

LOSSES

Losses can normally be set against other income in the year they are incurred and in the prior year. If other income is insufficient in the year when the loss occurs and in the prior year, unrelieved losses can be carried forward and set off against future profits from the same trade. Special rules apply to prevent abuse of loss relief provisions by 'hobby' farmers who are not running their farms on a commercial basis with a view to producing a profit: normally losses are disallowed against other income after 5 consecutive years of loss. Trading losses may be set against capital gains in the same year as the loss.

PROFIT AVERAGING

This relief is to enable farmers, other than companies, to average their taxable profits. Following a change from April 2016 there is an option to do this for either two or five two consecutive years.

Under the two-year option profits can be averaged if profits of one year are 75% or less of the profits of the other year. Total profits for the two years are equally divided between the two years.

Under the five-year option either the average of the first four years' relevant profits must be less than 75% of the last year's relevant profits or vice versa or the relevant profits of one or more of the five tax years to which the claim relates must be nil (or there is a loss).

4. CAPITAL GAINS TAX

APPLICATION AND RATES

Applies to capital gains made by an individual. Capital gains accruing to companies are chargeable to Corporation Tax. A capital gain is the difference between the acquisition value and the sale price. The first £12,300 of capital gains (for the 2021-22 year) realised by an individual in a tax year are covered by their annual exemption.

Disposals of non-business assets attract capital gains tax of 10% for Basic Rate taxpayers or 20% for Higher and Additional rate taxpayers. Rates of 18% and 28% respectively apply on gains from residential property which is not the main home.

The lower rates of CGT apply where total taxable gains and income, after taking into account all allowable deductions including losses, personal allowances and the CGT annual exemption, are less than the upper limit of the income tax basic rate band. The higher rate will apply to gains or any parts of gains above this limit.

Exempt assets include a principal private residence (e.g. farmhouse, if non-exclusive business occupation applies) if occupied as such, normal life assurance policies, animals and tangible movable properly (i.e. chattels) disposed of for £6,000 or less.

Capital Gains Tax is chargeable only on the disposal (including gifts) of assets. Capital Gains Tax is not payable on death. Payment of Capital Gains Tax is due on 31st January following the tax year of disposal.

RELIEFS

Losses

Should a transaction produce a loss, this may be set against any long-term chargeable gains arising in the same year or, if these are insufficient, those accruing in subsequent years. Losses brought forward will be used only to the extent necessary to reduce untaxed gains for the year to £12,300.

Where a trading loss can be set against other income in the same or prior year for income tax purposes, any unused loss can be set against capital gains for those years.

Improvements

Spending that has increased the value of the asset can be offset against any gain. In the case of agricultural property, allowance would be made for any capital expenditure undertaken to improve the property.

Indexation and Taper Relief

Indexation and Taper relief for individuals has now been abolished for any disposals taking place on or after 6th April 2008. Indexation allowance is still available for capital gains arising in companies.

Entrepreneurs Relief

Entrepreneur's relief applies to certain disposals of business assets by an individual. The relief, which must be claimed, gives an effective rate of Capital Gains Tax of 10% for eligible gains of up to £1m from 11th March 2020 (a £10m limit had previously applied from 6th April 2011). The limit is a lifetime limit per individual. The assets which qualify for entrepreneurs' relief are in line with those which qualified for business asset taper relief. This covers;

- a trading business carried on by an individual alone or in partnership;
- assets of such a trade following cessation;
- shares or securities in a trading company where the individual owns 5% or more and is an officer or employee

The conditions for the relief must have been satisfied throughout a qualifying period of a year before the disposal.

Editorial Note: The rules for Entrepreneurs' relief are complex, particularly in cases of disposals of part of the business. The rules are similar to the previous Retirement Relief and are particularly tricky in cases of disposals of farmland and related assets and trade. It is recommended that professional advice is sought where it is anticipated claiming this relief, particularly as given the increase in the lifetime allowance combined with the increase in tax rate for non-business assets, the tax savings can be greatly increased.

Rollover

Payment of tax may be deferred on gains accruing from the sale of business assets (including land and buildings occupied and used for trade purposes, fixed plant and machinery and from the sale of shares in a family business) if part or all of the proceeds are spent on acquiring new qualifying assets. The tax is deferred by deducting the gain from the acquisition price of the new asset. It can only be claimed if the new asset is acquired within 12 months before and 3 years after the disposal of the old assets. Disposal and acquisition dates for Capital Gains purposes are generally contract, not completion, dates.

Holdover

Payments of tax may be deferred where disposal is by gift. This relief only applies to gifts of business assets, land which qualifies for agricultural property relief at either the 100% or 50% rate under Inheritance Tax (see next section) and gifts which lead to an immediate charge to Inheritance Tax (e.g. gifts into a discretionary trust). The amount of the chargeable gain which would normally have accrued to the donor will be held over; the value at which the donee is deemed to acquire the asset will be its market value reduced by the amount of the donor's chargeable gain held over. Where deferral is not available, payment of tax by interest bearing annual instalments over 10 years will be allowed for gifts of land, controlling share holdings and minority share holdings in unquoted companies.

5. STAMP TAXES

'**Stamp taxes**' are levied on the sale and lease of property. The devolved regions of the UK now operate separate systems. The tax in England and Northern Ireland is Stamp Duty Land Tax (SDLT). In Scotland a separate Land and Buildings Transaction Tax (LBTT) applies. In Wales it is the Land Transaction Tax (LTT).

These taxes are levied on the value that falls into each bracket at the prevailing rate for both residential and non-residential property. The rates applicable are:

Residential				*Non-Residential (inc. Mixed Use)*			
Sale Value	SDLT*	LBTT	LTT	Sale Value	SDLT	LBTT	LTT
£0 to £125,000	Nil	Nil	Nil	£0 to £150,000	Nil	Nil	Nil
£125K to £145K	2%	Nil	Nil	£150K to £250K	2%	3%	1%
£145K to £180K	2%	2%	Nil	£250K to £350K	5%	3%	5%
£180K to £250K	2%	2%	3.5%	£350K to £1m	5%	4.5%	5%
£250K to £325K	5%	5%	5%	Over £1m	5%	4.5%	6%
£325K to £400K	5%	10%	5%				
£400K to £750K	5%	10%	7.5%				
£750K to £925K	5%	12%	10%				
£925K to £1.5m	10%	12%	10%				
Over £1.5m	12%	12%	12%				

A 3% supplement to the rates above is charged on purchases of residential property where the residence is not the buyers' main house and all purchases above £40,000 by corporates or trusts.

First Time Buyers exemptions are available on SDLT (first £300K of price) and LBTT (£175K).

all parts of the UK increased the nil-rate band for residential property for a limited period as a response to Covid-19. Rates have now reverted to the standard figures set out above.

SDLT, LBTT and LTT are payable on **leases** calculated according to the net present value of the rent payable over the term of the lease.

Stamp Duty is also charged on the transfer of shares and other securities at 0.5% of consideration paid (purchase by cash, other stocks or shares).

6. INHERITANCE TAX

APPLICATION AND RATES

This tax is charged on lifetime gifts and transfers on death. The rate for 2021-22 is 40%, on amounts chargeable to Inheritance Tax above the nil rate band of £325,000.

The nil rate band is potentially increased for surviving spouses or civil partners who died on or after 9th October 2007. From this date the nil rate band may be increased by the unused proportion of the deceased spouse or civil partner's nil rate band.

From the 2017-18 year a Main Residence nil rate band was introduced. This has risen to £175,000 for 2021-22. It is in addition to the usual nil rate band but only be applicable to the main house of the deceased if transferred to a direct descendent.

Any unused portion of the nil rate allowance (both the basic nil rate band and the residence nil rate band) can be transferred between spouses and civil partners.

Outright gifts to individuals are exempt from tax at the time of the gift. If the donor lives for a further seven years then the transfer is fully exempt. Gifts into accumulation and maintenance trusts and interest in possession trusts no longer receive special treatment - all other gifts will be taxed at half the above rates at the time of the transfer.

Tax is charged on the value of an individual's estate at death plus the value of all gifts made within seven years of death. Allowance is made for any tax paid on lifetime gifts included in the value of the estate on death. Relief is given for outright gifts made more than three years before death according to the following scale:

Years between gift and death	0-3	3-4	4-5	5-6	6-7
Percentage of the full tax charge	100%	80%	60%	40%	20%

Exemptions include: transfers between husband and wife; the first £3,000 of gift made by a donor in the income tax year and separately up to £250 per year to any number of persons; gifts made out of income which form part of normal expenditure; marriage gifts within limits of £5,000 for a parent, £2,500 for a lineal ancestor and £1,000 for other donors.

RELIEFS

Agricultural Property Relief

Relief may be available for agricultural land. Subject to a general rule that the agricultural land must have been occupied by the transferor (or by his controlled company) for two years, or owned by the transferor for 7 years and occupied for agricultural purposes by someone else before any relief is granted. The relief is at two different rates. If the basis of valuation is vacant possession (or there is the right to obtain it within 12 months), the taxable value of the land is reduced by 100%. If the basis of valuation is tenanted value, the taxable value of the land is reduced by 50% of that tenanted value. Ownership and occupation periods normally include prior periods of ownership or occupation by husbands and wives. From 1st September 1995, 100% relief applies to new lettings of agricultural land as Farm Business Tenancies. Agricultural Relief includes agricultural land in the European Economic Area (EEA).

Editorial Note: There has been much publicised activity and tax cases concerning APR claims, particularly attempts by the Inland Revenue to reduce or deny the relief on claims for farmhouses. Care must be taken to protect the relief particularly where the attached land is either let out on a Farm Business Tenancy or under a contract farming arrangement.

Business Property Relief

Relief is also available in respect to 'business property' transferred during lifetime or on death. The relief extends to the business assets of a proprietor and the interest of a partner or controlling shareholder in the business capital of a company. The value of such property, providing certain tests are satisfied (e.g. it has been owned by the transferor for two years preceding transfer), is reduced by 100%. Where a partner or controlling shareholder owns assets (e.g. land) that the business uses, the value will be reduced by 50%. Shareholdings in unquoted companies receive a 100% reduction in market value.

Lifetime gifts of property eligible for Agricultural and Business Property Relief have to be retained (or replaced by similar property) until the death of the donor (or earlier death of the donee) if those reliefs are to be available when the tax (or additional tax) becomes payable subsequent to the donor's death

In the case of the transfer of property eligible for APR and BPR, the tax can be paid by annual instalments over ten years free of interest.

7. VALUE ADDED TAX

Agricultural businesses with a turnover of taxable goods and services in excess of £85,000 per annum must register for VAT. Businesses with a smaller turnover can voluntarily register. Those with sales of less than £83,000 may apply for de-registration. The standard VAT rate has been 20% since January 2011. Most agricultural products are zero rated for VAT purposes. VAT has to be paid on certain inputs. Registered businesses are eligible to reclaim the tax paid where the goods or services purchased have been used in the production of zero-rated supplies.

A flat rate scheme is available to farmers as an alternative to registering for VAT. Farmers under the flat rate scheme do not have to submit tax returns or account for VAT and consequently cannot reclaim tax. They can, however, charge (and keep) a flat rate addition of 4% when they sell to VAT registered customers goods and services which qualify. This addition is not VAT but acts as compensation for losing input tax on purchases. The registered person paying the flat rate amount to the farmer can recover it as if it were VAT, subject to the normal rules for reclaiming. The local VAT office may refuse to issue a certificate to participate in the flat rate scheme if this would mean the farmer would recover substantially (£3,000) more than through the normal system.

A flat rate scheme operates for small businesses generally and is an alternative that farmers can use if they have taxable supplies of no more than £150,000. This scheme operates in a different way to the flat rate scheme for farmers in that a business charges the normal rate of VAT on sales. However, the VAT which the business has to remit to Customs and Excise is calculated by multiplying the value of gross sales by a rate specified for each particular trade sector. The rate for agriculture is 6.5% except for businesses supplying agricultural services, when the rate is 11%.

Editorial Note: *Farmers and landowners must always consider the VAT implications when considering any new or more farming activities on the land or within the buildings, particularly where supplies are made the public who cannot recover any VAT which may be charged on the service or goods provided from the farm.*

8. NATIONAL INSURANCE

The tables below set out the National Insurance contributions for the 2021-22 year;

Class 1 (not contracted out)

Employee's weekly earnings	Employee	Employer
£184 or less	Nil	Nil
£184.01 to £967	12%	13.8%
Over £967	2%	13.8%

Class 2 *Self-employed flat rate (for those earning over £6,515 per year)*		*£3.05 a week*
Class 3 *Non-employed (voluntary)*	*flat rate*	*£15.40 a week*
Class 4 Self-employed. On profits or gains	between £9,568 and £50,270	9%
	over £50,270	2%

VIII.   FARM BUSINESS MANAGEMENT

1.   DEFINITIONS OF FARM MANAGEMENT TERMS

VALUATIONS AND CAPITAL

Valuations

Valuation is essentially a process of estimation. Various methods are possible, according to the purpose intended. The basis should be consistent throughout the period or any series of figures.

1. *Saleable crops in store.* At estimated market value less costs still to be incurred, e.g. for storage and marketing. Both may be estimated either at the expected date of sale or at the date of valuation.

2. *Growing crops.* Preferably at variable costs to the date of valuation, although estimated total cost can alternatively be used.

3. *Saleable crops ready for harvesting* but still in the ground. Preferably as valued in point 1 above, less estimated harvesting costs, although they can alternatively be treated as described in point 2 above.

4. *Fodder stocks (home-grown).* Normally at variable costs when calculating gross margins although this can be misleading for management purposes. Estimated market value (based on hay-equivalent value according to quality for example) includes the opportunity cost of the fodder in the livestock margin. Fodder crops still in the ground, e.g. kale, treated as point 2 above.

5. *Stocks of purchased materials (including fodder).* Priced at cost (net of discounts).

6. *Machinery and equipment.* Original cost (net of grants and discounts), less accumulated depreciation to date of valuation – this gives a valuation on the 'historic' cost basis. Alternatively, at estimated market value.

7. *Livestock.* At current market value, less cost of marketing. Fluctuations in market value expected to be temporary should be ignored.

Capital

Tenant's Capital. The estimated total value of capital on the farm, other than land and fixed equipment. There is no easy way of determining this sum precisely and estimates are made in several ways depending on the information available and the purpose for which the estimate is required. One method is to take the average of the opening and closing valuations (at either market value or cost) of livestock, crops, machinery and stores (feed, seed, fertilisers). See also page 238 (following section).

Landlord's Capital. Value of the land and fixed equipment (including buildings).

OUTPUT TERMS

Revenue (or Income). Receipts adjusted for debtors at the beginning and end of the accounting period. Items such as CAP support, revenue grants, contract receipts and wayleaves are included.

Returns. Revenue including valuation changes (add closing, deduct opening, valuation) so if valuation goes up, this adds to the returns.

Gross Output. Returns plus the value of produce consumed in the farmhouse or supplied to workers for which no payment is made, less purchases of livestock, livestock products and other produce bought for resale.

Enterprise Output. The total value of an enterprise, whether sold or retained on the farm. It therefore equals Gross Output of the enterprise plus the market value of any of the products kept on the farm (transfers out). The Basic Payment should not be apportioned to individual enterprises. Products transferred from another enterprise to be used in the production of the enterprise whose output is being calculated are deducted at market value (transfers in). Instead of the accounting year the "harvest year" can be used for crops which means valuations may not be relevant.

(Enterprise) Output from Forage. Primarily the sum of the enterprise outputs of grazing livestock, but includes keep let and occasional sales, e.g. of surplus hay, together with an adjustment for changes in the valuation of stocks of home-grown fodder. However, fortuitous changes in stocks caused by yield variations due to the weather, the severity or length of the winter, or minor changes in livestock numbers or forage area can be either ignored (if small in relation to total annual usage) or included in miscellaneous output.

Adjusted Forage (Enterprise) Output. Output from Forage less rented keep and purchases of bulk fodder.

Standard Output. The average enterprise output per hectare of a crop or per head of livestock calculated from average yield data and either national or local average price.

INPUT TERMS

Expenditure. Payments adjusted for creditors at the beginning and end of the accounting period. Capital expenditure is not included.

Costs. Expenditure adjusted for valuation changes (add opening, deduct closing, valuation), with the following adjustments: Add; depreciation on capital expenditure including machinery, any loss made on machinery sales (add to depreciation) and the value of payments in kind to workers if not already included in their earnings. Deduct; purchases of livestock, livestock products and other produce bought for resale, any profit made on machinery (deduct from depreciation), allowance for private use of farm vehicles (deduct from machinery costs), the value of purchased stores used in the farmhouse (e.g. electricity) or sold off the farm (deduct from the relevant item).

Inputs. Costs with the following adjustments, made in order to put all farms on a similar basis for comparative purposes. Add: the value of unpaid family labour, including the manual labour of the farmer and spouse, and, in the case of owner-occupiers, an estimated rental value (based on average rents of similar farms in the area), less any cottage rents received. Deduct: any mortgage payments and other expenses of owner-occupation, interest payments and the cost of paid management. A proportion of the rental value of the farmhouse may also be deducted.

Fixed Costs. See pages from 209 whole Farm Fixed Costs.

Variable Costs. See page 2.

MARGIN TERMS

Management and Investment Income. Gross Output less Inputs. It represents the reward to management and the return on tenant's capital invested in the farm, whether borrowed or not. It is mainly used for comparative purposes, all farms having been put on a similar financial basis by the adjustments made to costs in calculating Inputs.

Net Farm Income. Management and Investment Income, less paid management, plus the value of the manual labour of the farmer and spouse. It represents the return to all tenant's type capital and the reward to the farmer for his or her manual labour and farmer's management.

Profit (or Loss). Gross Output less Costs. This represents the surplus or deficit before imputing any notional charges such as rental value or unpaid labour. In the accounts of owner-occupiers, it includes any profit accruing from the ownership of land.

Farm Business Income. This term is increasingly being used in FBS costings and is similar to 'Profit' above. It represents the return to all unpaid labour and to all their own capital in the farm business including land and farm buildings.

Gross Margin. See page 3.

Net Margin. A term sometimes used to denote Gross Margin less direct labour and machinery costs charged to an individual enterprise. This is not, however, nationally accepted terminology. Increasingly Net Margin in the enterprise context is being used to denote the profit of an enterprise by taking its gross output less its 'complete enterprise costs' but see page 2.

AREA TERMS

Total Hectares. All hectares comprising the farm.

Hectares. Total hectares less areas of woods, waste land, roads, yards, buildings, etc.

Adjusted Hectares. Hectares reduced by the conversion of rough grazing into the equivalent hectares of average quality grassland. This is the figure often used for lowland farms when calculating "per hectare" results.

Forage Hectares. Total hectares of forage crops grown, less any hectares exclusively used by pigs or poultry and the area equivalent of any home-grown fodder fed to livestock reared in cereal systems. Also, the area of rough grazing is converted to its grassland equivalent (see Adjusted Hectares). Forage crops are all crops including grass, rough grazing, maize and whole crops grown specifically for grazing livestock, but excluding catch crops and crops harvested as grain and pulses.

Adjusted Forage Hectares. Forage hectares adjusted as follows; add the area equivalent of keep rented, deduct the area equivalent of keep let; deduct the area equivalent of occasional sales of fodder, e.g. surplus hay, and seed cuts (note: hay and seed grown regularly for sale should be regarded as cash crops, not forage crops); add or deduct the area equivalent of planned changes in the valuation of stocks of home-grown fodder (fortuitous changes in stocks resulting from weather conditions may be ignored); convert rough grazing into their grassland equivalent if not already done. The following adjustments also may be made; add the area equivalent of catch crops and of grazing from cash crops of hay or seed: add the area equivalent of purchased fodder.

In calculations such as Gross Margins per Forage Hectare, Adjusted Forage Hectares are usually used. If the area equivalent of purchased fodder has been added, the cost of purchased fodder must not be charged as a variable cost: this is probably the best calculation for comparative purposes. Alternatively, when considering all the grazing enterprises taken together, purchased fodder can be deducted as a variable cost and no addition made for its area equivalent.

2. CAPITAL REQUIREMENT AND RETURN

TENANT'S CAPITAL

1. *Machinery.* Costs of new machinery are given from page 176. Written-down values (the depreciated, actual value of machinery on farm) in 2022 are likely to average £360-£1,450 per hectare (£145-£590/acre) of actively farmed land (excluding fallow and rough grazing) depending on farm types. Average values for different farm types for 2022 are detailed on the next page.

2. *Breeding Livestock.* The 2022 average of breeding livestock value per hectare could be anything up to £2,600 (£1050/acre) (say 2 high value cows per hectare) for an intensive (outdoor) dairy/livestock farm. Intensive (housed) pig and poultry units will be substantially more but a meaningless figure having minimal land. Approximate average market values of various categories of breeding livestock (of mixed ages in the case of adult stock) are as follows (actual value will vary according to average age and weight, quality, breed, time of year and market conditions):

Average market values of various breeding livestock

	Breeding Herd		
	Newly Calved	Average	Cull
Holstein/Friesian Dairy Cows	£1,630	£1,166	£702
Channel Island Dairy Cows	£1,300	£853	£405
Suckler Beef Cows: *	£1,600	£1,175	£750
Pure-bred Beef Cows *	£2,000	£1,469	£938
* Calf at Foot < 3 months			

	Replacements		
	Holstein Friesians	Ayrshires and C.I. Breeds	Beef Cattle
In Calf Heifers	£1,530	£1,200	£1,600
1-2 years	£1,230	£1,000	£1,040
6-12 months	£1,030	£800	£740
6 months	£590	£440	£540
Calf	£210	£116	£211

	Other Livestock		
	Young	**Average**	**Cull**
Ewes	£145	£105	£65
Rams	£500	£293	£85
Sows and In-Pig Gilts	£250	£171	£92
Boars	£1,250	£665	£80

3. *Working Capital* is the current assets of a business less its current liabilities. It is the liquid capital needed to finance the cash flow through the production cycle, the length of which varies considerably between different crop and livestock enterprises and different combinations of these enterprises. It can include the cost of purchased fattening stock, feed, seed, fertilisers, regular labour, machinery running costs, general overhead costs, rent and living expenses. This capital will vary between farm business types. Specialist root crop and vegetable farm businesses will have significantly higher working capital requirements than livestock and combinable cropping businesses. The only accurate way to estimate working capital requirement is to complete a full cash flow estimate for the production cycle of the business.

Average Tenants Capital per Hectare for different English farm types

Farm Type Group	Average Area	Breeding Livestock	Crops and Stores	Machinery and Equipment	Total Tenant's Capital	
	Hectares	**£/ha**	**£/ha**	**£/ha**	**£/ha**	**£/acre**
All Farms						
Small	115	207	356	578	2,071	*839*
Medium	151	272	454	952	2,462	*997*
Large	198	394	505	963	2,588	*1,048*
V. Large	376	505	551	1,084	3,064	*1,241*
Average	196	380	484	977	2,656	*1,076*
Mainly Dairying:						
Small	59	1,094	156	1,125	3,333	*1,350*
Medium	77	1,387	241	1,436	4,011	*1,624*
Large	113	1,502	284	1,388	4,243	*1,718*
V. Large	220	1,593	363	1,393	4,397	*1,781*
Average	160	1,549	334	1,388	4,315	*1,748*
Mainly Cereals:						
Small	183	24	570	1,073	2,329	*943*
Medium	277	28	648	948	2,336	*946*
Large	388	57	720	912	2,175	*881*
V. Large	916	51	712	776	2,195	*889*
Average	330	41	666	915	2,253	*913*
General Cropping:						
Small	137	-	548	743	1,834	*743*
Medium	192	28	519	1,045	2,074	*840*
Large	275	-	880	981	2,489	*1,008*
V. Large	739	48	731	989	2,428	*983*
Average	288	-	703	946	2,283	*925*
Mainly Sheep/Cattle (*Lowland*):						
Small	85	423	136	747	2,215	*897*
Medium	105	639	184	817	2,599	*1,053*
Large	152	588	166	837	2,529	*1,024*
V. Large	362	491	125	463	1,957	*792*
Average	126	518	149	702	2,286	*926*
Mainly Sheep/Cattle (*Upland Less Favoured Area*):						
Small	114	414	48	378	1,242	*503*
Medium	163	452	47	408	1,368	*554*
Large	267	443	62	398	1,438	*582*
V. Large	608	428	53	288	1,141	*462*
Average	194	431	52	361	1,276	*517*

Source; Farm Business Survey for England 2019/20
Average area is all commercial farms (above 1 full-time equivalent).

- Trading livestock, crops in store and other liquid assets are not included separately as they are not assets of production and vary according to marketing styles and time of year. They are included in the Total Tenant's Capital.

- Farm size is measured by Standard Labour Units; the amount of work nominally required on farms of these sizes: Small = 1-2 full time equivalent workers (FTE), Medium = 2-3 FTE, Large = 3-5 FTE and Very large = over 5 FTE. 'Very Small' (less than 1 FTE) has been omitted here. The average is for all farms of 1 FTE or more, considered 'full time farms'.

- The data is calculated from the Farm Business Survey for England. Some assets are excluded such as debtors. The variation in capital per farm size reflects the range of farming systems and the small sample numbers in some categories.

RETURN ON CAPITAL

Return on Tenant's Capital

Return on tenant's capital is calculated by taking the management and investment income (MII) of a business as a percentage of the tenant's capital (see definitions in section 1 of this chapter). Because MII is before deduction of any interest, this return is 'gross', i.e. before allowing for cost of finance. However, it should be borne in mind that MII includes no charge for management but that a rental value for owner-occupied land and the value of the unpaid labour of the farmer and wife have been deducted.

Return on Landlord's Capital

The return on landlord's capital is calculated by taking the rental income, less any ownership expenses (mortgage, insurance, repairs etc.), expressed as a percentage of the land value. With farmland in 2022 averaging possibly £22,000 per hectare (£8,900 per acre) (see page 216) with vacant possession (assuming no special amenity or house value), an average lowland existing rent of, say, £260 per hectare (£105 per acre) (see page 214), and assuming ownership expenses at £55 per hectare (£22 per acre), the (net) return of £205 per hectare (£83 per acre) averages 0.93%. This takes no account of land capital valuation change, tax implications or land trading costs.

Return on Capital to Individual Enterprises

On a mixed farm it is difficult to ascertain the return on enterprise capital, except perhaps for a full-time pig or poultry enterprise. It would also be of limited use. It would require the arbitrary allocation both of costs and capital inputs that are common to several, or all, of the enterprises on the farm.

What is relevant and important is the extra (net) return from an enterprise either to be introduced or expanded, as calculated by a partial budget, related to the extra (net) capital needed. The 'net' in brackets relates to the additional returns to gross margins less any additional (or plus any reduction in) 'fixed' costs, bearing in mind that another enterprise may have to be deleted or reduced in size; and, regarding capital, to the fact that deletion or reduction of another enterprise may release capital.

In most cases of 'marginal' substitution, it is differences in the value of breeding livestock and differences in variable costs that are particularly relevant, but the timing of both inputs and sales are also obviously very important.

'Marginal' Capital Requirements

These are for small changes in crop areas or livestock numbers and can be estimated as follows:

- Crops: variable costs until payment of sale.
- Dairy Cows and Egg Production: value of the cow* or hens, plus food until payment of product.
- Other Breeding Livestock: average value of stock*, plus variable costs to sale (payment) of the progeny (e.g. lambs) – or their transfer to another enterprise (e.g. weaners to the pig fattening enterprise).
- Rearing Breeding Livestock (e.g. heifers, shearlings, gilts, pullets): cost of the calf, lamb, weaner or chick, plus variable costs until they produce their first progeny/milk/eggs.
- Fattening Livestock and Production of Stores: cost of stock, plus variable costs till sale.

* Value of breeding stock, including dairy cows: either the average value over their entire breeding or milk producing life (see table on page 238) or their value when they first produce progeny can be taken. The latter will give the lower return on (marginal) capital and is thus the severer test.

Home-reared stock: where stock to be used for milk or egg production, breeding or fattening are home-reared, there are two possibilities:

(a) either they can be valued at variable costs of production when they are transferred from the rearing to the 'productive' enterprise; in this case the return on (marginal) capital will be estimated over the combined rearing and 'productive' enterprise.

(b) or they can be valued at market value at point of transfer. This is the procedure if one wishes to work out a return on (marginal) capital for the rearing and the 'productive' enterprises separately.

Return on 'Marginal' Capital

This is sometimes expressed as the gross margin less fuel and repair costs of the enterprise expanded as a percentage of the 'marginal', or extra capital. However, two points have to be remembered:

(a) If another enterprise has had to be reduced in size to enable the enterprise under consideration to be expanded, the capital released and the gross margin forfeited by reducing the size of the first enterprise must be brought into the calculation in estimating the net result of the change.

(b) All the above statements on 'marginal' capital refer to small changes. If the change is large enough to cause changes in labour, machinery, rent or building requirements, the capital changes brought about may be considerably greater.

Return on Investments in Medium-Term and Long-Term Capital

This calculates the Rate of Return and the Discounted Yield.

Example: If a £5,000 investment results in an annual net return of £500 (after deducting depreciation, but ignoring interest payments) and with no capital salvage value:

$$\textit{Rate of Return on Initial Capital} = \frac{500}{5,000} \times 100 = 10\%$$

$$\textit{Rate of Return on Average Capital} = \frac{500}{2,500} \times 100 = 20\%$$

Care has to be taken when using the return on '*average*' capital as the capital has still been spent, it is just that half has been written off. It is more accurate to calculate the '*Discounted Yield*', which is the discount rate that brings the present value of the net cash flows (which means ignoring depreciation) to the value of the investment. The tables from page 247 may be used.

'Short-Cut' Estimates of the Discounted Yield on Depreciating Assets

The Discounted Yield falls between the simple Rates of Return on Initial and Average Capital. In fact, for investments lasting 5 to 15 years, when the Rate of Return on Initial Capital is 10 per cent and on Average Capital 20 per cent, the Discounted Yield will be almost exactly halfway between, i.e. about 15 per cent. However, this is only so providing the anticipated annual net cash earnings are fairly constant — or fluctuate unpredictably around a fairly constant level.

There are three circumstances when the Discounted Yield will get closer to the Rate of Return on Initial Capital (i.e. the lower per cent return) and further from the Rate of Return on Average Capital:

(a)   The longer the life of the investment.

(b)   The higher the Rate of Return.

(c)   The higher the net cash flow is in the later years of the investment compared with the earlier years.

When the opposite circumstances occur, the Discounted Yield will be closer to the Rate of Return on Average Capital (i.e. the higher per cent return).

There are varying degrees of estimation and uncertainty in calculating future net annual earnings of investments. The following short-cuts might reasonably be used where the annual net cash earnings are expected to be fairly constant - or fluctuate unpredictably (e.g. through weather effects on yields) around a fairly constant level. (W.O. period = write-off period; R.R.I.C. = rate of return on initial capital).

1.   Where

(i)   the W.O. period is 5 years or less,

(ii)   the W.O. period is 6 - 10 years and the R.R.I.C. is 15 per cent or less,

(iii)   the W.O. period is 11 - 20 years and the R.R.I.C. is 10 per cent or less,

calculate the Return on Capital as being approximately midway between the Rates of Return on Initial and Average Capital, i.e. by calculating the Rate of Return on 2/3 of the original investment.

For example, following the earlier example above:

$$\frac{500}{3,333} \times 100 = 15\%.$$

2.   Where

(i)   the W.O. period is 6 to 10 years and the R.R.I.C. exceeds 15 per cent,

(ii)   the W.O. period is 11 to 20 years and the R.R.I.C. is between 10 per cent and 25 per cent,

(iii)   the W.O. period exceeds 20 years and the R.R.I.C. is 10 per cent or less,

calculate the Return on Capital on 80 per cent of the original investment.

For example, again following the earlier example:

$$\frac{500}{4,000} \times 100 = 12.5°\%.$$

3. Where

(i)   the W.O. period is 11 to 20 years and the R.R.I.C. exceeds 25 per cent,

(ii)   the W.O. period exceeds 20 years and the R.R.I.C. exceeds 10 per cent. Take the Return on Capital to be the R.R.I.C.

In borderline cases, use method 1 rather than 2, or 2 rather than 3 if there is a tendency for the cash flow to be higher in the earlier years, e.g. because of tax allowances on machinery. Take 2 rather than 1, and 3 rather than 2, if the likelihood is that the cash flow will be lower in earlier years and increase in later years.

Where annual cash flow is expected to vary (apart from unpredictable fluctuations) it is safer to make the full D.C.F. calculation. This is particularly so where the variation is both up and down and where further periodic investments are to be made during the project.

3.   INTEREST RATES

Rate of interest on Bank Loans

Overdraft borrowing rates are typically 1.5% to 3.5% above Base Rate. Extremes are likely to be 0.8% to 7% above. Particularly low margins over base have become rare, especially for new lending agreements. Annual arrangement fees based on the total facility and other charges can add substantially to the overall cost of borrowing. Base rate at the time of writing is 0.1%, an all-time low. It is always prudent for budgeting purposes to allow a rise of say 0.5% to 1% as changes can be fast if they are made. A 0.5% rise in base rate is now proportionally a large increase in borrowing rates.

Fixed Rate Mortgages

The table gives typical mortgage rates on domestic dwellings. Note that this is taken from the current mortgage marketplace. Each offering is different with varying retention clauses, booking fees or early redemption costs. The lowest interest rate is therefore not necessarily the best mortgage.

Typical Fixed Rates on Residential Mortgages

Fixed Rate	90% LTV*	80% LTV*	65% LTV*
2-year	1.9%	1.25%	1.15%
5-year	1.2%	1.5%	1.25%
10-year	4.0%	3.0%	2.0%

* *LTV = Loan to Value (the percent the financier loans against the capital value)*

Annual Percentage Rate (APR)

This is the effective rate of interest calculated on an annual basis and should be used when seeking to make a true comparison between interest charges on money borrowed from different sources. The APR allows for the fact that when interest is applied to accounts at half yearly, quarterly or monthly intervals an element of compounding will arise.

For example, £100 borrowed for one year at a quoted annual nominal interest rate of 6% (e.g. 5.25% over base rate of 0.75%) with interest charged quarterly, will lead to an accumulated interest charge of £6.136 (i.e., giving an APR of just under 6.14%). The higher the annual nominal interest rate and the more frequently the interest charges are applied to the account, the more pronounced the compounding element becomes. For example, an annual nominal interest rate of 10% produces an APR of 10.25% with half yearly charging, 10.38% with quarterly charging and 10.47% with monthly charging.

In the case of some loans and hire purchase agreements, interest charges may be quoted as a flat rate on the original amount borrowed. The APR will be considerably greater than the flat rate if the loan is repaid by equal periodic instalments, comprising part capital and part interest, so that the borrowing is completely repaid by the end of the agreed term.

The Real Rate of Interest.

When preparing profit and loss budgets to estimate how worthwhile an investment in a fixed asset (machinery, buildings, land) is, it is usual to price inputs and outputs at present-day values even when most costs and returns are expected to rise due to inflation over the life of the investment. Where this real-terms approach is adopted a more realistic estimate of the effect on profitability can be gained by basing charges for capital on the real rate of interest rather than the APR.

The real rate of interest is the APR adjusted for the annual rate at which prices relevant to the investment are expected to increase. A crude estimate of the real rate of interest can be obtained by simply subtracting the expected rate of price increase from the APR; for example, if the APR were 8% and the expected rate of inflation 3%, the real rate of interest would be $8 - 3 = 5\%$.

4.   FINANCIAL RATIOS

Common Ratios

The following ratios are standard guidelines using *'normalised'* output prices, i.e. those in an average year. These are used as guidelines for advisors, students, agricultural commentators and farmers alike:

% of Gross Output	Arable	Dairy	Mixed	Upland	Intensive stock
Variable Costs	32	39	37	47	65
Labour[+]	12	15	21	17	12
Machinery	18	17	19	14	5
Sundry Fixed Costs	9	9	10	12	4
Rent & Interest	12	13	9	8	4
Profit *	17	17	4	2	10
Basic Payment Support	12	5	13	17	2

+ *including drawings*

* *to cover, tax, capital repayments, reinvestments and drawings*

These are only rough guidelines and need to be considered with great care. Values vary with type and size of farm. Unpaid manual labour of the farmer and family has been included and a rental value has been allowed for owner-occupied land. Higher rent and finance can be justified on more profitable farm systems. In years when output is lower, all these percentages, other than profit, will rise.

The Basic Payment as a percentage of output is also included to compare against profit. Being greater than total farm profit in some cases, it identifies the dependence of several farm businesses to direct subsidy. This has started to decline.

Farm Survey Ratios

The following are rounded averages based on farm surveys in recent years on a large sample of all types of farm, assuming a Management and Investment Income (see page 236) of 10% of Total Output is made. It is to be noted that Total Output includes the market value of any production retained for use/consumption on the farm (e.g. cereals for feed or seed). Unpaid labour (value of manual labour by the farmer and spouse) is included. Rent includes the rental value of owner-occupied land and interest charges are not included in the costs.

Casual labour and all contract work are included in fixed costs. Costs are a lower proportion and the margin a higher proportion in profitable years (and on more profitable farms), and *vice-versa* in low profit years.

Average Financial Ratios calculated from Farm Business Survey (England)

	% Total Output			% Total Gross Margin			% Total Fixed Costs		
	2005	2017	2018	2005	2017	2018	2005	2017	2018
Gross Margin (*inc. Support*)	66%	65%	64%						
Variable Costs:									
(excl. casual labour and contract)	34%	35%	36%	52%	53%	55%	48%	58%	59%
Fixed Costs:									
Labour: Paid (inc. unpaid)	24%	19%	19%	37%	28%	29%	34%	31%	31%
Power & Machinery (inc. contract)	17%	18%	19%	26%	28%	30%	24%	31%	32%
Rent/Rental Value	21%	15%	15%	32%	23%	23%	30%	25%	25%
General Overheads	8%	8%	7%	12%	12%	11%	11%	13%	12%
Total Fixed Costs	70%	60%	60%	107%	91%	93%	100%	100%	100%
Margin	**-4%**	**6%**	**4%**	**-7%**	**9%**	**7%**	**-6%**	**10%**	**7%**

Lending Criteria

Another set of standards widely used by lending and leasing institutions looks at Total Finance Charges (rent, interest, leasing charges, etc.), as a percentage of Gross Output and Gross Margin;

Finance as a % of Gross Output	Finance as a % of Gross Margin	Lending Criteria
0-10%	0-15%	Normally very safe
11-15%	16-22.5%	Common range, should be safe
15%	24%	Average Farm
16-20%	23-29%	Care required
20% plus	30% plus	Potentially dangerous

As lenders will be well aware, these ratios must be regarded with caution and in conjunction with the farm's level of net worth (% equity) and its trend in recent years, recent trends in its profitability and the potential borrower's record of expenditure both on and off the farm, together with his or her character and potential. Also, some enterprises and types of farming are riskier than others.

DISCOUNTING TABLE A

Discount Factors for Calculating the Present Value of Future (irregular) Cash Flows

Year	Percentage																	
	2%	3%	4%	5%	6%	7%	8%	9%	10%	11%	12%	13%	14%	15%	16%	18%	20%	25%
1	0.980	0.971	0.962	0.952	0.943	0.935	0.926	0.917	0.909	0.901	0.893	0.885	0.877	0.870	0.862	0.847	0.833	0.80
2	0.961	0.943	0.925	0.907	0.890	0.873	0.857	0.842	0.826	0.812	0.797	0.783	0.769	0.756	0.743	0.718	0.694	0.64
3	0.942	0.915	0.889	0.864	0.840	0.816	0.794	0.772	0.751	0.731	0.712	0.693	0.675	0.658	0.641	0.609	0.579	0.51
4	0.924	0.888	0.855	0.823	0.792	0.763	0.735	0.708	0.683	0.659	0.636	0.613	0.592	0.572	0.552	0.516	0.482	0.41
5	0.906	0.863	0.822	0.784	0.747	0.713	0.681	0.650	0.621	0.593	0.567	0.543	0.519	0.497	0.476	0.437	0.402	0.33
6	0.888	0.837	0.790	0.746	0.705	0.666	0.630	0.596	0.564	0.535	0.507	0.480	0.456	0.432	0.410	0.370	0.335	0.26
7	0.871	0.813	0.760	0.711	0.665	0.623	0.583	0.547	0.513	0.482	0.452	0.425	0.400	0.376	0.354	0.314	0.279	0.21
8	0.853	0.789	0.731	0.677	0.627	0.582	0.540	0.502	0.467	0.434	0.404	0.376	0.351	0.327	0.305	0.266	0.233	0.17
9	0.837	0.766	0.703	0.645	0.592	0.544	0.500	0.460	0.424	0.391	0.361	0.333	0.308	0.284	0.263	0.225	0.194	0.13
10	0.820	0.744	0.676	0.614	0.558	0.508	0.463	0.422	0.386	0.352	0.322	0.295	0.270	0.247	0.227	0.191	0.162	0.11
11	0.804	0.722	0.650	0.585	0.527	0.475	0.429	0.388	0.350	0.317	0.287	0.261	0.237	0.215	0.195	0.162	0.135	0.09
12	0.788	0.701	0.625	0.557	0.497	0.444	0.397	0.356	0.319	0.286	0.257	0.231	0.208	0.187	0.168	0.137	0.112	0.07
13	0.773	0.681	0.601	0.530	0.469	0.415	0.368	0.326	0.290	0.258	0.229	0.204	0.182	0.163	0.145	0.116	0.093	0.06
14	0.758	0.661	0.577	0.505	0.442	0.388	0.340	0.299	0.263	0.232	0.205	0.181	0.160	0.141	0.125	0.098	0.078	0.04
15	0.743	0.642	0.555	0.481	0.417	0.362	0.315	0.275	0.239	0.209	0.183	0.160	0.140	0.123	0.108	0.084	0.065	0.04
20	0.673	0.554	0.456	0.377	0.312	0.258	0.215	0.178	0.149	0.124	0.104	0.087	0.073	0.061	0.051	0.037	0.026	0.01
25	0.610	0.478	0.375	0.295	0.233	0.184	0.146	0.116	0.092	0.074	0.059	0.047	0.038	0.030	0.024	0.016	0.010	.004
30	0.552	0.412	0.308	0.231	0.174	0.131	0.099	0.075	0.057	0.044	0.033	0.026	0.020	0.015	0.012	0.007	0.004	.001

Example: The Present Value of £2,000 received 10 years from now, at 8 per cent discount rate of interest = 2,000 x 0.463 = £926.

Conversely, £926 invested now, at 8 per cent compound interest, will be worth £2,000 in 10 years' time.

ANNUITY / DISCOUNTING TABLE B

Discount Factors for Calculating the Present Value of Future Annuity (i.e. Constant Annual Cash Flow) Receivable in Year 1 to n inclusive.

Year	Percentage																	
	2%	3%	4%	5%	6%	7%	8%	9%	10%	11%	12%	13%	14%	15%	16%	18%	20%	25%
1	0.980	0.971	0.962	0.952	0.943	0.935	0.926	0.917	0.909	0.901	0.893	0.885	0.877	0.870	0.862	0.847	0.833	0.80
2	1.942	1.913	1.886	1.859	1.833	1.808	1.783	1.759	1.736	1.713	1.690	1.668	1.647	1.626	1.605	1.566	1.528	1.44
3	2.884	2.829	2.775	2.723	2.673	2.624	2.577	2.531	2.487	2.444	2.402	2.361	2.322	2.283	2.246	2.174	2.106	1.95
4	3.808	3.717	3.630	3.546	3.465	3.387	3.312	3.240	3.170	3.102	3.037	2.974	2.914	2.855	2.798	2.690	2.589	2.36
5	4.713	4.580	4.452	4.329	4.212	4.100	3.993	3.890	3.791	3.696	3.605	3.517	3.433	3.352	3.274	3.127	2.991	2.69
6	5.601	5.417	5.242	5.076	4.917	4.767	4.623	4.486	4.355	4.231	4.111	3.998	3.889	3.784	3.685	3.498	3.326	2.95
7	6.472	6.230	6.002	5.786	5.582	5.389	5.206	5.033	4.868	4.712	4.564	4.423	4.288	4.160	4.039	3.812	3.605	3.16
8	7.325	7.020	6.733	6.463	6.210	5.971	5.747	5.535	5.335	5.146	4.968	4.799	4.639	4.487	4.344	4.078	3.837	3.33
9	8.162	7.786	7.435	7.108	6.802	6.515	6.247	5.995	5.759	5.537	5.328	5.132	4.946	4.772	4.607	4.303	4.031	3.46
10	8.983	8.530	8.111	7.722	7.360	7.024	6.710	6.418	6.145	5.889	5.650	5.426	5.216	5.019	4.833	4.494	4.192	3.57
11	9.787	9.253	8.760	8.306	7.887	7.499	7.139	6.805	6.495	6.207	5.938	5.687	5.453	5.234	5.029	4.656	4.327	3.66
12	10.58	9.954	9.385	8.863	8.384	7.943	7.536	7.161	6.814	6.492	6.194	5.918	5.660	5.421	5.197	4.793	4.439	3.73
13	11.35	10.635	9.986	9.394	8.853	8.358	7.904	7.487	7.103	6.750	6.424	6.122	5.842	5.583	5.342	4.910	4.533	3.78
14	12.11	11.296	10.563	9.899	9.295	8.745	8.244	7.786	7.367	6.982	6.628	6.302	6.002	5.724	5.468	5.008	4.611	3.82
15	12.85	11.938	11.118	10.380	9.712	9.108	8.559	8.061	7.606	7.191	6.811	6.462	6.142	5.847	5.575	5.092	4.675	3.86
20	16.35	14.877	13.590	12.462	11.470	10.594	9.818	9.129	8.514	7.963	7.469	7.025	6.623	6.259	5.929	5.353	4.870	3.95
25	19.52	17.413	15.662	14.094	12.783	11.654	10.675	9.823	9.077	8.422	7.843	7.330	6.873	6.464	6.097	5.467	4.948	3.99
30	22.40	19.600	17.292	15.372	13.765	12.409	11.258	10.274	9.427	8.694	8.055	7.496	7.003	6.566	6.177	5.517	4.979	4.00

Example: The Present Value of a constant annual net cash flow, for the next 10 years, at l2 per cent discount rate of interest = 500 x 5.650 = £2,825. This is the same answer that would be obtained by multiplying 500 by each discount factor (at 12 per cent) in Table A for each year from 1 to 10, and adding together the ten resulting figures.

To obtain the Discounted Yield of a constant annual net cash flow, divide this into the original investment and look up the resulting figure in the table above, against the number of years. Example: an investment of £1,000 is estimated to produce £80 a year additional profit over 10 years (before charging interest). Add £100 depreciation a year = £180 annual net cash flow. 1000 /180 = 5.56. This equals just over l2 per cent (the 10 years /12 per cent figure being 5.650).

COMPOUNDING TABLE A

The Future Money Value of £1 after n Years with no additional payments made

Rate of Interest %

Year	2%	3%	4%	5%	6%	7%	8%	9%	10%	11%	12%	13%	14%	15%	16%	18%	20%	25%
1	1.02	1.03	1.04	1.05	1.06	1.07	1.08	1.09	1.10	1.11	1.12	1.13	1.14	1.15	1.16	1.18	1.20	1.25
2	1.04	1.06	1.08	1.10	1.12	1.14	1.17	1.19	1.21	1.23	1.25	1.28	1.30	1.32	1.35	1.39	1.44	1.56
3	1.06	1.09	1.12	1.16	1.19	1.23	1.26	1.30	1.33	1.37	1.40	1.44	1.48	1.52	1.56	1.64	1.73	1.95
4	1.08	1.13	1.17	1.22	1.26	1.31	1.36	1.41	1.46	1.52	1.57	1.63	1.69	1.75	1.81	1.94	2.07	2.44
5	1.10	1.16	1.22	1.28	1.34	1.40	1.47	1.54	1.61	1.69	1.76	1.84	1.93	2.01	2.10	2.29	2.49	3.05
6	1.13	1.19	1.27	1.34	1.42	1.50	1.59	1.68	1.77	1.87	1.97	2.08	2.19	2.31	2.44	2.70	2.99	3.81
7	1.15	1.23	1.32	1.41	1.50	1.61	1.71	1.83	1.95	2.08	2.21	2.35	2.50	2.66	2.83	3.19	3.58	4.77
8	1.17	1.27	1.37	1.48	1.59	1.72	1.85	1.99	2.14	2.30	2.48	2.66	2.85	3.06	3.28	3.76	4.30	5.96
9	1.20	1.30	1.42	1.55	1.69	1.84	2.00	2.17	2.36	2.56	2.77	3.00	3.25	3.52	3.80	4.44	5.16	7.45
10	1.22	1.34	1.48	1.63	1.79	1.97	2.16	2.37	2.59	2.84	3.11	3.39	3.71	4.05	4.41	5.23	6.19	9.31
11	1.24	1.38	1.54	1.71	1.90	2.10	2.33	2.58	2.85	3.15	3.48	3.84	4.23	4.65	5.12	6.18	7.43	11.64
12	1.27	1.43	1.60	1.80	2.01	2.25	2.52	2.81	3.14	3.50	3.90	4.33	4.82	5.35	5.94	7.29	8.92	14.55
13	1.29	1.47	1.67	1.89	2.13	2.41	2.72	3.07	3.45	3.88	4.36	4.90	5.49	6.15	6.89	8.60	10.70	18.19
14	1.32	1.51	1.73	1.98	2.26	2.58	2.94	3.34	3.80	4.31	4.89	5.53	6.26	7.08	7.99	10.15	12.84	22.74
15	1.35	1.56	1.80	2.08	2.40	2.76	3.17	3.64	4.18	4.78	5.47	6.25	7.14	8.14	9.27	11.97	15.41	28.42
20	1.49	1.81	2.19	2.65	3.21	3.87	4.66	5.60	6.73	8.06	9.65	11.52	13.74	16.37	19.46	27.39	38.34	86.8
25	1.64	2.09	2.67	3.39	4.29	5.43	6.85	8.62	10.83	13.59	17.00	21.23	26.46	32.92	40.9	62.7	95.4	265
30	1.81	2.43	3.24	4.32	5.74	7.61	10.06	13.27	17.45	22.89	29.96	39.12	50.95	66.2	85.9	143	237	807

COMPOUNDING TABLE B

*The Future Money Value of £1 after n Years**

Year	Rate of Interest %																	
	2%	3%	4%	5%	6%	7%	8%	9%	10%	11%	12%	13%	14%	15%	16%	18%	20%	25%
1	1.02	1.03	1.04	1.05	1.06	1.07	1.08	1.09	1.10	1.11	1.12	1.13	1.14	1.15	1.16	1.18	1.20	1.25
2	2.06	2.09	2.12	2.15	2.18	2.21	2.25	2.28	2.31	2.34	2.37	2.41	2.44	2.47	2.51	2.57	2.64	2.81
3	3.12	3.18	3.25	3.31	3.37	3.44	3.51	3.57	3.64	3.71	3.78	3.85	3.92	3.99	4.07	4.22	4.37	4.77
4	4.20	4.31	4.42	4.53	4.64	4.75	4.87	4.98	5.11	5.23	5.35	5.48	5.61	5.74	5.88	6.15	6.44	7.21
5	5.31	5.47	5.63	5.80	5.98	6.15	6.34	6.52	6.72	6.91	7.12	7.32	7.54	7.75	7.98	8.44	8.93	10.3
6	6.43	6.66	6.90	7.14	7.39	7.65	7.92	8.20	8.49	8.78	9.09	9.40	9.73	10.07	10.41	11.1	11.92	14.1
7	7.58	7.89	8.21	8.55	8.90	9.26	9.64	10.03	10.44	10.86	11.30	11.76	12.23	12.73	13.24	14.3	15.50	18.8
8	8.75	9.16	9.58	10.03	10.49	10.98	11.49	12.02	12.58	13.16	13.78	14.42	15.09	15.79	16.52	18.1	19.80	24.8
9	9.95	10.46	11.01	11.58	12.18	12.82	13.49	14.19	14.94	15.72	16.55	17.42	18.34	19.30	20.32	22.5	24.96	32.3
10	11.17	11.81	12.49	13.21	13.97	14.78	15.65	16.56	17.53	18.56	19.65	20.81	22.04	23.35	24.73	27.8	31.15	41.6
11	12.41	13.19	14.03	14.92	15.87	16.89	17.98	19.14	20.38	21.71	23.13	24.65	26.27	28.00	29.85	33.9	38.58	53.2
12	13.68	14.62	15.63	16.71	17.88	19.14	20.50	21.95	23.52	25.21	27.03	28.98	31.09	33.35	35.79	41.2	47.50	67.8
13	14.97	16.09	17.29	18.60	20.02	21.55	23.21	25.02	26.97	29.09	31.39	33.88	36.58	39.50	42.67	49.9	58.20	86.0
14	16.29	17.60	19.02	20.58	22.28	24.13	26.15	28.36	30.77	33.41	36.28	39.42	42.84	46.58	50.66	60.0	71.04	109
15	17.64	19.16	20.82	22.66	24.67	26.89	29.32	32.00	34.95	38.19	41.75	45.67	49.98	54.72	59.93	71.9	86.44	137
20	24.78	27.68	30.97	34.72	38.99	43.87	49.42	55.76	63.00	71.27	80.70	91.47	103.8	117.8	133.8	173	224.0	429
25	32.67	37.55	43.31	50.11	58.16	67.68	78.95	92.32	108.2	127.0	149.3	175.8	207.3	244.7	289.1	404	566.4	1318
30	41.38	49.00	58.33	69.76	83.80	101.1	122.3	148.6	180.9	220.9	270.3	331.3	406.7	500.0	615.2	933	1418	4034

* Equal payments made at the beginning of each year.

AMORTISATION TABLE

Annual Charge to write off £1,000

Write-off Period	Rate of Interest																
	2	3	4	5	6	7	8	9	10	11	12	13	14	15	16	18	20
5 years	212	218	225	231	237	244	250	257	264	271	277	284	291	298	305	320	334
6	179	185	191	197	203	210	216	223	230	236	243	250	257	264	271	286	301
7	155	161	167	173	179	186	192	199	205	212	219	226	233	240	248	262	277
8	137	142	149	155	161	167	174	181	187	194	201	208	216	223	230	245	261
9	123	128	134	141	147	153	160	167	174	181	188	195	202	210	217	232	248
10	111	117	123	130	136	142	149	156	163	170	177	184	192	199	207	223	239
11	102	108	114	120	127	133	140	147	154	161	168	176	183	191	199	215	231
12	95	100	107	113	119	125	133	140	147	154	161	169	177	184	192	209	225
13	88	94	100	106	113	120	127	134	141	148	156	163	171	179	187	204	221
14	83	89	95	101	108	114	121	128	136	143	151	159	167	175	183	200	217
15	78	84	90	96	103	110	117	124	131	139	147	155	163	171	179	196	214
16	74	80	86	92	99	106	113	120	128	136	143	151	160	168	176	194	211
17	70	76	82	89	95	102	110	117	125	132	140	149	157	165	174	191	209
18	67	73	79	86	92	99	107	114	122	130	138	146	155	163	172	190	208
20	61	67	74	80	87	94	102	110	117	126	134	142	151	160	169	187	205
25	51	57	64	71	78	86	94	102	110	119	127	136	145	155	164	183	202
30	45	51	58	65	73	81	89	97	106	115	124	133	143	152	162	181	201
40	37	43	51	58	66	75	84	93	102	112	122	131	141	151	160	180	200

Example: £30,000 is borrowed to erect a building. The annual charge to service interest and capital repayment on the £30,000, repayable over 10 years at 12%, is 30 x £177 = £5,310. Where the write-off period of the building is equal to the repayment period of the loan (10 years), then the average annual depreciation plus interest will equal £5,310.

The proportion of the total annual charge representing the average amount of capital repaid per annum can be readily determined by dividing the sum borrowed by the number of years of the loan: (in the above example this is £30,000 ÷ 10 = £3,000/year). The remainder is clearly the average amount of interest paid per annum: (in the above example, £5,310 — £3,000 = £2,310/year). The year to year variations between the two items (i.e. capital repaid and interest) are shown in the Mortgage Repayment Data tables (2 pages further on) , which demonstrate the way the capital repayment part increases and the interest part decreases over time.

SINKING FUND TABLE

The sum required to be set aside at the end of each year to make £1,000

No. of Years	Rate of Interest																
	2	3	4	5	6	7	8	9	10	11	12	13	14	15	16	18	20
5	192	188	185	181	177	174	170	167	164	161	157	154	151	148	145	140	134
6	159	155	151	147	143	140	136	133	130	126	123	120	117	114	111	106	101
7	135	131	127	123	119	116	112	109	105	102	99	96	93	90	88	82	77
8	117	112	109	105	101	97	94	91	87	84	81	78	76	73	70	65	61
9	103	98	94	91	87	83	80	77	74	71	68	65	62	60	57	52	48
10	91	87	83	80	76	72	69	66	63	60	57	54	52	49	47	43	39
11	82	78	74	70	67	63	60	57	54	51	48	46	43	41	39	35	31
12	75	70	67	63	59	56	53	50	47	44	41	39	37	34	32	29	25
13	68	64	60	56	53	50	47	44	41	38	36	33	31	29	27	24	21
14	63	59	55	51	48	44	41	38	36	33	31	29	27	25	23	20	17
15	58	54	50	46	43	40	37	34	31	29	27	25	23	21	19	16	14
16	54	50	46	42	39	36	33	30	28	26	23	21	20	18	16	14	11
17	50	46	42	39	35	32	30	27	25	22	20	19	17	15	14	11	9
18	47	43	39	36	32	29	27	24	22	20	18	16	15	13	12	10	8
19	44	40	36	33	30	27	24	22	20	18	16	14	13	11	10	8	6
20	41	37	34	30	27	24	22	20	17	16	14	12	11	10	9	8	5
25	31	27	24	21	18	16	14	12	10	9	7	6	5	5	4	3	2
30	25	21	18	15	13	11	9	7	6	5	4	3	3	2	2	1	1
40	17	13	11	8	6	5	4	3	2	2	1	1	1	1	—	—	—

MORTGAGE REPAYMENT DATA

Items per £1000 invested; where I = Interest, P = Principal repaid, L = Loan outstanding

Loan of	3%			4%			5%			6%			8%			10%		
5 years	I	P	L	I	P	L	I	P	L	I	P	L	I	P	L	I	P	L
1	30	188	812	40	185	815	50	181	819	60	177	823	80	170	830	100	164	836
2	24	194	618	33	192	623	41	190	629	49	188	635	66	184	645	84	180	656
3	19	200	418	25	200	424	31	200	424	38	199	435	52	199	447	66	198	458
4	13	206	212	17	208	216	21	210	220	26	211	224	36	215	232	46	218	240
5	6	212	0	9	216	0	11	220	0	13	224	0	19	232	0	24	240	0
10 years																		
1	30	87	913	40	83	917	50	80	920	60	76	924	80	69	931	100	63	939
2	27	90	823	37	87	830	46	83	837	55	80	844	75	75	856	94	69	868
3	25	93	730	33	90	740	42	88	749	51	85	758	69	81	776	87	76	792
4	22	95	635	30	94	646	37	92	657	46	90	668	62	87	689	79	84	709
5	19	98	537	26	97	549	33	97	561	40	96	572	55	94	595	71	92	617
6	16	101	436	22	101	448	28	101	459	34	102	471	48	101	494	62	101	516
7	13	104	332	18	105	342	23	107	353	28	108	363	39	110	384	52	111	405
8	10	107	224	14	110	233	18	112	241	22	114	249	31	118	266	40	122	282
9	7	111	114	9	114	119	12	117	123	15	121	128	21	128	138	28	134	148
10	3	114	0	5	119	0	6	123	0	8	128	0	11	138	0	15	148	0

MORTGAGE REPAYMENT DATA (CONTINUED)

Loan of 20 years

years	3% I	3% P	3% L	4% I	4% P	4% L	5% I	5% P	5% L	6% I	6% P	6% L	8% I	8% P	8% L	10% I	10% P	10% L
1	30	37	963	40	34	966	50	30	970	60	27	973	80	22	978	100	17	983
5	25	42	802	34	39	818	43	37	833	53	34	847	72	30	872	92	26	893
10	19	49	573	26	48	597	33	47	620	41	46	642	58	44	683	76	41	722
15	11	56	308	15	58	328	20	60	347	26	61	367	38	64	407	51	66	445
20	2	65	0	3	71	0	4	76	0	5	82	0	8	94	0	11	107	0

25 years

years	3% I	3% P	3% L	4% I	4% P	4% L	5% I	5% P	5% L	6% I	6% P	6% L	8% I	8% P	8% L	10% I	10% P	10% L
1	30	27	973	40	24	976	50	21	979	60	18	982	80	14	986	100	10	990
5	27	31	854	36	28	870	45	25	884	55	23	897	75	19	920	95	15	938
10	22	36	686	30	34	712	38	33	736	47	31	760	66	27	802	86	24	838
15	16	41	490	22	42	519	29	41	548	37	41	576	54	40	629	72	39	677
20	9	48	263	13	51	285	18	53	307	23	55	330	35	59	374	48	62	418
25	2	56	0	2	62	0	3	68	0	4	74	0	7	87	0	10	100	0

MORTGAGE REPAYMENT DATA (CONTINUED)

Loan of	4%			5%			6%			8%			10%			12%		
	I	P	L	I	P	L	I	P	L	I	P	L	I	P	L	I	P	L
30 years																		
1	40	18	982	50	15	985	60	13	987	80	9	991	100	6	994	120	4	996
5	37	21	903	47	18	917	57	16	929	77	12	948	97	9	963	118	7	974
10	32	25	786	42	23	811	51	21	833	71	18	872	92	14	903	113	11	927
15	27	31	643	35	30	675	44	29	706	63	26	760	83	23	807	104	20	846
20	20	38	469	27	38	502	34	38	535	51	38	596	69	37	652	88	36	701
25	12	46	257	17	49	282	21	51	306	33	56	355	46	60	402	61	63	448
30	2	56	0	3	62	0	4	69	0	7	82	0	10	96	0	13	111	0
40 years																		
1	40	11	989	50	8	992	60	6	994	80	4	996	100	2	998	120	1	999
5	38	12	943	48	10	954	58	8	964	79	5	977	99	3	986	119	2	992
10	36	15	874	45	13	896	56	11	915	76	8	944	97	5	964	118	4	977
15	32	18	789	42	16	821	52	15	850	73	11	895	94	9	928	115	6	951
20	28	22	687	37	21	726	47	20	762	67	17	823	88	14	871	110	11	906
25	24	27	562	32	27	605	40	26	645	59	24	718	80	22	778	102	20	826
30	18	33	410	24	34	450	31	35	489	48	36	563	66	36	628	86	35	685
35	11	40	225	15	43	252	20	47	280	31	53	335	45	58	388	60	61	437
40	2	49	0	3	56	0	4	63	0	6	78	0	9	93	0	13	108	0

Note—All figures rounded to nearest £.

6.   FARM RECORDS

The following records should be kept for management purposes:

BASIC WHOLE FARM FINANCIAL POSITION

1. Cash Analysis Book, fully detailed.

2. Petty Cash Book.

3. Annual Valuation, including physical quantities of

    i.   Harvested crops in store

    ii.   Livestock (breeding and fattening) at (near) market value, less any variable costs yet to be borne.

    iii. Fertilisers, seeds, sprays, casual labour or contract work applied to growing crops should be recorded, but "cultivations" and manure residues can be ignored for management purposes.

    iv.   Fertiliser, seed, sprays and other sundry direct items in store,

4. Debtors and creditors at the end of the financial year.

OTHER FINANCIAL AND PHYSICAL RECORDS

5. Output (quantities and value) of each crop and livestock enterprise for the "harvest year" (or production cycle). It may be possible to get information of sales from a fully detailed cash analysis book (although, for crops, the financial year figures will then have to be allocated between crops from the current harvest and those from the harvest in the previous financial year in order to check on the accuracy of the opening valuation of crops in store; this is particularly a problem with Michaelmas ending accounts). The following records of internal transfers and consumption will also be required:

    (a) Numbers and market value of livestock transferred from one livestock category to another, e.g. dairy calves to dairy followers or beef enterprise, or dairy heifers to dairy enterprise.

    (b) Quantity and market value of cereals fed on farm and used for seed.

    (c) Quantity and market value of milk and other produce consumed by the farmer or his employees, used on the farm (e.g. milk fed to calves), or sold direct.

6. A monthly record of livestock numbers; reconciled with the previous month according to births, purchases, deaths, sales and transfers.

7. Costs and quantities of concentrate feed to each category of livestock, including home-grown cereals fed on the farm.

8. Allocation of costs of seed, fertiliser, sprays, casual labour and contract work specific to an enterprise. This is in order to calculate gross margins, where required.

9. Breeding record for cows, including bulling dates, date(s) served, type of bull used, pregnancy testing, estimated calving date, actual calving date, and date when dried off.

10. For each crop, total output and yield per hectare, in both quantity and value. Include each field where the crop has been grown and its approximate yield, where this can be satisfactorily obtained.

11. For each field, keep one page to cover a period of say, ten years. Record on this, each year, crop grown, variety sown, fertiliser used, sprays used, date sown, date(s) harvested, approximate yield (if obtainable), and any other special notes that you feel may have significance for the future.

12. A rotation record. On a single page, if possible, list each field down the side and say, ten years along the top. Colour each field-year space according to the crop grown, e.g. barley yellow, potatoes red, etc.

13. It is important to note that other farm records are required for legislative and cross compliance purposes including:

    i.   Livestock movements, identification, flock and herd records etc.

    ii.   Nitrate Vulnerable Zone (NVZ) records and calculations including livestock loadings, manure storage, fertiliser plans and usage etc.

    iii.   Pesticide application and storage records, risk assessments

    iv.   Farm waste storage and disposal records and necessary exemptions / permits / transfer certificates

    v.   Integrated Pollution and Prevention Controls (IPPC) records (for pig and poultry units)

    vi.   Soil Protection reviews and risk assessments

    vii.   Financial (HMRC) records including VAT, PAYE, NI etc.

IX. WHOLE FARM COSTINGS

1. COMMENTS ON WHOLE FARM COSTINGS

This chapter brings together the costings from the relevant parts of the Pocketbook to demonstrate what the farm profit and loss might look like for a 'typical' farm in some of the main sectors of UK farming. The farms are built up from the gross margin budgets for various enterprises shown in section II – Enterprise Data. These are then combined with the fixed (overhead) costs for specific farm types, as set out in section VI(1) – Whole Farm Fixed Costs. These figures are influenced by those in the Farm Business Survey. This produces a profit and loss schedule for the farm.

Costings are firstly shown for 'average' performance levels for each farm. The same farm system is then examined using the high-performance gross margins in the book coupled with the same overheads but have been reduced by a mere 10%. It is not always the case that more profitable farmers have larger gross margins and spend less on overheads, but it is common. The difference between the two sets of figures for comparable farm systems demonstrates the benefits of improving gross margin performance by raising technical performance (mostly increasing yields without changing variable costs) and making measured reductions in overhead costs. There are no other differences between the two sets of costings. In practice, as shown in the enterprise margins, higher performing farms may also have higher stocking rates, lower replacement rates and so no, making the overall returns for the better farms considerably better than shown.

The figures for whole-farm costings are shown in a standard format. Some specific points are worthy of mention:

1. The labour costs include an allowance for unpaid labour. This is for the manual labour of the proprietor and their immediate family. It covers the 'farm work' that is undertaken, but not the managerial input that the family makes to the farm as this management return comes from the profit and loss (as well as a return to the capital invested). Unpaid labour is obviously not a cash cost to farms, with proprietors of sole traders or partnerships taking a return through drawings (share of the profits). Such drawings may or may not relate to the actual amount of farm work undertaken. An average figure for unpaid labour is shown to illustrate the true profit and loss – even if a farming family chooses to 'work for nothing', the opportunity cost of this time should be reflected.

2. The labour figures, more than any other in these schedules, are particularly high for just farming and should be taken into consideration. They include a combination of overstaffing during quiet times in some parts of the year (almost all farms are inevitably inefficient being seasonal), farm capital works and considerable work on non-farming activities. The capital works are those that farmers might undertake with their own labour (e.g. laying cow tracks or building grain sheds etc.). The non-farming labour might include building diversified enterprises (such as converting barns, collecting rent, repairing gutters, improving roadways etc). Equally, with homes and farms often being the same places, a large component of labour is often actually private work, for example house and garden maintenance work is generally considered farm work but for those not living on a farm, the work still needs doing.

3. The machinery costs shown are average 'per hectare' figures based on survey data. In practice, resourcing machinery can be done in many ways, especially with regards to owning machinery versus the use of contractors. The split shown below would be typical. In several cases, replacing owned machinery (and labour) with contractors produces savings, in other circumstances it will be dearer.

4. The range of labour and machinery costs in UK farming sectors is very wide and is one of the main differences between high and low performing businesses. For aspirational power and labour costs, examine the Benchmark Power and Labour costs on page 199. The section has been generated from working with aspirational farmers in each sector, with a focus on identifying non-farming overheads and allocating them into private costs in the management accounts.

5. The capital structure of UK farms varies widely. Some are tenanted, some part-rented, and others fully owner-occupied. Of the owned land, some will have been purchased recently (and thus probably carry a large finance charge) whilst other land may have been purchased many generations ago and therefore incur little or no financing. For this reason, a 'Margin Before Rent and Finance' is shown. Such a measure puts all farms on the same basis and can be thought of as the return from the farming operation.

6. The rent shown in the costings below is an average based on survey data. This will cover a mix of tenanted and owner-occupied land (roughly a third of UK farmland is tenanted). As such it does not show a full rent for all the land on the farm. It can be argued that, like unpaid labour, a full economic cost of land rental for all land should be shown because, if farmers were not using it themselves, it could be let to someone else for an income. Rent and finance levels are assumed to be the same on both the 'average' and 'high performance' farms.

7. Income from the current Basic Payment Scheme is included separately from farming income as it is 'decoupled' from production. The figures shown are for the English scheme – refer to section III – Government Support for information on other GB regions. No income from environmental schemes is included in the arable and dairy systems as this is very farm specific. Such income tends to be particularly important on beef and sheep farms and especially in hill areas so is shown in these farm systems.

8. A notional income from diversification has been included in the costings. Again, this varies between farms, but is shown as non-farming revenue being an important venture of many real-life farming businesses. High performing farms are assumed to generate 10% more diversification income than average businesses.

9. Stocking rates are based on the details in the gross margins at the start of this book. This schedule highlights the importance of getting them right and the gains achieved from fitting the correct amount of farming on the land.

2. COMBINABLE CROP FARM

This model shows a combinable crop farm system of 375 hectares (*925 acres*). This farm is larger than the average (mean) of arable farms in the UK but is close to the average size for farms of 1 full time equivalent worker or more.

Enterprises:	Ha	*Average* GM/Ha	GM Total	*Higher Performer* GM/Ha	GM Total
Winter Feed Wheat	150	828	124,157	1,016	152,400
Spring Malting Barley	75	547	40,988	666	49,953
Winter Oilseed Rape	75	909	68,199	1,112	83,386
Spring Beans	75	509	38,203	632	47,428
Farm Gross Margin	**375**	**724**	**271,547**	**888**	**333,168**
Overheads					
Regular Labour (paid)		85	31,875	77	28,688
Regular Labour (unpaid)		80	30,000	72	27,000
Casual Labour		10	3,750	9	3,375
Total Labour		**175**	**65,625**	**158**	**59,063**
Machinery Depreciation		120	45,000	108	40,500
Machinery Running Costs		105	39,375	95	35,438
Contract		95	35,625	86	32,063
Total Power & Machinery		**320**	**120,000**	**288**	**108,000**
Farm Maintenance		35	13,125	32	11,813
Water & Electricity		65	24,375	59	21,938
General Overhead Expenses		75	28,125	68	25,313
Total Other Overheads		**175**	**65,625**	**158**	**59,063**
Total Fixed Costs		**670**	**251,250**	**603**	**226,125**
Margin before Rent & Finance		**54**	**20,297**	**285**	**107,043**
Rent & Interest		145	54,375	145	54,375
plus Basic Payment (England)		161	60,369	161	60,369
plus Diversification Income			15,000		16,500
Business Profit (Loss)		**110**	**41,291**	**345**	**129,537**

3. DAIRY FARM

This model shows a dairy farm with 180 milking cows plus followers. It is based on an All-Year Round production system and the total farm size is 115 hectares (*285 acres*).

Enterprises:	Head	Ha	*Average* GM/Ha	GM Total	*Higher Performer* GM/Ha	GM Total
All-Year Round Da	180	86	2,273	194,789	2,604	223,196
Dairy Youngstock	47	33	1,066	35,075	1,173	38,582
Farm Gross Margin		**119**	**1,938**	**229,864**	**2,207**	**261,779**
Overheads						
Regular Labour (paid)			200	23,723	180	21,351
Regular Labour (unpaid)			460	54,563	414	49,106
Casual Labour			35	4,152	32	3,736
Total Labour			**695**	**82,437**	**626**	**74,193**
Machinery Depreciation			205	24,316	185	21,884
Machinery Running Costs			210	24,909	189	22,418
Contract			170	20,164	153	18,148
Total Power & Machinery			**585**	**69,389**	**527**	**62,450**
Farm Maintenance			90	10,675	81	9,608
Water & Electricity			195	23,130	176	20,817
General Overhead Expenses			75	8,896	68	8,006
Total Other Overheads			**360**	**42,701**	**324**	**38,431**
Total Fixed Costs			**1,640**	**194,527**	**1,476**	**175,075**
Margin before Rent & Finance			**298**	**35,337**	**731**	**86,704**
Rent & Interest			200	23,723	200	23,723
plus Basic Payment (England)			177	20,971	177	20,971
plus Diversification Income				5,000		5,500
Business Profit (Loss)			**317**	**37,585**	**754**	**89,452**

4. LOWLAND GRAZING BEEF & SHEEP FARM

This model is a lowland beef and sheep farm on 110 hectares (*270 acres*). It has a herd of 75 autumn-calving suckler cows and the progeny of these are taken through to finishing over the following winter (housed so no per hectare margins). There is also a flock of 650 lowland ewes.

The average farm of this system is not profitable when rent and a cost for all the farmer's time is allowed but is cash flow positive making £20,000 if unpaid labour is not accounted for and £32,000 for an owner occupier. Whilst this does not fully account for the resources employed on the farm, it does explain how such businesses remain operational.

			Average		Higher Performer	
Enterprises:	Head	Ha	GM/Ha	GM Total	GM/Ha	GM Total
Sucklers (Autumn)	75	45	338	15,227	443	19,947
Beef Finishing	69	0	52 *	3,603	160 *	11,029
Lowland Ewes	650	65	557	36,196	881	57,273
Farm Gross Margin		**110**	**500**	**55,026**	**802**	**88,249**
Overheads						
Regular Labour (paid)			40	4,400	36	3,960
Regular Labour (unpaid)			360	39,600	324	35,640
Casual Labour			20	2,200	18	1,980
Total Labour			**420**	**46,200**	**378**	**41,580**
Machinery Depreciation			120	13,200	108	11,880
Machinery Running Costs			110	12,100	99	10,890
Contract			75	8,250	68	7,425
Total Power & Machinery			**305**	**33,550**	**275**	**30,195**
Farm Maintenance			45	4,950	41	4,455
Water & Electricity			80	8,800	72	7,920
General Overhead Expenses			60	6,600	54	5,940
Total Other Overheads			**185**	**20,350**	**167**	**18,315**
Total Fixed Costs			**910**	**100,100**	**819**	**90,090**
Margin before Rent & Finance			**(410)**	**(45,074)**	**(17)**	**(1,841)**
Rent & Interest			110	12,100	110	12,100
plus Basic Payment (England)			177	19,448	177	19,448
plus Agri-Environment Income				8,000		8,000
plus Diversification Income				10,000		11,000
Business Profit (Loss)			**(179)**	**(19,726)**	**223**	**24,507**
			* per head		* per head	

5. UPLAND GRAZING BEEF & SHEEP FARM

This model shows an upland beef and sheep farm on 180 hectares (*445 acres*), of which, 130 hectares are in-bye land, with a further 50 ha of hill land used for extensive summer sheep grazing. The farm has a herd of 40 spring-calving suckler cows with the progeny sold as stores and a flock of 950 upland ewes.

The average farm of this system, if taking all resources into full account are not profitable, but the cash position is positive if unpaid labour is not accounted for (£38,500) or nearly £50,000 If the farm owner occupied as well. It this does not account for the resources (labour and land) used on the farm fully but explains how farms remain viable.

Enterprises:	Head	Ha	Average GM/Ha	Average GM Total	Higher Performer GM/Ha	Higher Performer GM Total
Sucklers (Spring)	40	25	108	2,710	208	5,190
Upland Ewes	950	105	551	58,134	861	90,826
Hill Land		*50*				
Farm Gross Margin		**180**	**337**	**60,845**	**532**	**96,016**
Overheads						
Regular Labour (paid)			15	2,707	14	2,436
Regular Labour (unpaid)			235	42,406	212	38,165
Casual Labour			15	2,707	14	2,436
Total Labour			**265**	**47,819**	**239**	**43,037**
Machinery Depreciation			65	11,729	59	10,556
Machinery Running Costs			55	9,925	50	8,932
Contract			30	5,414	27	4,872
Total Power & Machinery			**150**	**27,068**	**135**	**24,361**
Farm Maintenance			20	3,609	18	3,248
Water & Electricity			40	7,218	36	6,496
General Overhead Expenses			35	6,316	32	5,684
Total Other Overheads			**95**	**17,143**	**86**	**15,428**
Total Fixed Costs			**510**	**92,030**	**459**	**82,827**
Margin before Rent & Finance			**(173)**	**(31,185)**	**73**	**13,190**
Rent & Interest			60	10,827	60	10,827
plus Basic Payment (England)			180 / 58	20,771	180 / 58	20,771
plus Agri-Environment Income				12,500		12,500
plus Diversification Income				5,000		5,500
Business Profit (Loss)			**(21)**	**(3,741)**	**228**	**41,133**

X.   EMISSIONS AND THE ENVIRONMENT

The environment, and in particular its care and repair, are attracting greater attention than ever before. And rightly so. Farming must decarbonise. It is not solely the greenhouse gasses that require our attention; the environment is a multi-faceted issue including water, biodiversity and use of other resources. Reducing production simply exports the problem. Consumption is the ultimate way to measure environmental impacts for that reason.

Emissions per hectare alone do not constitute the environmental footprint of the end product but make a major impact. When you consider yields over land area, the impact of the wider environment is brought into focus. Based on the gross margins at the start of this book, one hectare of lowland Britain can produce 7.9 tonnes of milling wheat per year (rotation complications aside). The beef gross margins suggest, the same hectare would provide about 250kg beef meat per year. It becomes clear, the environmental footprint then has to consider more than simple emissions, but wider considerations of land use. More work needs to be done to develop these figures.

This chapter presents a brief examination of the impact of farming on emissions and natural resources. It primarily considers GHG emissions both per field operation and per unit of food produced so including the processing of the good as well as the farm-level emissions, as this is how consumers view their sustainability. There are several other environmental aspects that are relevant to farming, many are covered in other parts of this book. For example, the first section of the chapter after this covers costs of environmental conservation (page 271), and the pulse section makes an estimate of nitrogen savings from leguminous crops in the rotation (p17).

1.   GREENHOUSE GAS (GHG) EMISSIONS

The focus on the environment and particularly greenhouse gas emissions has sharpened. The UK Government has set-out commitments to achieve zero net-emissions *'Net Zero'*, by 2050 and the NFU by 2040 (from agriculture) subject to receiving the Government support necessary. Even getting close to Net Zero will not be possible from tinkering at the edges of current farming systems, but by making major and fundamental changes to the way we farm. Addressing such challenges is central to the future of UK food and farming and all other areas of industry and life as we work through the 2020's, this is one of the major puzzles the world has to quickly solve.

Agriculture, as a process of gathering carbon into hydrocarbon molecules (as starch and cellulose in plants and then in all parts of animals) could be argued is a sequestrator of carbon (takes carbon dioxide from the atmosphere). However, this is then returned to the environment through respiration (breathing and simply, living), thus creating a cycle. To achieve this cycle, fuel is burned to move vehicles to cultivate, plant, harvest plants, and also from livestock farming. This then needs processing, moving, cooking, wrapping and chilling before the food reaches the consumer, thereby consuming much more carbon dioxide.

Beyond GHGs, agriculture has an intrinsically unavoidable environmental footprint; it is taking resources from the earth for consumption (such as land). However, that footprint can be minimised, and land can also sequestrate carbon, indeed should do (short term) to build soil organic matter and therefore fertility. As crops grow, they sequest (absorb) carbon and then animals (and people) release it. When plants stop growing and are used, eaten or decompose, the carbon is released as carbon dioxide. Different crops and technologies have differing GHG benefits and costs. Higher yields (per hectare for example), generally incur lower carbon costs per unit of production, especially if it means more output per unit of input.

There are seven main GHG groups that contribute to climate change, as covered by the Kyoto Protocol. The main GHGs in farming are Carbon Dioxide, Methane and Nitrous Oxide. Water vapour is the largest GHG by volume, but human interference has not changed its atmospheric balance meaning it is not contributory to climate change. GHG emissions are converted into a global warming potential (GWP) estimate using the Intergovernmental Panel on Climate Change (IPCC) guidelines for measuring the impact of GHGs. This is conventionally expressed as CO_2 equivalent (CO_2e) as summarised in the table below which expresses the GWP over 100 years as some gases persist in the atmosphere for longer than others.

Selected GHG Emissions Conversion Factors expressed in CO₂e Terms

	GHG	Lifetime (Years)	GWP over 100 Years
Carbon Dioxide	CO_2	*	1
Methane	CH_4	12	28
Nitrous Oxide	N_2O	121	265

Source: IPCC (2015),

* No single figure is available. It is a very stable molecule, so some experts believe that the lifetime of CO₂ can be infinite.

Carbon dioxide is a very stable molecule (it does not easily react with other gases). Methane is a substantially more potent GHG than carbon dioxide but breaks down in the atmosphere with a half-life of approximately 9 years. When it breaks down, one product is carbon dioxide. Most studies focus on the GWP over 100 years which means that a tonne of methane is 28 times more potent than a tonne of CO_2. Nitrous Oxide is more potent a GHG still and has an atmospheric half-life of about 110 years. Their contribution to the GHG emissions in terms of CO_2e in the UK and UK farming specifically are shown below.

Publications celebrate the largest reduction in GHG emissions in the UK in 2020 since records began in 1990, with reductions of 8.9% to 414mt CO_2e. Whilst that is a remarkable achievement, as the whole country was in lockdown or restrictions for most of the year, that was a small reduction.

Agriculture accounts for approximately 10% of GHG emissions in the UK. In 2019, human activity in the UK accounted for 455 million tonnes of GHG emissions (CO_2 equivalent), 2.8% down from 468mt in 2018. Agriculture accounted for 45.4mt CO_2e (2018), most of which comes from the enteric fermentation of ruminating animals (methane) and the use (and manufacture) of nitrogen fertilisers (nitrous oxides). The table below demonstrates this and identifies that the focus for agriculture is primarily to reduce methane and nitrous oxide emissions.

UK GHG Emissions 2019 (measured in million tonnes of CO₂ equivalence)

	GHG Total	Carbon Dioxide	Methane	Nitrous Oxide	Others
UK	**455**	365	54	22	14
UK percentage		80%	12%	5%	3%
UK Agriculture	**45.4**	6.0	25.2	15.0	0.0
Percentage	**10.0%**	1.6%	47%	68.0%	0%

Source; National Statistics, 2019 UK Greenhouse gas emissions, final figures

GHG EMISSIONS IN FOOD PRODUCTION

Several studies have examined GHG emissions from food and results vary wildly, even when calculated in a similar manner. For example, GHG emissions linked with beef production depend on factors such as the dietary regime, production system, genetic factors, country, age at slaughter etc. The results below are from a 2018 Oxford University study. They are based on global data so use with care when looking at UK agricultural emissions. These figures give a useful indication of performance ranges by product. More accurate estimating of CO_2e emissions at a UK level and by farming system is required.

Notes on the following table:

* GHG emission results focus on the *whole supply-chain* (i.e. farm, processing, retail etc.). For most products, the farm-level accounts for the majority of GHG emissions.

* *Differences by beef production system:* Beef from dairy calves has lower emissions because their mothers' emissions are attributed to milk production, whereas suckler beef cow's emissions are attributed solely to the fattening calf until the next is born. This means substantially higher emissions per unit of beef (emissions from 2 animals for one carcass). Differences in age at slaughter also have a big impact; dairy bulls tend to be fattened more intensively and slaughtered younger than grass-fed steers.

* *Variation by product:* 'Low' is based on 5th percentile scores from a 2013 IPCC study and 'High' is on the 95th percentile. There is a seven-fold variation in bovine meat from the beef herd and over 30-fold difference for tomatoes. This indicates substantial scope for performance improvement.

* *Ancillary products:* such as leather from beef or pig production need consideration. Some research suggests that CO2e emissions from leather are lower than synthetic alternatives, something which can be easily overlooked.

Estimated Global Variation in GHG Emissions by Food Group (Selected Products)

Product	Unit	Low	Median	High
			Kg CO_2e	
Starch-Rich Products				
Wheat & Rye (Bread)	per 1,000 kcal energy	0.3	0.5	1.1
Maize (Meal)	"	0.1	0.3	0.8
Oatmeal	"	0.3	0.3	1.6
Rice	"	0.3	1.0	2.8
Potatoes	"	0.1	0.6	1.0
Milk and Dairy Products				
Milk	per litre	1.5	2.7	7.0
Cheese	per 100g protein	4.6	8.4	26.6
Soymilk	per litre	0.5	0.9	1.7
Protein-Rich Products				
Bovine Meat (beef herd)	per 1kg protein	188	303	1,350
Bovine Meat (dairy herd)	"	76	173	287
Lamb & Mutton	"	118	203	301
Pig Meat	"	43	65	147
Poultry Meat	"	23	43	120
Eggs	"	26	26	42
Fish (farmed)	"	24	25	60
Other Pulses	"	4	6	19
Peas	"	2	4	08
Nuts	"	-25	-08	66

Product	Unit	Low	Median Kg CO$_2$e	High
Sugar Products				
Beet Sugar	per 1kg	1.0	1.8	2.6
Cane Sugar	per 1kg	0.6	3.2	5.6
Fruit and Vegetables				
Tomatoes	per kg	0.4	0.7	12.6
Onions & Leeks	"	0.3	0.4	0.8
Root Vegetables	"	0.2	0.4	0.6
Brassicas	"	0.2	0.4	1.2
Citrus Fruit	"	0.0	0.3	0.7
Apples	"	0.3	0.4	0.6
Berries & Grapes	"	0.6	1.4	2.9
Oils				
Soybean Oil	per litre	2.2	3.9	18.8
Palm Oil	"	2.8	7.2	13.1
Sunflower Oil	"	2.2	3.5	4.9
Rapeseed Oil	"	2.2	3.5	7.2
Alcoholic Beverages				
Barley (Beer)	per pint	0.2	0.4	0.8
Wine	per glass	0.1	0.2	0.7

Source: Poore & Nemecek (2018) Science

GHG EMISSIONS FROM FIELDWORK

This table makes an estimate of the amount carbon dioxide released as GHG from using tractor diesel for field operations. It is based on the assumptions used in the machinery chapter to calculate farmers' costings. The work rates make some allowances for down-time and repair times etc. but the delays are also considered in the fuel usage. Using the calculated amount of fuel used per hectare, the conversion into CO_2 emissions is based on 1litre diesel combusting to generate 2.598kg carbon dioxide. Diesel has a density of 835g/l, carbon content of diesel of 86.2% and molecular weights of carbon (12) and oxygen (16). This only accounts for the GHG from the fuel combustion, not the manufacture or disposal of the machine itself or from the release of CO_2 from the soil movement nitrous oxide from fertilising or the methane produced from rumens. Figures will vary according to the assumptions made in the previous chapter such as speed of operation. These figures are crude and an estimate from calculations, they are not from empirical evidence so should be treated with some care.

Estimated Emissions from diesel combustion when undertaking field operations.

Operation	detail	GHG Emissions kg CO2e/ha
Cultivations		
Plough Light Land	6-furrow	44
Heavy Land	6-furrow	55
Deep Plough	6-furrow	61
Inc. Furrow press	Light land	50
	Heavy land	61
Mole Ploughing	Single leg	45
Rotovate	Arable	47
	Grass	77
Subsoil		45
Stubble cultivating		31
Shallow disc		29
Heavy disc		40
Comb disc cultivating		39
Power Harrowing	4m + packer roller	41
	Shallow PH	26
Stubble Raking		6
Spring tine harrowing		14
Chain harrowing		11
Pressing		22
Rolling	Flat	15
	6m gang	6
Fertiliser	spinner	4
Drilling		
Cereals	plain	12
	Combi-drill	42
	Vaderstad Drill	20
	Direct Drilling	20
Grass	Broadcast	16

Operation	detail	GHG Emissions kg CO2e/ha
Spraying	24-35m trailed	4
	SP 36m	4
Baling	Small bales & Sled	28
	Big round Baler	16
	Big Square Baler	12
Sugar Beet Drilling		20
Destoning		90
Potato Planting		56
Ridging		44
Beet Harvesting	6-row tanker	52
Potato Harvesting		
2 row trailed manned/unmanned		116
inc. Carting 2 trailers		231
Combine Harvesting		
Hp	235	55
	275	55
	350	43
	550	45
Pea Viner	450	97
Grass Operations		
Grass Mowing		19
Topping		15
Raking		12
Tedding		12
Forage Harvesting	trailed	20
Quad Bike	Plus Slug Pelleter	0.7

MITIGATING GHG EMISSIONS

The data above record emissions 'spent' to produce something but not the potential for mitigating them. There are several techniques that generate lower emissions per unit of food production than others, several of which are also economically favourable. For example, keeping high stocking rates on grazing land and frequently moving stock to new pasture apparently helps grass absorb more carbon dioxide from the atmosphere than slower rotation grazing techniques, thus sequestering more carbon in the soil as organic matter. Keeping it in the soil is another challenge.

Lowering emissions in the future may be possible through improved genetics (genomics), better animal health; higher forage quality and feed processing; more effective manure usage and storage (including anaerobic digestion and decreased storage time of slurry); better housing systems for animals; utilisation of rainwater harvesting. Whilst farming must pursue all these actions, they are small adjustments and do not remove emissions totally. Major re-inventions of the way farming operates must be uncovered soon to bring GHG emissions down towards zero.

Being a land-based industry, farming also has the opportunity to sequestrate carbon dioxide. Tree-planting and peat conservation are the two obvious and most quoted examples. This is different to farming but sits aside it. Such sequestration activities are a good start but difficult to ensure permanence. Once a tree has matured or dies, there is little way to keep the carbon in the wood from returning to the atmosphere. Possibly the best agriculture can do at the moment is to reduce additional new emissions from fossil fuels by providing fuel from renewable sources and woodland. Other sequestration issues are additionality (doing *more* than the land occupant is currently doing which is carbon friendly) and quantification; how to measure it.

Opportunities for landowners and farmers have emerged from new industries created to reduce GHG emissions, many of which are well suited to agriculture. The renewable energy and energy storage industries are dependent on space, capital and enterprise, which offer good opportunities to agriculture. Refer to section on Renewable Energy on page 97 for information on these enterprises.

2. AMMONIA EMISSIONS

There are other agricultural pollutants. One is ammonia (NH_3) which is one of the main sources of nitrogen pollution and adversely impacts biodiversity. It causes soil acidification which can alter plants' susceptibility to frost, droughts and pathogens which can contribute to loss of habitats. In recent years, ammonia emissions from agriculture have been rising. A 2019 Defra report estimates a 3.5% increase on 2005 levels, despite an overall decrease of 7.5% since 1990. Other acidifying substances include sulphur dioxide (SO_2) which is particularly prevalent in post-farm processing activities. Eutrophication concerns the overloading of water courses (lakes, rivers, streams, seas etc.) with nutrients (principally nitrogen and phosphorous).

Estimated Ammonia Emissions from UK Agriculture 2017

Emissions source	'000t NH_3*	% of total
Cattle	115.8	47
Dairy	*57.1*	*23*
Beef	*58.8*	*24*
Sheep~	9.7	4
Pigs	18.6	8
Poultry	37.7	15
Horses	1.2	0
Fertiliser	44.9	18
Sewage sludge	4.2	2
Digestate	12.8	5
Total	244.9	

Source: Defra (2019)
~ *includes goats and deer,   * totals may differ to components due to rounding.*

Source: Guthrie. S., Giles. S., Dunkerley. F., Tabaqchali. H., Harshfield. A., Ioppolo. R., Manville. C.,(2018) The Impact of Ammonia Emissions from Agriculture on Biodiversity, An Evidence Synthesis *Pub: Rand Europe and The Royal Society*

3. FOOD WASTE

The first Coronavirus lockdown made consumers feel vulnerable and therefore more thoughtful with their food. After the initial immoral scramble for supplies by some shoppers, household food waste then fell by 25% compared with usual levels across all sectors. This equated to a greater volume of food than the total reduction of food bought by not going to restaurants or other venues where you can eat away from the home. Clearly, catering waste fell to almost zero too, food supplies were thus lower in 2020 per capita. The lockdown demonstrated how much more efficient society can be with food, and that so much is effectively 'wilfully' wasted as part of a lifestyle. This is evidenced by a survey by WRAP (Waste Resources & Action Programme) published in May 2020 called 'Citizens and Food During Lockdown'. Wastage inevitably rose again when the vulnerability of lockdown softened, and life became less threatening.

A 2019 WRAP report estimates 1.6 million tonnes of food is wasted annually in the UK at the farm level. This equates to 3.2% of all food harvested in the UK by volume. WRAP calculated this would be worth around £1.2 billion assuming the food is all in pristine condition and available when the market is buying. Most of this loss is because it either does not have a market or is not in top condition. Horticultural crops account for 54% by volume at the farm, cereals 30%, livestock 8% and milk 8%. Farmers do not elect to waste food, it is more likely a lack of workers to harvest goods or that the consumer demands food in pristine condition, which is difficult to achieve consistently in a natural environment.

Producing the precise quantities of foods, especially highly perishable horticultural goods, to meet the varying and demanding expectations of the consumer when appetites change dramatically when weather does, and the unpredictability of a natural production system, will inevitably lead to mismatches between supply and demand. Low value wastage of potentially edible crop parts such as external leaves may, in some cases, cost more to cart from fields and process for animal feed than to allow their decomposition as soil organic matter. Nevertheless, there is still work to do to reduce this wastage.

WRAP also estimates 2 million tonnes of food grown for human consumption is diverted to animal feed and other non-waste destinations (e.g. bio-based materials). This is also wasted food. As a guide, if the value of food falls by 80 percent when it becomes animal feed, we can assume it is 80 percent wasted.

Top-20 Food Waste Sectors from Primary Production by Volume (2017) ('000 tonnes)

Product/sector	UK production for human consumption	'Waste' at primary production	% wasted at primary production
Sugar beet	8,918	347	4%
Potatoes	6,218	335	5%
Carrots	968	152	16%
Milk	14,954	116	0.8%
Wheat	7,196	93	1%
Poultry	1,879	66	4%
Onions	380	66	17%
Oilseed rape	2,167	65	3%
Barley	2,301	30	1%
Cabbage	224	29	13%
Lettuce	104	26	25%
Apples	261	25	9%
Pigs	892	24	3%
Peas	135	23	17%
Parsnips	101	16	15%
Cider apples	301	15	5%
Strawberries	130	14	10%
Sheep	320	13	4%
Brussels sprouts	51	13	25%
Tomatoes	95	13	13%
Others	2,907	125	4%
Total	50,501	1,604	3%

Sources: various studies cited in WRAP (2019)

Plastics: WRAP estimated agriculture produced 13,000 tonnes of plastic in 2014 with plastic films (e.g. for silage wrapping) accounting for the majority (11,000t). The concern that the use of plastics is impacting ocean habitats and that micro-plastics are finding their way into the food chain has highlighted the single-use plastic industry. This has implications for both the on-farm usage of plastics and for how UK food is packaged and preserved as it moves through the supply-chain.

CONCLUDING REMARKS

There are other topics such as biodiversity and wildlife populations which also merit consideration in this chapter. More resource is required to calculate the impact of UK agriculture on the environment more accurately including both the positive and the negative impacts. These are emerging.

Caution is needed when interpreting the data shown above. One figure used in isolation can be taken out of context. For example, the climatic conditions in many parts of the UK are ideally suited to grazing livestock production and have few commercial (farming) alternatives. Forestry has a growing role in rural land use but is not the ideal solution for everywhere. Methods to remove emissions from livestock production in these areas are necessary. Overall, emissions and resource usage should be viewed in the context of wider cycles whether that be in terms of carbon dioxide, water or other resources. The estimates above present challenges for UK agri-food. The first step towards successfully managing these is to accurately measure their impact.

Measuring emissions from production are important, but as an economy, having shifted from a manufacturer of physical goods in the 1980's to a service sector driven economy now, that involves less heating and moving of heavy materials, it is easy to demonstrate reduced emissions from production. However, British consumers continue to gobble up as many goods simply imported from elsewhere and still involve carbon emissions. The emissions associated with that consumption now need to be measured and the consumer should be expected to pay for them through carbon taxes or similar economic devices. This is how behaviour patterns will change for the better.

XI. MISCELLANEOUS DATA

1. CONSERVATION COSTS

Conservation costs vary widely, depending on geographical location and the type and size of the job. Markets for such services can be highly localised, sparse in some areas, competitive in others. Also, refer to contracting charges on page 182.

Hedges

Hedge Cutting. Flailing £39/hour to £55/hour for sawblade cutting (contract charges). Average of 3-5 miles per day depending on trim quality and obstacles.

Hedge Laying (Making hedges stock proof and rejuvenated by selective cutting and positioning). Manual hedge laying approximately 20 to 40m/day depending on hedge thickness (single or double), amount of timber to clear, access to hedge, style of hedge and varieties in hedge. Cost ranges from £13 to £30 depending on location, density of hedges and tree population. NAAC quotes £15/metre for average hedge.

Hedge Planting. Single row = 3-4 plants per metre, double row 6 plants per metre

- Plants average 59p - £1.80 each (mixed species); spiral guards 40p; canes 30p.

- Labour: Planting up to £3.50-£4.50/metre, professional contractor up to 100-150 metres/day. Preferably October/March.

- Overall from £4.50/metre; unfenced, single width, self-planted;
  to £40/metre; double width & double rabbit fenced, contract planted.

Hedge Coppicing. By hand: 2 men and a chain saw, £7.00-£8.50 per metre plus burning debris. Contractor: tractor mounted saw, driver and 2 men, 12.5 metres per hour, £47.50/hour.

Devon Hedges. Maintenance, flailing annually and occasional mechanical recasting banks when eroded. Flailing costs as above and recasting with Backhoe excavator £45/hr.

Fencing

Fencing (labour and materials): stock proof post and 4-barb £6.25/metre, rabbit proof (dug in) £6.60/metre (per side). Post and 3 rails £16.00/metre

Dry Stone Walls

Dry Stone Walling. Highly variable cost depending on stone type, stone grading availability, structure, vehicular access and local competition (people pay more for private walls in gardens than fields). As a guide: Cost of graded stone from £250/tonne, varying enormously on local stone, type and availability. Some are priced in Square-Face-Yards (about 4SFY per tonne). Cost of wall building is from as low as £50 (highlands) to £300 (Cotswolds) per square metre (normally quoted per square metre but grants awarded per linear metre). Most are around £100-125/m^2. Partial grants might be available in some areas e.g. within National Parks. Wall repair about £30/m^2.

Trees

Amenity tree planting; (half acre block or less)

- Transplants average £1.50; shelter plus stake and tie £1.60; stake 67p; whip £1.00. Rabbit spiral guard 44p; netlon guard 65p; cane 21p.
- Trees per man day: farmer 200, contractor 400; (large-scale, 33-man days/ha). Optimal time November to April.

Shelter Belts; Per 100 metre length

- 100 large species (oak, lime, etc.) £60; 66 medium species (cherry, birch, etc.) £53; 100 shrubs, £42.50;
- 166 tree stakes, shelters and ties, £330;
  (site preparation, weed control, labour and fencing extra)

Woodland Establishment.

- Conifers £265/1,000 (2m spacing), broadleaves £500/1000 (3m spacing).
- To supply and plant transplants; conifer £3.80/tree, oak or beech £4.60-£5.20 each, (2-3ft tall) in tubes dependent on shelter size and species.
- Rabbit fencing £6.35/metre (dug in), deer fencing £9.25/metre, deer and rabbit fencing £12.00/metre
- Contract planting labour: Conifers at 2m £1,800/ha; broadleaves at 3m £1,200/ha.
- Mature Parkland trees £180 each

Forestry, General.

- 2-man tree surgery team £640/day
- Contract labour: chain sawing £35.00/hr,
- Brush cutting £16.80/hr,
- Extracting timber/pulp £6.00-£13.50/tonne,
- Chemical spot weeding 13p-17p/tree, or £3500/hectare
- Rhododendron control range from £900-£3,000/hectare or more dependent on stem diameter (largest over 7cm) density and accessibility.

Pollarding and Tree Surgery.

- Pollard: £150/mature tree; Pollarding: 2 or 3 trees/day. Pollard every 20-40 years.
- Tree surgery from £250/tree. Dependant on size and number. Best in winter.

Ponds and Ditches

Pond Construction. Butyl lining; 0.75mm £5.80/m^2 1.0mm £9.20/m^2. Contract labour: 150 Komatsu £40/hr.; bulldozer D6 LGP £60/hr, 13t 360° excavator £50/hr (excluding haulage), labour £15.50/hr.

Pond Maintenance. Hymac £50/hr.; Backhoe £30.00/hr. 100 m^2/day (contractor). Timing: probably winter; time depends on ground condition and species whose life cycles may be disturbed. Every 15 to 50 years.

Ditch Maintenance. Backhoe excavator £30.00/hr; 13t 360° excavator £50/hr (excluding haulage), labour £15.50/hr. Preferably in winter. Every 3 to 7 years on rotation.

Grassland

Permanent Grass Margins at Field Edges. To provide wildlife benefits and help control pernicious weeds, reducing herbicides at the field edge. (A sterile strip provides virtually no wildlife benefit and the initial establishment costs may be offset by savings in maintenance costs in future years.)

Seed costs per 100 metres of seeds as follows.

- 2m grass margins, £3.30 (4-6 year ley £160/ha)

- 6m grass margins, £9.50;

- beetle banks, £7.80 (6m wide) (£5.23/kg, 25kg/ha).

Establishment of Wildlife Grassland Meadow. £220-330/ha for ground preparation, depending on cultivations, weed burden and total area, more for heavy land or exceptional weed burden. Seed costs very variable, but as a guide:

- Native Perennial wildflowers and grasses, £18.00/kg, 21kg/ha = £378/ha

- Pollen and Nectar mix for bumble bees and butterflies £6.67/kg, 21kg/ha = £140/ha

- Bird Seed sward £4.00/kg, 50kg/ha = £200/ha for two year sward.

- Single species native grass seeds vary from £3.70/kg (e.g. Creeping Red Fescue) to £63/kg (Sweet Vernal).

- Single species native perennial wildflower seeds vary from £31/kg (Corn Cockle) to £720/kg (Cowslip)

- Buffer strip grass margin mix for cross compliance and agri-environmental features, £4.20/kg drilled at 25kg/ha = £105/ha. Costs of ground preparation and drilling are usually higher than the seed.

Acknowledgement: Thanks to Cotswold Seeds and the Forestry Commission

2. FIELD DRAINAGE

Field drainage is over-looked. Most agricultural land has been drained at some point, although some will have been over 100 years ago (clay pipes). Much was re-drained in the 1960's and 1970's when generous grants assisted with the capital cost. Despite the age of some of these systems, many still function but require regular maintenance. This may include clearing out-falls, ditches, or field drains (jetting). Some consider the lack of new field drainage prevents yield and productivity progress, which suggests there is a commercial case for farmers to drain fields at their own cost/investment.

The costs of installing drains per metre shown below include the cost of operating a trenching machine, supplying and laying perforated plastic pipe to an average depth of 800mm by trencher with 40/20mm cleaned washed porous fill (drainage stone) laid over the pipe to within 375mm of the surface:

60 mm diameter	£4.80 - £5.20/metre
80 mm diameter	£6.00 - £6.70/metre
100 mm diameter	£8.30 - £8.60/metre
160 mm diameter	£10.30 - £12.50/metre

In some soil types, soil can be used as backfill saving £2.80-£3.80 per metre depending on the trench depth required to get the falls correct and the type of drainage stone used. Porous backfill is much more common and improves drainage by keeping the openings in the pipe clear. The choice to use permeable backfill should depend on soil type not cost. The above rates apply to comprehensive schemes of 4 hectares or more. Smaller areas and patching up work can cost up to 50% more because of the cost of transporting and tracking trenching equipment across fields for small areas of work. Patching up / repairing old drainage systems is common practise as a cheaper alternative to new comprehensive systems. 100mm diameter drainage pipe costs approximately £1 per metre.

Digging new open ditches (1.8m top width, 1.25m depth) costs £2.50-£3.50 per metre compared with improving existing ditches at £1.45 to £2.00 per metre depending on the amount of material that needs to be removed. However, most contractors charge on an hourly basis for this work with a 360 digger at approximately £45/hour.

Mole draining costs in the region of £70-£110 per hectare (see contractor charges). It is effectively a secondary drainage method which is used where a drainage system already exists. The mole plough creates a cavity for the water to travel through. This is best suited to heavy land / clay-based soils, where mole cavities will remain in place for some time.

Total costs per hectare for complete schemes vary on the distance between laterals, soil type, area to be drained, region of the country and the time of year when the work is to be undertaken.

- The cost of a scheme with 20m spacing between laterals and using permeable backfill will typically be in the range of £2,500 to £3,500 per hectare (£1,000-£1,420 per acre).

- Comprehensive schemes using little / no permeable backfill cost about £1,400 - £2,000 per hectare.

Certain soil types which are particularly suitable for mole drainage may permit spacing between laterals to be increased to 40m or even 60-80m in some instances.

Acknowledgement: thanks to Rob Burtonshaw 01926 651540

3. FERTILISERS & SOIL IMPROVERS

FERTILISER PRICES

Compounds

Analysis			Price per tonne
N	P_2O_5	K_2O	£
0	26	26	347
0	24	24	322
0	18	36	320
0	20	30	312
0	30	15	336
0	30	20	357
5	24	24	362
8	24	24	385
10	26	26	427
11	15	20	314
13	13	20	313
15	15	20	346
16	16	16	346
20	10	10	301
25	5	5	277
26	0	15	283

Straights

	Price per tonne
Ammonium Nitrate: UK (34.5% N)	275
Ammonium Nitrate: Imported (34.5% N)	264
NS grade: UK (27% N, 30% SO_3)	256
Sulphate of Ammonia (21% N, 60% SO_3)	249
Urea (46% N.): granular/ prills	367
Liquid Nitrogen (26% N, 5% SO_3)	214
Triple Superphosphate (TSP) (46% P_2O_5)	400
DAP (18/46/0)	516
Muriate of Potash (MOP) (60% K_2O)	250
Keiserite (50% Sulphate, 25% MgO)	

Average price (p) per kg nutrient			
	N :	79.7	(UK AN)
	P_2O_5 :	87.0	(TSP)
	K_2O :	41.7	(MOP)
	SO_3 :	13.6	(from SNH_3)

The prices are for fertiliser delivered in 600kg bags; delivery in bulk averages £7.50/tonne less; collection of bags by farmers £8/tonne less. They are based on forward prices quoted in August 2021; they vary according to area and bargaining power. They assume delivery in 25-27 tonne loads; add approximately £5.00/tonne for 10 tonne loads, £9.50 for 6-9 tonne loads, £21 for 4-5 tonne loads.

FERTILISER COSTS IN CROPS

This table summarises the fertiliser usage in the gross margins at the start of the book. They are based, largely on RB209 recommendations, using a soil index of 2 and replacing the nutrient taken off the land through the crop. It assumes straw is incorporated.

	kg/Ha			£/Ha
	N	P	K	
Feed Winter Wheat	190	56	47	220
Milling Winter Wheat	250	51	43	262
Second F. Wheat	184	62	44	205
Spring Wheat	150	53	74	196
Winter Feed Barley	140	62	77	198
Winter Malting Barley	100	57	70	158
Spring Malting Barley	80	48	68	134
Winter Oats	130	55	101	194
Spring Oats	70	50	92	138
Winter Oilseed Rape	190	49	39	210
Spring Oilseed Rape	80	32	25	102
Winter Beans	0	47	52	63
Spring Beans	0	43	47	57
Blue Peas	0	36	40	48
Marrowfats	0	32	36	43
Maincrop Potatoes	179	50	292	379
Early Potatoes	113	31	151	200
Sugar Beet	100	62	131	238
1-2 year Grass Ley	250	35	120	280
Intensive 3-5 year Ley	200	33	113	235
Long Term Ley	150	29	101	187
Improved Permanent Pasture	100	25	84	136
Low Input Pasture	50	19	65	83
Maize	70	28	88	117
Clover Ley	0	30	30	39
Kale	90	27	113	142
Swedes	150	50	90	104
Fodder Beet	90	30	30	201
Forage Rape	60	50	125	110
Maincrop Turnips	100	30	35	143
Stubble Turnips	60	25	84	120

FERTILISER VALUE OF SLURRY & MANURE

Nutrient Values of Common Farmyard Manure (FYM) Types

	Dry Matter (kg N/t)*	Total	Total (kg P_2O_5/t)	Available	Total (kg K_2O/t)	Available
Cattle	25	6.0	3.2	1.9	9.4	8.5
Pig	25	7.0	6.0	3.6	8.0	7.2
Sheep	25	7.0	3.2	1.9	8.0	7.2
Duck	25	6.5	5.5	3.3	7.5	6.8
Horse	25	5.0	5.0	3.0	6.0	5.4
Goat	40	9.5	4.5	2.7	12.0	10.8

* Crop-available nitrogen depends on application timing, and time taken to incorporate, but RB209-2017 quotes 10% of total N in most conditions, 10-50% for poultry.

** Refer to RB209 for different dry matter FYMs.

Note: these nutrient contents are for guidance only and will vary between different livestock systems and storage methods. Analysis should be performed to understand the specific values of manure.

Source: RB209-2017

Manure Output per Head during the Housing Period

	Undiluted excreta t or m³	Total Kg N	P_2O_5	K_2O
1 dairy cow (*6,000 to 9,000l milk yield*	11.6	60	26	46
1 beef cow (*>500 kg*)	8.2	41	15.5	33
1 finishing pig (*per place, 86% occupancy*)	1.6	10.6	5.6	5.6
1,000 broiler hens (*per place, 85% occupancy*)	19	330	220	340

Note: These figures should not be used for calculating NVZ compliance as they only allow for the time spent in the buildings and therefore exclude manure deposited in fields during grazing.

The housed periods are October to 1 April (6 months) for pigs and poultry, 1 October to 1 March (5 months) for other livestock. Refer to the DEFRA NVZ guidance, for NVZ calculation methodology and annual manure output tables.

LIME

Lime is sold at £5-10 per tonne, plus delivery of £7-8/tonne. The complete delivered and spread prices average around £26.00 delivered with an application rate of 4-6 tonnes per hectare per application, typically every 4 years.

Lime price varies according to type of dressing, grade of mineral (such as particle size and consistency), location and ease of spreading and could be as low as £4.00 per tonne ex-quarry to £30.00 ex-quarry. A short haul would cost about £6.00 and spreading approximately £5.00 per tonne, adding about £10 to the ex-quarry cost.

BIOSOLIDS (SEWAGE SLUDGE)

Biosolids act as good soil conditioner and fertiliser to farmers, whilst providing the most environmentally favourable method for water companies to dispose of the sludge. Biosolids vary in nutritional composition depending on processing and location, but RB209 (2017) describes its content as follows:

Biosolid and Green Compost Key Composition

	Digested Cake	Thermally Dried Pellets	Lime Stabilised	Green Compost
Dry Matter	25%	95%	25%	60%
Total Nitrogen *kg/t*	*11*	*40*	*8.5*	*7.5%*
Total Phosphate (kg P_2O_5/t)	*11*	*55*	*7.0*	*3.0*
Total Potash (kg K_2O /t)	*0.6*	*2.0*	*0.8*	*6.8*
Available N *kg/t (10-20%)*	1.6	6	1.2	0.0
Available P_2O_5 *kg/t*	5.5	28	3.5	1.5
Available K_2O *kg/t*	0.5	1.8	0.4	5.4
Available SO_3 *kg/t*	8.2	23	7.4	
Guideline Price £/t applied*†	£7.50	£33.00	£5.20	£4.50

Nutrient data taken from Fertiliser Manual RB209 (2017)

*   *Prices can be much lower depending on region and Water Company.*

†   *These are solely chemical values; the value of the organic matter could be more.*

Application rates vary according to terrain, soil analysis and plant need, but an application of 25 tonnes dry solids per hectare is the typical maximum rate. Thermally dried and lime stabilised cakes are far less common than digested cake. A Biosolids Assurance Scheme makes the product considerably more acceptable for use on land used to grow grains for high-value processing which has not been the case in many firms to now.

COMPOST

The new RB209 (2017) has a detailed section on the nutrient value of compost. It summarises typical nutrient values of green compost (non-food) as follows. It sensibly points out that nutrient provided by compost (or other organic matter) will probably not precisely match the nutrient requirement of the following crop so all added nutrient might not have the same economic value. Equally, some other fertiliser might still be required. RB209 also comments on typical figures for food compost and digestate from anaerobic digestion, entire and separated.

The values of organic fertiliser in this section are calculated based on their equivalent value for chemical component in bagged synthetic and mineral fertilisers. They take no account of the considerable value of the biological organic matter, which, in many cases will outstrip the chemical components. This is critical to soil health but difficult to value.

CATCH AND COVER CROPS

A 'catch' crop is grown between two 'cash' crops to catch nutrients which might otherwise be lost from weather erosion. A cover crop is grown over winter to protect and enrich soil. Cover and Catch Crops clearly have a cost of establishment and destruction (although some graze it) and can act as a green bridge, resulting in a build-up of pests. But they also have several benefits:

- Correcting soil C:N ratio (see below)
- Fixing soil nitrogen
- Increasing soil organic matter which helps to retain soil nutrients and moisture facilitating crop establishment and higher yields for following crops
- Improving soil structure, which reduces cultivation requirements
- Providing a canopy to reduce soil erosion and slow nutrient loss
- slowing leaching of nutrients (eutrophication) and volatilisation of nitrogen compounds

A C:N ratio compares the ratio of carbon to nitrogen in organic matter. The ideal C:N for soil is 24:1. The ratio for wheat straw and microorganisms is 80:1 and 8:1 respectively. Thus, land farmed for cereals crops often has a C:N above optimum, and leafy crops help to reduce it. Fertiliser does the same but at a cost.

Crop	Seed Cost £/kg	Seed Rate kg/ha	Cost £/ha
Black Oats*	1.75	25	44
Forage Rye*	1.00	40	40
White Mustard*	1.95	12	23
Lucerne*	6.60	25	165
Phacelia*	3.70	10	37
Vetch*	1.55	25	39
Clover	5.10	10-15	51 – 77
Radish	2.55	12	31
Oilseed Radish*	8.60	12-15	103 – 130

*EFA Cover and Catch Crop Compliant

4.   AGROCHEMICALS

AGROCHEMICAL COSTS

Names of the active ingredients are given below, with their principal use. These materials should be applied in accordance with the manufacturers' recommendations. Application rates vary and there are differences between the prices of various proprietary brands. The list is not intended to be exhaustive and there is no implied criticism of materials omitted.

The variation in costs per hectare is because of varying application rates rather than price variation between suppliers. It is priced on the purchase of chemical alone, i.e., not the agronomy service.

Chemical Name	£/litre	Application l/ha	Cost £/ha
CEREALS			
Herbicides, General			
Tri-allate	2.80	15.0	42.00
Flufenacet and Pendimethalin	10.50	2.0 - 4.0	21.00 - 42.00
Metsulfuron-Methyl + Tribenuron	66.90	in a 4ha pack	16.73
Mesosulfuron Iodosulfuron	30.00	1.2	36.00
Diflufenican	27.00	0.2 - 0.3	4.05 - 6.75
Flufenacet + Diflufenican	49.60	0.3 - 0.6	14.88 - 29.76
Mecoprop-P (isomeric)	6.25	1.0 - 2.3	6.25 - 14.38
Amidosulfuron	491.66	0.0 - 0.0	14.75 - 19.67
Florasulam & Fluroxypyr	14.52	1.0 - 1.5	14.52 - 21.78
Pinoxaden + Cloquintocet-mexyl	54.33	0.8 - 1.1	43.46 - 59.76
Clodinafop-propargyl	84.00	0.1 - 0.1	6.72 - 10.50
Fenoxaprop-P-ethyl	16.72	1.0 - 1.3	16.72 - 20.90
Flurasulam + Pyroxsulam	23.00	0.8 - 1.0	17.25 - 23.00
Growth Regulators			
Chlormequat	1.78	1.0 - 2.0	1.78 - 3.56
2-chlorethylphosphonic Acid	12.06	0.5 - 1.0	6.03 - 12.06
2-chlorethylphosphonic acid & Mepiquat Chloride	11.32	1.0 - 2.0	11.32 - 22.64
Trinexapac - ethyl	22.00	0.2 - 0.4	4.40 - 8.80
Fungicides			
Azoxystrobin	21.00	0.8 - 1.0	16.80 - 21.00
Epoxiconazole	16.30	0.8 - 1.0	12.23 - 16.30
Tebuconazole 250gm	9.60	0.8 - 1.0	7.20 - 9.60
Prothioconazole	44.80	0.4 - 0.8	17.92 - 35.84
Folpet	6.87	1.0 - 1.5	6.87 - 10.31
Mefentrifluconazole & Fluxapyroxad	49.50	0.8 - 1.5	39.60 - 74.25
Pyraclostrobin	23.00	0.3 - 0.6	6.90 - 13.80
Prothioconazole & Bixafen	32.50	1.0 - 1.3	32.50 - 40.63
Epoxiconazole & Fluxapyroxad	31.50	1.0 - 1.3	31.50 - 39.38
Bixafen, Fluopyram and Prothioconazole	32.50	1.2 - 1.5	39.00 - 48.75
Benzovindiflupyr and Prothioconazole	47.00	0.6 - 0.8	28.20 - 37.60

Chemical Name	£/litre	Application l/ha	Cost £/ha
Aphidicides			
Pirimicarb	38.50	0.3	10.78
Lambda-Cyhalothrin	65.00	50.0	3.25
Molluscicides			
Ferric-Phosphate	2.73	5.0 - 7.0	13.65 - 19.11
Metaldehyde 3%	1.80	3.0 - 3.5	5.40 - 6.30
Oilseed Rape			
Herbicide			
Propyzamide	12.30	1.4 - 1.7	17.22 - 20.91
Metazachlor	10.00	1.5 - 2.5	15.00 - 25.00
Clomazone	78.00	0.2	15.60
Aminopyralid + Propyzamide	22.50	1.7 - 2.0	38.25 - 45.00
Quizulop-P-tefaryl	10.90	0.5 - 2.3	5.45 - 24.53
Insecticide			
Deltamethrin	13.14	0.3 - 0.3	3.29 - 3.94
Pirimicarb	38.50	0.3 - 0.4	10.78 - 16.17
Cypermethrin	29.08	0.1 - 0.1	1.45 - 1.45
Lambda-Cyhalothrin	65.00	0.1 - 0.1	4.88 - 6.50
Fungicide			
Tebuconazole	9.60	0.5 - 1.0	4.80 - 9.60
Metconazole	25.43	0.4 - 0.8	10.17 - 20.34
Boscalid	73.03	0.3 - 0.5	18.26 - 36.52
Arylex	105.00	0.3 - 0.5	26.25 - 52.50
Dessicant			
Glyphosate	2.03	3.0 - 5.0	6.09 - 10.15
Potatoes			
Herbicide			
Metribuzin	25.54	0.8 - 1.5	19.16 - 38.31
Prosulfucarb	5.90	3.0 - 5.0	17.70 - 29.50
Metobromuron	17.88	1.5 - 4.0	26.82 - 71.52
Aclonifen	14.60	1.5 - 1.8	21.90 - 25.55
Clomazone	78.00	0.2	15.60
Blight Control			
Cymoxanil + Mancozeb	5.30	2.0	10.60
Mancozeb + Dimethomorph	8.70	2.0	17.40
Cyazofamid	39.60		
Haulm Dessicant			
Carfentrazone	38.66	0.6 - 1.0	23.20
Insecticides			
Fosthiazate	16.22	15.0 - 30.0	243 - 487

Chemical Name	£/litre	Application l/ha	Cost £/ha
Sugar Beet			
Herbicides			
Metamitron	18.71	1.5 - 3.0	28.07 - 56.13
Tri flusulfron-methyl	85.76	30.0 - gm	21.44
Phenmedipham	7.51	1.5 - 3.0	11.27 - 22.53
Insecticide			
Pirimicarb	38.50	0.3	10.78
Beans			
Herbicide			
Pendimethalin	5.20	2.5 - 3.0	13.00 - 15.60
Clomazone	78.00	0.2	15.60
Fungicide			
Tebuconazole	9.60	1.0	9.60
Azoxystobin	21.00	1.0	- 21.00
Peas and Beans			
Herbicide			
Pendimethalin & Imazamox	13.50	3.0 - 4.0	40.50 - 40.50
Insecticide			
Pirimicarb	38.50	0.3	10.78
Lambda-Cyhalothrin	65.00	0.1 - 0.1	4.88
Maize			
Herbicide			
Nicosulfuron	21.23	0.5 - 0.8	10.62 - 15.92
Mesotrione	10.80	1.0	10.80
Brassicas			
Herbicides			
Metazachlor	10.00	1.5	15.00
Pyridate	37.29	2.0	74.58
Broadleaved Crops			
Grass Weeds & Volunteer Cereals			
Clethodim	19.00	1.0 - 1.0	19.00 - 19.00
Propaquizafop	17.40	0.7 - 1.5	12.18 - 26.10
Cycloxydim	36.69	0.8 - 1.3	27.52 - 45.86
Grassland			
Herbicides			
MCPA	3.70	3.0 - 5.0	11.10 - 18.50
Clopyralid + Triclopyr	24.74	0.5 - 1.0	12.37 - 24.74
Fluroxypyr + Triclopyr	21.00	1.0 - 2.0	21.00 - 42.00
General			
Glyphosate	2.03	3.0 - 4.0	6.09 - 8.12
Clopyralid + Fluroxypyr + Triclopyr	22.60	2.0 - 2.0	45.20 - 45.20

The above prices are based on retail prices paid by farmers (August 2021) and reflect the discounts available where there are competing products from several manufacturers. The range in prices per hectare reflects the varying application rates. Average rates for agronomy only are £13.00/ha for cereals or maize only and rising to £21.50-£33/ha for potatoes and other vegetable and perishable crops.

Acknowledgement: Many thanks to Bartholomew's

AGROCHEMICAL RATES

This table summarises the agrochemical spend for the main crops in Chapter 2, with a breakdown of what each figure is comprised of. Clearly the variation can be considerable between soil-types, regions, farms and even fields, but this offers a starting point from which individual costings can be derived.

£/Hectare	Herb-icides	Fung-icides	Insect-icides	PGR	Other	Total Ag-chemical
Feed Winter Wheat	103	121	8	18	6	255
Milling Winter Wheat	103	127	8	18	9	264
Second F. Wheat	113	127	8	18	6	272
Spring Wheat	65	55	8	18	6	151
Winter Feed Barley	81	83	8	18	6	195
Winter Malting Barley	81	83	8	18	6	195
Spring Malting Barley	65	55	8	18	6	151
Winter Oats	57	44	8	17	6	131
Spring Oats	37	34	7	9	6	93
Winter Oilseed Rape	113	80	8	18	15	234
Spring Oilseed Rape	54	57	8	18	15	152
Winter Beans	65	50	8	0	10	132
Spring Beans	65	44	11	0	10	130
Blue Peas	81	55	11	0	10	157
Marrowfats	70	97	11	0	17	195
Maincrop Potatoes	32	200	50	0	300	582
Early Potatoes	17	103	26	0	260	406
Sugar Beet	200	57	39	28	7	331

5. SEEDS

GRASS, FORAGE AND ENVIRONMENTAL SEED

(for 2021)

Crop	Price £/kg	Seed Rate kg/ha		Cost £/ha
Grass Leys				
1-year silage ley	£2.85	35		99
2-year silage ley	£3.07	35		107
3-4-year silage ley	£4.14	35		144
4-6-year leys	£4.76	35		166
Permanent grass	£5.36	32.5		174
Drought resistant	£6.16	32.5		200
Red Clover ley	£3.07	55		169
Overseeding				
Short-term Ryegrass	£3.26	25		81
Long-term Ryegrass	£4.08	25		101
White Clover overseed	£10.86	5		54
Fodder Crops				
Forage Maize: Silage				190
Fodder Kale	£9.80	5		49
Swedes	£42.80	3.80		160
Stubble Turnips	£3.80	4.70kg	drilled	18
		5.0 kg	broadcast	19
Maincrop Turnips	£11.40	3.75 kg	drilled,	45
		5.0 kg	broadcast	57
Fodder Beet	55.90	3.8		210
Rape	£3.75	10		37
Rape/Kale Hybrid	£4.60	7.50		34
Countryside Stewardship				
Buffer Strip	£6.88	25		172
Legume Fallow	£5.76	30		172
Flower Rich Margin	£14.20	20		284
Winter bird food 1-year	£4.76	12.5		59
Bird and bee mix	8.99	12.5		112
Mustard	6.0	15		90
Game & Equine				
Game Cover mixture	£4.75	20		95
Game Maize	£2.97	32.50		97
Vetch	£1.73	75		130
Quinoa & Kale mix	£12.00	7.5		90
Field Corner mixture	£16.80	25		420
Horse grazing	£5.23	32.5		170
Gallop mixture	£4.95	125-400		618 - 1,980

SEED ROYALTY RATES

Seed Royalty rates for autumn 2021 and spring 2022

	£/ha	£/tonne		£/ha
Wheat	10.34	52.63	Beans	14.16
Winter Barley	9.48	49.69	Oilseed Rape	10.39
Spring Barley	10.38	53.82	Linseed	5.70
Oats	6.77	42.40	Triticale	9.27
Peas	10.11	43.37		

Seed purchased from a merchant includes a royalty for the seed breeder. Farmers who home save seed are legally obliged to pay the royalty irrespective of the purpose of the sowing (e.g. includes cover crops). If seed is cleaned and dressed, the royalty is taken at this point (per tonne), if not, the farmer is responsible for paying (per hectare). Some older varieties no longer have royalty charges. It is illegal to sell or buy seed (such as between farmers) unless licensed. View eligible varieties at BSPB website

HOME SAVED SEED COSTS

	Value of Old Crop £/t	Cleaning & Dressing Sack £/t	Testing £/t	Royalty £/t	Total Cost £/t
Feed Wheat	160	88	1.70	53	**302**
Milling Wheat	171	88	1.70	53	**314**
Spring Wheat	171	88	1.50	53	**313**
Winter Feed Barley	142	88	3.40	50	**283**
Winter Malting Barley	156	88	3.40	50	**297**
Spring Malting Barley	157	88	3.40	54	**302**
Winter Oats	142	88	6.80	42	**279**
Spring Oats	142	88	6.40	42	**279**
Winter Rape	405	750	108.10	2433	**3,696**
Spring Rape	405	750	216.10	2433	**3,804**
Winter Beans	195	22	5.30	60	**282**
Spring Beans	205	22	5.30	60	**292**
Blue Peas	230	22	4.50	43	**300**
Marrowfats	325	22	5.90	83	**435**

The old crop seed is from 2021 harvest. Cleaning and dressing figures are based on costs for a mobile cleaner on a 350-hectare farm, and likely amounts of seeds required for each crop (the lower the tonnage, the higher the cost). Single purpose or basic seed treatments included. Testing costs assume a single test (one variety) per species (Germination only; £40/test). Royalty rates as above.

6.   FEED

FEED PRICES

Prices are delivered May-October 2022 set in July 2021; there is a range of differences in the ingredients and delivery destinations. For hauls over 10 miles in 25 tonne loads. Additional farm delivered cost for bags ranges from £23 to £30 per tonne.

			£/Tonne
Cattle	Dairy:	High Energy Parlour (21% CP)	295
		Dairy Concentrate 41%	375
		Medium Energy Blend (18% CP)	255
	Beef	Pellets (16% CP)	275
		Concentrate (34% CP)	349
	Calf	Milk Substitute (bags)	1,909
		High Fat Replacer (bags)	1,765
		Calf Weaner Pellets.	345
		Calf Rearer Nuts (16% CP)	277
Sheep		High Energy Lamb Pellets (17% CP)	310
		Medium Energy Sheep Feed (16% CP)	287
		Lamb Finisher Nuts	278
		H.E.Ewe Feed 19%	307
Horses		Horse and Pony Pencils/Cubes (15kg bags)	750
Pigs		Sow Nuts (17% CP)	285
		Early Grower Pellets (22% CP)	345
		Grower/Finisher Pellets (19% protein)	299
		Sow Concentrate (43% CP)	380
		Grower Concentrate (45% CP)	398
Poultry		Chick Crumbs	362
		Layers Pellets 18%	295
		Broiler Grower Feed	345
		Turkey Grower Feed	337
Straight Feeds		Fishmeal (66/70% CP)	1,350
		Soya Bean Meal (Hipro; 50% CP)	380
		Rapeseed Meal (34-36% CP)	270
		Palm Kernel Meal/Cake (17% CP)	195
		Sunflower S Ext 36%	290
		Soya Hull Pellets	185
		Wheatfeed Meal (14-18% CP)	185
		Wheatfeed Pellets (14-18% CP)	190
		Maize Gluten (19-20% CP)	230
		Molasses (Cane) (5% CP)	205
		Sugar Beet Pulp (Molassed Nuts/Pellets)	210
		Brewers' Grains	45

Feed Prices (Continued)

Distillers Wheat Pellets	275
Corn Distillers Meal	250
Maize (Whole)	230
Wheat (May / June)	208
Barley (May / June)	190
Beans (May / June)	245

FEEDSTUFF NUTRITIVE VALUES

Typical Energy and Protein Contents of Some Common Feeds and cost per unit

Type of Feeds	£/T	Dry Matter g/kg	ME MJ/kg DM	CP g/kg DM	p/kg DM	p/MJ ME	p/g CP
Forages:							
Barley Straw	60	860	7	10	6.98	1.00	0.70
Grass Silage (typical clamp)	28	250	10.8	150	11.36	1.05	0.08
Hay (typical meadow)	80	850	8.8	100	9.45	1.07	0.09
Maize Silage	27	300	11	90	8.90	0.81	0.10
Pasture (rotational grazed)	10	180	11.5	160	5.75	0.50	0.04
Whole-crop Wheat (fermented)	48	350	10.5	95	13.74	1.31	0.14
Cereals:							
Barley (home grown *)	142	860	13.2	120	16.51	1.25	0.14
Oats (home grown *)	142	860	12.5	120	16.51	1.32	0.14
Wheat (home grown *)	160	860	13.6	130	18.60	1.37	0.14
Roots:							
Fodder Beet	7	180	12	60	4.11	0.34	0.07
Potatoes	35	200	13.3	100	17.50	1.32	0.18
Wet By-Products:							
Brewers Grains	45	260	11.5	250	17.31	1.51	0.07
Straights:							
Cane Molasses	205	750	12.7	40	27.33	2.15	0.68
Distillers Maize Grains	230	900	14	310	25.56	1.83	0.08
Distillers Wheat Grains	275	900	13.5	340	30.56	2.26	0.09
Dried Molassed Sugar Beet Pulp	210	900	12.5	100	23.33	1.87	0.23
Field Beans	185	880	13.3	290	21.02	1.58	0.07
Maize Gluten Feed	230	880	12.8	210	26.14	2.04	0.12
Palm Kernel Meal	195	900	11.4	200	21.67	1.90	0.11
Wheat-feed	185	880	11.3	190	21.02	1.86	0.11

* Home grown feed should be costed to the livestock enterprise at the value the grain could otherwise be sold at, i.e. the opportunity cost of the crop.

7. AGRICULTURAL STATISTICS

These basic agricultural statistics relate to the UK farming and food sectors. The main source of data is the Defra Publication 'Agriculture in the UK 2020'. All figures are for the UK and relate to the 2021 year unless otherwise stated.

INDUSTRY STRUCTURE

Agriculture's Economic Contribution	2018	2019	2020
Gross Output (£m)	26,752	27,481	26,717
Total Income from Farming* (£m) ...	4,735	4,886	4,119
Agriculture's Share of the Economy .	0.51%	0.51%	0.49%
Agriculture's Share of Employment..	1.47%	1.45%	1.44%

* *Total Income from Farming (TIFF) is essentially profit of the farming sector, provisional figures.*

Agriculture accounted for £9.435bn to national gross value-added (GVA) in 2020. The wider agri-food sector (including farming, food manufacturing, wholesaling, retailing and catering) contributed £127.5bn or 6.4% GVA in 2019, and employed about 4 million people, about 13% of the total UK workforce.

The average expenditure on food and drink (including alcohol), per person per week in 2018/19 was £46.60, £32.12 consumed in the house, £14.48 eaten out. (*Defra Family Food 2018/19*). Excluding alcohol, it was £28.32 in the house and £11.12 out.

Agricultural Workforce	*2015*	*2018*	*2019*	*2020*
Regular Full-time	73,000	-	-	
Regular Part-time*	43,000	-	-	
Seasonal, Casual and Gang	67,000	-	-	
Total Employees	183,000	181,000	177,000	171,000
Farmers, Partners Directors and Spouses				
Full-time	142,000	145,000	144,000	147,000
Part-time*	152,000	152,000	155,000	153,000
Farmers, Partners Directors & Spouses	294,000	296,000	299,000	301,000
Total Labour Force	476,000	477,000	476,000	472000

* *Part-time is less than 39 hours in England and Wales, less than 38 hours in Scotland and less than 30 hours in Northern Ireland.*

Average Farm Size - Hectares

	All Sizes	Part Time	Full Time	Small	Medium	Large	Very Large
All Farms	149	70	196	115	151	198	376
Cereals	191	90	330	183	277	388	916
General Cropping	230	61	288	137	192	275	739
Horticulture	26	6	31	13	8	22	66
Dairy	160			59	77	113	220
Grazing Livestock Lowland	89	59	126	85	105	152	362
Grazing Livestock LFA	164		194	114	163	267	608
Pigs	76				53	112	185
Poultry	58		72	27	24	51	116

This is a summary from the Farm Business Survey 2019/20, Taking account of contracting arrangements and other collaborations, the decision-making body is likely to be responsible for larger areas.

* FTE: Full Time Equivalent: Farm size is measured by the amount of agriculture on each farm, measured by total work to be done. This means that extensive farms covering a large area can be compared with intensive farms on a small hectarage. a Full Time Equivalent is what one worker would 'normally' be expected to achieve.

Percentage of Rented Farmland

	All Sizes	Part Time	Full Time	Small	Medium	Large	Very Large
FTE *		0.5 < 1.0	> 1	1 < 2	2 < 3	3 < 5	= > 5
All Farms	39%	19%	44%	41%	40%	44%	46%
Cereals	35%	17%	39%	41%	39%	41%	37%
General Cropping	41%			47%		38%	44%
Horticulture	34%		36%			24%	46%
Dairy	48%			43%	43%	38%	52%
Grazing Livestock Lowland	38%	19%	49%	40%	41%	45%	70%
Grazing Livestock LFA	55%		60%	53%	44%	64%	72%
Pigs	28%					13%	32%
Poultry	18%		18%			30%	16%

This is a summary from the Farm Business Survey 2019/20, Not all data is available. It shows the percentage of farmed land in each farm system and size that is tenanted. The rest will be owner-occupied.

UK Farmed Areas '000 Hectares

'000 Ha.	2000	2010	2019	Actual 2020	Estimate July 21 2021	Forecast 2025	Forecast 2030
Wheat	2,086	1,939	1,816	1,387	1,803	1,761	1,686
Winter Barley	589	383	453	312	395	414	404
Spring Barley	539	539	710	1,076	740	799	839
ALL BARLEY			1,163	1,388	1,135	1,213	1,243
ALL OATS	109	124	182	210	210	230	255
Mixed Corn, Triticale, Rye	25	29	51	53	58	62	67
Total Cereals (excl. maize)	**3,348**	**3,014**	**3,212**	**3,038**	**3,206**	**3,266**	**3,251**
Oilseed Rape	332	642	530	379	331	353	353
Linseed	72	44	15	33	25	25	25
Peas (harvested dry)	84	42	41	52	52	56	65
Field Beans	124	166	137	181	190	202	217
Potatoes	166	138	145	142	139	140	137
Sugar Beet	173	118	108	111	95	99	96
Veges & Salad grown in ope	117	119	115	118	120	120	120
Top & Soft Fruit	38	34	35	34	34	34	34
Other Horticulture	16	14	14	14	14	14	14
Maize	104	164	228	228	230	242	257
Other Arable Crops	75	102	135	147	132	144	159
Bare Fallow	533	174	224	362	270	250	250
Total Tillage	**5,182**	**4,771**	**4,939**	**4,839**	**4,838**	**4,944**	**4,979**
Temporary Grass (<5 years)	1,226	1,232	1,193	1,181	1,250	1,145	1,114
Total Arable	**6,408**	**6,003**	**6,132**	**6,020**	**6,088**	**6,089**	**6,093**
Permanent Grass (>5 years)	5,364	5,925	6,207	6,118	6,149	6,194	6,244
Total Grass*	6,590	7,157	7,400	7,299	7,399	7,339	7,358
Total Tillage & Grass*	**11,772**	**11,928**	**12,339**	**12,138**	**12,237**	**12,283**	**12,337**
Sole Right Rough Grazing	4,445	4,055	3,986	3,924	3,974	3,790	3,690
Common Rough Grazing	1,228	1,228	1,197	1,194	1,194	1,194	1,110
Total Rough Grazing	**5,673**	**5,283**	**5,183**	**5,118**	**5,168**	**4,984**	**4,800**
Land for Outdoor Pigs	0	10	10	10	10	11	13
Utilisable Agric.l Area (UAA)	**17,445**	**17,221**	**17,532**	**17,266**	**17,416**	**17,279**	**17,149**
Woodland	499	773	1033	1065	1090	1190	1275
Other Land on agric.l holdings	279	274	284	293	300	325	382
Total Agricultural Area	**18,223**	**18,268**	**18,849**	**18,624**	**18,806**	**18,794**	**18,806**

*   *Excluding Rough Grazing*

**   *2021 estimate and forecasts provided by The Andersons Centre*

The Utilisable Agricultural Area (UAA) comprises around 71% of the total UK land area. Of the remaining 29%, 4% is woodland. The 25% of 'non-agricultural/wood' land broadly splits equally between forest, urban areas and 'other' land uses. The latter includes villages, small towns, transport infrastructure, non-urban wasteland, and inland water. The total UK land area is approximately 24.3 million hectares.

UK Livestock Numbers

Historic data from Defra June Survey, estimates by The Andersons Centre

'000 Head	2005	2010	2019	Actual 2020	Estimate 2021	Forecast 2025
Total Cattle and Calves	**10,770**	**10,170**	**9,739**	**9,615**	**9,625**	**9,241**
of which: Dairy Cows	1,998	1,830	1,871	1,850	1,843	1,815
Beef Cows	1,751	1,668	1,527	1,509	1,499	1,459
Total Sheep and Lambs	**35,416**	**31,084**	**33,580**	**32,697**	**31,556**	**30,356**
of which: Breeding Ewes	16,935	14,740	16,035	15,370	15,170	14,370
Total Pigs	**4,862**	**4,460**	**5,078**	**5,055**	**4,750**	**4,937**
of which: Female Breeding	470	427	413	402	406	422
Poultry	**173,909**	**163,867**	**187,072**	**181,957**	**191,442**	**189,851**
of which: Table Fowl	111,475	105,309	124,544	125,197	125,864	124,970
Laying Flock	49,034	47,107	54,008	54,158	54,378	53,866
Other Poultry	13,400	11,451	10,750	10,025	11,200	11,015
Farmed Deer	33	31	*32*	*32*	*32*	*32*
Goats	96	93	*100*	*100*	*100*	*100*

Age of English Farmers

Data from Farm Business Survey 2018/19 shown below suggests older farmers tend to farm part time and younger people manage larger fulltime farms:

Age of English Farmer (Years-Months)	Part Time	Full Time Farms			
		All F.T Farms	Small	Medium	Large & V Large
All Farm Types	63-2	58-3	59-4	58-2	57-5
Cereals	62-7	57-4	58-7	57-5	55-11
General cropping	65-2	58-9	57-7	59-10	59-1
Horticulture	67-9	61-3	60-1	65-4	60-6
Dairy		56-11	53-5	55-5	57-5
Grazing livestock (lowland)	62-7	59-1	59-12	57-11	57-8
Grazing livestock (LFA)	65-11	58-5	59-11	58-7	55-10
Pigs		56-7		57-10	56-6
Poultry		55-10	59-3	53-1	55-6

Size Distribution of 'commercial' Holdings - 2019

By Area on Holding	Holdings - '000	Area - '000 Ha	% of Holdings	% of Area
Under 20 hectares	103	705	47	4
20 to 50 hectares	42	1,390	19	8
50 to 100 hectares	32	2,280	15	13
100 hectares and over.....................	41	13,277	19	75
Total..	217	17,637	100	100

FINANCE

Total Income From Farming (TIFF)

	TIFF £ Million	TIFF per Entrepreneur £ Million
1975	7,647	25,115
1980	4,897	17,424
1985	3,782	13,814
1990	3,600	14,028
1995	8,236	33,740
2000	2,135	9,706
2005	3,063	15,299
2010	4,617	24,060
2011	5,978	30,756
2012	5,372	27,626
2013	6,115	31,740
2014	5,829	30,237
2015	4,278	22,128
2016	4,218	21,901
2017	6,215	31,969
2018	5,114	26,030
2019	5,169	26,056
2020	4,119	20,562

* *TIFF per full-time entrepreneur equivalent. DEFRA Data. Real terms*

TIFF is Total Income from Farming. It is the business profits plus remuneration to farmers, partners and directors and others with an entrepreneurial interest in the business. It is calculated on a calendar year basis and is the main aggregate measure of UK farming's income (profitability). There are no imputed charges (such as a rental value for owned land or value of the farmer's own labour).

Average English Farm Business Income (FBI) (Real Terms 2019/20 Prices)

Farm Type	2017/18	*2018/19*	*2019/20*
Cereals..................................	64,500	*68,600*	*60,500*
General Cropping..................	90,500	*108,400*	*80,500*
Dairy.....................................	123,000	*81,200*	*70,000*
Grazing L'stock (Lowland)...	21,300	*12,700*	*10,500*
Grazing Livestock (LFA)......	28,000	*15,800*	*19,500*
Specialist Pigs......................	30,900	*30,200*	*39,500*
Specialist Poultry..................	95,500	*76,100*	*88,000*
Mixed....................................	45,000	*46,400*	*25,500*
All Types..............................	*49,500*	*45,000*	*39,000*

FBI is the main farm-level measure of farming income (profitability). It is similar to TIFF but is based on a March to February year and calculated per farm rather than aggregated for TIFF.

TIFF Accounts - Inputs and Outputs (2019)

Inputs	£m	Outputs	£m	%
Animal Feed	5,586	Wheat	1,550	5.19%
Seeds	977	Barley	1054	3.53%
Fertilisers	1,147	Oats and other cereals	155	0.52%
Plant Protection Products	1097	Oilseed rape	358	1.20%
Veterinary expenses	460	Potatoes	824	2.76%
Hired labour	2,767	Sugar beet	172	0.58%
Depreciation: equipment	2,117	Fresh vegetables	1,611	5.39%
Depreciation: buildings	1058	Fruit	1041	3.48%
Depreciation: livestock	1,451	Plants and flowers	1,358	4.54%
Maintenance: materials	1,068	Other crops	896	3.00%
Maintenance: buildings	755	Cattle	3,710	12.42%
Fuels	835	Sheep	1,616	5.41%
Electricity & heating fuel	455	Pigs	1,447	4.84%
Agricultural services	1,341	Poultry	3,048	10.20%
Net rent	544	Milk	4,383	14.67%
Interest and finance fees	444	Eggs	730	2.44%
Other goods and services	3,661	Other products	95	0.32%
		Other livestock	43	0.14%
		Other agricultural	1,341	4.49%
		Non-ag income	1,239	4.15%
		Total Gross Output	**26,671**	
Total Inputs	**25,763**	Single P.t/Subsidy	3,212	10.75%
Total Income From Farming	4,119	**Total Output**	**29,883**	100.00%
Balance	**29,882**	Total crops	5,009	18.78%
		Total horticulture.	4,010	15.04%
		Total livestock	9,821	36.82%
		Livestock products	5,113	19.17%
		Other	2,718	10.19%

Balance Sheet of UK Agriculture *(2018 – latest data)*

			2018	2019	
			£m	£m	£m
Assets:					
	Fixed:	Land	219,184	231,095	
		Buildings, plant, machinery	37,548	37,813	
		Breeding livestock	6,175	6,211	
	Total Fixed Assets:		*262,907*		*275,119*
	Current	Trading livestock	4,086	4,073	
		Crops and stores	4,340	4,166	
		Debtors and cash deposits	6,980	7,005	
	Total Current Assets:		*15,406*		*15,244*
		Total Assets:	**278,313**		**290,363**
Liabilities:					
	Long term:	Bank, Building Society loans	11,508	11,926	
	Med-term:	AMC and SASC	2,552	2,795	
		Other (inc. family loans)	639	730	
	Long and Medium Liabilities		*14,699*		*15,451*
	Short-term	Bank overdrafts	2,166	2,055	
		Trade credit	2,408	2,239	
		Hire purchase and leasing	1,582	1,591	
		Other	48	56	
	Total Short-term Liabilities:		*6,204*		*5,941*
	Total Liabilities:		**20,903**		**21,392**
Net Worth:			**257,410**		**268,971**
% Equity (Net worth as a % of Total Assets):			92.49%		92.63%
Total Income from Farming (TIFF) 2019 as % of					
	a) Net Worth:		1.60%		1.53%
	b) Total Assets:		1.48%		1.42%
	c) Tenants Capital:		6.97%		6.95%

Note: no charge has been made for farmers' own labour or management

PRODUCTIVITY

UK Crop Yields

							Average - Harvest Year		
(tonnes per hectare)	2010	*2014*	*2015*	*2016*	*2017*	*2018*	*2019*	*2020*	*14-20*
Wheat	7.7	8.6	9.0	7.9	8.3	7.8	9.0	7.0	8.2
Barley (all)	5.7	6.4	6.7	5.9	6.1	5.7	7.0	5.9	6.3
Winter Barley	6.4	7.2	7.7	6.4	7.0	6.8	7.8	6.2	7.0
Spring Barley	5.2	5.9	6.0	5.6	5.6	5.2	6.3	5.8	5.8
Oats	5.5	6.0	6.1	5.8	5.4	5.0	5.9	4.8	5.6
Oilseed Rape	3.5	3.6	3.9	3.1	3.9	3.4	3.3	2.8	3.4
Field Beans	3.5	4.2	4.4	3.7	4.0	2.6	4.0	4.0	3.8
Dried Peas	3.5	4.0	4.1	3.7	4.0	2.8	3.9	3.9	3.8
Potatoes (all)	44	47	49	45	49	42	45	45	46
Sugar Beet*	55	80	69	66	83	69	75	57	71

* *Adjusted to 16% sugar A new method of Sugarbeet yield is introduced in 2022 including more tops. This is not included yet.*

UK Livestock Output

(kg unless stated)	2015	2016	2017	2018	*2019*	*2020 Prov'*
Milk Yield (litres/cow) *	7,894	7,559	7,893	7,959	8,122	8,204
Beef Carcase Wt.**	*355*	*352*	*349*	*341*	*346*	*346*
Lamb Carcase Wt. Δ....	*20*	*19*	*19*	*19*	*20*	*20*
Pig Carcase Wt. ♦.........	*81*	*82*	*83*	*83*	*85*	*87*

* *litres per annum*   ** *Carcase weight; steers, heifers & young bulls*
Δ *Carcase weight; clean sheep and lambs*   ♦ *Carcase weight; clean pigs*

FOOD

Self sufficiency of all food in 2020 = 60%
Self sufficiency of all 'indigenous' foods in 2020 = 74%

Self Sufficiency* (%)	2004	2018		2004	2018
All Food **.................	*62*	*60*	Indigenous-type Food	*75*	*77*
Crops:..........................			*Livestock:*		
Wheat............................	111	99	Beef and Veal........	70	86
Barley	110	127	Mutton and Lamb..	85	109
Total Cereals **...........	103	96	Pig-meat................	49	66
Oilseed Rape	194	86	Poultry-meat..........	91	89
Potatoes........................	77[+]	68	Milk.......................	103	106
Sugar............................	74	61	Hen Eggs...............	87	93
Fresh Vegetables..........	57[+]	53			
Fresh Fruit....................	14[+]	16			

* *ratio of UK production to UK human consumption*   ** *2003 and 2016,* [+] *2011*

Food Spend (current terms)*

Food Spending	2010	2012	2014	2015	2015/16	2016/17	2017/18	2018/19
Food and Drink at Home	27.57	29.29	29.57	29.24	29.26	30.07	31.39	32.12
Eating-Out Expenditure	11.66	12.09	12.40	13.18	12.98	13.96	13.92	14.48
All food and Drink	39.2	41.4	42.0	42.4	42.2	44.0	45.3	46.6

Details of Food Spend for consumption in the Home

Milk and Milk Products	2.68	2.69	2.63	2.54	2.54	2.63	2.71	2.80
Meat	5.72	6.06	6.23	5.91	5.95	6.11	6.26	6.31
Fruit. Veg. & Potatoes	5.54	5.82	5.92	5.90	5.95	6.20	6.38	6.56
Bread	1.16	1.23	1.17	1.13	1.11	1.12	1.19	1.18
Alcoholic Drinks	3.07	3.30	3.30	3.32	3.28	3.51	3.85	3.80

Expenditure on Food and Non-alcoholic Drinks (£ per person per week) DEFRA

Farmer's share of retail price (per cent) DEFRA.

Producers Share	1990	2000	2010	2014	2015	2016	2017
Basket of Goods	43	35	37	38	36	37	41
Wheat (bread)	16	10	8	9	8	8	8
Potatoes..................	31	27	20	17	18	26	25
Carrots	31	38	41	35	48	60	54
Apples....................	51	40	42	32	32	34	38
Milk	35	28	32	39	32	30	38
Beef.......................	57	44	48	50	49	49	51
Lamb......................	57	43	56	52	48	51	51
Pork	55	47	39	40	35	35	42
Chicken..................	44	37	38	39	41	44	47
Eggs.......................	36	29	27	27	30	27	38

Latest Figures are for 2017

8. RATE OF INFLATION; PRICE AND COST INDICES

INFLATION DATA

Calendar Year	RPI*: % yearly change	RPI: Index 1987=100	CPI** % yearly change	CPI Index 2015=100	Food & N.A. Drink; % y/y change ^	Agricultural Prices Index, 2015 = 100	
						Outputs	Inputs
1988	4.9	107	-	50		66.1	49.6
1989	7.8	115	5.2	52	5.6	70.5	52.3
1990	9.5	126	7.0	56	8.1	71.8	54.7
1991	5.9	134	7.5	60	5.2	70.7	56.7
1992	3.7	139	4.3	63	2.1	70.6	58.2
1993	1.6	141	2.5	64	1.2	74.6	60.5
1994	2.4	144	2.0	65	1.3	75.1	60.7
1995	3.5	149	2.6	67	3.9	81.9	62.1
1996	2.4	153	2.5	69	3.1	79.8	65.4
1997	3.1	158	1.8	70	-0.1	69.7	63.8
1998	3.4	163	1.6	71	1	65.2	61.2
1999	1.5	165	1.3	72	0.3	62.5	60.9
2000	3	170	0.8	73	-0.5	60.6	62.0
2001	1.8	173	1.2	74	3.8	65.6	63.9
2002	1.7	176	1.3	75	0.8	62.6	63.5
2003	2.9	181	1.4	76	1.2	66.8	64.6
2004	3	187	1.3	77	0.7	68.2	68.2
2005	2.8	192	2.1	78	1.5	66.3	70.5
2006	3.2	198	2.3	80	2.5	68.9	73.1
2007	4.3	207	2.3	82	4.5	78.3	79.4
2008	4	215	3.6	85	9.1	94.3	96.7
2009	-0.5	214	2.2	87	5.4	90.6	89.8
2010	4.6	224	3.3	89	3.4	95.3	93.6
2011	5.2	235	4.5	93	5.5	108.1	105.1
2012	3.2	243	2.8	96	3.2	113.2	106.9
2013	3.0	250	2.6	99	3.8	119.9	109.5
2014	2.4	256	1.5	100	-0.2	109.3	105.0
2015	1.0	258	0.0	100	-2.6	100.0	100.0
2016	1.8	263	0.7	101	-2.4	99.8	97.5
2017	3.6	272.5	2.7	103.4	2.2	110.9	102.5
2018	3.3	281.6	2.5	105.9	2.1	115.1	110.9
2019	2.6	288.8	1.8	107.8	1.4	113.4	112.7
2020	1.5	293.1	0.85	108.7	0.65	118.5	112.6
2021*	2.4	300.2	1.32	110.2	-0.83	121.0	119.3

*Retail Price Index, ** Consumer Prices Index, ^ N.A. = Non-Alcoholic*

Inflation of food-based Component of CPI

Per Cent	2000	2005	2010	2015	2017	2018	2019	2020	Jun-21
CPI (Overall Index)	0.8	2.1	3.3	0.0	2.7	2.5	1.5	0.8	2.4
All goods	-0.8	0.3	3.1	-2.0	2.7	2.6	1.5	-0.3	2.8
All Services	3.3	4.1	3.6	2.4	2.7	2.4	2.5	1.5	2.1
Food & non-alcoholic drink	-0.5	1.5	3.4	-2.6	2.2	2.1	1.4	-1.4	-0.6
Food	-0.4	1.7	3.0	-2.8	2.5	1.9	1.1	0.5	-0.4
Bread & Cereals	-0.2	1.3	2.1	-2.8	2.6	1.1	1.3	1.4	1.3
Meat	0.4	0.7	0.9	-3.1	1.8	1.0	-0.2	1.7	-1.6
Fish	2.2	1.6	6.6	-3.5	8.9	3.8	1.7	1.3	-3.3
Milk, Cheese & Eggs	-0.6	2.7	0.2	-4.4	2.0	2.4	0.2	-0.3	-0.2
Oils & Fats	-1.2	-2.2	6.7	-4.6	6.2	5.9	4.1	-2.7	0.9
Fruit	0.4	1.2	7.9	-0.2	2.6	2.9	0.5	1.4	-0.1
Vegetables inc. Potatoes	-3.5	3.0	2.9	-4.0	2.1	2.0	3.5	-1.3	-1.1
Sugar, Jam & Sweets	0.7	2.8	5.6	-0.2	1.5	1.6	1.2	0.8	0.5
Alcoholic Beverages	0.0	-0.8	3.2	-2.5	2.4	0.9	1.0	1.1	1.4

Weighting of food-based Component of CPI

parts per 1000	2000	2005	2010	2015	2017	2018	2019	2020	2021
CPI (Overall Index)	1000	1000	1000	1000	1000	1000	1000	1000	1000
All goods	591	536	549	532	525	519	519	510	566
All Services	409	464	451	468	475	481	481	490	434
Food & non-alcoholic drink	121	106	108	110	103	101	100	99	114
Food	109	93	96	97	91	90	88	88	101
Bread & Cereals	19	15	16	16	15	15	14	16	19
Meat	27	23	22	22	20	20	19	18	21
Fish	5	4	4	4	4	4	4	3	4
Milk, Cheese & Eggs	14	13	14	14	12	12	11	10	11
Oils & Fats	2	2	2	2	2	2	2	2	2
Fruit	9	8	9	10	9	9	10	11	12
Vegetables inc. Potatoes	18	14	15	14	13	13	13	13	15
Sugar, Jam & Sweets	12	12	11	12	13	13	13	12	14
Alcoholic Beverages	26	20	18	19	20	20	19	20	23

AGRICULTURAL PRICE AND COST INDICES

2015 = 100	2000	2010	2016	2017	2018	2019	2020	2021
All Outputs	61	95	100	111	115	113	122	129
Crop products	60	97	105	114	122	123	133	147
Cereals	59	97	98	118	136	127	152	165
Wheat - Feeding	57	99	99	123	136	132	158	171
Barley - Feeding	62	94	99	115	143	123	132	145
Potatoes	60	94	132	125	121	131	111	132
Oilseed Rape	46	105	110	127	119	124	139	164
Sugar Beet	84	91	95	92	101	100	100	104
Fresh Vegetables	64	94	110	107	120	125	117	137
Fresh Fruit	68	99	108	115	119	130	161	243
Dessert Apples	51	96	102	116	123	126		
Animals and animal products	61	94	97	109	111	108	115	121
Cattle (clean)	47	78	97	103	103	97	112	121
Pigs	73	108	98	120	111	114	113	110
Sheep and lambs	50	101	106	108	118	109	125	170
All Poultry	69	96	101	103	107	106	108	109
Milk	69	101	92	117	120	118	124	119
Eggs	54	84	85	84	82	82	93	99
Wool clip	59	120	85	71	71	71	74	81
Total Inputs	62	94	97	103	110	112	115	120
Seeds	73	105	101	100	105	105	116	118
Energy and lubricants	49	99	95	107	119	123	114	122
Fertilisers and soil improv	40	99	83	90	101	104	91	112
Plant protection products	90	98	100	107	117	116	144	143
Animal feedingstuffs	57	92	97	105	113	114	124	129
Other goods and services	65	92	101	104	107	110	111	112
Machinery and other equip	66	82	100	101	106	108	113	123
Tractors	84	96	102	103	108	109	110	123
Buildings	60	93	99	103	108	110	112	120

Source: DEFRA Agricultural Price Index; 100= 2015

9. METRIC CONVERSION FACTORS

Metric to Imperial   *Imperial to Metric*

Area

1 hectare (10,000m²).... 2.471 acres	1 acre .... 0.405 ha
	1 square mile .... 259 ha
1 square km.............. 0.386 sq. mile	1 square mile .... 2.590 sq. km
1 square m.............. 1.196 sq. yard	1 square yard .... 0.836 sq. m
1 square m.............. 10.764 sq. feet	1 square foot .... 0.093 sq. m

Length

1 mm............................. 0.039 inch	1 inch.................................... 25.4 mm
1 cm .... 0.394 inch	1 inch.................................... 2.54 cm
1 m................................. 3.281 feet	1 foot.................................... 0.305 m
1 m................................. 1.094 yard	1 yard .... 0.914 m
1 km............................ 0.6214 mile	1 mile .... 1.609 km

Volume

1 millilitre .... 0.0352 fluid oz	1 fluid oz .... 28.413 ml
1 litre........................ 35.2 fluid oz	1 fluid oz .... 0.028 litre
1 litre............................. 1.76 pints	1 pint .... 0.568 litre
1 litre............................ 0.22 gallon	1 gallon............................. 4.546 litres
1 cubic m .... 35.31 cu feet	1 cubic foot.......................... 0.028 cu m
1 cubic m .... 1.307 cu yard	1 cubic yard........................ 0.765 cu m
1 cubic m .... 220 gallons	1 gallon............................... 0.005 cu m
1 ha of 10mm water .22,000gallons	1 acre-inch .... 102.75 m³

Weight

1 gram............................ 0.0353 oz	1 oz...................................... 28.35 gm
1 kg................................. 35.274 oz	
1 kg................................. 2.205 lb	1 lb .... 0.454 kg
50 kg............................... 0.984 cwt	
1 tonne (1,000 kg).......... 19.68 cwt	1 cwt..................................... 50.80 kg
1 tonne .... 0.984 ton	1 ton .... 1.016 tonne

Milk

1 litre................................. 1.03 kg	
1kg................................. 0.971 litre	
1 litre........................... 1.709 pints	1 pint .... 0.585 kg
1 tonne..................... 213.63 gallon	1 gallon................................. 4.681 kg

Yields and Rates of Use

1 tonne/ha. .... 0.398 ton/acre	1 ton/acre .... 2.511 tonnes/ha
1 tonne/ha. ....7.95 cwt/acre	1 cwt/acre .... 0.125 tonne/ha
1 gram/ha ....0.014 oz/acre	1 oz/acre ....70.053 g/ha
1 kg/ha .... 0.892 lb/acre	1 lb/acre.............................1.121 kg/ha
1 kg/ha ....0.008 cwt/acre	1 cwt/acre ....125.5 kg/ha
1 kg/ha (fert.) .... 0.797 unit/acre	1 unit/acre...........................1.255 kg/ha
1 litre/ha................. 0.712 pint/acre	1 pint/acre........................ 1.404 litre/ha
1 litre/ha...................0.089 gal/acre	1 gal/acre .... 11.24 litres/ha

Power, Pressure, Temperature

1 kW .... 1.341 hp	1 hp ....0.746 kW
1 MW............................ 1,000kW	
1 kilojoule...................... 0.948 Btu	1 Btu............................. 1.055 kilojoule
1 therm......................... 10,000 Btu	1 Btu............................... 0.0001 therm
1 lb f ft .... 1.356 Nm	1 Nm ....0.738 lb f ft
1 bar...................... 14.705 lb/sq.in.	1 lb/sq.in............................... 0.068 bar
°C to °F ....x1.8, + 32	°F to °C ....-32, ÷ 1.8

INDEX